THE *Shih Tzu* HERITAGE

BY
JON FERRANTE

Edited by
William W. Denlinger and R. Annabel Rathman

Cover Design by
Bob Groves

Translation

Shih Tzu,

from whence

they

originate.

獅
子
狗
的
由
來

DENLINGER'S PUBLISHERS, LTD.
Box 76, Fairfax, Virginia 22030

Reproduced on the front cover of this book is a photo of Ch. Choo Ling's Red Royalty (Duke), owned by Bill and Dottie Campbell, Choo Ling Shih Tzu. Photo courtesy Lone Star Dog Food Company. Reproduced on the back cover (lower right) is a poster which was sent to the State Department, Washington, D.C., by the American Consul in Canton. It illustrates the Chinese view of the combined foreign powers encircling China. The artist is unknown. The poster is reproduced here with the compliments of the United States Marine Corps National Museum to Jon Ferrante for *The Shih Tzu Heritage.*

The Foo Dog, the Shih Tzu, and the lion are symbolically interrelated as defenders of laws and protectors of sacred buildings. Depicted above is the male Foo Dog, holding with his left paw a spherical object. The ball, the sun, and the egg are symbolic of dual powers over nature and precious stones, and also symbolic of energy, valor, and wisdom. A female Foo Dog is depicted holding a young dog with her paw, symbolic of playing with and protecting her young, and disciplining her young to realize eternal experience, ultimate joy, and immortal spirit.

Library of Congress Cataloging-in-Publication Data

Ferrante, Jon C.
    The Shih Tzu heritage.

    1. Shih tzu.   I. Denlinger, William Watson.
II. Rathman, R. Annabel.   III. Title.
SF429.S64F47   1989   636.7 '   88-30895
ISBN 0-87714-132-0

The City of Kashi is located where the Hindu Kush, Tian Shan, and Himalayan mountain ranges converge on the Ancient Silk Route. Through the centuries, this city, in the farthest western portion of China, was a meeting place of Chinese, Indians, Persians, and Tibetans. A theory has been advanced that ancestors of the modern Shih Tzu were presented by Tibetan Lamas to Kashi's visitors from Chinese courts and taken by them back to Peking, where they were nurtured and cherished as prized possessions of emperors and members of the court.

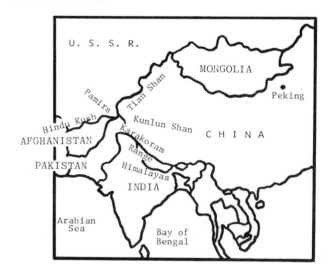

DEDICATION

This book, *The Shih Tzu Heritage,* is dedicated to Tzu Hsi, Orchid, of the Yeonala Family, Empress of the Western Palace, Dowager Empress of China, Shih Tzu breeder and patroness;

to Betty J. Munden, whose strength, courage, knowledge, and integrity are truly exemplary;

and to Gay Widdrington, Lhakang Kennels, England, who for almost fifty years, throughout the traumatic years of World War II to the present, has served as modern day Shih Tzu breeder and patroness throughout the world. As friend and counselor to many breeders, as author and judge, she has developed, maintained, and promoted her own high ethical standards, yet has worked ceaselessly to extend the work of Lady Brownrigg and the Dowager Empress to heed quality and preserve the treasured Lion Dog for posterity.....

"Thank you"

Acknowledgements

Thomas E. Wilgus, Reference Specialist, Heraldry and Military History, Library of Congress, Washington, D.C.

Lulie Maeshiro, Chinese Desk, Library of Congress, Washington, D.C.

The United States National Archives, Washington, D.C.

J. Michael Miller, The United States Marine Corps Museum, Boxer Rebellion Exhibition, Washington, D.C.

The Freer Gallery of Art, Washington, D.C.

The Arthur M. Sackler Gallery of Asian Art, Washington, D.C.

The "Army-Navy Times" (Modern Chinese Palace Art and Photographs of the Great Wall of China), Washington, D.C.

Cultural Attache, The Embassy of the Peoples Republic of China, Washington, D.C.

The Archives Bureau, Peking, China.

The Palace Museum, Peking, China.

Roberta Vesley, Head Librarian, and Ann Sergi and Marie Fabrizi, Librarians, The American Kennel Club Library, New York, New York.

The Folger Shakespeare Library, Washington, D.C.

Maxwell Riddle, for the "Foreword."

Carol Baynton Phelps, Halcaldee Collies, Artist and Sculptor par excellence, for inside composite drawings of House of Visconti Shih Tzu and skeletal background studies.

Antoinette Buxton, Chopmist Harlequin Great Danes and Arabian Horses, Geneticist.

Sandy Tremont, President, Professional Handlers Association.

Tom Allen, Photographer, for the photograph of the Visconti Coat of Arms.

Garrett Crissman, Jubilation Shih Tzu and Punchbrook Arabian Horses.

Jean Lade, Professional Handler.

Mary Hutchinson, Hi Vu Collies.

Janice Wanamaker, Candray Keeshonden, Collies, and Shih Tzu.

Paul and Coni Nickerson, Copa Shih Tzu.

Lone Star Dog Food Company, for the front cover photograph.

Kari Fox, Studies and Lectures on Genetics and Color Inheritance.

Gay Widdrington, Lhakang Shih Tzu, for information and compilations — English champions and breeders.

Susan Sandlin, Petit Point Yorkshire Terriers and Maltese.

Del and Connie Smart, Conwynn Shih Tzu, for Elfann photographs.

James Cavallaro, for permission to include the chapter titled "Whelping a Shih Tzu," written by Richard Paisley.

Peggy Hogg, Dragonfire Shih Tzu, for her chapter titled "Conditioning the Coat — Grooming the Shih Tzu."

R. Scott Dickinson, for German translations

Lorraine De Salvo, Bilor Shih Tzu, for the map of the Ancient Silk-trade Route.

Elaine Meltzer, Lainee Shih Tzu, for copy for the new AKC Standard of the Shih Tzu.

Judith Sirinsky, Nan-A-Ju Shih Tzu, Editor, American Shih Tzu Club Historical Record Book.

Mary Warren Lea, China Trade Shih Tzu.

Patti Link, Link's Shih Tzu and Bearded Collies, for Shih Tzu historical memorabilia.

Dave and Mary Robertson, Kamira, Reg., Shih Tzu, for statistics—Canadian Shih Tzu.

Trudy Kerr, Ta Ya Chai Shih Tzu, for details of Erika Geusendam's kennels and other European breeders' kennels.

Peggy Easton, Chumulari, Reg., Shih Tzu, photos from the Reverend D. Allan Easton's mission to China.

Ruth Laakso, Zizi Shih Tzu, for information from Scandinavia.

Astrid Jeppesen, Bjorneholm Shih Tzu, for her years of devotion to the breed and her "very best wishes" for *The Shih Tzu Heritage.*

The Visconti coat of arms.

The City-State of Milan, Italy was ruled for nearly a century by Dukes of the Visconti family. The eagle and dragon (or serpent) on the Visconti shield were sanctioned by the Holy Roman Empire. The author adopted his paternal grandmother's family name, Visconti, for his show kennel's official name. He has bred and/or owned champions in three of the seven Groups of dogs designated by the AKC, and is an AKC judge.

Ch. Marco Polo di Visconti. *Dog World* magazine's representation of the Shih Tzu Standard, 1978 and 1979.

Foreword

During some forty years as a reporter-columnist for the "Cleveland Press" and other newspapers, I promoted all phases of the sport of purebred dogs — breeding, exhibiting, care, training, obedience, field work, and junior showmanship. The latter, if reported at all in most news summaries, comes last. There is a reason for this.

You can divide this activity into three classes. First there are the juniors who are being driven into competition by parents who wish to bask in the glory of their children's victories, and who may blast the judges who do not place the boy or girl First. Such children — and their parents — quickly disappear from the dog world. They are replaced quickly by others with similar temporary interest.

In the second group are children who are genuinely interested for a time, but who turn to other interests — athletics, music, stamps, and academic prowess. In the third category are those juniors who grow up to follow their parents into dog breeding. A few of them parlay their handling skills into professional handling in the show ring, become obedience handlers or trainers, and sometimes go into field training and handling.

One day at my office at the "Cleveland Press" came a twelve-year-old boy. He wanted to meet me, and I wanted to meet him. He had been spectacularly successful in showing and had been best junior handler at three or four shows in succession. I wanted to interview him, and to get his picture for publication.

He wanted to grow up to become a breeder, owner, and handler of Collies. I encouraged him, although, as time was to prove, he needed no encouragement. When next he visited me, he had become successful as a career professional in the federal government in Washington. But most important to me, he had become successful in showing several breeds, and guiding dogs to their championships.

He had become successful as a breeder and exhibitor of the Shih Tzu. He had combined his extraordinary thirst for knowledge with an incomparable ability to research ancient records through the Library of Congress and many other sources. All this has been combined to give you a very successful account of the heritage of a popular dog breed, the Shih Tzu.

Maxwell Riddle

Maxwell Riddle presenting First in Group award to Ch. Daybreak At Wyvern, owned by Mr. and Mrs. A. Dickson. Mr. Riddle is the world's top living authority on dogs.

Pavilion of Green Ripples in the Imperial Garden, Forbidden City, Beijing (formerly Peking), China. It was here that ShihTzu romped with each other, the eunuchs, and the Empress and her attendants. The Shih Tzu was a "highly valued, prized companion and Palace pet."

故宫

Above: Reproduction of actual front cover inscription by curator— ''The Palace Museum'' in abbreviated form. Below: ''The Palace Museum''—inscription in full.

故宫博物院

Gate of Heavenly Purity, Forbidden City. It was here that R. Annabel Rathman, Editor-in-Chief for Denlinger's Publishers, Ltd., personally presented two front covers of this book for signature by a curator of the Palace Museum. A crowd of Chinese people gathered here on the steps as this unprecedented event took place on October 8, 1988. Arrangements were made on behalf of the author by the Cultural Attache of the Chinese Embassy in Washington, D.C.

Contents

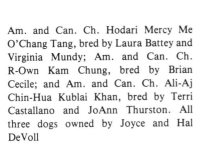

Am. and Can. Ch. Hodari Mercy Me O'Chang Tang, bred by Laura Battey and Virginia Mundy; Am. and Can. Ch. R-Own Kam Chung, bred by Brian Cecile; and Am. and Can. Ch. Ali-Aj Chin-Hua Kublai Khan, bred by Terri Castallano and JoAnn Thurston. All three dogs owned by Joyce and Hal DeVoll

The Summer Palace, Peking (now called Beijing), 1901. Here during summer months, the Dowager Empress ruled her Empire. Her favorite animals, including her Shih Tzu, and her favorite attendants resided here with the Dowager Empress throughout her annual stay.

Contrary to widely held beliefs, an American was among the very first to receive a Shih Tzu as a gift from the Dowager Empress. Sarah Conger, wife of American Minister to China Edwin H. Conger, received the Shih Tzu from the Dowager Empress about the time this photo was taken in 1903. Mrs. Conger is pictured here to the immediate right of the Dowager Empress.

Abbreviations

The following abbreviations are used in text and listings in this book.

AKC—American Kennel Club. The registry body of breeds recognized in the United States; the governing body of shows and registrations.

AM./Can./Ber./Mex. Ch.—Championships in all countries specified, i.e., Am.—American; Can.—Canadian; Ber.—Bermudian; Mex.—Mexican.

(B)—Bitch.

BIS—Best in Show. The winner chosen from the Group winners as the best dog or bitch shown that day.

BOB—Best of Breed. The dog or bitch chosen as best from all class dogs and champions competing in the breed that day.

BOS—Best of Opposite Sex. The best from the sex opposite that chosen BOB.

BOW—Best of Winners, i.e., the best of the WD and WB.

CACIB—*Certificat d'Aptitude au Championat Internationale.* The certificate awarded for a win in an F.C.I. show. After receiving a specified number of such certificates, the dog is awarded the title of International Champion (Int. Ch.).

C.C.—Challenge Certificate, awarded in England. It is necessary to obtain three in order to win the title of champion. In England, champions and class dogs compete together for the C.C.

C.D.—Companion Dog. The first title awarded in obedience competition to a dog with a specified number of passing scores in Novice classes.

C.D.X.—Companion Dog Excellent. The next title awarded in progression for qualifying scores in Open classes.

Ch.—Champion of Record, title awarded by AKC upon winning fifteen points, with two major wins.

(D)—Dog.

F.C.I.—*Federation Cynologique Internationale.* The organization which licenses certain shows to award international championships. The national kennel clubs of every European country (with the exception of England), every South American country, Japan, and South Africa are members of the F.C.I.

HIT—High in Trial; highest scoring dog in obedience competition.

HSD—Highest Scoring Dog for the day in obedience competition.

Int. Ch.—International Champion. The title awarded a dog that competes and wins in a specified number of F.C.I. shows.

Nord (or Nordic)—Norwegian and Swedish Champion. Formerly was Norwegian, Swedish, and Finnish Champion, but in Finland there currently can be no competition for this title because of Finland's new quarantine restrictions.

O.T.Ch.—Obedience Trial Champion, pronounced "OTCH." A dog that has won the required points and First Place awards specified in current Obedience Regulations.

R.O.M.—Register of Merit. An award for breeding excellence.

RWB—Reserve Winners Bitch. Awarded to the bitch deemed second best in the classes. If, for any reason, the WB is disqualified, the RWB will be awarded the championship points.

RWD—Reserve Winners Dog. Awarded to the male deemed second best in the classes. If, for any reason, the WD is disqualified, the RWD will be awarded the championship points.

S Ch.—Swedish Champion.

Sf Ch.—Finnish Champion.

T.D.—Tracking Dog. This title is awarded for running a qualifying track.

T.D.X.—Tracking Dog Excellent. An advanced degree of tracking.

U.D.—Utility Dog. The title awarded for the specified number of passing scores in Utility competition, the most advanced and difficult of the obedience classes. This title may be combined with the T.D. and shown as the U.D.T.

WB—Winners Bitch. The female chosen as best in the classes. Awarded championship point(s), depending on the number of bitches in competition.

WD—Winners Dog. The male chosen as best in the classes. Awarded championship point(s), depending on the number of males in competition.

Note the similarity between the Maltese puppy (left) and the White Shih Tzu (right). This Shih Tzu's color is a "throwback" resulting from the genetic influence of infusion of Maltese bloodlines, centuries ago when East met West on the Ancient Silk Trade Route. A number of breeds evolved when various Maltese type dogs were mated with Oriental type dogs.

Courtyard scene, 1903. Center, Tsu Hsi, the Dowager Empress, with her ladies in waiting. Various eunuchs are on either side. At right is Chief Eunuch Li Lien-Yang, who helped guide the Shih Tzu breeding program. At the Empress' feet is Hai Ling (Sea Otter), the solid black Shih Tzu, the Empress' favorite, who sired many Shih Tzu of various colors within the Palace. This rarity is the only known photo of Tsu Hsi with any of her Shih Tzu.

History of the Shih Tzu

There is strong indication that the Shih Tzu is a breed developed in China from ancient lines of dogs of Tibet. One theory is that these ancestors of the modern Shih Tzu were presented by Tibetan Lamas to royal visitors from Chinese courts and taken by them back to Peking, where they were nurtured and cherished as prized possessions of the emperors and members of the court. A somewhat parallel theory, also to be given credence, is that the dogs were exchanged by royal travelers and merchants — representatives of many cultures and societies — who met as they traveled along that segment of the ancient "Silk Trade Route" that runs in a generally west to east route from Lhasa, Tibet, to Peking (now known as Beijing), China.

Tibet, with its fabled city of Lhasa and its magnificent lamasery and luxurious Potala Palace, has been shrouded in mystery, romance, and intrigue for centuries. Because of its extreme inaccessibility, most attempts by Europeans (Feringhi) to discover and record Tibetan history and geography have been unsuccessful.

The world's highest mountain ranges border Tibet. The Hindu Kush, Himalayas, Tian Shan, Kunlan Shan, and Karakorams form natural geographic barriers that have kept Tibet relatively free of outside influences throughout the ages. And continuing on into modern times these natural barriers have prevented amalgamation of Eastern and Western cultures. It is this area which the Persians call the "Roof of the World," partly because of its extremely high altitude and partly because of its secluded nature.

The Hindu Kush, Tian Shan, and Himalaya mountain ranges converge in the area known as the Pamirs. Here, on one of the highest plateaus in the world, lies the city of Kashi. This city, in the farthest western portion of China, is surrounded by the U.S.S.R., Afghanistan, and Pakistan. Through the centuries it was a meeting place of travelers, merchants, and representatives of many cultures and empires. Chinese, Indians, Persians, and Tibetans congregated in Kashi to rest and barter goods before continuing their journey to the largest cities of the East.

While natural barriers discouraged travelers from entering Tibet, it is man-made barriers that have kept outsiders from the Inner City of Peking for many hundreds of years. The Inner City, separated by a high wall from the Outer City, is further divided by high walls into three parts, the innermost being the "Forbidden City," a nest of palaces and buildings into which "barbarians" were seldom permitted to enter. This imperially determined exclusion of the outside world, continued for centuries, led, of course, not only to narrowness of

social and political outlook but also to intensive evolvement in religious, scientific, and cultural spheres.

Tibetan Lamas were wandering constantly, searching for "Truth." Respect for and fear of the Chinese emperors made presentation of tribute gifts the usual procedure for fending off trouble. There is no doubt that "temple dogs" — revered symbols of Lamaism — were among "tribute gifts" presented by Tibetan Lamas to representatives of Chinese emperors at Kashi as well as at other gathering places along the ancient Silk Route.

For centuries, ruling classes and aristocrats in most areas of the world have honored the toy breeds. In Rome and in Egypt, as well as in China, long before the Christian era, Maltese, Italian Greyhound, and Pekingese type dogs were depicted on vases and other art objects, and in paintings and drawings. Toy breeds represented one avenue for displaying high social status because they were not bred for utilitarian purposes and therefore served as symbols of wealth and position.

All Oriental dogs had forms which were quite similar. This was a direct result of the influence of Buddhism. The lion was said to have been Buddha's constant companion and on several occasions saved him from death or capture by his enemies. According to his followers, Buddha could summon lions to protect him at any time the occasion arose. Buddha could simply stretch forth his hand and his fingers would change into five lions, which, roaring with a combined voice which shook the heavens, brought his enemies into subjection.

Because the Chinese considered the lion symbolic of Buddha, they used "the King of the Beasts" as a model in breeding their dogs. Among the Oriental dogs so produced are the Shih Tzu, the Pekingese, the Chow Chow, the Lhasa Apso, the Spitz, and the Pug. The latter, although it does not have the lion-like mane which so many Oriental breeds possess, has a body which closely resembles the form of the lion, and the common colors of the breed are those that are lion-like.

The lion was not native to China, so early Chinese had little concept as to what the lion actually looked like. It is probable that early Chinese sculptors carved lions from descriptions they had received about the beasts, and that the Chinese dogs were bred to look like the statues rather than like lions themselves.

As the lion became more and more a symbol of spiritual and physical protection, the "lion dogs" became increasingly an extension of that symbolism. The status of such dogs is said to have influenced the conversion to Buddhism of China's Emperor Ming Ti.

There is evidence that Maltese type dogs were present in China as early as 8000 B.C. Chinese excavations in the Northern Desert revealed "a model of a Maltese dog thought to be a child's toy," proving the antiquity of the breed. There is strongly based conjecture that

Reproduction of painting depicting combat between Krishna on the mighty bird Garuda and Indra on a white elephant, watched by other gods in the sky. This symbolism is in part the basis for Buddhist symbolism and mysticism.

The Great Wall of China seen through an aperture at one of the observation points at a lookout tower.

Reproduction of painting—Freer Gallery of Art. Manjusri, Goddess of Mercy, from whom the Manchus of the Manchu Dynasty (including the Dowager Empress) derived their mysticism.

12

Melitaic dogs (later known as Maltese) were brought into China and Tibet in the first century B.C. over the Karakoram Highway by traders and diplomats on missions between East and West.

Although there is some belief that small dogs of the Maltese type may have originated in China and were carried to the Mediterranean area by traders, it is considered more probable that these small dogs appeared in the West as "descendants of the Spitz race, which were descended from the March, or Turf Dog of the Swiss Lake Dwellers."

These Maltese type or Fu-lin dogs may very well have been interbred in Tibet with Tibetan Terriers to produce the Lhasa Apso type temple dogs. Certainly there is no doubt that dogs — both small and large — became "tribute gifts" from Tibetan Lamas to Chinese Emperors. Those presented by the wandering Lamas were more than likely bred with the existing flatter-faced Pekingese type dogs. The Maltese type and the Lo Sze ancestor of the Pug undoubtedly also were crossed with them.

The Tang Dynasty (618-907) is noted for territorial expansion, especially cultural contact with Central Asia, the highest development of Chinese poetry, the first development of printing, and the political as well as the religious importance of Buddhism. During the Tang Dynasty, K'iu T'ai, King of Viqur, gave the Chinese court a pair of dogs which presumably were from the Byzantine Empire. A few paintings and art objects dating back to the seventh century depict dogs resembling the Shih Tzu. Documents of the tenth century also mention dogs presented to the Chinese court.

In 747 Khrisrongldebtsan, King of Tibet (743-798), brought to Tibet "the real founder of Lamaism," Padmasambhava, who introduced magic and mysticism (saturated with Hindu Sivaism), which found its way to Mongolia and China. The King was converted to Buddhism by his mother, a Chinese Princess, and became a powerful supporter of it. The mysteries of Lamaism, with its Buddhist "Wheel of Life" philosophy, has remained an enigma to Westerners.

When Kublai Khan accepted the Lamaist form of Buddhism in the thirteenth century, Lhasa Apso type dogs were given as tribute to his court in China by the Tibetan Lamas. Also, the Fo-lin or Fu-lin type dogs from the Byzantine Empire were brought into the court in Peking. "Fo" and "Fu" mean Buddha, and ceramic representations of the ancient Fo and Fu Dogs portray them as somewhat distorted in conformation.

Tracings of the exchange of various ancestors of our present day breeds of dogs generally are to be classified only as legend and conjecture. But Marco Polo, as Emissary of the Great Tartar Emperor Kublai Khan, wrote in the thirteenth century of the Tartars as "having

the best falcons in the world and also the best dogs in the world." He wrote, too, of magnificent lions owned by Kublai Khan and trained to hunt wild boar, oxen, bear, stags, roebuck, and other animals. He described how small dogs were housed with the lions and familiarized with them in order to keep the lions calm when they were not hunting.

The multi-century-old awe and respect for the lion as the most courageous of beasts contributed to the continuing tendency for the Chinese to breed dogs to resemble the lion. The breeding of dogs with flattened muzzles, undershot bites, bowed legs, wrinkled faces, protruding eyes, and fierce expressions, presumably was for the purpose of strengthening the resemblance to the lion.

During the Ming Dynasty (1368-1644) the Shih Tzu type dog was a cherished pet — highly favored by the royal family. Real fanaticism and a cult-like worship for the "lion dog" developed at this period. Eunuchs were charged with the duties of breeding and rearing the beautiful royal pets. Competition among the eunuchs to gain royal favor became fierce, as each tried to breed the best, most lion like, and most ferocious looking specimens.

Surgery was used to shorten noses and other unnatural means were used to alter size and appearances. Women who bore female offspring were used to nurse puppies after their babies were murdered mercilessly so as not to disrupt an abundantly even flow of milk from human nurses to nursing puppies.

The Ming Dynasty was marked by the development of the arts, especially in porcelain, textiles, and painting. Still extant are sculpture, hangings, and paintings from this time period, depicting dogs resembling Shih Tzu.

The Manchu Dynasty extended from 1644 to 1912. Throughout this period, tribute gifts of pairs of Lhasa Apso "Lion Dogs" are known to have been sent to Chinese rulers from the Potala Palace. Also from lamaseries in Tibet, Tibetan Spaniels, Tibetan Terriers, and Tibetan Mastiffs were sent as tribute gifts to lesser persons — Chinese nobles, dignitaries, and emissaries residing outside the Chinese Imperial Palace.

Through the first two centuries of the Manchu Dynasty, the Shih Tzu and the Lhasa Apso were more similar than they are today — although even now people unfamiliar with the two breeds often confuse them initially. But it probably has been only in the last hundred or hundred fifty years that specialized breeding programs in the Forbidden City and in the West have established uniformity in conformation to really individualize the two breeds in their uniqueness.

In the mid-1800s, the Emperor of China proclaimed Tibet off limits to Europeans, Judeans, and even Buddhists from other countries. Only a select few outsiders were permitted entry and the country was

13

under the rule of the lamas, who much of the time were under the dominance of Emperors of China.

Accounts written in 1905 described the general populace of Tibet as "monks, women and dogs," in that order of descending numbers. At that time many dogs were described as of stunted mangy Mastiff types that roamed the streets, whereas the nobles fond of dogs favored what was probably a combination of Lhasa Terrier and Chinese Spaniel. Palace guard dogs were well-cared-for Mastiffs, with huge lion-like manes — magnificent to behold. Owners honored their guardians with names translated as "Bullbear" and "Supreme Strength." Bitches were said often to be called by a name equivalent to "Mary."

The Shih Tzu went through several stages while its breeding was confined to the palaces of the Chinese Emperors. For centuries prior to the Boxer Revolution (which occurred in 1900), the royal family included a very large retinue of sub-royalty and servants. They traveled from their summer courts to their winter quarters in procession — complete with household and personal possessions, which, of course, included their Shih Tzu and other pets. The description of this massive semiannual exodus which is included in Princess Der Ling's book, *The Old Buddha,* is reminiscent of a very large circus parade.

The Shih Tzu came into its heyday as the pampered darling of the Chinese Imperial Palaces during the reign of the last Empress, who came into power in 1861 and continued as Empress until her death in 1908.

In her youth she was known to her family as Orchid, of the Yehonala family. She was of Manchu, not Chinese, background and was of humble origin. At seventeen years of age she became the beautiful concubine of the Emperor in the Forbidden City. In the Palace of Surpassing Brightness she was elevated from concubine to consort and named by the Emperor "Tzu Hsi," Empress of the Western Palace. As the mother of the Emperor's first-born son, she gradually rose to power as a brilliant strategist. Eventually she ruled with absolute power over millions of people. In later years she was known as the earthly embodiment of the Goddess of Mercy, and as the "Old Buddha." And this great personality was the patroness of the Palace Dog — the Shih Tzu.

Tzu Hsi had other prized breeds of "Lion Dogs." Among them were huge white Mastiff type dogs of Tibetan descent as well as Pekingese and Lhasa Apsos. Also, the Empress was still receiving Tibetan dogs occasionally from the Lamasery in Tibet.

Eunuchs and their personal hierarchies actually ran the Imperial households, but it was Li Lien-Yang whom Tzu Hsi named Chief Eunuch and made responsible for overseeing the breeding and Shih Tzu selections to be presented to her and perhaps to become part of her "Shih Tzu entourage." The Empress insisted that complete pedigrees and descriptions of physical markings be kept for all dogs used as breeding stock within the Imperial household, as well as for all puppies whelped.

Imperial selections of "best specimens of Shih Tzu" were based on health, temperament, conformation, and markings. For aesthetic and religious reasons, particolors with perfect facial marking and perfect saddle were held in high esteem by the Empress. But solid colors were prized equally by her.

Many of today's breeders have assumed that Empress Tzu Hsi, from the time she came into power in 1861 until her death in 1908, had surrounded herself with gold and gold-white dogs only. This assumption is totally without foundation. A favorite Shih Tzu, a male who followed her everywhere — from her private apartments to the Palace of Heavenly Purity — was a solid black. His name was Hai Ling, which translated into English means "Sea Otter." A photo of the Dowager Empress and Sea Otter is reproduced in this book.

Tzu Hsi was wise to the laws of color inheritance. She knew of the importance of the darker shades of brindle and silver and of black in maintaining pigmentation of eye color and coat color. Whether or not she knew of the then-new theories and laws of Mendelism, she was well aware of basic breeding tenets. One must remember that the Chinese had been producing pure lines of dogs for centuries before the practice became prevalent in the West.

Intrigue flourished in the Palace among nobility, concubines, and eunuchs. Spies and counterspies reported rumors and counter-rumors to the Empress daily. Payoffs were made continually in the forms of position, status, and recognition by the Empress, but she had an ongoing fear and hatred of treason. Even more than treason Tzu Hsi feared and hated the influence of "Foreign Devils" who were invading her country and disturbing her peace of mind throughout most of her reign. When a Chinese secret society, the Boxers, brutally tortured and murdered Westerners at the turn of the century, the Empress supported and condoned their actions, for their slogan, "Support the Throne and annihilate the foreigners," was a reflection of her own convictions.

The Empress feared that the Foreign Devils would encourage foreign ways and destroy traditional Chinese values. Opium trade was being encouraged in China by the British, and the Empress feared it would lead to extensive use of the drug by the Chinese, to further contaminate and destroy their minds. Consequently, she supported her subjects totally when they became embroiled in the "Opium Wars" against the British.

Although the Empress entertained wives of various ambassadors and diplomats from time to time, and

After the death of the Dowager Empress, some of the eunuchs fled, concealing top quality Shih Tzu and smuggling them out of the Palace in order to sell them.

Pu Yi, the last Chinese Emperor, too young in 1908 to realize treasures were being stolen and smuggled out of the Imperial Palace. Photo, United States National Archives.

Funeral procession of the Dowager Empress, 1908. This rare photo provides a glimpse of the eunuchs' sorrowful duty to their protectoress, who had fostered the security of those closest to her. The Dowager Empress' death marked a new era for China, her faithful attendants, and her beloved Shih Tzu. Photo courtesy the Marine Corps Museum, Washington, D.C.

bestowed upon them valuable gifts, she gave them attention only for political reasons. In the beginning Shih Tzu were not among the gifts, despite the apparent interest the foreign ladies showed toward the dogs. Following the end of the Opium Wars, several Pekingese from the Imperial Palace were taken to England by returning members of the diplomatic community. Eventually, a few of the Shih Tzu were given as gifts to foreigners, but there is some evidence that the eunuchs fed powdered glass to the dogs to cause death rather than permit them to leave China.

Westerners living in China at the time considered association with the Dowager Empress to be the highest form of status. The lavish attention she received from visitors may have been instrumental in Tzu Hsi's decision to present some of her treasured Shih Tzu to her admirers.

By the early 1900s, whether because of the changing political atmosphere or the mellowing of the jealous spirit of the Dowager Empress, several Shih Tzu were introduced into Europe by returning diplomats and ladies. Also, the eunuchs assigned to breeding, whelping, and general maintenance of the Imperial Shih Tzu would do anything for financial gain. Indications are that falsified breedings took place and that puppies were bartered and sold outside the Forbidden City to affluent Chinese and even to the Foreign Devils.

It has been speculated that the Dowager Empress had the Emperor Kuang-hsu secretly murdered just hours before her own death so that she would be the last Imperial Ruler of China. With her death and with the ascension of the new child Emperor, Pu Yi, the fate of the breeding programs of all her animals became tenuous. Many of the eunuchs who had become expert breeders during the half century of Tzu Hsi's guidance were dismissed. Some of them fled the Forbidden City and found employment with nobles in Peking, Shanghai, and Hong Kong.

American diplomat R. Gordon Sloan reported happenings to the American Department of State in Washington, D.C. These files are part of the treasure trove of records of the Archives of the United States. Mr. Sloan says, "It is a tragedy of sorts to see the pillaging of Palace treasures such as objets d'art, jewelry and even the 'Old Buddha's' clothing, her birds and her beloved shag dogs which resemble the gargoyles outside and on the trimmings of the Palace. Bedlam has changed the aura of discipline in the Palace to chaos. Fire has destroyed animals and large portions of the inner chambers. It is believed that Palace servants are responsible for causing the fires to conceal their thieving and looting."

The eunuchs who fled prior to the fires within the Palace took much of the Shih Tzu breeding stock and finest specimens to sell to foreigners and Chinese noblemen who would pay handsome prices for dogs and treasures of the Palace. This was survival money for the eunuchs until they could relocate into Chinese society.

In Peking the Comtesse d'Anjou was the recipient, third hand, of some of the Palace stock. Also in Peking, Mrs. Lorenz had two black Shih Tzu, Mei-mei and Moer in the 1930s. Mrs. Lorenz owned a Shih Tzu kennel of almost all black dogs, and one of her studs, Chu Po, a solid black with a strong gold gene behind him, was a great grandson of Hai Ling (Sea Otter), a favorite of the Empress.

When the Emperor was overthrown by the Communist Chinese in 1949, many of the dogs were destroyed. Before taking their own lives, some members of the royal family cut the throats of their dogs so that they might not fall into the hands of the conquerors. This exemplifies the great love they had for their Shih Tzu.

And, certainly, our present day Shih Tzu exemplify the great love the Dowager Empress, Tzu Hsi, had for the breed. Under her half century of direction and influence, the Imperial Shih Tzu flourished and developed in uniformity. These intelligent little beings brought great happiness to her at times of excessive loneliness and sorrow, and in the frenzied circumstances when her Empire crumbled before her eyes. A multi-faceted person of great depth, the Empress lives on as spiritual guide and patroness of the Shih Tzu.

Blow, blow thou winter wind,
Thou art not so unkind
As man's ingratitude.
William Shakespeare, As You Like It, II. 7.174

The purest treasure mortal times afford
Is spotless reputation.
William Shakespeare, Richard II. I. 1.178

16

THE SHIH TZU AND BUDDHIST/HINDU SYMBOLISM

The Buddhist religion and its philosophy and symbolism (particularly as related to the lion), were in part responsible for the awesome respect accorded the "Lion Dogs" in the Forbidden City. Known as Ab-bah Go (dogs owned by the revered ones, or ones of royal status), Shih Tzu were seen to have a number of characteristics that were believed to be comparable to characteristics of Buddha. Following are descriptions of some of the symbols perceived by the Shih Tzu's royal owners.

The white mark on the forehead of the Shih Tzu, perceived as the energy center, often called the third eye or sixth chakra, is symbolic of the trinity, oneness of mind, universalism, salvation for all, and the three mystical areas (body, mouth, and mind). Positive qualities were believed to exude from the Shih Tzu: intuition, perception, optimism, and vision.

The top knot, the crowning glory of the Shih Tzu, symbolically represented creativity, mysticism, charm, magical powers, wisdom, and love.

The luxurious featherings on the Shih Tzu head and face were perceived as symbolic of the rays of the sun and of the sacred adumbara flower which blooms once in three thousand years.

The white neck and front of the Shih Tzu were believed to be symbolic of Buddha's swelling cape of dignity. The cape permitted its wearer, as administrator of the sun, moon, and stars, the privilege of attending to purity, justice, and virtue. Upon the cape are the Rosary of the Goddess of Mercy and the three rings of the Buddha.

The draping coat or skirt of the Shih Tzu was seen as symbolic of light, strength, and courage. The Buddha's flock must never reject their children, their parents, those who love them, or those whom they have loved, lest they never reach Nirvana or Heaven. Buddha-like, the Shih Tzu was considered symbolically the guardian of wisdom so that all may reverse their imperfections.

Am. and Can. Ch. Lou Wan Farrah Faucet, owned by Louis and Wanda Gec.

A marking may be present in the middle of the back or there may be one that extends from the upper back to the end of the back or nearly as far as the tip of the tail. This blanket or saddle effect was believed symbolic of the saddle or blanket upon which Buddha is seated as minister of the sun, moon, and stars. It also was believed symbolic of the three vehicles of learning leading to wisdom: discipline, knowledge, and meditation. Pegasus-like, the Shih Tzu is to carry his rider through the air to realize material gain of wealth and jewels.

The heavily plumed tail which forms a graceful arch over the back represents one of the five Royal Insignia attributable to anointed kings and holy men. This umbrella-like feature is depicted in symbolic representations of Buddha, covering his form, protecting him from worldly imperfections.

The white feet were considered reminiscent of the Buddha's shoes, embroidered with jewels, to convey the wearer one hundred miles without fatigue and give the wearer the ability to glide across water without wetting the feet.

Lady Brownrigg, who imported two Shih Tzu from China in 1930, pictured at the W.E.L.K.S. Championship Show in 1939 with three of the first Shih Tzu whelped in England.

Arnold Leadbitter with Eng. Ch. Greenmoss Chin-Ki of Meo and Jeanne Leadbitter with Eng. Ch. Ko Ko Saki of Greenmoss.

Lady Brownrigg in 1932 with Hibou (left), one of the first imports from China; Yangtze of Taishan (center), Hibou's son; Shu-Ssa (right); and puppies from two litters.

Development of the Breed in England

Following the political upheaval in China and the burning of the Imperial Palace, several Shih Tzu were found alive by members of the British embassy staff and were taken by them to England. The first Shih Tzu introduced there were brought from Peking by General Sir Douglass and Lady Brownrigg in 1930. These two, a dog and a bitch, were Hibou and Shu-Ssa. About the same time, Miss Madelaine Hutchins imported a Shih Tzu named Lung-Fu-Ssu into Ireland. These three became the foundation stock for the well-known Taishan strain of Shih Tzu. Some later imports were bred to the original strain in order to consolidate the type.

Shih Tzu had been introduced in Scandinavia by Mme. Henrik Kauffman. Norway's Queen Maud brought one of Mme. Kauffman's puppies, Choo Choo, to England and presented her to the Duchess of York — later to become Her Majesty The Queen Mother. Another Shih Tzu, Tashi of Chouette, a bitch, was brought to England by the Earl of Essex in 1938 and was bred successfully. Three bitches were imported by General Telfer-Smollett. They were Ming (in 1939), Ishuh-Tzu (in 1948), and Hsing-Erh (in 1952). Also, Mr. R. P. Dobson imported a bitch, Hsi-Li-Ya (in 1952).

The English Kennel Club recognized the breed in 1934. Later that same year, the Irish Kennel Club recognized the Shih Tzu. About this same time, the English Shih Tzu Club was organized under the presidency of the Countess of Essex, with Lady Brownrigg as the secretary. The English Kennel Club granted the breed championship status in 1940.

Within a few years, Shih Tzu from English kennels were being shipped to America, Canada, Australia, and European countries, where they were shown and used as breeding stock.

In all breeds and in all countries there are a few kennels whose lines are widely used and therefore appear frequently in pedigrees of top winners and top producers. Other kennels survive only briefly and may or may not have lasting impact on the breed. In England there have been four kennels that produced outstanding Shih Tzu that are now found in pedigrees in all countries where Shih Tzu are being bred and exhibited. The four kennels are Lhakang, Elfann, Telota, and Greenmoss.

Lhakang Kennel was founded just after the outbreak of World War II and now (in 1989) is the oldest Shih Tzu kennel in existence.

Gay Widdrington's love story with the Shih Tzu began when she bought a black and white bitch from Lady Brownrigg — ostensibly for a pet — to keep her company after her husband was called into military service.

The breed was very rare at that time and Lady Brownrigg would part with the puppy only on condition that Gay promise to help her establish the breed. The puppy — Mee Na of Taishan — was only the second generation from the first three Shih Tzu imported into the British Isles from China in 1930.

Mee Na was quite captivating. She sat in the doorway looking like a fluffy baby owl, so the promise was quickly made — and it is one that Gay has never regretted, for it led to an absorbing, lifelong interest.

Gay has vivid recollections of those early dogs and has done her best to preserve their essential characteristics. After the war ended in 1946, she helped Mona Brownrigg rebuild the Shih Tzu Club, trace the members, and rekindle enthusiasm among the war-weary.

Breeding stock was at a low ebb, and already very inbred. Mee Na had one litter during the war, but the only available male had been her own father! Luckily, newly imported lines soon became available.

Lhakang Kennel carried out careful selective breeding over a period of many years to help introduce and stabilize these new lines so that the breed could be established on a broader basis. It is due in great part to Gay's efforts that the breed today is one of the few in the British Isles free of serious hereditary problems.

In 1946 the "Lhakang" kennel name, meaning "Temple of the Gods," was registered. In 1952, one of Mee Na's daughters, Ch. Mao-Mao of Lhakang, produced an outstanding black and white litter, four of whom became champions. This litter really established the Lhakang Kennel and founded an important continuing line.

In the ensuing years, Lhakang Kennel produced many more champions, and by the beginning of the sixties, was the top-winning kennel in the British Isles.

In the late forties Gay and her mother decided to establish a true-breeding rich gold strain through the line of Ishuh Tzu, who had been imported from Shanghai. That line transmitted the color, and it still flourishes in the Lhakang Kennel after four decades!

Gay is more interested in breeding and rearing Shih Tzu than in showing them. Her aim has always been to produce reliable breeding stock, and she has helped to establish many other kennels. In 1964, after Ch. Soong of Lhakang, a black and white, gained her title, Gay retired from active showing.

A dog who made his mark in the United States was Ching-Yea of Lhakang, also a black and white, and out of the same dam as Soong. He went to America in 1966 — several years before the Shih Tzu was officially recognized by The American Kennel Club — and so never gained his title. However, Ching-Yea was listed as an all-time top producer and gained his Registry of Merit award (ROM) for siring eleven American champions.

Soong had a beautiful son, Sing-hi of Lhakang, fawn and white, who himself produced two famous sons: International Ch. Greenmoss Golden Peregrine of Elfann, gold, silver, and white, and Ch. Jen-ki-ko of Lhakang, black and white. Both made an impact on the breed.

In 1971 Gay produced her popular *Shih Tzu Handbook* — a small book giving essential information on the breed and illustrated by her daughter.

A bitch whom Gay values very highly is her red-gold Lhakang Cherubim. She is the dam of English and Finnish Ch. Lhakang Cassius, now owned by Eija Verlander in Finland, and of Nordic Ch. Lhakang Celandine, owned by Major Hasle in Norway and the top Shih Tzu for 1986 and 1987. A younger sibling is Finnish Ch. Lhakang Casper, who is owned by Ansa and Olli Pennanen. All three were sired by the beautiful little Tor Ra Lon, similar to Sing-hi in type.

Gay became a Specialist Judge for Shih Tzu in 1951 and has judged at Championship Shows regularly ever since. During the seventies and eighties she received many invitations to judge in countries abroad, and consequently she has enjoyed seeing the progress of the breed world-wide.

Every summer Gay arranges a Shih Tzu gathering held at Newton Hall in aid of the N.E. Rescue organization. Gay and her husband, Francis, live at Newton

Jemima of Lhakang, bred in England by Miss M. McMullen for Gay Widdrington, and later owned in the United States by Peggy Easton. Jemima was the great-great-granddaughter of Mai-Ting, who was shipped out of China on a British naval vessel just before the Communists seized control in 1949.

Hall, the Widdrington ancestral estate in the wilds of Northumberland. Her dogs live as family pets and are never confined. For this reason she prefers to place her puppies in homes where they will continue to live as members of the family, even if they are never shown.

Elfann Kennel was owned by Elfreda Evans, who swept into the Shih Tzu breed in 1951 like a ball of fire, took a cursory look at the state of the breed in the British Isles, and decided she must do something drastic to improve it! The following year, without asking advice of any of the established breeders, let alone the members of the Shih Tzu Club, she mated a black Shih Tzu bitch, Elfann Fenling of Yram, to the black and white Pekingese dog, Philadelphus Suti-T'sun of Elfann, who had unusually straight front legs for a Pekingese. As a puppy, he had been gold and white.

"Freda" had an excellent eye for beauty as well as that subtle thing — quality! She considered that the Shih Tzu she had seen were too big, leggy, rangy, plain in the face, and often wild in temperament. They certainly would not have pleased the Dowager Empress! In China, she had heard, the shaggy Lion Dogs which came as tribute from Tibet had been crossed with Pekingese every few generations. She decided to do likewise to keep the breed on the right lines.

There was shocked outrage among some (had they become a little kennel blind?) at this extraordinary action by a complete newcomer — but others saw it as a possible way out of an impasse.

At that time the English Kennel Club permitted the introduction of an outcross to another breed, providing each generation, mated back to the pure one, was registered under "Crossbreeds" in the Kennel Gazette. The fourth generation from the outcross could be registered as "Purebred."

Elfreda had previously bred Griffons and Pekingese, and she was a close friend of Mary de Pledge (Caversham Pekingese). Elfreda had founded her Pekingese kennel on Alderbourne and Caversham lines, and her brilliant breeding had resulted in a top class kennel of more than thirty show and brood bitches, including seven homebred champions. She had bred the all-time great, Ch. Ku-chi of Caversham, twice Best in Show, All Breeds, at Crufts, and winner of more than thirty challenge certificates. When Pekingese became almost too perfect, she looked around for another breed she could develop, and she chose the Shih Tzu.

Elfreda was born in Wales in 1894, and from an early age had a strong desire to succeed in life. She trained as a nurse, qualifying as a Sister Tutor. At the outbreak of World War II, she and a nursing colleague, Rossie Selth, took over the South Eden Surgical Nursing-Home in Paignton, Devon. She continued with her canine interest as a sideline. With her medical knowledge, she became an expert on all aspects of whelping and rearing, and her advice was both keenly sought and freely given. She was very outspoken and was not concerned about what others thought of her.

In 1961 Elfreda moved to Northumberland and lived with Captain and Mrs. Widdrington (Lhakang Kennel). They worked in partnership for five years. But the harsh northern climate proved too much for her, and she rejoined her former colleague in Somerset, where she ended her days.

Elfreda had been keen to establish a really good gold line in Shih Tzu. When she left Northumberland, she took with her two bitches: a pretty gold and white, Golden Bobbin, and a solid gold, Sunshine of Greenmoss. From these two she established a very successful line, using Lhakang, Greenmoss, and Tricina studs. Several of the offspring were exported to the United States — in fact, Golden Bobbin earned the Registry of Merit award (ROM), for producing four American champions.

Some of the best known Elfann Shih Tzu exported to the United States are Ch. Greenmoss Golden Talon of Elfann, Ch. Elfann Golden Puffball, and Ch. Elfann Golden Beau Brummel. The well known Canadian Ch. Elfann Golden Adonis was a Bobbin son from her last litter.

By this time — twenty years later — the Pekingese outcross was in practically all British Shih Tzu lines and undoubtedly had done much to beautify the breed.

Elfreda died March 13, 1985, just before her ninety-first birthday. Her close friend Gay Widdrington points out that some of Elfreda's admirers abroad have called her ''a prophet without honor in her own country....''

Telota Kennel is owned by Olive Newson. Olive became ''hooked'' on the Shih Tzu breed after she had caught sight of a little black and white Shih Tzu looking up at her from its bench at the Windsor Show in 1957. She discovered that a fellow Pekingese breeder, Elfreda Evans, had a litter of Shih Tzu puppies and immediately reserved a bitch. This was black and white Chin Shih of Elfann, small and sturdy, who came from Freda's good line of black and black and white Shih Tzu. Chin Shih was out of Yulan of Elfann by Wen Shu of Lhakang — the latter being the fifth generation from Elfann Kennel's Pekingese outcross.

In the same year, Olive obtained a handsome silver and white dog with a particularly beautiful head and expression — Choo-Choo of Telota. He was bred by Miss S. E. Gill (Darli Kennel), a retired postmistress who lived on the Yorkshire moors. The Darli dogs were based on Taishan, Chasmu, and Lhakang lines. Choo-Choo's dam, Coral of Airlea, was a beautiful and typical little bitch who took her name from her brilliant red and white coloring, which was then so rare.

Chin Shih and Choo-Choo produced a notable son,

Choo T'Sun of Telota (owned by Doug Hodgkinson, Brownhills Kennel). This dog rose to fame as sire of the all-time great Ch. Greenmoss Chin-Ki of Meo, who sired thirteen English champions and many more overseas, and who stamped his own excellence on his descendants.

Olive believed in careful linebreeding, so Chin Shih had another litter, this time by a black dog, Tackla Sahib of Lhakang (a son of Bimbo). He was black and white and was Chin Shih's maternal grandfather and also at stud in the Lhakang Kennel. The latter had an interesting history because he was the grandson of a lemon and white bitch, Hsi-la-ya, imported from China via India. Lady Brownrigg had liked this little bitch so much that she allowed one of her black and white dogs, Ch. Choo-ling, to be mated to her. Hsi-la-ya's daughter was in due course bred to Ch. Wang-poo of Taishan, son of Choo-ling, thus fixing the good type of the Taishan line.

The liaison of Chin Shih with Tackla Sahib produced a very stable line for the Telota Kennel, descending through their son, Tensing of Telota, Tensing Tu of Telota, and Ch. Tensing of Shanreta. The beautiful bitch Ch. Domese of Telota gained her title in 1965. She was a daughter of Tensing of Shanreta, and she acquired her title a few days before her father acquired his! Domese was out of Sien Sing of Pagodaland, who doubled back again to Bimbo. Domese really fixed the good Telota type, for she also went back, through her sire, to Choo T'Sun of Telota.

Further success came in the next generation through a notable son of Domese, Ch. Dominic of Telota. He was not a big dog, but he was a very important one, for he sired six English champions and his line helped establish several other kennels on the right lines. A granddaughter of Dominic, Ch. Telota Anouska, became the foundation bitch of the thriving Harropine Kennel. Another famous dog from Olive Newson's stock was Ch. Telota Simon Chen, who was Best in Show two years running at the Ottawa All-Breeds Championship Show in Canada.

Dominic was sired by Ch. Antarctica Chan Shih of Darite, a grandson of Jungfaltets Jung Ming, imported from Sweden, and was also linebred back to Elfann stock. Another paternal ancestor was Mr. and Mrs. Ken Rawlings' famous dog, Ch. Pan Wao Chen of Antarctica.

The Telota dogs have been traditional both in type and coloring, and have come mostly in the black and white or gray and white of the original Taishan strain. Occasionally a brilliant coral color has appeared, tracing back to the delectable Coral of Airlea. This kennel has done much for the betterment of the breed, and its line continues strongly in today's Shih Tzu in England.

Olive was a Founder Member of the Manchu Shih

Tzu Society, also a Committee Member and Area Correspondent for many years, and her husband, Ben, served as Treasurer. She was judge-elect for the Society's very first Championship Show in 1969.

Soon after her husband's death in 1982 (and Dominic's the same year), Olive retired from active participation in Shih Tzu affairs but still retained a great interest in the breed. She has published a valuable booklet, *A.B.C. of Dogs*, setting out "do's and don'ts" based on her own wide knowledge and experience. She still lives in her cottage at No. 1, Great North Road — an address which has intrigued many people, since the Great North Road stretches from London to Edinburgh — a distance of more than four hundred miles!

Greenmoss Kennel is owned by Jeanne and Arnold Leadbitter, who first met when both were serving in the Air Force. Jeanne is the fourth generation of dog breeders in her family and was schooled in the very competitive world of Terriers. The Greenmoss prefix was first taken out in 1949 for a kennel of Cairns.

Jeanne and Arnold obtained their first Shih Tzu in 1960 from the late Mrs. Emma Roberts after a two-year wait. This first Shih Tzu was Yu-li-Ching of Wyndtoi, a sturdy black and white dog whose show career was ended when one eye was damaged. The Leadbitters continued building up their kennel on Wyndtoi, Lhakang, and Elfann bloodlines, and by 1963 had made their first champion, Mei-saki of Greenmoss, son of Yu-li-Ching, also a black and white. By well-thought-out linebreeding, Greenmoss quickly became one of the leading British kennels.

The introduction of stock from Brownhills and Telota bloodlines further strengthened the kennel. Brownhills Yu Honey, red-gold and white, proved a marvelous brood bitch and helped establish some striking gold shades.

In 1965 the Leadbitters had the good fortune to find an outstanding young dog in a pet home — Ch. Greenmoss Chin-Ki of Meo, who remains the all-time Number One Top Producer of English Shih Tzu champions. He was gray and white but threw both black and white and bright gold shades. There are few leading sires who have stamped their own excellence on their progeny as has this dog, and he had a remarkable influence on stabilizing the breed. He descended strongly from the 1952 Pekingese outcross on both sides of his pedigree and was everything Elfreda Evans hoped this outcross would achieve.

Chin-Ki sired thirteen British champions and many more exported overseas, including seven who went to the United States. This earned him the coveted ROM award. At the age of twelve he sired a fine black and white dog — Ch. Greenmoss Chinki's Fling — a real "chip off the old block" who carried on his sire's prepotency.

In 1966 Jeanne and Arnold purchased ten-month-old Greenmoss Golden Peregrine of Elfann from Gay Widdrington, and he quickly won his title. He was a very glamorous dog — gold, silver, and white, and had the best of British and Scandinavian qualities. Peregrine sired four English champions before going to the late Signora Belli in Italy, where he had a sensational show career, gaining his International crown. He also sired three American champions, the best known being Fay and Ray Wine's Ch. Greenmoss Gilligan, ROM, who sired seven American champions.

Ch. Greenmoss Glory Bee, grandson of Chin-Ki, was the first solid gold ever to gain the title of champion in England. He became a champion in 1974. Chinki's Fling and Glory Bee notched up about ten champion offspring each. The Leadbitters campaigned three of Glory Bee's puppies — the "Bee" family! They were Ch. Greenmoss Bee-in-a-Bonnet, Ch. Surely Bee (Best of Breed at Crufts in 1983), and a striking dog, Ch. Bees Knees. All three were gold and white and all were out of a remarkable little bitch, Wyesarge Jade Lotus Bud (bred by the late Madge Coppage), and were produced in three successive litters. Glory Bee's color was deep reddish gold.

Ch. Glory Bee doubled back on another of the Leadbitters' well-known studs — Holmvallee Lao Yeh of Lhakang, bred from golds, although dark gold-brindle himself.

Chin-Ki's line also fanned out through his brilliant red-gold son Ch. Chin Ling of Greenmoss, who sired four champions and founded an important continuing line before going abroad.

Many top-quality Greenmoss dogs have been exported world-wide, somewhat depleting their stock at home. One of the most famous is International and Nordic Ch. Greenmoss Titfer Tat (a son of Chinki's Fling ex Bee-in-a-Bonnet), who made a big impact in Scandinavia. He is owned by Anita Berggren, Anibes Kennel, Sweden.

Although Jeanne and Arnold are less active these days, they continue to breed on a small scale, and to judge at home and abroad. In 1984 they acquired a solid gold bitch, Fugama Amber Gem, descended from their stock and formerly owned by the late Eunice Fox. This bitch produced the young winning dog Ch. Greenmoss Song of Bee. He and other top winners of Greenmoss extraction are owned by Danielle Ulrich in France and have been campaigned all over the Continent of Europe.

The Leadbitters hold the view that Shih Tzu should be strong, sturdy little dogs, sound fore and aft, and able to cover the ground; that they should have long luxurious coats shining with good health; that they should have jolly, outgoing personalities; and that they should always go to homes where they are loved and understood.

Gay Widdrington and Shih Tzu at Newton Hall, 1954.

Patti Link, longtime American breeder, at Newton Hall, September 1986. Patti has visited England many times. This quiet moment at the ancestral home of Captain and Mrs. Widdrington is one of sheer relaxation.

Gay and Francis Widdrington in the conservatory at Newton Hall with some of their Shih Tzu, 1986.

23

BRITISH SHIH TZU CHAMPIONS, 1949–1987

Dog	Breeder(s)	Owner(s)
1949		
Ch. Ta Chi of Taishan (B)	Lady Brownrigg	Breeder
1950		
Ch. Yu Mo Chaug of Boydon (D)	Mrs. H. Moulton	Lady Brownrigg
Ch. Choo Ling (D)	Gen. Telfer-Smollet	Lady Brownrigg
1951		
Ch. Shebo Tsemo of Lhakang (D)	Mrs. G. Widdrington	Mrs. S. Bode
Ch. Sing Tzu of Shebo (B)	Mrs. G. Garforth-Bless	Mrs. S. Bode
Ch. Mao Mao of Lhakang (B)	Mrs. G. Widdrington	Breeder
1953		
Ch. Ling Fu of Shuanghsi (B)	Mrs. J. Hopkinson	Mr. & Mrs. Rawlings
Ch. Hong of Hungjao (D)	Gen. Telfer-Smollet	Mrs. H. Eaden
Ch. Pa-Ko of Taishan (B)	Mrs. S. Bode	Lady Brownrigg
Ch. Tensing of Lhakang (D)	Mrs. G. Widdrington	Mr. & Mrs. K. B. Rawlings
1956		
Ch. Maya Wong of Lhakang (B)	Mrs. G. Widdrington	Breeder
Ch. Yi Ting Mo of Antarctica (D)	Mr. & Mrs. K. B. Rawlings	Breeder
Ch. Lily-Wu of Lhakang (B)	Mrs. G. Widdrington	Mrs & Mrs. K. B. Rawlings
Ch. Wang-Poo of Taishan (D)	Lady Brownrigg	Breeder
1957		
Ch. Yano Okima of Antarctica (D)	Mr. & Mrs. K. B. Rawlings	Breeder
Ch. Shu-Ssa of Michelcombe (B)	Miss O. Nichols	Mrs. R. A. Clarke
1958		
Ch. Shu-She Yu of Lhakang (B)	Mrs. G. Widdrington	Mrs. Haycock
Ch. Elfann Ta-To of Lhakang (B)	Mrs. Mather	Mrs. Murray-Kerr
Ch. Sindi-Lu of Antarctica (B)	Mrs. A. L. Dadds	Mr. & Mrs. K. B. Rawlings
1959		
Ch. Choo Choo of Cathay (D)	Mrs. J. Ross	Mrs. A. O. Grindey
1960		
Ch. Tzu-An of Lhakang (B)	Mrs. F. M. Bunk	Mrs. A. O. Grindey
Ch. Shebo Wen Yin of Lhakang (D)	Mrs. Widdrington	Mrs. S. Bode
Ch. Suki of Mavesyn (B)	Mrs. M. Cope	Mr. & Mrs. K. B. Rawlings
Ch. Tien Memsahib (B)	Mrs. T. Morgan	Mrs. G. Widdrington
1961		
Ch. Clystvale Kari of Snowland (D)	Mrs. A. L. Westcott	Miss E. Clark
Ch. Kuan Ti of Antarctica (D)	Mr. & Mrs. K. B. Rawlings	Breeder
Ch. Jou-Li of Lhakang (B)	Mrs. Widdrington	Mr. P. Beeley
1962		
Ch. Ellingham Kala Nag (D)	Lady Haggerston	Mrs. J. Lovely
Ch. Pan Wao Chen of Antarctica (D)	Mrs. St. John Gore	Mr. & Mrs. K. B. Rawlings
1963		
Ch. Li Ching Ku of Snaefell (D)	Mrs. A. Dadds	Breeder
Ch. Teresa of Tinkertown (B)	Mr. Beeley	Mrs. Balmforth
Ch. Su Si of Snaefell (B)	Mrs. A. Dadds	Breeder
Ch. Sumi San of Darli (B)	Miss S. Gill	Mr. & Mrs. Jobson
1964		
Ch. Shang Wu of Antarctica (B)	Mr. & Mrs. Rawlings	Mr. J. Moody
Ch. Soong of Lhakang (B)	Mrs. Widdrington	Breeder
Ch. Talifu Fu Hi (D)	Mr. & Mrs. C. Boot	Breeders
Ch. Shiraz of Ellingham (B)	Lady Haggerston	Miss E. Evans
Ch. Mei Saki of Greenmoss (B)	Mrs. E. Roberts	Mr. & Mrs. Leadbitter
Ch. Susie Wong of Antarctica (B)	Mr. and Mrs. K. B. Rawlings	Mr. & Mrs. K. B. Rawlings
1965		
Ch. Domese of Telota (B)	Mrs. Preedy	Mrs. O. Newson
Ch. Tensing of Shanreta (D)	Mr. & Mrs. J. R. Smith	Breeders
Ch. Talifu Bossy Boots (D)	Mr. & Mrs. C. Boot	Breeders
Ch. Cathay Nicholas of Kashmoor (D)	Mrs. Ross	Mrs. A. O. Grindey
Ch. Chi-Ma-Che of Antarctica (D)	Mrs. M. Longden	Mr. & Mrs. K. B. Rawlings

An informal international gathering of Shih Tzu breeders: dinner at the Hotel Cumberland, London, February 19, 1988. From left, Eija Verlander, Finland; Sylvia Hoyle Rawlings (Lansu), England; Elaine Meltzer (Lainee), United States; Gay Widdrington (Lhakang), England; and Gilbert Kahn (Charing Cross), United States.

Ch. Choo Lang of Telota, being awarded Best in Show at Canada's invitational show, the Show of Shows, Toronto. Bred by Olive Newson, and owned by Peter Federico and William Guzzy, Choo Lang also was Breed winner at the Westminster Kennel Club Show.

Dog	Breeder(s)	Owner(s)
1966		
Ch. Kuang-Kuang of Antarctica (D)	Mr. & Mrs. K. B. Rawlings	Breeders
Ch. Dott of Gorseycop (B)	Mrs. Bennett	Mrs. M. Hoare
Ch. Ling Fu of Antarctica (B)	Miss E. L. Bennett	Mr. & Mrs. K. B. Rawlings
Ch. Greenmoss Chin-Ki of Meo (D)	V. Reynolds	Mr. & Mrs. Leadbitter
Ch. Katrina of Greenmoss (B)	A. & J. Leadbitter	Breeders
1967		
Ch. Susella of Banwee (B)	Ms. Tomlinson & Godson	Mrs. T. E. Morgan
Ch. Antarctica Chan Shih of Darite (D)	Mrs. Copplestone	Mr. & Mrs. Rawlings
Ch. Quan-Shu of Edsville (D)	Mr. E. Openshaw	Breeder
1968		
Ch. Ah Hsueh Li-Chan of Cathay (D)	Mrs. A. O. Grindey	Breeder
Ch. Golden Peregrine of Elfann (D)	Miss E. M. Evans	A. & J. Leadbitter
Ch. Fleeting Yu Sing of Antarctica (D)	Mrs. M. Garrish	Mr. & Mrs. K. B. Rawlings
Ch. Lochranza Cho-Ling of Cathay (B)	Misses MacMillan & Coull	Mrs. A. O. Grindey
1969		
Ch. Yuh Chin Wong (B)	Mr. C. Howe	Breeder
Ch. Cherholmes Singing Lady of Wysearge (B)	Mrs. Reithermann	Mrs. M. Coppage
1970		
Ch. Jen Kai Ko of Lhakang (D)	Mrs. Widdrington	Mrs. E. Fox
Ch. Che Ko of Antarctica (B)	Mr. & Mrs. K. B. Rawlings	Breeders
Ch. Sue Lin of Bridgend (B)	Mr. & Mrs. E. Carter	Breeders
Ch. Ya Tung of Antarctica (D)	Mr. & Mrs. K. B. Rawlings	Breeders
Ch. Cha Saki of Antarctica (B)	Mr. & Mrs. Rawlings	Breeders
Ch. Dominic of Telota (D)	Mrs. O. Newson	Breeder
Ch. Greenmoss Golden Sunbeam of Elfann (B)	Miss E. M. Evans	A. & J. Leadbitter
1971		
Ch. Chin Ling of Greenmoss (D)	J. Mangles	A. & J. Leadbitter
Ch. Ko Ko Saki of Greenmoss (B)	A. & J. Leadbitter	Breeders
Ch. Tricina Wen Mo of Bridgend (B)	Mr. & Mrs. E. Carter	Breeders
Ch. Fei Ying of Greenmoss (B)	A. & J. Leadbitter	Breeders
Ch. Antarctica Don Juan of Telota (D)	Mrs. O. Newson	Mr. & Mrs. K. B. Rawlings
1972		
Ch. Kuire Hermes of Antarctica (D)	Mrs. R. D. Johnson	Mr. & Mrs. K. B. Rawlings
Ch. Cherholmes Golden Samantha (B)	Mrs. Reithermann	Breeder
Ch. Zeus of Bridgend (D)	Mr. & Mrs. E. Carter	Mrs. Thornton
Ch. Newroots Nankipoo of Snaefell (D)	Misses Fenner & Thomas	Mrs. A. Dadds
Ch. Whitethroats Chinese Gem (B)	Mrs. E. Fox	Breeder
Ch. Mu Tang of Antarctica (B)	Mr. & Mrs. K. B. Rawlings	Breeders
Ch. Bowstones Shapur of Cathay (D)	Mrs. I. Booth	Mrs. A. O. Grindey
1973		
Ch. Greenmoss Socket Tumi (D)	A. & J. Leadbitter	Breeders
Ch. Sarawana Chiu Mei of Taonan (B)	Mrs. I. E. & Miss S. M. Wigglesworth	Mrs. D. B. Harding
Ch. Kushi Palhi of Shasheen (B)	Miss D. Bridge	Mrs. M. Turnbull
Ch. Keytor Sweet Charity (B)	Mrs. E. M. Johnson	Breeder
Ch. Antarctica Ta T'Ung Fu (B)	Miss K. Willeby	Mr. & Mrs. K. B. Rawlings
Ch. Wyesarge Chin Ki Tuo of Greenmoss (D)	Mr. & Mrs. Leadbitter	Mrs. E. M. Johnson
Ch. Simone of Sandown (B)	Mrs. W. E. Donaldson	Mr. B. Halton
Ch. Santosha Rambling Rose (B)	Mr. & Mrs. D. Crossley	Mr. & Mrs. Wilkinson
1974		
Ch. Su Tung Po of Antarctica (B)	Miss K. Willeby	Mr. & Mrs. K. B. Rawlings
Ch. Sherzo of Shimisu (D)	Miss K. Willeby	Miss M. Cole
Ch. Greenmoss Glory Bee (D)	A. & J. Leadbitter	Breeders
Ch. Patsy Do of Hyning (B)	Mrs. Rowling	Mr. & Mrs. Richardson
Ch. Tricina Tai Haku (D)	Mr. & Mrs. E. Carter	Miss J. Papps
Ch. Sampa Ke-Ke-Ru Zimba of Shasheen (D)	Miss D. Bridge	Mrs. M. Turnbull
Ch. Golden Summertime of Elfann (B)	Miss E. M. Evans	Mr. T. Hoyle
Ch. Keytor Midas (D)	Mrs. E. M. Johnson	Breeder

Eng. Ch. Ta Chi of Taishan, the first Shih Tzu to become an English Champion.

Eng. Ch. Lansu Fragrant Cloud, owned by the Hoyles.

Arnold Leadbitter with Greenmoss Daisy Tu, July 1986.

Irish Ch. Lyre Limerick Lace, whelped in 1973. Owned by Miss Myrna Russell.

Patti Link with Gay Widdrington at Newton Hall, September 1986.

Dog	Breeder(s)	Owner(s)
1975		
Ch. Elfann Golden Posy of Lansu (B)	Miss E. M. Evans	Mr. T. Hoyle
Ch. Kareth Krishna (B)	Mr. J. Peat	Breeder
Ch. Sandown Yolande (B)	Mrs. Donaldson	Mr. B. Halton
Ch. Merrygarth Mai-Suzi (B)	Mr. & Mrs. R. Atwill	Breeders
Ch. Whitethroat Suna of Berinshill (D)	Mrs. E. Fox	Mesdames Waugh & Boyle
Ch. Golden Heidi of Elfann (B)	Miss E. M. Evans	Mr. T. Hoyle
1976		
Ch. Crowvalley Tweedledum (D)	Mrs. S. & Mr. L. A. Williams	Breeders
Ch. Hartend Dill (D)	Misses Overend & Hartharn	Mrs. G. Moston
Ch. Whitethroat Little Missee (B)	Mrs. E. Fox	Breeder
Ch. Greenmoss Chinki's Fling (D)	A. & J. Leadbitter	Breeders
Ch. Shasheen Lorelei (B)	Mrs. M. Turnbull	Breeder
Ch. Gorseycop Turnip Top (D)	Mrs. M. Hoare	Breeder
Ch. Sandi Quai Lu of Antarctica (D)	Mrs. J. Broadbent	Mr. & Mrs. K. B. Rawlings
Ch. Greenmoss Gideon (D)	Mrs. I. Duncan	Mr. K. Thompson
Ch. Khumar China Silk of Darralls (B)	Mrs. J. Edwards	Mrs. D. Gurney
Ch. Merrygarth Kan Do of Cathay (D)	Mr. & Mrs. Atwill	Mrs. A. O. Grindey
1977		
Ch. Pensmoor Jade Prince (D)	Mrs. Young	Breeder
Ch. Unistev Mei-Way (B)	Mr. B. Halton	Breeder
Ch. Montzella's Tsi Chou (D)	Mr. & Mrs. J. Carter	Breeders
Ch. Jamart Ki Ming (D)	Mrs. M. L. K. Fourt	Breeder
Ch. Juling Mings Golden Slipper (B)	Mrs. W. Elder	Mrs. R. Barlow
Ch. Khumar Kiss Me Kate (B)	Mrs. J. Edwards	Breeder
1978		
Ch. Bellakerne Suki Sue (B)	Mr. & Mrs. Richardson	Mr. & Mrs. T. Richardson
Ch. Lansu Fragrant Cloud (B)	Mr. T. Hoyle	1. Mr. T. Hoyle, 2. Mrs. S. Hoyle (Rawlings)
Ch. Bowstones Crowvalley Shang Tang (B)	Mr. & Mrs. Williams	Mrs. I. Booth
Ch. Ling Chee Jay Tung (D)	Mrs. G. Ling	Breeder
Ch. Bellakerne Inca Do (B)	Mr. & Mrs. Richardson	Breeders
Ch. Meriadoc Kahedin (D)	Miss J. Wray	Breeder
Ch. Shou Shang of Antarctica (B)	Mr. & Mrs. K. B. Rawlings	Breeders
Ch. Bellakerne Zippity Do (D)	Mr. & Mrs. Richardson	Breeders
Ch. Santosha Bewitched (B)	Mr. & Mrs. Crossley	Breeders
Ch. Bowstones Meena of Attocyl (B)	Mrs. I. Booth	Mrs. M. Kaye
Ch. Trisula Chioh Koh of Antarctica (B)	Mrs. B. Todd	Breeder
Ch. Crowvalley Poseidon (D)	Mrs. S. & Mr. L. A. Williams	Breeders
1979		
Ch. Philwen Mi Boi of Antarctica (D)	Mr. & Mrs. Behan	Mr. & Mrs. K. B. Rawlings
Ch. Greenmoss Bee in A Bonnet (B)	A. & J. Leadbitter	Breeders
Ch. Fishponds Soo Sze (B)	Mrs. Coulson & Mrs. Carey	Breeders
Ch. Kadwen Yan Tsi (D)	Mrs. E. Sellers	Mrs. M. Devine
Ch. Telota Anouska (B)	Mrs. O. Newson	Mr. & Mrs. Harper
Ch. Shirwen Han-Sum-Bee (D)	Mr. & Mrs. R. Lewis	Breeders
Ch. Santosha Sundown (B)	Mr. & Mrs. Crossley	Breeders
1980		
Ch. Tercero's Enchantress (B)	Mrs. E. Egan	D. S. Iley
Ch. Darralls Felicity (B)	Mrs. D. Gurney	Breeder
Ch. Telota Simon Chen (D)	Mrs. O. Newson	Mrs. & Miss W. Greves
Ch. Buttons of Snaefell (D)	Mrs. I. May	Mrs. A. Dadds
Ch. Crowvalley Pegasus (D)	Mrs. S. & Mr. L. A. Williams	Breeders
Ch. Kareth Kestral of Ritoung (D)	Mr. J. Peat	Mrs. M. Young
Ch. Jaivonne Glimmer of Hope (B)	Mrs. S. Yates	Mrs. E. Stephenson
Ch. Debridge Golden Gemini at Crowvalley (D)	Mesdames Budd & Wilson	Mrs. S. & Mr. L. A. Williams & Mrs. E. Wilson
Ch. Fernell Spring Bandit (D)	Mrs. J. E. Ellis	Breeder
Ch. Greenmoss Bees Knees (D)	Mr. & Mrs. A. Leadbitter	Breeders

Above: Eng. Ch. Dominic of Telota, bred by Olive Newson, Telota Kennels.

Above: Elfann Golden Sunrise at 11 months.

Above: Choo T'Sun of Telota, owned by Douglas Hodgkinson, England. Choo T'Sun sired Ch. Greenmoss Chin-Ki of Meo, all-time top producer of English champions. Choo T'Sun excelled in movement.

Below: Eng. Ch. Elfann Golden Posy, bred by Miss E. M. Evans, owned by Mr. Tom Hoyle.

Above: Eng. Ch. Telota Anouska (daughter of Ch. Dominic of Telota), bred by Olive Newson.

Below: Eng. Ch. Crowvalley Tweedledum with trophy won at Crufts, 1977, for Best of Breed and Reserve in the Group. Bred and owned by Mrs. S. and Mr. L. A. Williams.

Dog	Breeder(s)	Owner(s)
1981		
Ch. Montzella's Chink To Chen (D)	Mr. & Mrs. J. Carter	Breeders
Ch. Hiona Hoosa Babee of Cijena (B)	Mrs. G. Moston	Mrs. J. Heath
Ch. Elanzo Chao Fu Of Sarosim (B)	Miss A. Martin	Mrs. P. Brook
Ch. Eastern Promise of Honeylee (D)	Mr. & Mrs. J. Foster	Miss J. Papps
Ch. Bellakerne Zoe Do (B)	Mr. & Mrs. T. Richardson	Mrs. T. Morgan
Ch. Crowvalley Jessica (B)	Mr. & Mrs. L. Williams	Breeders
Ch. Yakee Chang Yeh (B)	Mr. A. Easdon	Mr. A. Easdon & Mr. P. Martin
Ch. Gorseycop Splendid Summer (B)	Mrs. M. Hoare	Mrs. A. Pickburn
Ch. Keytor Sweet Dreamer (B)	Mrs. E. Johnson	Mrs. E. & Miss S. Johnson
Ch. Queensfield Tutsi Wong of Chelhama (B)	Mrs. F. Wood	Mrs. V. Goodwin
Ch. Ragoosa Golden Raffles (D)	Mrs. T. Lewis	Mrs. H. S. Baxter
Ch. Wentres Jay Cee Valencee (D)	Miss W. Greves	Breeder
Ch. Keytor Trische Trasche (B)	Mrs. E. Johnson	Mrs. E. & Miss S. Johnson
Ch. Santosha Sunking (D)	Mr. & Mrs. D. Crossley	Breeders
Ch. Keltina Ssu Shih Wen Shu (B)	Mrs. L. Johnson	Breeder
1982		
Ch. Kareth Khoir Angel (B)	Mr. J. Peat	Breeder
Ch. Bellakerne Melisa Do (B)	Mr. & Mrs. T. Richardson	Breeders
Ch. Eastelms Teo Chi (B)	Mrs. N. J. Gardner	Breeder
Ch. Emrose Spinning Wheel (D)	Mrs. R. and Miss J. Howard	Breeders
Ch. Paora Suki Shoo of Chaulin (B)	Mr. & Mrs. K. Draper	Mr. & Mrs. P. Jackson
Ch. Claropie Peter Pan At Crowvalley (D)	Mrs. A. Aiken	Mr. & Mrs. L. Williams
Ch. Fernell Mista Magic (D)	Mrs. J. E. Ellis	Breeder
1983		
Ch. Greenmoss Surely Bee (B)	Mr. & Mrs. A. Leadbitter	Breeders
Ch. Jardhu Waffles Wu (D)	Mrs. J. Grugan	Mr. & Mrs. J. Grugan
Ch. Lyntor Eastern Magic (D)	Mrs. R. Barlow	Breeder
Ch. Santosha Bewitching Of Janmayen (B)	Mr. & Mrs. D. Crossley	Breeders
Ch. Snaefell Charm (B)	Mrs. A. L. Dadds	Breeder
Ch. Harropine China Town (D)	Mr. M. & Mrs. D. Harper	Breeders
Ch. Hyning Barbaby Bee Of Rabart (D)	Mrs. M. Rowling	Mr. R. Slater
Ch. Charka Of Kuire (B)	Mrs. Smetherham	Mrs. J. Johnson
Ch. Grandavon Maeli (B)	Mrs. M. Martin	Breeder
Ch. Mort Of Bella-Kerne At Lharing (D)	Mrs. T. Morgan	Mr. & Mrs. T. Harvie
Ch. Snaefell Imperial Imp (B)	Mrs. A. L. Dadds	Breeder
1984		
Ch. Lhakang Cassius (D)	Mrs. G. Widdrington	Mrs. Y. Brooker
Ch. Sengusi Rosalita Of Rossvale (B)	Mr. D. Iley	Mrs. S. Brown
Ch. Montzella's Rosa Lin (B)	Mr. & Mrs. J. Carter	Breeders
Ch. Chelhama Ajax Olympius (D)	Mrs. V. Goodwin	Breeder
Ch. Lingcape Gemini (B)	Mr. P. Capeling	Breeder
Ch. Crowvalley Perdita (B)	Mr. & Mrs. L. Williams	Breeders
Ch. Harropine Christmas Carol (B)	Mr. M. Harper & Mrs. D. Harper	Breeders
Ch. Greenmoss Yu Tu (D)	Mr. & Mrs. A. Leadbitter	Breeders
Ch. Snaefell Katrina Of Janmayen (B)	Mrs. A. Dadds	Breeder
Ch. Kuire Secret Simon (D)	Mrs. J. Johnson	Breeder
1985		
Ch. Kareth Kumuppance (D)	J. Peat	Breeder
Ch. Santosha Royal Flush (D)	Mr. & Mrs. Crossley	Breeders
Ch. Jorhecas Kevins Feelings (D)	C. Saevich & J. Caram	Mrs. M. Newell
Ch. Sunny Boy Of Tanibet (D)	Mrs. P. Whitehead	Miss D. Howland
Ch. Gold'n Delicious Of Rossvale (B)	Mr. Orchard	Mrs. S. Brown
Ch. Sweet Cindy Lou Of Fernell (B)	Mrs. Nafi	Mrs. J. Ellis
Ch. Janmayen Bianca (B)	Mrs. Pickburn & Mrs. Duke	Breeders
Ch. Yakee Joie De Vive At Meracon (B)	P. Martin & A. Easdon	Mrs. S. McNab
Ch. Valardy Chan Ting (B)	Mrs. C. Alferoff	Breeder

Above: Golden Bobbin of Elfann, bred by Mrs. H. Mitchell and owned by Miss E. M. Evans, England. Pictured here at 6 months of age, she acquired the R.O.M. title for producing four American champions.

Above: Eng. Ch. Greenmoss Bees Knees, bred and owned by Mr. and Mrs. Arnold Leadbitter.

Above: Eng. Ch. Greenmoss Chinki's Fling, bred and owned by Mr. and Mrs. Arnold Leadbitter.

Above: Eng. Ch. Greenmoss Bee In A Bonnet, bred and owned by Mr. and Mrs. Arnold Leadbitter.

Below: Eng. Ch. Wentres Jay Cee Valencee, Best of Breed at Crufts, 1981. Bred and owned by Miss W. T. Greves, England.

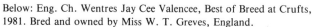

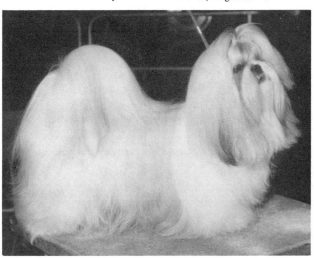

Below: Eng. Ch. Soong of Lhakang, bred and owned by Gay Widdrington.

Dog	Breeder(s)	Owner(s)
1986		
Ch. Harropine Super Trooper (D)	Mrs. D. & Mr. M. Harper	Mrs. P. Lord
Ch. Boufalls The Brigadier At Crowvalley (D)	Mrs. B. Taylor	Mr. & Mrs. L. Williams
Ch. Keytor Any Questions (D)	Mrs. E. & Miss S. Johnson	Breeders
Ch. Harropine Chaka Khan At Antarctica (D)	Mrs. D. & Mr. M. Harper	Mr. & Mrs. K. B. Rawlings
Ch. Firefox Of Santosha (D)	Mr. B. Easdon	Mr. & Mrs. D. Crossley
Ch. Harropine Lord Of The Rings (D)	Mrs. D. & Mr. M. Harper	Breeders
Ch. Orlando Of Kuire (D)	Mrs. M. Droogan	Mr. & Mrs. N. Stevens
Ch. Amylots Wai Wai Wonder (B)	Mr. & Mrs. D. Williams	Mrs. P. Woodbridge
Ch. Rosaril Modesty Blaize (B)	Miss A. Stephenson	Breeder
Ch. Anibes Puttin' On The Ritz (B)	Mrs. A. Berggren	Breeder
Ch. Harropine Odyssey (B)	Mrs. D. & Mr. M. Harper	Breeders
1987		
Ch. Koun Billy Buntch Of Yashnee (D)	Mrs. M. D. Ross	Mr. & Mrs. K. Dyson
Ch. Senousi Be Bop deLux (B)	Mr. D. S. Iley	Breeder
Ch. Bowstones Shu Shan (B)	Mrs. I. Booth	Mrs. P. Maule
Ch. Lharing Moon-Mischief (B)	Mr. & Mrs. T. Harvie	Breeders
Ch. Kareth Kismet of Lyre (B)	Mr. & Mrs. G. Hickey	Mr. J. Peat
Ch. Wendolyn Wild Ginger (B)	Mrs. J. W. Wood-Jones	Breeder
Ch. Zuthis Moonlight Shadow (B)	Mr. & Mrs. B. J. Roberts	Breeders

Eng. and Braz. Ch. Crowvalley Poseiden. Bred by Mrs. S. and Mr. L. A. Williams. Owned by Mr. M. Schneider, San Paulo, Brazil. Poseiden was Best in Show in England several times before leaving for Brazil in May 1978. He was named Dog of Dogs in Brazil in 1978.

Nord Ch. Furuglantans Golden Biley, owner Ritva Nissila.

Conwynns Beau Geste, owner Connie Smart.

Left: Ch. Chinai's Starlord at 6 months, owners David and Chris Jones.

Right: Ch. Mar-Lin's Ginger Lee, owner Patricia Jones.

Ch. Yingsu Charleston Blue, owner Sue Miller.

Ch. Bon D'Art Adore Ring of Fancee, owner Marilyn Sue Woodward; and Ch. Bon D'Art Amour Ring of Fancee, owners Wheeler and Guggenheim.

Left: Ch. China Chimes Slew of Gold, owner Kathryn Heilman.

Right: Am., Can., and Jap. Ch. Lainee Edipus Complex of Nova, owners Meltzer and Novak, then exported to Japan.

Left: Visconti The Duchess of York, "Fergie," owner Dan Haley.

Right: Ch. Chin Yu Tristan of Jonafins, owner Eleanore De Maio.

Left: Ch. Ambelon's Son Of A Gunther, owner Janeth Nyberg.

Right: Ch. Dragonfire's Red Raider, owner Peggy A. Hogg.

Am. and Can. Ch.
Strawberry Blond
Luvncare, owner
Rosemary Hoo.

Ch. Kee-Lee's Red
Baron of Mar-Del,
owners Keenan,
Lee, and
MacIntosh.

Ch. Char-Nick's U
Gotta Believe,
owner Gloria
Camileri.

Ch. Mar-Del's Ring
A Ding Ding, owner
Margaret Edel
MacIntosh.

Ch. Emperor's
Thing Ah-Ma Ying,
owners Dr. and
Mrs. J. Wesley
Edel.

The British Royal
Family in the late
1930s with their
Shih Tzu, Choo-
choo.

Ch. Char-Nick's I Gotcha, owners Mr. and Mrs. Louis Sanfilippo; and Ch. Char-Nick's Be-Wit-Ching of Copa, owner Macada Kennels.

Ch. Snobhill's Free Lance, owner Sharon Milligan.

Am. and Can. Ch. Mei San Theo-Dorable Cameo, owner Betty Meidlinger.

Witch's Wood Shot In The Dark, handler Alan Harper.

Ch. Bel Air Ace of Spades, owner Diane Backovich.

Ch. Aagalynn's I'm A Dandy, owners Keenan and Lee.

Ch. Laksana's Bubblin' Brown Sugar, owner Victor Joris.

Ch. Taylwag's P B R Donimie, owners Taylor, Wagner, and Crissman.

Am. and Can. Ch. Ta Ya Chai's Emeer von Arvind, owner Trudy Kerr.

Ch. Cabrand's Agent Orange v. Lou Wan, owner Robert Koeppel.

Am. and Can. Ch. Shente's Brandy Alexander, owners Brown and Ehricht.

Ch. Wenrick's Tini Tina, owners Wendy and Richard Paquette.

Ch. Rockee Vollee Scarlet Angel, owner Helen Mueller.

Ch. Dragonwyck The Great Gatsby, owner Robert Koeppel.

Am. and Can. Ch. House of Wu U Know Who, owner Gay D. Eckes.

Can., Am., Ber. Ch. Kaduna's Sewzi-Q Lan-Sing, C.D., owners Corbett and Sniderman.

Ch. Sanchi's Kokutan Of Si-Kiang, owner Bonnie Miller, D.V.M.

Ch. Vilenzo Red Rover, Red Rover, owners Vilas and Savio.

Ch. Afshi's Gunther, owners Joly and Torriello.

Ch. Emperor's All That Glitters, owners Dr. and Mrs. J. Wesley Edel.

Ch. Kee-Lee's Strut 'N Stuf of Mar-Del, owner Julia Mech.

Am. and Can. Ch. Imua's Guava Jam, owner Rosemary Hoo.

Ch. Dragonwyck Danielle's Delite, owners Patton and Constantino.

Ch. Chang Tang's Elusive Jeffrey, owners Joyce and Hal DeVoll.

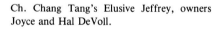

Am. and Can. Ch. Samalee's Reflections of Baron, owners Marnie and Ron Oystrick.

Ch. Lou Wan Rebel Rouser, owners Gec, Gunning, and Wheeler.

Ch. Chumulari Chin Te Jih, owner Victor Joris.

Am. and Can. Ch. Ch'Ang Ch'U Apollo, owners Tony and Linda Barrand.

Ch. Shen Wah's Turn It Loose, owners Mr. and Mrs. Joe C. Walton.

Ch. Lainee O.D.'D At Charing Cross, owner Gilbert S. Kahn; breeder and co-owner Elaine Meltzer.

Ch. Ambiance A Head Of The Crowd, owners David and Stockstell.

Ch. Wingate's Never Say Dye, owner Jody Neal.

Am. and Can. Ch. Regal's Dr. Spock, owners Wendy and Richard Paquette.

Ch. Show Off's I've Got Rhythm, owners Ena and Bruce Lane.

Ch. Mei San Tuf E Nuff, owner Betty Meidlinger.

Ch. Dragonfire's I'm Bucko, owner Laura Gidusko.

Brownhills Teresa.

Sing-Hi of Lhakang and Ch. Soong of Lhakang with Golden Peregrine of Elfann (later a champion) and Jenny Wren.

Ch. Greenmoss Glory Bee, bred and owned by the Leadbitters, Greenmoss Kennels.

Elfreda Evans in 1961 with Elfann Fu-ling of Lhakang and Akela of Ellingham.

Ch. Golden Summertime of Elfann, bred by Elfreda Evans, owned by Sylvia and Tom Hoyle.

Am. Ch. Elfann Golden Sunmaiden, owned by Connie Smart.

33

Above: Swedish Ch. Anibes Li-Missee, bred and owned by Anita and Kurt Berggren.

Above: Int. and Nordic Ch. Kurt's Boy of Lansu with his daughter Int. and Nordic Ch. Formaregardens Q-Ti-Pie.

Above: Mrs. Erne Jungfeldt and children, Sweden, 1957, with Jungfaltets' Shih Tzu.

Below: Ch. Jungfaltets Bo-Chi-Li, owned by Kurt and Anita Berggren.

Above: Froken Astrid Jeppesen, owner of Bjorneholm Kennel, Denmark, photographed in 1984.

Below: Major Hasle, Norway, with his English-bred foundation stud, Nord Ch. Lhakang Jolyon.

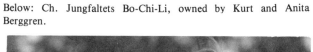

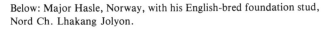

Shih Tzu International

SCANDINAVIA

Shih Tzu were introduced to Scandinavia by Mme. Henrik Kauffman when her husband, who had been Danish Minister to China, was transferred from Peking to Norway in 1932. Mme. Kauffman had acquired a Shih Tzu, a black and white bitch named Schauder, a short time before. Schauder was one of several Mme. Kauffman came across that were about to be burned in what she believed to have been a religious ceremony — perhaps as part of a funeral ritual.

Mme. Kauffman managed to acquire only Schauder at that time, but she became so intrigued with the breed that she set about searching for others, and before leaving China, she acquired two more.

Schauder was whelped in Shanghai in 1931. She was by Aidzo-Hu out of Hu-Luh. Aidzo, also black and white, was a male whelped in Peking in 1930. He was by Law Hu out of Lun-Geni. Leidza, a golden bitch, had been whelped in the Imperial Palace in 1928. She was by Chin Tai out of Wu-Hi, and has been described as the only European breeding stock known to have come directly from lines bred in the Imperial Palace. Pedigree information given Mme. Kauffman consisted only of the names of the sires and dams, and dates and places of whelping. The Kauffmans' three dogs and their offspring were interbred in Scandinavia for almost twenty years without infusion of other lines. One of the best known of the progeny of Aidzo and Schauder was Lingen. Lingen's granddaughter Norwegian and Swedish Ch. Voksenliast Shih-Tzu was mated to her sire, Norwegian Ch. Law Hu II, and to her son Yun Toy, and the resulting progeny exerted great influence on the breed. The Danish Consul's wife, Mrs. Elsie Grum, was fascinated by the Kauffmans' Shih Tzu and acquired Ting-a-Ling, who was by Lingen out of Leidza.

One of the names by which the breed had been known in China was Lhasa Terrier, and it was by that name that the breed was first recognized in Norway. The breed had been recognized in 1934 by the Federation Cynologique Internationale (F.C.I.) under the name Shih Tzu. And in 1939 the Norwegian Kennel Club approved the changing of the name in Norway to "Shih Tzu."

Noted judge Tore Edmund began judging the breed in 1952. His wife also judged the breed.

Included among early breeders in Norway were Mrs. Adele Heyerdahl, who established her Flinthaugs Kennel after being given her first bitch by Mme. Kauffman. Mrs. Heyerdahl continued her line until her death some thirty years later.

Mrs. Aasta Helliksen established her Voksenliast Kennel in the early days of the breed in Norway. Her foundation bitch was Voksenliast Pareblomst, by Law Hu II out of Bijou, and was whelped in 1939.

John Norman, another early breeder in Norway, established his Dux Kennel about the same time. He started with Ling Tzu av Dux, who was whelped in 1941 and was by Psiupsia out of Mi-tzu.

Extended pedigrees of Shih Tzu in Scandinavia and elsewhere include dogs from these kennels as well as those of early kennels in Denmark, Sweden, and Finland.

Miss Astrid Jeppesen established her famous Bjorneholm Kennel in Denmark with the purchase of Mai Ling Tzu av. Dux from Norway. Beginning in the forties, she linebred, using Scandinavian lines without outcrossing. Her dogs had a tremendous impact on the breed through the years, and in many countries. Her Bjorneholms Pippi became the foundation bitch for Mrs. Erma Jungefeldt's kennel in the midfifties. Mrs. G. Wedege established her Lindevangens Kennel in Denmark during this same early period.

Outside lines were introduced in 1951 when Fru Hansa Anderson imported a dog and a bitch from England. The dog was Shebo Schunder of Hungjao, a large black Shih Tzu. The bitch was Looching of the Mynd. She also was large, and gray and white. The Shih Tzu was judged in the Non-Sporting Group in Great Britain but in the Toy Group in Scandinavia (as in some other countries) and it is to this difference in Groups that the difference in size is attributed, because dogs competing in the Non-Sporting Group traditionally are larger than dogs competing in the Toy Group.

Before being exported to Denmark, Looching was mated with Ch. Shebo Tsemo of Lhakang. Soon after arrival in Denmark, Looching whelped five puppies. The two imports and their progeny proved influential in a number of breeding programs, in spite of their somewhat larger size.

In Sweden, a pioneer breeder was Walter Ekman, who brought a male Shih Tzu with him when he returned from a trip to China. Shortly thereafter he purchased Amoy, a bitch by Tangtz of Taishan out of Tzu Hsi of Taishan, from Lady Brownrigg's Taishan line.

Baron Carl Leuhusen imported Flinthaugs Da-Wa from Mrs. Heyerdahl's kennel in 1950. This gold colored dog, of course, went back through the Flinthaugs Kennel lines to the Kauffmans' Shih Tzu.

Mrs. Anna Hauffmann established her Shepherds Kennel as one of the earliest Swedish kennels that specialized in breeding Shih Tzu. Mrs. Hauffmann imported Lindevagens Choo-Li, a bitch by Flinthaugs Wu Hi out of Bjorneholms Karma, and Wu-Lung Fengsao, a male by Shebo Tsemo of Lhakang out of Looching of the Mynd.

Above: Charing Cross Prince Andrew, bred by Gilbert Kahn, Florida, and exported to Vaclav Mazanek in Czechoslovakia in 1980.

Above: Cocoandrew Golem, by Charing Cross Prince Andrew ex Etana Chicatita. Etana was the Mazaneks' foundation bitch.

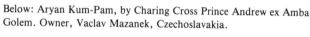

Above: Nord Ch. Boreas Elfline Lodestar, owned by Eija Verlander, Finland.

Below: Aryan Kum-Pam, by Charing Cross Prince Andrew ex Amba Golem. Owner, Vaclav Mazanek, Czechoslavakia.

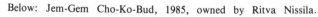

Above: Shih Tzu Specialty Show, 1980, Norberg, Sweden. Judge, Gay Widdrington. Best in Show, Int. and Nord Ch. Bellakerne Suki Sue, handled by Paul Stanton. Best of Opposite Sex, Int. and Nord Ch. Anibes Li-Tom-Boi, handled by Kurt Berggren.

Below: Jem-Gem Cho-Ko-Bud, 1985, owned by Ritva Nissila.

36

Bjorneholm stock served as foundation Shih Tzu for several other Swedish kennels, including Mrs. U. B. Wifalk's Wi-Lu's Kennel; Mrs. M. Larson's Nankings Kennel; and Mrs. E. Jungefeldt's Jungfaltets Kennel.

The Jungfaltets' strain was founded in the early fifties on Bjorneholms Pippi and her litter brother Bjorneholms Megg, who were by Bjorneholms Kesang and out of Bjorneholms Dott. A few years later, Mrs. Jungefeldt imported from England Fu-Ling of Clystvale, a small black and white Shih Tzu, in order to reduce the size of the Swedish strains — some of which weighed as much as eighteen pounds. An influential stud, Fu-Ling sired many C.C. winners.

Jungfaltets Jung Wu completed her French championship under the ownership of Ingrid Colwell, and then came to America to become a foundation bitch of the Si Kiang Shih Tzu in the United States.

Flinthaugs Lung Toy was imported from Mrs. Heyerdahl's Kennel. He sired Ch. Ting-e-Ling av Brogyllen out of Ch. Shepherds Si Kiang. Ting-e-Ling became the foundation bitch for a strong, winning line. Another import from Mrs. Heyerdahl's kennel was Flinthaugs Li Tze, but this dog's impact was not so great as Ting-e-Ling's.

International and Nordic Ch. Beldams Fu Mao Thing was another bitch who played an important part in establishing Swedish lines. She was bred by Mrs. K. Sandberg of Beldams Kennel and owned by Mrs. M. Berg of Marinas Kennel. She was the first Swedish bred international champion bitch and a number of her offspring became champions as well as continuing as producing stock. Among her champion get are Ch. Chendru and International and Nordic Ch. Nuff-Chang-Tzu. The latter sired numerous progeny who were successful in the show ring.

International and Norwegian Ch. Tempel-gardens Mia-Bela-Tzu not only was a top producing Shih Tzu, but ranked high among top producing bitches in all breeds. She produced thirteen champions in Lundehill Kennel.

Anita and Kurt Berggren established an outstanding line in their Swedish Anibe Kennel. They started their Shih Tzu breeding from pure Scandinavian lines from the Bjorneholm and Jungfaltet Kennels in 1962. Later they decided it was necessary to introduce other strains and purchased Kurt's Boy of Lansu from Mr. Tom Hoyle of Lansu Kennel in England. That dog became an International and Nordic champion and produced outstanding offspring when bred to Scandinavian bitches. He was top winning stud dog, all breeds, in Sweden for 1977, 1978, and 1979. The Berggrens also imported English bitches, one of which became English, International, and Nordic Ch. Bellakerne Suki Sue, multiple Best-in-Show winner and top winning Toy Dog in

Scandinavia in 1978 and 1979, as well as second top winning dog, all breeds, in Sweden in 1979.

Foundation stud dog for Major Borre Hasle's Boreas Kennel is Nordic Ch. Jolyn, sire of many champion Shih Tzu. Boreas stock includes famous English lines such as Elfann, Lansu, Lhakang, and Whitethroat.

Ruth Laakso (Zizi Shih Tzu) of Drammen, Norway, has for many years been one of Scandinavia and Europe's finest breeders of Shih Tzu. Hers is one of the oldest active kennels in Europe. Her Norwegian Ch. Zizi's Law-Hu is out of her Best-in-Show Scandinavian Ch. Zizi Tara, who is one of the "winningest" bitches in Scandinavia. Tara's sire was International and Scandinavian Ch. Marinas Muff-Lung Feng, also a Best-in-Show winner, and out of International, Scandinavian, and Danish Ch. Zizi's Lhamo.

The Swedish Shih Tzu Society was founded in March 1969 and accorded official recognition in 1981.

The breed was introduced into Finland in 1955. The first imports were Shepherds Yen-Psung, a bitch whelped in 1954, and Shepherds Hien Kiang, a dog whelped in 1953. Both were bred by Mrs. Hauffmann of Sweden and imported into Finland by Mrs. Irja Kunnari.

Mr. Antti Seppala imported Chow-Ah-Ling as foundation bitch for his Capella Kennel. The first litter from this Norwegian-bred bitch was whelped in 1961. Mr. Seppala also imported dogs from England, including International and Nord Ch. Edsville Fu Yung of Elanzo. The first Shih Tzu in Finland to acquire the title of International Champion, this outstanding dog has sired many champions. Among them are International and Nordic Ch. Genius Pei-Pik, Scandinavian Ch. Marella Tatzang, and Scandinavian Ch. Capella Cu Ling. Shih Tzu which Mr. Seppala imported from the Liliencrons Kennel owned by Mrs. B. Larsen-Rosvall in Sweden include the outstanding Ch. Liliencrons Lord Maurice and International and Nordic Ch. Liliencrons Capella. Another import from the Liliencrons line is International and Nordic Ch. A-Abracadabra, procured from Mrs. Fossenius in Sweden. A-Abracadabra was among Mr. Seppala's most outstanding dogs — ranking as top winning Shih Tzu in Finland for 1980 and 1981.

Mr. H. Mutanen of Marella Kennels owned International and Nordic Ch. Capella Jim, who was bred by Mr. Seppala. This outstanding dog was the top winning Shih Tzu in Finland in 1978 as well as winner of the Club Specialty that year.

Mr. Pekka Vaissi imported Nordic Ch. Nankings O-Fe-Lia in 1963 as foundation bitch for his Kauhakuusen Kennel. A daughter of Fu Ling of Clystvale, she was winner of seven CACIBs and produced Ch. Kauhakuusen Tzu-En-Lai and Ch. Kauhakuusen Tsang-Sha. Mr. Vaissi imported Ch. Lochranza Khan Du in 1966. This dog was bred by the

Scandinavian Ch. Zizi's Tara, owned by Ruth Laakso, Norway.

Int. and Nord Ch. Anibes Li-Tom-Boi, owned by Mr. and Mrs. Sven Ake Angnell, Sweden.

Norwegian Ch. Zizi's Law-Hu, bred and owned by Ruth Laakso, Norway.

Six champion Shih Tzu owned by Ruth Laakso, Kennel Zizi, Norway.

Danish Ch. Bjorneholm's Lovi-She-Ling, owned by Merete C. Kjaer, Denmark.

Misses McMillan and Coull in England. He sired a number of champions including International and Nordic Ch. Scedessan Da-Zaza and International and Nordic Ch. Kauhakuusen Wen-Tai. Khan Du sired a litter of five whelped in 1968 out of O-Fe-Lia. Included were Kauhakuusen Charles, who was exported to France, plus three outstanding champions — one of which, Camilla, won the Club Specialty in 1976 and 1977.

In 1971 Mr. Vaissi imported Ch. Law Hu van de Blauwe Mammouth from Holland. He sired a number of champions.

Ch. Kauhakuusen Casse, bred by Mr. Vaissi, was the foundation bitch for Mrs. Sirkka Lahdenpera's Sirklahden Kennels. Following her purchase in 1968, Casse produced a number of champions for Mrs. Lahdenpera. Mrs. Lahdenpera mated her Ch. Sirklahden Kadri-Lee to Mrs. Berggren's International and Nordic Ch. Kurt's Boy of Lansu. This breeding produced Ch. Sirklahden Pa-Ya and Sirklahden Po-La, both of whom produced champions.

Mrs. Lahdenpera imported Ch. Lansu Tribute to Heidi from the Hoyles in England, and Ch. Anibes Pee Wee Peony from the Berggrens in Sweden. Through her successful breeding program using these Shih Tzu and some from her earlier breedings, Mrs. Lahdenpera developed an outstanding line. In 1980 and 1981 she was winner of the Club's "Top Shih Tzu Breeder of the Year" award. And among the outstanding champions she has bred is Wu-Ling, who was Best of Breed at the Club Specialty in 1981 and 1982.

A bitch imported by Miss Pakarinen in 1977 became Top Winning Shih Tzu in Finland in 1979. This outstanding Shih Tzu is International and Nordic Ch. Boreas Mei Hsi Ch'iao, bred by Major Hasle in Norway. In her first litter, Mei Hsi Ch'iao produced two puppies who eventually acquired international titles and two who gained championships in two countries.

The Shih Tzu Club of Finland was founded in 1971. In Finland, as in all countries of Europe (with the exception of England), Shih Tzu are judged by the Federation Cynologique Internationale Standard.

Int. and Nord Ch. Lansu Heidi's Fair Lady, bred by Mr. T. Hoyle, England, owned by Kurt and Anita Berggren, Sweden.

Sf Ch. Sirklahden Zeus, bred by Mrs. Sirkka Lahdenpera and owned by Miss Marja Nurmi, Finland.

Boreas Imperial Dibalove, owned by G. M. Soderholm, Sweden; and Ch. Boreas Majormagic, owned by Major B. Hasle, Norway.

Danish Ch. Gaya's Khe-Tuo-Zi-Ling, owned by Kirsten and Preban Larsen, Denmark.

Danish Ch. Gaya's Lin-You-Yue, owned by Kirsten and Preban Larsen, Denmark.

Trashi-Lhunpo Chiuming, owned by Merete C. Kjaer, Denmark.

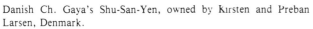

Danish Ch. Gaya's Shu-San-Yen, owned by Kirsten and Preban Larsen, Denmark.

Ch. Bjorneholm's Leidsa, Sweden.

Above: Carin, owned by Misako Kanno, Japan.

Above: Vogelflight Mop 'N Glo, bred by Mary Vogel, owned by Misako Kanno, Japan.

Above: Jap. and Am. Ch. TiGi's Blazen Fury, bred by Tim Glaven.

Above: Grand Ch. Castle Morozumis A P Ton O Thunder, owned by Seishi Niiyama, bred and co-owned by Mami Nakae, Japan.

Above: Jap. and Am. Ch. Lainee The Raven Maniac. Bred by Elaine Meltzer and Judith Boyles. Owned by Elaine Meltzer.

Below: Ch. Jen-Mi's Gee Whiz, Best in Show at the 1988 F.C.I., Osaka, International Show. Owner, Takehi Watanabe. Handler, Hiroshi Osumi. Breed judge, Mrs. Tomie Hashimoto. Group judge, Mr. Robert Forsyth. BIS judge, Mrs. Jane Forsyth.

THE NETHERLANDS

The Netherlands was home to the world renowned Oranje Manege Kennel owned by Miss Eta Pauptit. Her studious approach paid off, for in the sixties she was the leading Dutch fancier and breeder of Shih Tzu. She bred many winners and producers. International and Dutch Ch. Hang Shu v.d. Oranje Manege was one of her most illustrious stud dogs. His influence, and that of other Oranje Manege Shih Tzu, is evident in pedigrees of outstanding dogs throughout the world.

The Baronesse Beatrice V. van Panthaleon Van Eck-Klasing was also an avid and successful Shih Tzu fancier for many years. She was the breeder of International Ch. Quang Te v.d. Blauwe Mammouth, one of the most titled Shih Tzu ever. Owned and campaigned in Europe by M. L. Rentzing-Stouten, Quang Te, under the guidelines of the F.C.I. and the German Kennel Club, won the title of "Deutsche Bundessieger" in 1975 in Stuttgart, West Germany. In Paris in 1974, he had been awarded the "Diplome de Champion de l'Exposition Mondiale (World Champion, F.C.I.)." Quang Te was later imported to the United States by the Reverend and Mrs. D. A. Easton.

Above: Am., Ger., and Int. Ch. Entang Shu v.d. Oranje Manege, a darker faced particolor, shows us that Europeans judge conformation and movement first, rather than color or markings. They have set a good example.

Above: Kwan Tan Djo v. Ebbinks Lhoewe (left) and Quesnay Wang v.d. Kleine Oosterling, owned by Mevr. Renzing, Holland.

Below: Netherlands and Int. Ch. Lon Shu v.d. Oranje Manege (left), bred by Eta Pauptit in The Netherlands; and Chumulari Hoo T'ee, bred by the Reverend and Mrs. D. Allan Easton.

Below: Eta Pauptit, owner of the Van Der Oranje Manege Kennels in The Netherlands, is shown here at an F.C.I. Show in Switzerland with Am., Ger., and Int. Ch. Entang Shu v.d. Oranje Manege. This European winner was imported to the United States and is owned by Dr. Barbara S. Merickel.

FRANCE

Among the first Shih Tzu to be seen in Europe was Mei-Yun, who belonged to Mme. Graeffe, wife of the Belgian ambassador to Peking. Probably the first to be entered in a show in Europe, Mei-Yun won first prize at the 1929 Exposition Canine de Paris, when the Graeffes were on home leave.

Although the Graeffes had a number of the breed throughout their years of residence in China and other countries, none of their stock seems to have continued in Europe.

Currently Mme. Chantal Mery of le Vesinet is breeding and exhibiting very successfully. International Ch. Muna vom Tschomo-Lungma, whelped in 1977, is the foundation bitch of this outstanding kennel located near Paris. Muna won the World Championship in Berne in 1979. Of excellent quality, Mme. Mery's stock has been exported to several countries in Europe and to the United States. She has exhibited at various F.C.I. World Championship Shows.

Above: French Ch. Jungfaltets Jung-Wu, owned by Ingrid Colwell. One of Ingrid's original imports from Europe, Jung-Wu was an important part of her foundation stock in America.

Above: French Ch. Muna v. Tschomo-Lungma. Bred by Frau Erika Geusendam, Germany. Owned by Mme. Chantal Mery, Paris.

Below: Pukedal's Do Dat, sire of Ingrid Colwell's first import.

Below: Int. and French Ch. Kanda v. Tschomo-Lungma, owned by F. Dichmann, France.

43

WEST GERMANY

The Shih Tzu world has been proud of the revered name of Frau Erika Geusendam of Lubeck, West Germany. Her world famous Tschoma-Lungma Kennels, named after the lofty mountains in the Himalayan system, have been in existence since the 1950s.

Frau Geusendam's knowledge of horse breeding in West Germany contributed to her astuteness in pulling together the tight genetic pool that has made her strain so dominant throughout Europe and the Americas. She has exported her Shih Tzu to at least fifteen countries, including the U.S.S.R.

The influence of the Bjorneholm dogs played an important part in Frau Geusendam's foundation breeding stock. International Ch. Bjorneholm Pif was bred by Fru Jeppesen of Denmark but was later owned by Frau Geusendam, who in turn, exported him to the United States. Pif's titles included that of "Bundessieger," which he won in Frankfurt, Germany, in 1965. The title of "Bundessiegerin" was won by International Ch. Tang-la vom Tschomo-Lungma (litter sister to Tangra, who was exported to the Eastons in whelp to Pif). Tang-la won the coveted "Bundessiegerin" title at the same show. Pif and Tangra won the titles "Sieger and Siegerin der Weltausstellung" (World Champions), in Brun, Czechoslovakia, in 1965.

The titles "Sieger" and "Siegerin" are awards to the "select" dog and "select" bitch, respectively, at a German regional show. "Bundessieger" and "Bundessiegerin" are awards made yearly to one dog and one bitch, respectively, in each breed competing at the National Bundessieger Show in the Federal Republic of Germany. The awards represent excellence above all other males or females in that breed. The title "World Champion" is an F.C.I. award given at an annual show held at a different location in the world each year. A dog may compete only if registered in a country whose national kennel club is a member of the F.C.I.

Tangra became the dam of American and Canadian Ch. Chumulari Ying Ying. Tang-la became the dam of the famous European winner and producer, International Ch. Sopon vom Tschomo-Lungma, who was later exported to the Bom Shu Kennels to become an important producer in the United States.

Tang-la was defeated only once during her show career, and that was when she was competing against International champions, so one can appreciate her outstanding qualities. She went on to win Toy Groups, which were competitions held only in Benelux Countries and Scandinavia.

Other famous Tschomo-Lungma dogs have included the fabulous bitch Naga, a Tang-la daughter; Ollo, a Pif son; and the heavily titled, two times "World Champion" Faran Vom Tschomo-Lungma.

Although Erika has stayed true to the direct line from China in her genetic pool, she found it necessary to import a litter of four males and one bitch from Gay Widdrington. This litter was from an English Lhakang bitch and was by Juan of Lhakang (Choo Choo of Telota ex Jo-Ann of Lhakang). Both parents of the litter were free of any Peke cross and were pure descendants from the original stock from China introduced into Norway in 1932, and then into England in 1948 and 1949 by Mr. and Mrs. Rowland Morris (Lunghwa). From this Lunghwa line, a descendant went to the English Royal Family.

The bitch Hsi-la of Lhakang (one of the litter of five puppies from Gay Widdrington) was bred by Frau Geusendam to her International Ch. Ollo Vom Tschomo-Lungma, thus producing Dhuti Vom Tschomo-Lungma.

In 1989, Erika is breeding but on a very limited basis. Trudy Kerr has imported outstanding stock into Canada from the Tschomo-Lungma Kennels and has based her Ta Ya Chai Kennels solely on Frau Geusendam's stock.

Above: Swiss, Czech., and Can. Ch. Tangra v. Tschomo-Lungma, dam of Chumulari Ying Ying.

Below: Int. Ch. Faran v. Tschomo-Lungma, champion in Germany, Denmark, and The Netherlands, and World Champion (F.C.I.) 1979 and 1981. Owned by Frau Erika Geusendam, Germany.

Bundessieger Show, Essen, Germany, 1979. Left, Mahal v. Tschomo-Lungma with owner H. Stupp. Center, Ch. Faran v. Tschomo-Lungma with breeder/owner E. Geusendam. Right, Ch. Oruro Shu v.d. Oranje Manege with owner P. Vlieghuis, The Netherlands.

AUSTRALIA

For the first twenty-five years following breed establishment "Down Under," Australian Shih Tzu winners were primarily from stock derived from inter-breeding of the original English imports and their progeny. By the early seventies, there was infusion from some later imports.

Tony and Soo Dobson were the first Shih Tzu breeders in Australia. They established their Wawnehill Kennels in New South Wales in 1954. Their original stock was from three top English kennels of the day: Wen Chin of Lhakang (chestnut and white male puppy); Pei Ho of Taishan (black and white male who already had two English C.C.s to his credit); and Chloe of Elfann (black bitch). Eventually, all three became Australian champions. Tony Dobson qualified as a Shih Tzu judge and continued to serve in the show ring for many years.

Mrs. Dot Avery imported Lee Lisan of Lhakang, an outstanding sire who was an important addition to the stock she had acquired from the Dobson imports to establish her Newglen Kennels.

Mrs. Gwen Teele established her Geltree Kennels with dogs from the original imports. Then in 1958 she imported Hia Nan of Snaefell, a black and white bitch. In 1959 she imported Ty Yung of Antarctica, a black and white male. In 1963 Mrs. Teele imported Ch. Skoal of Eyeworth, a gray and white grandson of Jungfaltets Jung Ming. All three of these imports became Australian champions. Stock from Geltree Kennels is to be found in Shih Tzu pedigrees throughout the world.

Mrs. Joan Reeves acquired Ch. Geltree Ty Ching, a black and white dog who became an extraordinarily successful sire. He also was outstanding in the show ring and became the first Shih Tzu to win the award Best Exhibit in Show, All Breeds, in Australia.

Mrs. J. Gaspero acquired Australian Ch. Geltree Cheng Liu. This black and white bitch had numerous Best-in-Show and Group wins.

Australian Ch. Tsuyung Fanci That.

Stock from early kennels was to be found throughout Australia and New Zealand within a few years, and Shih Tzu were winning in show rings in all states. Some of the winning dogs and bitches were imported from England — notably from lines originated in such kennels as Lhakang, Telota, Greenmoss, Crowvalley, and Chasmu. The infusion of these lines is still obvious in characteristics of outstanding Shih Tzu "Down Under."

Below: Australian Ch. Tsuyung Ming Dynasty.

Below: Australian and American Ch. Skywalker Milinia. Owned by Gilbert S. Kahn, Florida.

45

Importations of dogs were barred for several years following a rabies scare in 1969. It was not long after the ban was lifted and importations were resumed in the seventies that Australian Shih Tzu made an impact world-wide. One of the first big wins following the lifting of the ban was made by imported Ch. Saffron of Greenmoss. She won the award for All Breed Best in Show in 1970 under Mr. W. G. Siggers, a famous International judge.

John Sheppard's Ch. Tsuyung So Sweet Sum Wun was under nine months of age when she was awarded her title. She had spectacular success in the ring, going Best in Show and winning multiple Groups.

Through the seventies important breeders and owners included Mrs. Joan Reeves; Mrs. Bales; Mr. John Sheppard; Mr. L. Walsh; Shirley Leach; Paul and Julie Nash; Dr. Cunningham; and the Gardiners, who owned the remarkable Shemara Autumn Leaves, a multi-Best-in-Show winning bitch whose wins included Best in Show at the prestigious Victoria Shih Tzu Club Championship Show. A bitch owned by King and Wood, Ch. Louanne Chen Hsing, was another multi-Best-in-Show winner. Paul and Julie Nash's Ch. Garaig Ko Ko (bred by Shirley Leach) made outstanding wins in the late seventies in New South Wales. He was Best-in-Show, All Breeds, in 1977.

In the eighties, Mrs. Pan Bales had Ch. Tao Ting-A-Ling , who was bred by Mrs. Loretta Walsh. Among Ting-A-Ling's winning sons were Ch. Tilcha Link Intime (owned by Mrs. Rosemarye D'Agostine) and Ch. Tsuyung Ming Dynasty (owned by Greg Royall). Both were multiple Best-in-show winners and sired winning stock.

Among Ting-A-Ling's winning and producing daughters were Ch. Janju Coloured Gold (owned by Mrs. Bales), Best-in-Show winner at the 1980 New South Wales

Australian Ch. Geltree Ty Ching.

Above: Australian Ch. Crowvalley Minerva.

Above: Australian Ch. Erintoi Autumn Haze. Bred and owned by the Sheppards.

Shih Tzu Club's Championship Show; and Ch. Tsuyung Petit Point (owned by Mr. John G. Glen), Best-in-Show winner at the 1981 New South Wales Shih Tzu Club's Championship Show.

Greenmoss dogs have continued to be among imports that have attained Australian championship titles. Also among them are Shih Tzu from Crowvalley, Lhakang, and Taonan Kennels.

Australia has a number of "Royal" Shows — most famous of which are the Melbourne Royal and the Sidney Royale. Ch. Peking Pan Lu (owned by Mrs. Clay Hutcheson), first to win Best Puppy in Group, made that win at the 1976 Melbourne Royal Show. Another outstanding winner is Ch. Tsuyung Fanci That (owned by Mrs. Joan Reeves), first to win Best in Show, All Breeds. He made that outstanding win at the 1978 Victoria Show. And Ch. Shemara Sho-Em-How (owned by the Gardiners), was the first Shih Tzu to win Best in Group at a Royal Show. He made that win at the 1981 Adelaide Show.

An outstanding winner bred in Australia is Australian and American Ch. Skywalker Milinia. She was exported to her new owner in the United States — Gilbert S. Kahn, of Miami, Florida.

Above: Philippine Ch. Achilles Yogi Bear. Handler/owner Wally Cham. Judge Mike Wirtz.

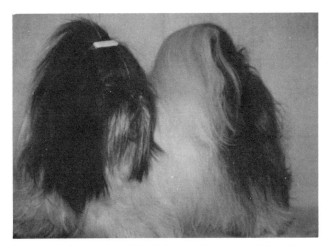

Above: San Yen Foo Jin Nikol, imported from the United States. Owned by Wally Cham.

Above: Philippine Ch. Bletilla of Akane. Owned by Lucianne Cham.

Above: Achilles Yogi Bear winning Best Philippine Born in Show. Judge, Mrs. Edith Cho, Singapore.

Below: Winners Dog competition. From left, Lainee's Floyd Boy O'Potpourri; Achilles June Peanuts; BW2 of Golden World King; Achilles Yogi Bear. Judge at extreme right, Mr. Swabe, from Japan.

Left: Ch. Greenmoss Jezebel, owned by Betty Meidlinger, United States.

Above: Can. Ch. Elfann Golden Adonis, owned by Del and Connie Smart, United States. Adonis, from the last litter of Golden Bobbin of Elfann, was imported at 12 weeks of age. His plushness and profuse coat developed after he was a year old. This was an "Elfann" trait, according to Freda Evan's remarks to Connie Smart.

Left: Int. Ch. Ruli Shu v.d. Oranje Manege, owned by Sally Murphy, United States.

The Shih Tzu Comes to North America

Early breeders in the United States were members of the Armed Forces who had seen the Shih Tzu in England during World War II and finally obtained some. Colonel and Mrs. James E. Lett had purchased several Shih Tzu while Colonel Lett was stationed in England. When they returned to the United States, Colonel Lett was stationed in Texas. The Letts brought their dogs with them, and when the dogs were bred, they sold a number of puppies to other military personnel. The Letts used the kennel name "Tamworth."

Other early breeders in Texas were Charles Gardner and his wife. Thus there were two sources in Texas through which the breed became available.

Colonel and Mrs. Harry Atkinson had early contact with the breed. Their first knowledge of the Shih Tzu also came through the Colonel's service with the United States Armed Forces. He had managed to bring a pair of Shih Tzu out of China when the Communists took over the Chinese government and he was required to return to the United States. When the Colonel was left a widower, he stopped breeding the dogs, and the people to whom he gave his dogs did not continue.

Mr. Murdoch and his sister Miss Maureen Murdoch, who lived in the Philadelphia area, also were early breeders of the Shih Tzu. Most of the dogs owned in the East in the early days can be traced to the breedings of the Murdochs.

There were separate groups that kept very accurate records with the aim of eventually having the Shih Tzu accepted by The American Kennel Club. The Shih Tzu Club of Texas was formed at San Antonio for this purpose. Colonel Lett was elected president and Mrs. Wittaker served as registrar. In the East, Shih Tzu fanciers formed an organization they called the American Shih Tzu Club. Mr. Curtice, a Shih Tzu fancier in Ossining, New York, kept a third studbook.

The three groups were attempting to gain breed recognition from The American Kennel Club, when they were told that a unified effort would best serve the interests of the breed. Accordingly, the groups merged and were called the American Shih Tzu Club.

Encore Charlie Chan — co-owned by William Kibler and Jane Fitts — was the first Shih Tzu given much publicity. He was entered in the Madison Square Garden Show in 1962 and was selected Best of the Miscellaneous Classes. He was handled at the Garden by William Kibler's wife, Joan. A few weeks later, Mrs. Kibler showed Encore Charlie Chan at the Chicago International Kennel Club Show, and the win was repeated.

The first Shih Tzu match show to take place in the United States was held June 27, 1964, at the home of Ingrid Colwell in Middleton, Pennsylvania. Fifty Shih Tzu were present at this show, which was sponsored by the Penn-Ohio Shih Tzu Club. At that time there were said to be about four hundred Shih Tzu in the United States.

Classes were judged by Mrs. Eunice Clark. Best adult was Si Kiang Tashi, an all black Shih Tzu owned by Margaret Easton and bred by Ingrid Colwell. Best of Opposite Sex was French Ch. Jungfaltets Jung Wu, a Swedish import bred by Erna Jungefeldt and owned by Ingrid Colwell. Jung Wu was handled by Ann Anderson Hickok (Warner).

Tashi and Jung Wu were descendants of International and Scandinavian Ch. Bjorneholm Wu-Ling, who was a grandson of Leidza. As noted elsewhere in this book, Leidza was the only Shih Tzu used as breeding stock in the West who had been whelped in the Imperial Palace — and therefore the only Shih Tzu in direct line back to the dogs owned by the Dowager Empress.

It also is noted elsewhere in this book that Ch. Bjorneholm Wu-Ling was the sire of Ch. Bjorneholm Pif and grandsire of Ch. Chumulari Ying Ying.

The first annual meeting of members of the American Shih Tzu Club was held in Chicago in conjunction with the Chicago International Show in April 1965. At this meeting many of the early breeders were present, and there was very good representation of members from several sections of the United States. Seventeen dogs and eleven bitches were shown by club members. Joan Kibler showed her own dog, Encore Chop Sticks, to the top win in the Miscellaneous Classes.

Will C. Mooney was a columnist for a major Texas newspaper for many years and authored *Your Shih Tzu,* one of the first books devoted exclusively to the breed. Mr. Mooney's Bill Ora Shih Tzu were pioneers among breed championship winners. They were descended from dogs from Mrs. Widdrington's Lhakang Kennel in England. The style of the Shih Tzu has changed considerably since then, but in the early days of the breed in the United States, Mr. Mooney described the great diversity of type and the great diversity of breeder opinion concerning type. Today, uniformity in breed type is quite general, yet the dogs now being produced continue to retain the fine qualities which make the breed personality attractive.

Left: Ingrid Colwell, Si Kiang Kennels, the original American matriarch of the breed. Tragically, Ingrid died in a fire, January 18, 1968.

Right: Peggy Easton with Ch. Chumulari Ying Ying and the Reverend D. Allan Easton with a Ying Ying son, Ch. Chumulari Sheng-Le Che.

Left: Chumulari Trari (Si Kiang's Tashi ex Wei-Honey Gold of Elfann). Owned by the Eastons.

Right: The Mandarin di Visconti (by Ying Shu V.D.O.M.) at 12 years of age. Breeder, Louise Weber. Owner, Sarah Lowe.

Left: Ch. Talifu Bobby Dazla, imported from England. Owned by Patricia Link. Bobby's influence has been noteworthy.

Right: Am. and Can. Ch. Ma-Tu's Most Happy Fella. Owned by Marjorie Hansen.

American Lines

The Shih Tzu winning in the American show rings today truly reflect the huge success American Shih Tzu breeders have experienced in their efforts to maintain inherent breed characteristics while improving over-all quality.

Major European and British kennels were the source of early imports to the United States and Canada. Several early Shih Tzu came directly from China to the United States. Although they were unregistered, they were, of course, from ancestry that goes back to the Imperial Palaces of China and the Lamaseries of Tibet.

While English, Scandinavian, Dutch, and more broadly, European influences have contributed to American lines, American-bred Shih Tzu, in turn, have been exported to all of those countries as well as to Japan, the Philippines, and South America. This chapter concentrates on American kennels that have established lines, rather than on individual owners and winning Shih Tzu.

The American Kennel Club approved the original Shih Tzu Standard in 1969. Because of breed size and type, many fanciers expected the Shih Tzu to be placed in the Non-Sporting Group. Early Shih Tzu in the United States were large as compared to the type being shown today. Placing the Shih Tzu in the Toy Group changed breed direction, for many fanciers then bred for a smaller Shih Tzu which would better fit into the Toy Group.

Jack and Mary Wood (Mariljac Kennels) imported English Ch. Talifu Fu Hi and International Ch. Bjorneholm Pif. A smaller type than many imported from England, Pif was purchased from Frau Erika Geusendam of West Germany. He had been bred by Astrid Jeppeson, Bjornholm Kennels, Denmark. Pif not only was a top producer of winners in Europe, he also sired eighteen American champions. As the first American champion of the breed, he exerted great influence on pedigrees and on style throughout the United States.

The Reverend D. Allan Easton and his wife, Margaret, of the famed Chumulari Kennels, had imported several fine Shih Tzu from major kennels in England. Prior to recognition of the breed in the United States, the Eastons had imported International Ch. Tangra V. Tschomo-Lungma, an outstanding bitch bred by Frau Geusendam. Tangra was imported in whelp to Pif, who was still in Europe. A son from the litter, whelped in America, became the famous American and Canadian Ch. Chumulari Ying Ying, a gold and white dog who won Best in Show at the first show held after breed recognition. All told, Ying Ying sired twenty-nine American champions, six of which won Best in Show in the United States and Canada.

Ch. Sopon V. Tschomo-Lungma, a Pif son imported from Europe, was owned in the United States by Jean Gadberry of Bom Shu Kennels. Sopon sired seventeen champion offspring and influenced quality greatly on the West Coast. Sopon's dam was Tangra's litter sister, the fabulous Ch. Tang-la V. Tschomo-Lungma, who was awarded the coveted German title Bundessiegerin.

Ingrid Colwell, a Swedish-born devotee of the Shih Tzu, was the daughter of Mrs. Engstrom, who bred Shih Tzu in Sweden. And Ingrid had been breeding Shih Tzu before she came to live in the United States.

Many American Shih Tzu breeders (including some who are now judges) were attracted to the breed by Ingrid's enthusiasm and started with stock purchased from her Si Kiang Kennels. Ingrid's foundation studs, Stefengardens Jenn Ling (a silver-gold bred by L. Svensson of Sweden) and Jungfaltet's Wu Po (a black and white bred by Carl Jungefeldt, also of Sweden) provided early breeding stock for some of the most notable kennels in the United States.

Jenn Ling was a small, solid colored dog whelped in Europe. He and Pif were half-brothers by their common sire, International Ch. Bjorneholm Wu-Ling. Jenn Ling and Pif also were very closely related genetically through their dams, so they had great chromosome likeness. Pif was exhibited in America after breed recognition, but Jenn Ling was not — although he was acclaimed for his superb movement with a free flowing, slightly swashbuckling gait.

Some English imports were smaller and more refined than others, and Ingrid's Swedish whelped Wu Po was larger and coarser than most Scandinavian imports. Although he did not appear to be a particularly good specimen, many of his progeny were of excellent quality.

A Wu Po son from Ingrid's black bitch, Si Kiang's Mi-Tze, went to Margaret and Harry Edel's Mar Del Kennels. A gold and white whelped in 1965, he turned black and white as an adult. He had a compact body and a very appealing facial expression and a short nose. He became the American and Bermudian Ch. Chow Mein, notable as the foundation of the unique and celebrated Mar Del strain.

Ch. Mar Del's Ring A Ding Ding was a Best-in-Show winning and top producing Chow Mein son. He was bred by Margaret Edel MacIntosh. Ringy was bred to Richard Paisley's Chow Mein daughter, Ch. Paisley Petronella. The resulting litter from this half-brother/half-sister breeding included three champions, one of which was Group-winning Ch. Paisley Ping Pong, owned by Nanjo Kennels and for several years America's Number One top producer of champions.

The Char Nick line is another strain based on stock

51

originally from Ingrid Colwell's Si Kiang Kennel. This distinctive line is truly excellent in structure. It was several generations after purchasing their first stock from Ingrid that Louis and Florence Sanfilippo bred Ch. Char Nick's I Gotcha. As a ten-month-old puppy, he was Best of Winners at the 1972 Westminster Show. With relatively few breedings he became a top producer and sired twenty-one American champions, three of which were American all-breed Best-in-Show winners. Another exceptionally lovely Char Nick dog in early days of breed recognition was Ch. Char Nick's My Sin.

Eta Pauptit of the Netherlands exported many of her Van De Oranje Manege (V.D.O.M.) winners to the United States. Eleanore Eldredge of Shang T'ou Shih Tzu received many of them.

Through Ruth Ragle (Lakoya), Raymond Antonucci purchased Ch. Parquins Sartezza, who was bred by Anne Koenig out of Lakoya's Lu Lu. Sartezza was owned for most of his life by Len and Bonnie Guggenheim.

Sartezza produced several puppies that became champions and then was bred to one of his daughters. A puppy from this litter, Ch. Parquins Pretty Boy Floyd, set off a major trend toward a new style and look in the Shih Tzu breed. Raymond sold this striking puppy to judge/breeder Jay Ammon, who finished him to his championship title. Floyd had the ability to produce lovely sons and daughters and was used heavily at stud. He sired several puppies that became top producers and Specialty and Toy Group winners.

Stock came to the United States from such notable English kennels as Lhakang, Elfann, Greenmoss (and combinations of these three), Chasmu, and Antarctica. Ching Yea of Lhakang, imported by Brenda Ostencio but acquired by Ingrid Colwell shortly afterward, was the English element of Ingrid's triumvirate stud force — although most of her dogs were from Scandinavia. The quality of Ching Yea's get was excellent — particularly in head and in body substance — when he was bred to pure Scandinavian stock. Ching Yea became a multiple-champion producer.

American Ch. Talifu Bobby Dazla came from England, and he also left his mark on the breed. He was small — about eight pounds — with superb head and expression, which he passed on to his get. He was imported by Roku Kennels, then sold to Patricia Link who exhibited him to his American championship. Bobby sired Ch. Yoshi's Ah So Omar (multiple-Group winner) as well as Witch's Wood Guru, who in turn sired American and Bermudian Ch. Witch's Wood Yum Yum (winner of forty all breed Best-in-Show awards and for many years the top winner in the breed). Bred by Judi Merrill, Yum Yum was a stud-fee puppy to Marilyn Guiraud, who owned Ch. Witch's Wood

Socket Tumi, Best-in-Show and Westminster Best-of-Breed winner. Marilyn also owned Witch's Wood Guru.

Dr. and Mrs. J. Wesley Edel purchased Yum Yum and used her in establishing their Emperor Kennels, promoting her all the way to the top. In 1973, Yum Yum won the coveted Quaker Oats Award for winning more Groups than any other Toy Dog during one full year. She won a total of 136 Group Firsts during her show career.

Dr. and Mrs. Edel founded their Emperor Kennels with stock from some of the first Shih Tzu kennels established in the United States. This included dogs from Mar Del, Mariljac, Hillside Acres, and, of course, Witch's Wood, from which they purchased Yum Yum. The Edels introduced into their line the Group winning Ch. Emperor's Ping Pong Partner, a Ch. Paisley Ping Pong son. Also, they bred out to Ch. Chumulari Ying Ying and to Ch. Marco Polo di Visconti. After retirement from the ring in 1974 at the age of five, Yum Yum produced three litters. The first was sired by Best-in-Show winning Ch. Emperor's Qwapaw Quarter Emp; the second by the Edel's Ping Pong Partner; and the third by Ch. Marco Polo di Visconti.

Emperor Kennels finished and/or bred some forty champions, including three Best-in-Show winners: Ch. Emperor's Thing A Ma Ying (a Ying Ying son); Ch. Emperor's Qwapaw Emp; and Ch. Emperor's All That Glitters (a Ping Pong Partner son). Another notable champion bred by the Edels was Ch. Emperor's Super Trooper, a beautifully marked, gold and white male of superb structure and excellent movement. He was Number Five in competition for wins one year, but his show career unfortunately was cut short.

The Emperor banner has been carried on under the care of Ornah Jordan of South Carolina through three generations represented by Trooper's son Ch. Emperor's Fashion Designer; Fashion Designer's son

ASTC National Specialty. Judge Elfreda Evans (Elfann Kennels), England. Gin Doc's Kojac handled by Dottie White.

52

Shana Mar-Lins Bun Hopp, owned by Julie Seibert.

Chinai's Nice and Easy, owned by David and Chris Jones.

Judge Jim Glavan awarding BOS to Rockee Vollee Raddy Radcliffe at Twin Cities Area Shih Tzu Sweepstakes, 1987.

Am. and Can. Ch. Jaisu Ling-Ho Chinese Junk, owned by Donna Fritts. A Floyd son out of Ch. Lansu Magnolia, who was imported from England by Jay Ammon.

Ch. Pen Sans Parti Toi, owned by Gloria Busselman.

Encore Chopsticks, owned by Joan and Bill Kibler. The top winner at important competitions when the breed was still in the Miscellaneous Class, Choppy was BOB for six years at the ASTC National Specialties.

Ch. Emperor's Top Line Designer; and Top Line Designer's son Ch. Emperor's Designer's Image, who is out of the Marco Polo ex Yum Yum daughter Laura of Avignon. Designer's Image was handled to his championship by Jim Blackburn of the notable Ming Dynasty Kennel. Jim and Gloria Blackburn have steadily increased their numbers of homebred champions over the past ten years.

Among other English imports who contributed to the excellent quality of early winners and producers in the United States was American Ch. Greenmoss Gilligan, owned by Winemaker Kennels. He sired their multiple Best-in-Show winning American and Canadian Ch. Winemaker's Pla-Boi. Bred to the lovely Ch. Gin Doc Suzie Wong, Pla-Boi sired two Best-in-Show winning bitches: Ch. Gin Doc's Champagne-Ladi and Ch. Gin Doc's Suzi of Sanguish. This combination of Scandinavian and English bloodlines included Pif, Ying Ying, and Chin-Ki as progenitors.

American and Canadian Ch. Choo Lang of Telota, another English import, won Best of Breed at Westminster and Best in Show at Canada's "Show of Shows." (The latter show is limited to dogs that have won Best in Show in Canada during the previous year.) Choo Lang's son Ch. Anjo's Yu Tu was bred by Ann McGovern. He sired Best-in-Show winning Ch. Jaisu Humdinger of Loriel. Another Choo Lang son was Ch. V.I.P. Confucious, a multiple Group winner. Humdinger and Confucious were results of English and Scandinavian genetic unions, and both had impressive movement from strong, sound rear assemblies.

With forty-five American all-breed Best-in-Show wins, Ch. Dragonwyck The Great Gatsby is the top winner in that category. Ch. Witch's Wood Yum Yum won forty American all-breed Best-in-Show awards. Ch. Cabrand's Agent Orange v. Lou Wan is the top Toy Group winner of all time, all Toy breeds, with one hundred sixty Toy Group Firsts.

Gatsby, sired by Ying Ying, is a top producer of champions. During his show career, Gatsby was owned by Robert Koeppel. He was bred by handler/breeder (now AKC judge) Norman Patton. Initially, Norman handled for Mariljac Kennels and took Ch. Mariljac Chatterbox to Best-in-show wins, and Ch. Mariljac Maripet to one Best-in-Show win. Norman bred several Best-in-Show winners in addition to Gatsby. He and J. Chip Constantino are owners of Dragonwyck Shih Tzu.

Peggy Hogg, who handled Gatsby during his show career, used him successfully as foundation stud for her Dragonfire line. Peggy established her successful line with her Ch. Car Lins Foxy Lady as foundation matron. Foxy Lady was bred by Carla Morgan from Bom Shu stock.

Louis and Wanda Gec began their Lou Wan line with Chumulari stock. They and their son Ted and his wife Cathy (Cabrand Kennels) have worked together. Ch. Lou Wan Casinova, Best-in-Show winner at the 1977 American Shih Tzu Club National Specialty, is linebred on Ying Ying five times. The Gecs have gone out for breedings to Ch. Mariljac Maripet and Ch. Paisley Ping Pong. They also bred to the multiple Best-in-Show winning American and Canadian Ch. Yingsu Johnny Reb, who brings Floyd and Gatsby into their line. A result is the multiple Best-in-Show winning Ch. Lou Wan Rebel Rouser. Then, having bred back into their own Lou Wan line, the Gecs produced the Rebel Rouser son, multiple Best-in-Show winning Ch. Lou Wan Rebel Yell, winner of the Group at the 1983 Westminster Show. Rebel Rouser not only is the all time top producer of American Shih Tzu champions, with well over one hundred champion progeny, but also is the sire of several American all-breed Best-in-Show winners.

The Gecs' dogs are noted for their deep color, generally high quality, and elegant style. Their handler, Emily Gunning, and Emily's husband, Sean, have achieved high plateaus as breeders/handlers. Their Ch. Long's Bronze Bandit of Gunning, a Ringy son from Ch. Long's Little Lick, has influenced many kennels. Ch. Gunning's Better Half, a Bandit granddaughter, continues as the top producing dam of American Shih Tzu champions.

Jackie and Jim Peterson (Jazmin Kennels) purchased a bitch puppy of Floyd and Gatsby background, who as a nine-month-old puppy was Best in Show. Bred by Gerraldine Ikola of Canada, she is Ch. Erincroft Qu Ti Pi of Jazmin. Another top win for Qu Ti Pi was Best of Opposite Sex at the 1978 National Specialty. Mated in the United States to Gatsby, Qu Ti Pi produced Ch. Jazmin Maxi Million, who was Best of Winners at two major Specialty events — including the 1979 American Shih Tzu Club Specialty. Maxi was sired by Gatsby and linebred on him. His outstanding champion get are characterized by showmanship, style, and flowing movement. Maxi's son American and Japanese Ch. Jazmin's High Calibre was evaluated by this author at a very young age. He was a spectacular puppy and as an adult was a Specialty and Best-in-Show winner in Japan. Jackie has bred out to Ch. Lainee Sigmund Floyd, Ch. Dragonfire Red Raider, Ch. Hodari Lord of the Rings, and Ch. Chang Tang Elusive Jeffrey.

Ch. Lainee Sigmund Floyd, a Pretty Boy Floyd son bred and owned by Elaine Meltzer (Lainee Kennels), ranked for years as the top producer of champions. A multiple Specialty winner, he was never shown in breed competition after he acquired his American championship. Obviously, his stature as a founder of a strain with appealing faces and body compactness has affected the type of Shih Tzu shown in the United States. Elaine, herself, has topped the charts with a number of breeder's awards given by the ASTC. Her high ethical standards and intense interest in the breed have been praiseworthy for many years. Her work guiding the new Shih Tzu Standard to approval by the AKC has been exemplary.

Another Pretty Boy Floyd son, Ch. Ming Toi P. V. Spunky, is out of a dam descended from Bobby Dazla. Bred and owned by Judy Boyles, Spunky made his mark as an excellent producer. A son, Ch. Gunning's Semi-Spunky of Nova, bred by Emily Gunning and owned by Taunnie Novak (Nova Kennels) sired champions and Specialty Show winners. Taunnie's Best-in-Specialty-Show Ch. Nova's Magnificent Obsession is a Semi-Spunky granddaughter and a Sigmund Floyd daughter. Linebred on Floyd, Semi-Spunky is out of Ch. Gunning's Highway Robbery, who is a daughter of Ch. Long's Bronze Bandit of Gunning and the dam of Gunning's Better Half.

Charles and Janet Long (Long/Charjalong Kennels) bred Bronze Bandit, a Ringy son out of Ch. Long's Little Lick. Chuck and Janet had developed a strain of their own based on stock descended from Greenmoss and Chumulari dogs. Their Ch. Long's Chiny Chin Ah Chop Chop was noted as a producer of American champions. Chiny's daughter Ch. Long's Bedeviled Bedazzled was Best in Show at the first ASTC National Specialty. The Longs bred out and bought outside their own stock in order to achieve certain goals. Their efforts produced the bitch Ch. Charjalongs Kiki Kid, who was Best of Breed at the 1980 Westminster Show.

Ch. Winward's Wheeler Dealer was a Chiny son owned by Mimi Bump. His gorgeous daughter, Ch. Hodari Imperial Lin, was Winners Bitch at Westminster in 1977. Laurie Battey (Hodari Kennels), owner of Imperial Lin, bred her to Sigmund Floyd. Ch. Hodari Lord of the

Ch. Hodari Lord of the Rings, owned by Joyce DeVoll.

Rings, one of Sigmund Floyd's most beautiful sons, resulted from that breeding. A compact, stunning Shih Tzu with excellent expression, he is a top producer of champions.

Bonnie Guggenheim (Bon D'Art Kennels) and Dolly Wheeler (Fancee Kennels) bred their original Shang T'ou bitch, Bon D'Art Cachet of Shang T'ou, to Ringy. The results were two lovely gold and white bitches: Ch. Bon D'Art Adore Ring of Fancee and Ch. Bon D'Art Amour Ring of Fancee. Bred to Ch. Ming Toi P.V. Spunky, Amour Ring produced two males: Ch. Bon D'Art Tu Tone Fancee, a multiple Group winner, and Bon D'Art Caio of Fancee. Ch. Fancee Dari Heir of Bon D'Art is also from Ming Toi ex Amour Ring. She is the dam of Best-in-Show and Best-in-Specialty-Show winning Ch. Fancee Heir Mhale Bon D'Art. Heir Mhale was Best of Breed at Westminster in 1982.

Bonnie and Dolly with their Bon D'Art/Fancee combination are examples of two breeders who dwell in separate households but capitalize on combining talents and resources — and both are AKC licensed judges of Shih Tzu. The Bon D'Art/Fancee Shih Tzu have combined balance and soundness with good expression and type. Bonnie owns the Best-in-Specialty-Show bitch Ch. Lukens All Fired Up, bred by Jean and E. R. Luchenbach (Luken Kennels). Firey's pedigree shows her relationship to dogs of the Bon D'Art/Fancee line.

Chow Mein and Ringy are found frequently in American pedigrees, emphasizing the importance of these two Shih Tzu — father and son. The name Mar Del has been mentioned several times, and one of the most charismatic bitches ever shown in America was the late Ch. Mar Del's Tempel Bells, a Chow Mein daughter and a point winner at Westminster. In her only litter, Tempel Bells produced the bitch Ch. Mar Del's Tempel Chimes, owned by Margaret Edel MacIntosh, and Mar Del's

Ch. Lainee Hallucination, owned by Elaine Meltzer.

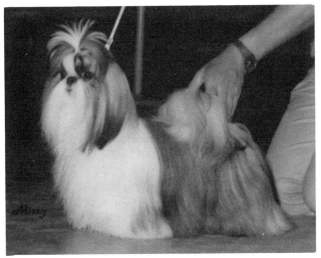

Wind Chimes, owned by the author. Ch. Meadowbrook Pudee Fu, a black and white stud with a lovely head, was purchased by Mar Del and incorporated into the line. He was bred to Ringy and Chow Mein daughters, including Tempel Bells. Margaret also bred out to Ch. Royale Hu-Lu (a Jenn Ling grandson) and to Ch. Char Nicks I Gotcha. The latter, bred to Ch. Mar Del's Samantha, produced Ch. Mar Del's U Betcha, owned by Joe Cannon (Cannonade Kennels), and Ch. Hil Ton's Fortune Cookie, owned by Sylvia Hilton.

Warren Lee and Tom Keenan (Kee Lee Kennels) built their strain largely by linebreeding on Ch. Mar Del's Chow Mein and Ch. Mar Del's Ring A-Ding Ding. American and Canadian Ch. Aagalynn's I'm a Dandy, one of their original purchases, was a multiple Best-in-Show winner and Westminster Best-of-Breed winner. An appealing and beautifully marked black and white male, Dandy was owner handled by Warren throughout his show career. Dandy's pedigree combines grand-parents Chow Mein and Chumulari Shiao Choo (a Ying Ying litter sister). Other Westminster winners owned and handled by Warren and/or Tom have been De Neergard's Golden Ming and the lovely bitches Ch. Kee-Lee's Munday's Child and Ch. Kee-Lee's Pre Chaun Sundae. Ch. Kee Lee's Red Baron of Mar Del (co-owned with Margaret Edel MacIntosh) is by Ringy out of a Dandy daughter. Another Best-in-Show and Best-in-Specialty-Show winner, Red Baron is the sire of the Best-in-Show winning bitch Ch. Kee-Lee's Munday's Fame and a top winning Canadian Shih Tzu, Ch. Samalee's Reflection of Baron.

The Visconti strain began shortly after breed recognition with the author's purchase of the lovely male Ch. Mar Del's Golden Sunset from Mar Del Kennels. Golden Sunset easily became an American champion and attained his ROM award as a top producer. His sons Ch. Marco Polo di Visconti and Ch. Kublai Khan di Visconti represented the ideal Shih Tzu for four years in *Dog World* magazine. Many of the Visconti champions were beautifully handled in the ring by Betty Munden, who is now an AKC judge.

Marco Polo sired Ch. Rex Landor di Visconti, a multiple Group winner bred by the author and handled by co-owner Billy L. Baker. Rex sired Best-in-Specialty-Show winner Ch. Romano of Landor di Visconti and the 1978 National Specialty Winners Bitch Ch. Chaka Khan di Visconti. The latter won her major points over the largest entry of bitches at one show in the history of the breed. The dams of Romano and Chaka Khan were bred by Constance Smart (Conwynn Kennels) and are granddaughter and great-granddaughter of English Ch. Greenmoss Chin-Ki of Meo. Other Visconti notables are Ch. Visconti The Enlightened One, whose grandsire is imported Ying Shu Van de Oranje Manege; the 1980

Westminster Winners Bitch and Best of Winners, Visconti The Mean Betty Jean; and Ch. Visconti The Godfather.

Joe Cannon (Cannonade) began breeding Shih Tzu in the early days, about a year before breed recognition. The bitch Ch. Cannonade Wun Dey Atta Tyme, sired by Ch. Adair's Tek of Paisley (Ping Pong's litter brother), was Joe's first homebred Shih Tzu champion. Joe recognized the quality of Marilyn Guiraud's puppy which later became Best-in-Show winning Ch. Witch's Wood Soket Tumi. Joe was the first to breed a bitch to Soket, thus proving him. Later Joe purchased the Got-cha son Mar Del's U Betcha, who finished his cham-pionship partly handled by his owner. Joe incorporated several of Bonnie Miller's dogs into his breeding pro-gram, then bred several of his bitches to Ch. Hodari Lord of the Rings. He kept what he felt to be the best of the male puppies — Cannonade Razzle Dazzle, a lovely, structurally superb, gold and white dog.

Hilde Pittelli (Joylin Kennels) began her breeding program with Mar Del stock. Her Ch. Joylin's Golden Masterpiece brings Gatsby and Golden Sunset into the pedigrees. Hilde owned and finished the striking bitch Ch. Gunning's Semi-Sparkle of Joylin, a Spunky daughter. Ch. Joylin's Exstra Terrestrial was sired by Semi-Spunky. Ch. Joylin's Rebel Reflection was sired by Ch. Lou Wan Rebel Rouser and is out of linebred Ch. Joylin's String of Pearls. Hilde has outcrossed to use Rebel in her breeding program. She usually handles her dogs in the ring.

Rae and Gay Eckes (House of Wu) are examples of fanciers who breed infrequently but whose stock is of exceptionally good quality. The outstanding Best-in-Show bitch Ch. House of Wu Mai Mai exemplifies quality. She was bred by House of Wu and owned by breeder/AKC judge Ann Hickok Warner. Both Ch. House of Wu Hai U, who was a Best-in-Show winner and Ch. House of Wu Boi Named Tzu were structurally sound with excellent rear assemblies and strong move-ment. The Eckes' success has been achieved by stockpil-ing in-house genes with little utilization of other lines. They did, however, breed to Ann Hickok Warner's Ch. Rosemar's Very Bismark, the sire of Mai Mai and the Best-in-Show winning Ch. House of Wu Outrigger. Original House of Wu stock were dogs bred by Mary Smithburn (Shaadar). Janet Long's foundation bitch, Little Lick, was out of a Shaadar bitch.

Carol Davis (Macada Kennels) has achieved success by linebreeding on Ch. Char Nick's I Gotcha. Carol, together with Coni Nickerson (Copa Kennels), purchased the Best-in-Show and National Specialty Best-in-Show bitch Ch. Char Nick's Be Witching of Copa from the San-filippos. Handled by Jean Lade and campaigned by Carol, "The Witch's" style and showmanship won her many admirers. Carol's stud dog, Ch. Macada's Tribute to Char Nick (a Gotcha son) has been a tribute to her prowess as a breeder. Her Best-in-Show winning bitch, Ch. Zip, the Tempest in a Teapot, was sired by Tribute and bred by Patsy Williams and Coni Nickerson out of Chow Mein daughter Donna Foo Young of Floridonna. Carol's outcrosses to Ch. Lainee's Sigmund Floyd were successful.

Sylvia Hilton (Hil Ton Kennels) had success linebreeding on I Gotcha. Ch. Mar Del's Fortune Cookie, a Gotcha daughter out of Ch. Mar Del's Samantha, was Sylvia's foundation bitch. Bobbie and Joe Walton (Shen Wah Kennels) campaigned their Gotcha son, Ch. Char Nick's Spiffee Larree, to Best-in-Show wins. Ch. Char Nick's Studley Durite is another of their successful and winning studs. The Waltons' Ch. Shen Wah Turn It Loose is a homebred who is setting his pace winning Best in Show.

With their champion-producing stud Ch. Paisley Ping Pong, AKC judge Ann Cowie and daughter Joan (Nanjo Kennels) have been a major force in the American Shih Tzu rings. Ping's daughter Ch. Nanjo's Ah So Sweet Sum Wun was a prize foundation bitch. A Westminster point-winning bitch and top producing dam, she was bred to Ch. Char Nick's I Gotcha. This breeding is the basis for a line credited with excellent front assemblies. Best-in-Show winning Ch. Char Nick's Oh Mai Gosh and Group-winning Ch. Char Nick's Swing Ehr of Copa, both Gotcha sons, have been notable producers for the Nanjo Line.

Best-in-Show winning Ch. Hullaballou J. Ray of Nanjo, a Ping son owned and campaigned by Jay and Linda Ballou, brought credit to the Ballous and Nanjo Kennels. Joan Cowie's Nanjo Pao Chai's Designer By Dior predictably should be on the rise as a very notable Shih Tzu. She is probably one of Nanjo's finest products sired by Shente's Christian Dior out of the Nanjo bitch Nanjo Desiree.

Dee Shepherd (Stylistic Kennels) handled Ch. Afshi's Gunther, an Oh Mai Gosh son. He was the Best-of-Breed winner at the 1978 National Specialty and was Best-in-Show at three all-breed shows. He was Number One Shih Tzu in 1978 (all systems) and won twenty-three Toy Group Firsts. A Ringy descendant, Gunther sired some lovely champions. Dee chose Gunther as the dog around which to continue the Stylistic line. Later he was shipped to Japan where his new owner is Mrs. Michee Onda. Gunther is sire of American and Canadian Ch. Shente's Brandy Alexander and the striking Ch. Ambelon's Son Of A Gunther.

J. Herbert Kaye (Kayesett Kennels) had noteworthy success with his Westminster Show Winners Dog, Ch. Kayesett Michelangelo, and the typey bitch, Ch. Kaysesett Mona Lisa. Both were sired by Gunther. Ch.

Kayesett Zebadiah, a Sigmund Floyd daughter out of Ch. Kayesett Mona Lisa, is a lovely bitch owned by Barbara and Robert Flaharty of Robara Farms Shih Tzu.

The Flahartys also own Ch. Kayesett's Michelangelo and Ch. Kayesett Dragonfall's Salute, a Zebadiah son co-owned with Kohki Iijima. Ch. Robara's Monkeydo, the Flahartys' first homebred champion, was sired by Hillside Acres Toy Visconti (a Yum Yum grandson) out of a Ch. Mariljac Maripet granddaughter. This extremely sound black and white dog has a background built on older lines.

Marian Russell (Granville) of Richmond, Virginia, has done some excellent breeding on Char Nick lines with some infusion of Joylin breeding and Rebel Rouser. Marian's recent champions, often handled by Trisha Fox (Foxfire), have been very appealing and certainly are indicative of their excellent background. Best-in-Show winning Ch. Char Nick's Be Witching of Copa is prominent in pedigrees of dogs bred by Carol Davis (Macada), who is her owner, as well as dogs bred by Marian Russell. Ch. Granville Fa Pitti Sake is one of the latest of Marian's homebred champions and a really lovely bitch.

Ohio has been a cradle of enthusiasm and love for the Shih Tzu, and many outstanding dogs have been bred there. The Penn-Ohio Shih Tzu Club had long fostered knowledge of the breed with symposium-type gatherings open to the public. The Club sponsored the first Shih Tzu Specialty Match in America before recognition of the breed. Remember the names Jazmin, Jaisu, Parquins, Anjo's, Fancee, Bon D'Art, and, of course, Conwynn.

Connie and Del Smart (Conwynn) imported several puppies from Elfann and Greenmoss Kennels in England. Their Ch. Elfann Golden Beau Brummel and Canadian Ch. Elfann Golden Adonis (last son of Elfann Golden Bobbin) were among the last Shih Tzu bred by the grand dame of the breed in England, Freda Evans, who was responsible for the original Peke/Shih Tzu cross in England. The Smarts' bitch Ch. Conwynn's Tabetha, was Best of Winners and Best of Opposite Sex at Westminster. Ch. Conwynn's Rolls Royce, bred by Connie, exemplifies quality and type. His dam is the lovely English import, Ch. Elfann Golden Sunmaiden, who was handled for the Smarts by Freeman (Bud) Dickey.

Joan Buck (Mi Kennels) has a typey representative of the breed, Ch. Mi Clyde Chin Chiny. His sire, Ch. Illenids Le Pre Chin Chiny (now in Japan), is a son of Ch. Long's Chiny Chin Ah Chop Chop out of Ch. Kee Lee's Le Pre Chaun Sundae. This line carries profuse coat, traditional with Kee Lee and Charjalong stock.

A notable breeder in Ohio is Beverly Kim (Ann Wei Kennels), with her Ch. Jazmin's Drummer Boi of Ann

Above: Ch. Emperor's Designers Image, owned by Marie Waterfield.

Above: Ch. House of Wu Windjammer, owned by Gay D. Eckes and Clay Williams.

Above: Ch. Nanjo Hi Point, owned by Nanjo Kennels.

Above: Ch. Char Nick's San Fu Li Po, owned by Mr. and Mrs. Louis Sanfilippo.

Below: Ch. Char Nick's Executive Action, owned by Abacus Kennels.

Below: Nanjo Avenger, owned by Joan Cowie.

58

Wei and Ch. Fancee Put'n On Heirs Bon D'Art (litter brother to Heir Mhale). Beverly has had some excellent results by linebreeding and inbreeding on lines similar to the Jazmin line of Jackie Peterson. Beverly's Specialty winning bitch, Ch. Anh Wei Rum Pa Pa Pum is from a brother to sister breeding — which demonstrates that inbreeding can be successful. When genes are pulled together tightly and backed by soundness, quality, and vitality, these traits can be intensified.

Other Ohio breeders who deserve credit for developing strong lines and who also have strengthened their genetic pools by breeding to improve what they already have produced are Carla Morgan (Car Lin Kennels); former Ohioan Barbara Rourke (Barbarella Kennels); and Mary Hollingsworth (Fang Chu Kennels). Mary's foundation stud is American and Canadian Ch. Fang of Shang T'ou, who was bred by Eleanore Eldredge and beautifully displayed in breed magazines with Phyllis Diller, Eleanore's friend. Eleanore's late husband, John Eldredge, was a well known motion picture actor. Eleanore's friends in the motion picture industry (including actor Yul Brynner, owner of several Shih Tzu) have helped spread breed fame. Zsa Zsa Gabor, Eva Gabor, and Elizabeth Taylor also are Shih Tzu lovers and owners and have helped draw national attention to the breed. Their Shih Tzu have appeared in numerous magazine articles and have been seen on Johnny Carson's "Tonite Show." Mary has been breeding for type and color, having incorporated offspring from Char Nick related stock, including Ch. Macada's Tribute to Char Nick as well as Donna Foo Young of Floridonna, a Chow Mein daughter owned by Patsy Williams and Coni Nickerson. Mary also has bred out to Ch. Bon D'Art Tu Tone Fancee. Her Gunther daughter has produced very well for her. Her Ch. Fang Chu's Five Card Stud, sired by Tribute, is an excellent example of type and balance.

Toledo, Ohio, breeder Nancy Tripp (NanCee Kennels) gained notice as an exhibitor with her Group winning bitch Ch. NanCee's Saucy San San. Handled by Virgina Makuc (Vams Kennels), who also owned and handled several of her own dogs to their titles, San San won over some of the breed's top winners. Nancy also bred and owns Ch. NanCee's Vanilla Confection, a showy little daughter of Ch. Kublai Khan di Visconti. Nancy and her husband, Tom Tripp, owned Ch. Visconti The Enlightened One, a Marco Polo son with spectacular movement who was later sold to John Bohm of Michigan.

Diane Kijowski's Best-in-Show winning studs include her black male, Ch. Chateau's San Souci of Jolei, bred by Billie Forsman (Chateau Kennels). Diane's National Specialty Best-in-Show and all-breed Best-in-Show winner, Ch. Jolei Chinese Checker, was owner handled.

The Jolei line was established in part with champion bitches sired by Ch. Paisley Ping Pong, with Ch. Jolei The Artful Dodger as foundation stud. San Souci, or "Blaka," as he is known, is a son of Group winning Ch. Emperor's Ebony Blak-a-Moor, a direct descendant on the tail-male line of Stefengarden Jenn Ling. Diane, notable as a junior handler and later as a young adult, has won many admirers with her handling talents and professionalism.

Harold and Joyce DeVoll (Chang Tang) are relatively new to the breed, but because of excellent counseling and first rate stock, their presence is being felt. They own Ch. Hodari's Lord of the Rings, a top American producer. Joyce DeVoll and Bonnie Schaffer are co-breeders of the exquisite Ch. Chang Tang Elusive Jeffrey, owned by Harold and Joyce. Jeffrey's sire, Ch. Dragonfire's Red Raider, a top producer, is owned by Peggy Hogg. Harold and Joyce's first champion, American and Canadian Ch. R-Own Kam Chung, was doubled on Ch. Visconti The Enlightened One.

Minnesota has some of America's foremost Shih Tzu breeders, as well as 10,000 lakes. Coincidentally, the Chinese praised their Emperors and Empresses with lauds of 10,000 years of life and sovereignty.

Helen Mueller (Rockee Vollee), Forest Lake, Minnesota, has been successful with her homebred champions, and her bitches and studs have been excellent producers of champions. Her Ch. Rockee Vollee Irish Red Bayly attained his coveted ROM, giving Helen her fifth ROM Shih Tzu. Bayly's sire is Ch. Cabrand's Agent Orange v. Lou Wan and his dam is Ch. Sun Loon Ms. of Rockee Vollee.

A successful breeder in Afton, Minnesota, is Betty Meidlinger, whose homebred champions, well over thirty in number, are proof of her quality breeding program. Substance is much of the continuing Mei San story, originating from Betty's foundation bitch, Ch. Greenmoss Jezebel.

Along with Yum Yum and Gatsby, Robert Koeppel's winner, Ch. Cabrand's Agent Orange v. Lou Wan, stands as part of the top winning American Shih Tzu triumvirate. With twenty-three Bests in Show, one hundred sixty Group Firsts, and twelve Specialty Bests in Show (including two National Specialties), "O.J." was the Toy Group recipient of the Quaker Oats Award in 1986. He was expertly handled by Darryl Martin, who had apprenticed as a junior handler under her mother — professional handler Rena Martin — then as a young adult, and now is skyrocketing to fame as a professional handler herself. Darryl and Rena campaigned many dogs for Peggy Rust (Pentara) and for Dalai Kennels, making Ch. Dalai Razzle Dazzle a top winning bitch with fifteen Group Firsts.

The western part of the United States is vast, indeed,

Above: The King of Siam and Shang T'ou, bred by Eleanore Eldredge.

Above: Int., Am., and Mex. Ch. Dynasty's Toi-Ying, owned by N. Sherri Newkirk.

Above: Ch. Dynasty's Wind-Up Toi, owned by Dynasty Kennels.

Above: Ch. Char Nick's Mr. Chit Chat, owned by Mr. and Mrs. Louis Sanfilippo.

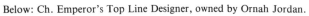

Below: Ch. Emperor's Top Line Designer, owned by Ornah Jordan.

Below: Ch. Bel Air Tara Tu, owned by June Chapin.

and there the vastness of quality in the breed is apparent also. Bel Air is the line begun in the West by handler/breeder Cathie Phillips and being continued by Diane Backovich. Aa Li Wang De Kleine Oosterling was imported from the Netherlands and became the foundation stud for the Bel Air line. Many champions from Cathie Phillips' breedings have helped improve the breed in various parts of the United States and Canada.

Best-in-Show winner Ch. Bel Air Ace of Spades, a beautiful solid black dog, is helping to improve the quality of solid blacks seen in the ring today. He, along with his sire, Gardner's Black Devil, has become a powerful force, for few solid blacks have ever been exhibited or done much winning. Black Devil is owned by Susan Bar of San Yen Kennels.

California breeders of note are increasing in numbers continually. When Pretty Boy Floyd and his owner, Jay Ammon, relocated from Ohio to California, Floyd was used at stud by a number of California breeders. There is no question that in addition to the quality of Shih Tzu descended directly from the Longs' homebred stock, the influence of Pretty Boy Floyd is noticeable.

Jody Neal (Wingate) has risen to prominence as an established breeder in a relatively short period. Her Shih Tzu have won in extremely competitive national shows. Her Ch. Wingates Never Say Dye won points at local and National Specialty Shows and acquired several all-breed Best-in-Show awards.

The 1987 top breed point winner is owned by Californians Ena and Bruce Lane. Best-in-Specialty-Show Ch. Show Off's I've Got Rhythm made a beautiful appearance at the 1988 American Shih Tzu Club National Specialty Show in Maryland. Rhythm, bred by Georgianna Williams, is a stud dog with prospects of considerable influence in the future. Ch. Show Off's Flying Sparks, by Rhythm out of Ch. Lou Wan Fancee Gunning Et Al, was bred by the Lanes and is owned by Pamela L. Mazette, also of California. The blending of the Rebel Rouser and Sigmund Floyd lines is producing beautifully pigmented Shih Tzu with gorgeous eyes. Rebel Rouser and Sigmund Floyd are the all time top producers of champions of the breed in America. This combination may ultimately produce a strain in itself.

Brenda McNight (Loubren) has successfully blended offspring from several top producing lines. American and Canadian Ch. Loubren's Code of the West is a son of Best-in-Show and Westminster Group winner Ch. Lou Wan Rebel Yell, a Rebel Rouser son. His dam goes back on the Kijowski's Jolie line. Brenda bred Sigmund Floyd to Ch. Loubren's Love Bandit to produce the flashy Ch. Loubren Doctor Ruth, a beautifully marked bitch with brilliant color.

Sharon Heuser (Jen Mi Kennels) not only has an active interest in the breed but also in the American Shih Tzu Club. Her Best-in-Show bitch Ch. Tipton's Lady Jen Mi is the foundation for her California-based kennel. Floyd played a large part in this line, along with Chow Mein. Lady's son Ch. Jen Mi's Give 'em Hell Harry was sired by Floyd.

Helen — Kitty — Strom (Din Ho Kennels) bred a whirlwind puppy who became the very typey Ch. Din Ho Wind Jammer of Ric Mar, owned and campaigned by Rick Banks. Kitty owns the Best-in-Specialty-Show winning Ch. Winward's Free Wheeling (a Wheeler Dealer son), and Ch. Din Ho Me Tu Great Balls Afire.

Barbara Pennington (Copper Penny Kennels) is another California-based breeder. Her stock, mostly owner-handled, has done well consistently in the ring. With careful, close linebreeding, Barbara's Ch. Copper Penny Cur-I-Oh-So sired three champions in one litter: Copper Penny An De, An Ge, and An Ne. The young male Copper Penny Dalai Free N Easy, sired by Ch. Snobhill's Free Lance ex Dalai Sunset Sweet Charity, is a tribute to two fine kennels, and owners/breeders Barbara Pennington and Marion Mabry (Dalai Kennels).

Bruna Stubblefield (Beedoc Kennels), in Washington State, is noted for Best-in-Show winning Ch. Beedoc's Bangaway. He was handled by Dee Shepherd.

Shih Tzu breeder/judge Evelyn Koch (Ah So Kennels) is in Colorado. Her Best-in-Show winning Ch. Ah So Su Suki was Best of Breed at Westminster. Evelyn began with a centrum of English stock, then reached out to several top producers, including Gatsby and Floyd, but stayed mainly within her original stock — as did Rae Eckes (House of Wu Kennels) also in Colorado.

Judge Gloria Busselman (Pen Sans Kennels) is receiving national attention because of Specialty winners she bred and/or owned. Ch. Garvin's Topaz of Runkel, one of her foundation bitches, caught many an eye when her photo was displayed in an advertisement years ago. In addition to incorporating Ch. Mariljac Maripet into her line, Gloria has maintained elements of Emperor and Mar Del stock.

Additional breeders in Eastern states deserve recognition. Ruth Di Nicola (Mandarin) has been breeding Shih Tzu successfully for many years. She has bred out to other lines but has maintained the discernible Mandarin look and has bred several top producing dams. She has Specialty winning Ch. Mandarin's Sassy Samantha and Best-in-Show winning Ch. Mandarin Sunni Side Up.

Jo Ann Regalman (Regal) began breeding under the tutelage of Ruth Di Nicola and is a breeder of definite note. Ch. Regals Jack in the Box, bred by Jo Ann, is owned by Kathy Kwait (Tu Chu). He is the sire of the bitch Sunni. Ruth and Jo Ann purchased a grandson of Witch's Wood Guru and great-grandson of Bobby Dazla, named Camelot's Beau Brummel. Generations later, it is astonishing to see what Bobby Dazla did to improve head type and expression in the United States. The heads of Jo Ann's winners generally are exquisite. Her American and Canadian Ch. Mandarin's Salt N Pepper, a true black and white, is a Best-in-Show winner in Canada.

Terri Castellano (Ali Aj Kennels) has developed outstanding winners. Included is Ch. Ali Aj Holy Smoke of Dragonfire, Best of Winners at Westminster. Terri began with Gatsby and Gotcha related stock, and later incorporated Wheeler Dealer and Floyd related stock.

Shirley Utstein (Sharn Kennels) deserves recognition for developing a distinctive look in her Shih Tzu. Longtime breeder Mary Frothingham merits recognition, too. She purchased Winward's Sly Fox from Mimi Bump and he became a champion. American and Canadian Ch. Ambelon Samantha, a champion producing bitch, also is worthy of notice. Samantha, basically Greenmoss linebred, is a credit to stock originally imported from England.

American, Canadian, Mexican, International Ch. Dashi's My My is of larger type. Best-in-Show winner My My is owned by Connecticut resident Catherine Pouliot. He is a descendant of Ringy with some Chumulari background. His daughter Ch. Woodsmoke's Enchantment is beautifully marked.

Dr. Sam and Billie Shaver were successful Lhasa breeders before their entry into the Shih Tzu arena. Their Ch. Loubren I'm a Billie's Follie was bred to Code of the West to produce their Best-in-Show bitch Ch. Billie's Follie Little Shaver. Bred back to grandfather/great-grandfather Rebel Rouser, she produced 1988 Westminster Best-of-Breed and multiple Best-in-Show winner Ch. Billie's Follie 'Lectric Shaver. In 'Lectric Shaver, the Shavers have built a tight genetic pool and his success as a stud dog should easily come to the fore. Their Billie's Follie Rapid Shave, from a repeat of the breeding which produced 'Lectric Shaver, is another to watch.

Bill and Dottie Campbell (Choo Ling) are Texans who began their breeding program in the late 1970s and who own the Number Two ranking top producing bitch of all time. A champion, Barrington's Wind Song of Choo Ling is a blend of Nanjo and Char Nick lines, with I Gotcha and Ping Pong prominent in her pedigree. "Windy's" litters are characterized by topnotch puppies each time she is bred. The Campbell's Ch. Choo Ling Red Royalty (Duke) is pictured on the front cover of this book. He is a son of Best-in-Show Ch. Vilenzo Red Rover out of Windy's sister. Duke is appealing and naturally photogenic because the pigmentation of his eyes and vibrant coat is dark. His muzzle is broad and square, emphasizing the good head type we seek in the Shih Tzu.

The Eastern portion of the United States continues to

Jean Gadberry handling one of her Bom Shu Shih Tzu.

be an exciting area in which to breed and show dogs. Lorraine De Salvo (Bilor) had as her foundation bitch Dominique di Visconti. The total of three American champions and three Canadian champions proves that the Dominique and Duster Buster combination produces well together, and the resiliency of the Shih Tzu has been well demonstrated by Dominique. Lorraine's bitch Ch. Bilor's Stardust was bred to American and Canadian Ch. Shente's Brandy Alexander, thus continuing to incorporate a high degree of quality into her breeding program.

Kathryn Heilman and Irene Strap (China Chimes) have a breeding program that obviously has worked,

Ch. Charing Cross Ching El Chang. Owners Troy and Lillian Phillips. Breeders Gilbert S. Kahn and George Sanchez. Handler Norman Patton. Ching's record includes 7 BIS awards, all breeds; 28 Group Seconds; and 60 BOB wins.

Ch. Choo Ling's Wind Brook, owned by Bill and Dottie Campbell.

Bon D'Art Ciao of Fancee, owned by Bonnie Guggenheim. Both Ciao and his brother Ch. Bon D'Art Tu Tone of Fancee are in the pedigree of Ch. Gunning's Better Half, top champion producing bitch.

Yingsu's Soy Sauce, owned by Sue Miller.

Pako's Lotus Blossom, owned by Mr. and Mrs. Louis Sanfilippo.

Above: Ch. Ming Toi Bab-Ling Babs, owned by Elaine Meltzer and Judith Boyles.

Below: Ch. Parquins Sartezza, owned by Len and Bonnie Guggenheim; and Bon D'Art Cachet of Shang Tou, owned by Bonnie Guggenheim.

Ch. Robara's Domino Monkeydo, owned by Barbara A. and Robert E. Flaharty.

Above: Barbara, owned by Misako Kanno, Japan.

Below: Ch. Kai Shih's Call Me Paddington, owned by Laurie Semple.

Above: Ch. Loubren Doctor Ruth, owned by Brenda McKnight.

Below: Ch. Jaina vom Tschomo-Lungma, owned by Trudy Kerr, Canada.

with a record of fifty percent eventual champions from a litter of perhaps every two years. Their Ch. China Chimes Slew of Gold, a Rebel Yell son, has been owner handled to five Best-in-Show awards. He is proof that excellence can come from kennels with very limited breeding programs. Slew of Gold has Ping Pong, Ch. Charing Cross Ching El Chang, and Emperor stock on his dam's side of his pedigree.

As judge, exhibitor, and breeder, Gilbert Stanley Kahn has given very generously of his talents, resources, and energy to the American Shih Tzu Club and the breed, as well as to breeders in the United States, Great Britain, and Europe. Gilbert has been responsible for the importation of several fine Shih Tzu from England, including his American Ch. Elfann Golden Puff Ball and American and Australian Ch. Skywalker Milinia. He bred the multiple Best-in-Show winning Ch. Charing Cross Ching El Chang, who was handled by Norman Patton. His help in securing Mrs. Evans and others from abroad to judge National Specialties has been greatly appreciated by American fanciers. Gilbert's talents as judge, breeder, and exhibitor have been extolled from the United States to Eastern European countries and England.

Garrett Crissman not only has had several fine champions of his own breeding but also has owned fine Shih Tzu purchased from other kennels. He has become an avid breeder of Arabian horses but is continuing to promote an occasional Shih Tzu when he feels the quality deserves recognition. Now in Arkansas, Garrett was a co-owner of the Best-in-Show winning Ch. Taylwag PBR Donimie, who was handled by Sandy Tremont.

Donna Steapp, of Texas, has been a strong supporter of the American Shih Tzu Club. She now is the banner bearer of the Bom Shu line, which originated with the late Jean Gadberry, who devoted much time to the breed. Donna has now incorporated several other strains into the line, including both English and Scandinavian stock.

Coni Nickerson, who lives in Virginia, has assisted several breeders in securing outstanding stock for breeding and exhibiting. She has always been an unselfish devotee of the Shih Tzu breed. Her kindness and her positive attitude have long been inspirations to others to strive for the best.

Lise Miller (Lisel Kennels) was responsible for the importation to America of two elegant European champion bitches, although much of her stock is linebred to Ying Ying. From the Netherlands, Lise imported Ch. Zim Shu Van de Oranje Manege, now also an American champion, and Ch. Hoppa Shu Van de Oranje Manege. Both bitches did considerable winning in the United States as Specials and both have won all-breed Best-in-Show awards. Lise is breeding fine, well balanced dogs.

Ch. Wes-Ro's Sunday Prime Time, bred and owned by Rose Marie Boggess.

Two examples are her male, Ch. Lisel's Rock N'Rye, and her bitch, Ch. Lisel's Not Coffee But Sanka.

Jane Forsyth, considered for many years America's foremost handler, is besieged by breed clubs to judge Specialty Shows so that her expertise will resound ultimately in breeding programs in the United States and Canada. According to Jane, Shih Tzu quality is outstanding and many kennels in the United States and Canada are breeding excellent specimens. Such were her remarks at the 1988 ASTC National Specialty annual awards dinner, after having judged Dogs and Intersex Classes.

Am., Can. and Ber. Ch. Rambutan Sabrena Fair, owned by Jim and Jane Frances.

WESTMINSTER KENNEL CLUB SHOW WINNERS

1970—Judge, L. E. Murray
  BOB—Ch. Chumulari Ying Ying (D), Easton
  BOS—Ch. Chumulari Hsuan Shou (B), Roberts
  WD—Dougal Of Telota, Federico & Guzzy
  RWD—Fan Ci Mei Tu, Terroux & Winslow
  WB, BOW—Chumulari Peng Yu, Lindblom
  RWB—Petwill Ah Mei Of Brynhall, Prymas
1971—Judge, Mrs. E. N. Hellerman
  BOB Gr 4—Ch. Witch's Wood Soket Tumi (D), Guiraud
  BOS—Ch. Mar Del's Titwillow (B), Edel
  WD—Fluff And Stuff Of Paisley, Marsh
  RWD—Chang Of Kandu, Kahn
  WB, BOW—Mar Del's Tempel Bells, Edel
  RWB—Chumulari Jen Tung, Bibbo
1972—Judge, H. R. Hartley
  BOB Gr 3—Ch. Choo Lang Of Telota (D), Federico & Guzzy
  BOS—Ch. Char Nicks Sesame Of Sam Chu (B), Sanfilippo
  WD, BOW—Char Nicks I Gotcha, Sanfilippo
  RWD—Chumulari Chung Hsia Te, Evans
  WB—Nanjo's Ah So Sweet Sum Wun, Cowie
  RWD—Char Nick's My Sin, Sanfilippo
1973—Judge, E. W. Bivin
  BOB, Gr 2—Ch. Mariljac Maripet (D), Wood
  BOS, WB, BOW—Conwynn's Tabetha (B), Smart
  WD—Mei Tu Of Lou Wan, Gec
  RWD—Char Nick's Mr. Chit Chat, Cowie
  RWB—Mandarin's Royale Rhapsody, Di Nicola & Whittington
1974—Judge, T. Stevenson
  BOB, GR 3—Ch. Witch's Wood Yum Yum (B), Edel
  BOS—Ch. Char Nick's I Gotcha (D), Sanfilippo
  WD—Mistybank Ouzo V Zervlistan, Zervoulis & Banga
  RWD—Parquin's Pretty Boy Floyd, Ammon
  WB, BOW—Car Lyn's Foxy Lady of Cambalu, Morgan & Kaye
  RWB—Mistybank Santi Sin, Banga
1975—Judge, Mrs. J. E. Clark
  BOB, Gr 4—Ch. Carrimount Ah Tiko Tiko (D), Long
  BOS, WB, BOW—Kee Lees Le Pre Chaun Sunday (B),
    Lee & Keenan
  WD—Hajji Baba of Floridonna, Ellis
  RWD—Dragonwyck The Great Gatsby, Patton
  RWB—Dunkel Havens Luv Li Wun, Guggenheim

Ch. Lou Wan Make My Day, owned by Louis and Wanda Gec.

1976—Judge, Miss V. E. Sivori
  BOB—Ch. Dragonwyck The Great Gatsby (D), Koeppel
  BOS—Ch. Zim Shu V D Oranje Manege (B), Miller
  WD, BOW—Ming Toi Tuf Lil Jin Ail, Crissman
  RWD—Carrimount Ah Chunki, Johnstone
  WB—Gin Docs Champagne Ladi, Weber
  RWB—Shan Shui of Spruce Brook, Easton
1977—Judge, D. C. Rayne
  BOB, Gr 2—Ch. Dragonwyck The Great Gatsby (D), Koeppel
  BOS—Ch. Kee Lees Mundays Child (B), Munday & Keenan
  WD—De Neergaards Golden Ming, Gabriel
  RWD—Visconti The Godfather, Crissman
  WB, BOW—Hodari Imperial Lin, Battey & McClarnon
  RWB—Ah So Georgie Gyrl of Hsu Jih, Miller
1978—Judge, Mrs. E. N. Hellerman
  BOB—Ch. Aagalynns I'm A Dandy (D), Lee & Keenan
  BOS—Ch. Pombos Fancy Pants (B), Pombo
  WD, BOW—Imua Guava Jam, Hoo
  RWD—Nat Sams Hevenly Dynasty Wajima, Marcum & White
  WB—Cha Ming Sugar Plum Fairy, Merrill
  RWB—Lou Wan Shanghai Lilly, Gec

Ch. Mar-Lin Smart Alec, owned by Lynne Milstein.

Visconti The Mean Betty Jean, owned by Jon Ferrante.

65

Ch. Conwynn's Tabetha.   Owned by Del and Constance Smart.

Ch. Mar Del's Titwillow, owned by Margaret Edel MacIntosh.

Above: Westminster Kennel Club Show, 1978. Ch. Kee Lee's Munday's Fame, handled by Warren Lee.

Below: Ch. Visconti The Godfather, owned by Virginia Makuc and Jon Ferrante.

Above: Ch. Li Ming's Ameretta, owned by Robert P. Parker.

Below: Ch. Gin Doc's Champagne Ladi. Owned by Louise Weber, then Mimi Bump. Handled by Dottie White.

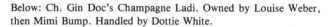

66

Raintree's Oriental Rose, owned by Shirley Rainee.

Ch. Lou Wan Rebel Yell, owned by Mr. and Mrs. Louis Gec, the only Shih Tzu to win the Group at the Westminster Kennel Club Show.

Above: Ch. Mar Del's Tempel Bells, owned by Harry Edel.

Above: Ch. Aagalynn's I'm A Dandy, owned by Tom Keenan and Warren Lee; and Ch. Pombo's Fancy Pants, owned by Vinny and Chris Pombo.

Below: Ch. Nanjo Ah So Sweet Sum Wun, owned by Joan Cowie.

Below: Ch. Char Nick's I Gotcha, bred and owned by Mr. and Mrs. Louis Sanfilippo.

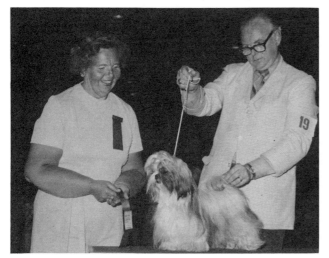

Ch. Laksana's Li Ning, owned by Victor Joris.

Ch. Billie's Follie 'Lectric Shaver, owned by Dr. and Mrs. Samuel Shaver. Closely linebred on Ch. Lou Wan Rebel Rouser, 'Lectric Shaver is a multiple BIS winner and was BOB and Group Fourth at the 1988 Westminster Show.

Ch. Kee Lee's Munday's Fame, owned by Helen D. Munday and Tom Keenan, conditioned and presented by Warren Lee.

Ch. Conwynn's Tabetha, daughter of Ch. Tucker of Fiddler's Green and granddaughter of Ch. Greenmoss Chin-Ki of Meo. Owned by Del and Constance Smart.

Above: Ming-Toi Tuf Lil Jin Ail, owned by Garrett Crissman.

Below: Ch. WenShu's Mona Lisa. Breeders/owners, Donna and Floyd Gerl. Co-owner, Miriam Thompson.

Below: Ch. Hajji Baba of Floridonna, owned by Edgar and Donna Ellis.

Above: Ch. Kayesett Michaelangelo, owned by Mr. and Mrs. Robert Flaharty.

Below: Ch. Hodari Imperial Lin, owned by Laurie Battey.

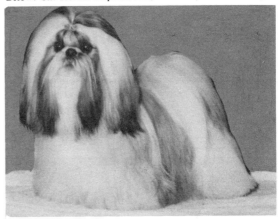

Below: Ch. Fancee Heir Mhale Bon D'Art, owned by Diana Alverson and Dolly Wheeler.

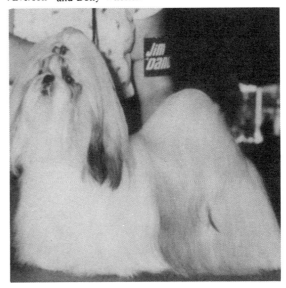

1979—Judge, Mrs. W. Hunter
  BOB, Gr 3—Ch. Afshi's Gunther (D), Joly & Toriello
  BOS—Ch. Kung Fus Happi With Gunning (B), Brewer, Lehman
      & Gunning
  WD, BOW—Kee Lee's Show Stopper of Wei Tu, Whitney
  RWD—Gunning's Semi Tough, Silveira
  WB—Li Ming's Ameretta, Collins & Parker
  RWB—Rain Tree's Oriental Rose, Rainey
1980—Judge, Mrs. S. B. Tietjen
  BOB—Ch. Charjalongs Kiki Kid (B), Long
  BOS—Ch. Illenids Le Pre Chin Chinny (D), Buck
  WD—Kayesett Michaelangelo, Kaye
  RWD—Dragonwyck Dragonfire, Patton & Constantino
  WB, BOW—Visconti The Mean Betty Jean, Ferrante
  RWB—Dragonwyck Desire, Caliento
1981—Judge, E. R. Klinckhardt
  BOB—Ch. Ah So Sue Suki (B), Ledoux
  BOS, WD, BOW—Paramount Rhett Butler (D), Moncion,
      Patton & Constantino
  RWD—Mar Del's Ring Leader, Edel & Lee
  WB—Carousels Second Hand Rose, Touzel & Edwards
  RWB—Fran Oaks Midnight Magic, Francis
1982—Judge, Miss I. De La Torre Bueno
  BOB—Ch. Fancee Heir Mhale Bon D Art (D), Alverson
      & Wheeler
  BOS—Ch. Kee Lees Mundays Fame (B), Munday & Keenan
  WD, BOW—Ali Aj Holy Smoke O Dragonfire, Castellano
  RWD—Dragonwyck Lord Dragonfire, Constantino & Patton
  WB—Grayarlin's Gingerbread Girl, Forsyth
  RWB—Anh Wei Rum Pa Pa Pum, Kim
1983—Judge, Mrs. G. J. Wanner, Sr.
  BOB, Gr 1—Ch. Lou Wan Rebel Yell (D), Gec
  BOS—Ch. Kee Lees Mundays Fame (B), Munday & Keenan
  WD—Dansin Heart To Heart, Sinnamon
  RWD—Shonapings Argonaut Era, Cornett
  WB, BOW—Stylistic Miss Clairol, Rubino & Shepherd
  RWB—Loubren's Tarsha Of Chin Chu, Mederios

Ch. Pen Sans Eye Of The Thai Ger, owned by Gloria Busselman.

1984—Judge, F. T. Sabella
  BOB—Ch. Wen Shu's Mona Lisa (B), Bartlett
  BOS—Ch. Lou Wan Rebel Yell (D), Gec
  WD—Terdel's Woodsmoke Chant, Miller
  RWD—Pen Sans Eye Of The Thai Ger, Busselman
  WB, BOW—Dragonwyck Dominique, Patton, Constantino &
      Moncion
  RWB—Laksana's Bubblin Brown Sugar, Joris
1985—Judge, Miss A. Seranne
  BOB, Gr 2—Ch. Terdel's Woodsmoke Chant (D), Martin
  BOS—Ch. Wen Shu's Mona Lisa (B), McMichael
  WD—Bon D'Art Nose In The Heir, Guggenheim
  RWD—Mirra's Ceasar Of Kee-Lee, Kogan
  WB—Beswick's Brandy Alexandria, Horton
  RWB—Dragonfire's Lady Rebeca, Hexom & Hexom
1986—Judge, G. P. Newell
  BOB, WD, BOW—Chin-Chu's Risin' Son (D), Mederios
  BOS—Ch. Kayesett Zebadiah (B), Flaharty & Kaye
  RWD—Bryant's Rebellion Of Lou Wan, Bryant
  WB—Shentes Flash Dance Benard, Marshall
  RWB—Peking's Just About Perfect, Connaughton & Bradshaw
1987—Judge, Mrs. E. Young
  BOB—Ch. Wen Shu's Mona Lisa (B), McMichael & Crosby
  BOS—Ch. Cabrand Agent Orange v. Lou Wan (D), Koeppel
  WD, BOW—Laksana's Li Ning, Shakofsky & Joris
  RWD—Achilles Dang Sal Dragonfly, Cham
  WB—Briden's Golden Hussey, Vinacco
  RWB—Kual Lo Stylistic Tapestry, Illiesco & Shepherd
1988—Judge, Dr. Jacklyn E. Hungerland
  BOB Gr 4—Ch. Billie's Follie 'Lectric Shaver (D), Shaver
  BOS—Ch. Dragonfire's Shotgun Bunny (B), Hogg
  WD—Lou Wan Make My Day, Gec
  RWD—Mar-Lin Smart Alec, Milstein
  WB, BOW—Shali-Hi's Lyda Rose, Goss
  RWB—Wingate's Miss Demednor Sujo, Watson

Ch. Kavesett Zebadiah, owned by Barbara A. and Robert E. Flaharty.

70

Ch. Nanjo Good As Gold, owned by Joan E. Cowie.

Ch. Char Nick's Sesame of Sam Chu, owned by Mr. and Mrs. Louis Sanfilippo.

Ch. Mar Del's Chink Chink Chinaman, owned by Margaret Edel MacIntosh.

Ch. Mandarin's Jet Set di Visconti, owned by Jo Ann and Kris Regelman. Jet's dam was a litter sister to Ch. Witch's Wood Soket Tumi.

Ch. VAM's Joss Hotei, a Pif son owned by Virginia and Al Makuc.

Ch. Conwynn's Roll's Royce, bred by Connie Smart and owned by Pam Fleener.

REGISTRY OF MERIT AWARDS

The Registry of Merit (ROM) award is bestowed by The American Shih Tzu Club on any sire who has produced six or more champions, and on any dam who has produced four or more champions. The title is even more important than that of champion, because a champion that does not produce is unable to contribute to the improvement of the breed.

All dogs and bitches who have earned ROM awards through 1987 are listed below.

Ch. Aagalynn's I'm A Dandy (D)
Aa-Li-Wang de Kleine Oosterling (D)
Ch. Afshi's Gunther (D)
AagaLynn's Three Rum Collins (B)
AagaLynn's Water Chestnut (B)
Ah-So Lizzie Borden (B)
Ch. Ali-Aj Wildfire of R and R (B)
Ch. Ali-Aj Holy Smoke O'Dragonfire (D)
Ch. Ambelon's Son Of A Gunther (D)
Avalon's Choo Moo (B)
Bambu Tibetan Blossom (B)
Barbara's Ming Tu (B)
Ch. Barrington's Windsong of Choo Ling (B)
Ch. Beedoc's Bangaway (D)
Ch. Beedoc's Chueh Shih Tei Jen
Ch. Bel Air Tigherson of Shang T'Ou (D)
Ch. Bjorneholm Pif (D)
Bon D'Art Ciao of Fancee (D)
Ch. Bon D'Art Tu Tone of Fancee (D)
Ch. Brownhills Yolan of Greenmoss (B)
Cabrand's Ciara of Lou Wan (B)
Camelot's Beau Brummel (D)
Ch. Caralandra's Passing Fancy (B)
Ch. Car Lyn's Foxy Lady of Cambalu (B)
Ch. Carrimount Ah Chop Chop (D)
Ch. Carrimount Ah Crepe De Chine, CDX (B)
Ch. Charjalongs Bronze Bandit (D)
Ch. Charjalong's Thai of Phildore (D)
Char-Nick's Aliage of Shen Wah (B)
Ch. Char Nick's Executive Action (D)
Ch. Char-Nick's I Gotcha (D)
Ch. Char-Nick's Sesame of Sam Chu (B)
Ch. Char-Nick's Studley Durite (D)
Ch. Char Nick's S'Wing-Erh of Copa (D)
Cha-Shu van de Oranje Manege (D)
Ch. Chateau's White Peony of Arlys (B)
China Chimes Jasmine N Jade (B)
Ch. Ching Tsu of Marlen (D)
Ching-Yea of Lhakang (D)
Chumulari Ch'Ing Fu (B)
Ch. Chumulari Chin-Te (B)
Ch. Chumulari Chin Te Jih (D)
Ch. Chumulari Chung Hsia Te (D)
Chumulari Hsiao Choo (B)
Chumulari Pao Shih (B)
Chumulari Phola (B)
Ch. Chumulari Sheng-Li Che (D)
Chumulari Trari (B)
Ch. Chumulari Ying Ying (D)
Copper Penny Tas Si (B)
Ch. Dang Sai Angie Dickens (B)
Ch. Dashi's My My (D)
Ch. Davanik's Classic Reflection (D)
DeVilbiss Wind Song (B)

Diandee Kee Mo No (B)
Din Ho Wan Shih Poppy (B)
Donna Foo Young of Floridonna (B)
Ch. Dragonfire's I'm Mahalia (B)
Ch. Dragonfire's I'm No Lady (B)
Ch. Dragonfire's Red Raider (D)
Ch. Dragonfire's The Great Draco (D)
Ch. Dragonwyck The Great Gatsby (D)
Ch. Dun Kee Wang Socket Tu Ya (B)
Ch. Emperor's Ping Pong Partner (D)
Ch. Emperor's First Lady Ch'Eng (B)
Ch. Emperor's Top Line Designer (D)
Ch. Emps Cloisonne Glitter Ying (D)
Encore Chopsticks (D)
Ch. Encore Flower Child (B)
Ch. Fancee Dari Heir of Bon D'Art (B)
Ch. Fancee Heir Mhale Bon D'Art (D)
Ch. Fashions JC Superstar (D)
Ch. Forest Farm's Scheherazade (B)
Gardner's Black Devil (D)
Ch. Garvin Topaz of Runkel (B)
Glenka Tzi v Klein Vossenburg (B)
Golden Bobbin of Elfann (B)
Greenmoss Chin-Ki of Meo (D)
Ch. Greenmoss Gilligan (D)
Ch. Greenmoss Golden Talon of Elfann (D)
Ch. Greenmoss Jezebel (B)
Ch. Gunning's Better Half (B)
Gunning's Hi Eye Cue (B)
Ch. Gunning's Highway Robbery (B)
Ch. Gunning's The Eighth Wonder (B)
Ch. Gunning's Tyopgrafical Errer (B)
Heavenly Dynasty's Wan Chi (B)
Ch. Heavenly Dynasty's Olivia (B)
Ch. Hee Shee's Wee Bel Ange (B)
Ch. Highland's Spice and Ice (B)
Ch. Ho Chi's Ring Leader (D)
Ch. Hodari Lord of the Rings (D)
Ch. Hodari Tam Lin of Moonling (B)
Ch. Imperial Ping Tan (B)
Ch. Imperial Pong Tan (D)
Ch. Imua's The Gatsby's Pride O'Ali-Aj (D)
Ch. Jaisu Ling-Ho Chinese Junk (D)
Ch. Jaisu Ling-Ho Plai-Toi O'Dynasty (B)
Ch. Jaisu Ling-Ho X-Rated of Lainee (D)
Ch. Janiric's Jumbo-O-Laya (D)
Ch. Jazmin's Drummer Boi of Anh-Wei (D)
Ch. Jazmin's Maxi-Million (D)
Ch. Jolei Chinese Checker (D)
Ch. Jolei Lucille (B)
Ch. Jolei The Artful Dodger (D)
Ch. Joy Tu Ring of Fire of Luken (D)
Juling Miss-Chief (B)
Ch. Kachina's Sugar and Spice (B)

Ch. Parquins Sartezza, owned by Len and Bonnie Guggenheim.

Ch. Long's Chiny Chin Ah Chop Chop, owned by Chuck and Janet Long.

Am. and Ber. Ch. Mar Del's Chow Mein. Owned by Margaret Edel MacIntosh. Bred by Ingrid Colwell.

Ch. Mar Del's Golden Sunset. Foundation stud of the Visconti line, he is the sire of Ch. Marco Polo di Visconti. Owner, Jon Ferrante.

Ch. Mariljac Maripet, owned by Mary L. Wood. Sired by Ch. Chumulari Ying Ying, Maripet's pedigree doubles on Ch. Bjorneholm Pif.

Can., Am., and Ber. Ch. Carrimount Ah Chop Chop, owned by Mr. and Mrs. Jeffrey G. Carrique.

Ch. Kee Lee's Munday's Child (B)
Ch. Kee Lee's Red Baron of Mar-Del (D)
Ch. Ku Che Toi of Antarctica, CD (D)
Ch. Lainee Sigmund Floyd (D)
Ch. Lansu Magnolia Time (B)
Ch. Lilibet Golden Dawn (B)
Ch. Li-Ming's Bell Bottoms (B)
Ch. Li-Ming's Carouser (D)
Ch. Long's Chiny Chin Ah Chop Chop (D)
Ch. Long's Kiko Lady (B)
Ch. Long's Little Lick (B)
Ch. Loubren Pippi Longstockings (B)
Ch. Loubren's Code of the West (D)
Ch. Lou Wan Casinovia (D)
Ch. Lou Wan Tootsie (B)
Louwan Forget-Me-Not (B)
Ch. Lou Wan's Rebel Rouser (D)
Ch. Lou Wan Rebel Yell (D)
Ch. Lou Wan Tootsie (B)
Louwan's Red Lady (B)
Ch. Luken's All Fired Up (B)
Ch. Lyckobringarens Guy of Vitahund (D)
Ch. Macada's Tribute to Char Nick (D)
Mandalay's Blockbuster (D)
Ch. Mandarin's Royale Rhapsody (B)
Ch. Mandarin's Sassy Samantha (B)
Mandarin's Sweet N'Sassy (B)
Ch. Mar Del's Chow Mein (D)
Ch. Mar Del's Golden Sunset (D)
Ch. Mar Del's Moo Goo Gai Pan (D)
Ch. Mar Del's Ring A Ding Ding (D)
Ch. Mariljac Chatterbox (D)
Mariljac En-Chant-Ress (B)
Ch. Mariljac Kwang K'Whae (D)
Ch. Mariljac Ledgend of Bomshu (D)
Ch. Mariljac Marilyn Of Chusanho (B)
Ch. Mariljac Maripet (D)
Ch. Mariljac Tinker Town Toi (B)
Ch. Ming Dynasty's Bamboo Shoot (D)
Ch. Ming Toi Bab-Ling Babs (B)
Ch. Ming Toi P V Spunky (D)
Mistik Mylan Pao Kuei (B)
Ch. Monki Doodle of Midhill (B)
Moon-Ling's Tang Lee of T'Ien Tan (B)
Ch. Mundy's Ama Yo Yo's Yum Yum (B)
Ch. Mundy's Ama Yummers Bummer (D)
Ch. Nanjo Hi-Hope of Joy-Fu-Li (D)
Nanjo Ming Tiger Tu (B)
Nanjo Miss Wiggles (B)
Ch. Nanjo Oh Mai Gosh of Char Nick (D)
Nanjo Pien Tue (B)
Ch. Nanjo Ping's Pat-Ti-Cake (B)
Ch. Nanjo's Ah So Sweet Sum Wun (B)
Ch. Nanjo Wild Honey (B)
Ch. Nova's Miss Dee Fying Min Dee (B)
Orgs Ama Rangers Tempest (B)
Ch. Paisley Petronella (B)
Ch. Paisley Ping Pong (D)
Pako's Lotus Blossom (B)
Ch. Parquins Pretty Boy Floyd (D)
Ch. Parquins Sartezza (D)
Peersun's Evening Ember (B)
Pen Sans Parti Crasher (B)
Ch. Pen Sans Parti Pet (D)
Ch. Pen Sans Parti Toi (D)

Pen Sans Parti-Ying (B)
Ch. Phildore's Woo-Fie Do (D)
Ch. Regal's Dr. Doolittle (D)
Ch. Regal's Jack N'The Box (D)
Rockee Vollee Ailee Ali (B)
Rockee Vollee Marzi-Pan (B)
Ch. Rockee Vollee Velvetier (D)
Rockee Vollee Victoria (B)
Ch. Sabar Snowfire of Marcliff (D)
Sam Tsus Ta Shi (B)
Ch. Sanchi's Vhima (D)
Shaadar's Happi Boi Sam (D)
Sharn's Chantilly Lace O'Ali-Aj (B)
Ch. Shente's Brandy Alexander (D)
Shentes Manhattan Lady (B)
Si Kiang's Ester-Wu (B)
Si Kiang's Gumpy (D)
Si Kiang's Prci-Phe (B)
Ch. Sopon Vom Tschomo-Lungma (D)
Ch. Sparkle Plenty for David (B)
Stony Lane's Imported Crystal (B)
Ch. Stylistic Make Mine Cashmere (B)
Ch. Suki Mei Ling (D)
Ch. Sun Canyon Hi Hopes (B)
T'Ai T'Ai of Shang T'Ou (B)
Talifu Fu-Hi (D)
Taramont I Went Wong (B)
Taylwag's Brandywine (B)
Ch. Taylwag's PBR Donimie (D)
Ch. Thompson's Tun Pu (B)
Ch. Tipton's Lady Jen-Mi (B)
Toryglen How Sweet It Is (B)
Ch. Tu Chu Golden Happiness Marja (D)
Ch. Tu Chu's Mesmerized (B)
Ch. Tu Chu's You Only Live Twice (D)
Ch. Tzi Tzi Shu (D)
Vilenzo Copper Penny Etc. Etc. (B)
Ch. Vilenzo Hsing Ah Muk (B)
Ch. Willoway's Good Samaritan (D)
Ch. Wingate's Debutante (B)
Ch. Winward's Free Wheeling (D)
Ch. Winwards Wheeler Dealer (D)
Ch. Wyndee Cheerleader of Ho Chi (B)
Yen Sing of Graywood (B)
Ch. Yingsu's Johnie Reb (D)
Yingsu Lucky Lindy Bear (D)
Ch. Yosha Toddie Mikko (D)
Ch. Yoshi's Ah So Omar (D)

Minnesota's first Specialty Show, 1985. Rockee Vollee Velvetier, owned by Helen Mueller, with Rockee Vollee champions.

74

AMERICAN SHIH TZU CLUB ALL-TIME TOP WINNERS

Breed Points Only — Through December 1987
<u>American Kennel Gazette</u>

Rank		Dogs Defeated
1.	Ch. Cabrand Agent Orange v. Lou Wan (D)	4,437
2.	Ch. Dragonwyck The Great Gatsby, ROM (D)	3,496
3.	Ch. Wen Shu's Mona Lisa (B)	3,131
4.	Ch. Witch's Wood Yum Yum (B)	3,112
5.	Ch. Lou Wan's Rebel Rouser, ROM (D)	2,625
6.	Ch. Beedoc's Bangaway, ROM (D)	2,331
7.	Ch. Afshi's Gunther, ROM (D)	2,073
8.	Ch Lou Wan Rebel Yell, ROM (D)	2,051
9.	Ch. Winemaker's Pla-Boi (D)	2,000
10.	Ch. Ah So Suki Sue (B)	1,918

Ch. Cabrand's Agent Orange v. Lou Wan, owned by Robert Koeppel, handled by Daryl Martin.

Ch. Dragonwyck The Great Gatsby. Bred by Norman Patton. Owned by Robert Koeppel. Handled by Peggy Hogg.

Ch. Witch's Wood Yum Yum, owned by Dr. and Mrs. J. Wesley Edel, handled by John Murdock, conditioned by Georgia Moore.

ALL-TIME TOP WINNERS — TOY DOGS
Kennel Review System

Irene K. Schlintz developed the original idea on which the point system is based. Data she compiled were published from 1956 through 1968. In 1969 the Kennel Review System was initiated. It is the only national all-breed system maintained continuously since that time.

Under the Kennel Review System, all placements are determined on the basis of points acquired through show wins for the year given. Since breed recognition, there have been four instances when a Shih Tzu was named Top-winning Toy Dog of the year. They are:

Year	Dog	Points
1973	Ch. Witch's Wood Yum Yum	24,324
1976	Ch. Dragonwyck The Great Gatsby	22,411
1977	Ch. Dragonwyck The Great Gatsby	20,635
1986	Ch. Cabrand Agent Orange v. Lou Wan	22,196

AMERICAN SHIH TZU CLUB ALL-TIME TOP PRODUCERS
Through December 1987   American Kennel Gazette

Sires	Number of Champions	Dams	Number of Champions
Ch. Lou Wan Rebel Rouser, ROM	96	Ch. Gunning's Better Half, ROM	14
Ch. Lainee Sigmund Floyd, ROM	66	Ch. Barrington's Windsong of Choo Ling, ROM	10
Ch. Paisley Ping Pong, ROM*	43	Glenka Tzi v Kleine Vossenburg, ROM*	10
Ch. Dragonwyck The Great Gatsby, ROM*	39	Ch. Long's Little Lick, ROM	10
Ch. Chumulari Ying Ying, ROM*	30	AagaLynn's Water Chestnut, ROM*	9
Ch. Long's Chiny Chin Ah Chop Chop, ROM*	30	Ch. Mariljac Tinkertown Toi, ROM*	9
Ch. Hodari Lord of the Rings, ROM	26	Ch. Caralandra's Passing Fancy, ROM	8
Ch. Char Nick's I Gotcha, ROM*	22	Ch. Ali-Aj Wildfire of R and R, ROM	7
Ch. Mar Del's Ring A Ding Ding, ROM*	22	Chumulari Trari, ROM*	7
Ch. Nanjo Hi-Hope of Joy-Fu-Li, ROM*	19	Din Ho Wan Shih Poppy, ROM*	7
Ch. Parquins Pretty Boy Floyd, ROM*	19	Ch. Dun Kee Wang Soket Tu Ya, ROM	7
		Ch. Gunning's Highway Robbery, ROM	7
		Ch. Gunning's The Eighth Wonder, ROM	7
		Ch. Imperial Ping Tan, ROM*	7
		Ch. Ming Toi Bab-Ling Babs, ROM	7
		Taylwag's Brandywine, ROM	7

*Deceased

*Deceased

Ch. Paisley Ping Pong. Bred by Richard Paisley. Owned by Joan E. Cowie. Sired by Ch. Mar Del's Ring A Ding Ding out of Ch. Paisley Petronella (a Chow Mein daughter), Ping Pong's pedigree triples on Jungfaltet's Wu Po, a grandson of Int. Ch. Bjorneholm Wu Ling.

Ch. Parquins Pretty Boy Floyd. Bred by Raymond Antonucci. Owned by Jay Ammon. Sired by Ch. Parquins Sartezza, Floyd was a product of a father-daughter breeding and readily produced his own likeness, which was reminiscent of Ch. Si Shu V.D.O.M., Sartezza's sire.

Can. Ch. Bilor's Golden Elegance, owned by Lorraine C. De Salvo.

Ch. Char Nick Masterpiece O'Sesame, owned by Mr. and Mrs. Louis Sanfilippo.

Ch. Wingate's Carrot Top, owned by Jody Neal.

Ch. Kee Lee's De Ja Vu Moonlight Lady, owned by Brenda Lee and Dean Kiernan.

Ch. Ming Dynasty Chinese Silk, owned by Mr. and Mrs. J. Blackburn.

Ch. Pen Sans Peaches N' Cream, owned by Gloria Busselman.

AMERICAN SHIH TZU CLUB NATIONAL SPECIALTY SHOW WINNERS

1973—Portland, OR, May 5. Judge, F. H. Stern
  BOB—Ch. Longs Bedeviled Bedazzled (B), Long
  BOS—Ch. Bel Air Tigherson of Shang Tou (D), Phillips
  WD, BOW—Laineux Wunk Hungh Loh, Hansen & Kelly
  RWD—Carrimount Ah Flip Flop, Lambert & Repice
  WB—Charjalongs Lotus Flower, Camberis
  RWB—Bel Air Bali Hai, Atkinson
1974—Marlborough, MA, May 31. Judge, J. Faigel.
  BOB—Ch. Char Nicks Be Wit Ching of Copa (B), Davis
  BOS—Ch. Geodans Ron Eric (D), Crissman
  WD, BOW—Winemakers Plai-Boi, Wine & Gazdzicki
  RWD—Rondelay Chin Ki, Dabrowski
  WB—Winemakers Mingboi of Lou Wan, Gorab & Gec
  RWB—Windsor Gayelyn Jade of Nika, Hager
1975—Houston, TX, March 14. Judge, Mrs. J. E. Clark.
  BOB—Dragonwyck The Great Gatsby (D), Koeppel
  BOS—Ch. Moonlighter So Sweet Sum Wun (B), Burch
  WD, BOW—Jaisu Ling Ho X-Rated of Lainee, Meltzer
  RWD—Winemakers Pla Ting, Gazdzicki & Wine
  WB—De Rays Our Gal Pentara, Anderson & Johnson
  RWB—Greetings Bitsy Bee, Brewer & Lehmann
1976—Miami, FL, April 16. Judge, Dogs & Inter-Sex Competition,
    E. Jungfeldt. Judge, Bitches, Elfreda Evans.
  BOB—Ch. VIP Confusious (D), Slatkin
  BOS—Ch. Gin Docs Champagne Ladi (B), Weber
  WD, BOW—Abacus Chairman of the Board, Pier
  RWD—Bomshu Born Flee, Zervoulis
  WB—Ramurkas Hocus Pocus, Murphy
  RWB—Cabrands Confection of Bourne, Wardell & McCord

Ch. Wenrick's M's Kelly N' Sou Yen, owned by Patti and Mark Paquette.

Ch. Loubren Pretti Sassy of Toma, owned by Brenda McKnight.

1977—Saint Louis, MO, March 4. Judge, Dogs & Inter-Sex Competition, E. E. Biven. Judge, Bitches, Mrs. J. E. Clark.
  BOB—Lou Wan Casinova (D), Gec
  BOS—Ch. Jen Mi Kis Sing Kin of Mig Toi (B), Heuser
  WD, BOW—Cabrands Midnight Special, Gec
  RWD—Greylocks Razz Ma Tazz, Goldberg
  WB—Ah So Georgie Gyrl of Hsu Jih, Miller
  RWB—Charing Cross Peek A Boo, Kahn & Sanchez
1978—New Carrollton, MD, April 21. Judge, Dogs & Inter-Sex Competition, Mrs. Keke Blumberg. Judge, Bitches, Joseph Gregory.
  BOB—Ch. Afshi's Gunther (D), Joly & Toriello
  BOS—Ch. Erincroft Qu Ti Pi Of Jazmin (B), Peterson
  WD, BOW—Pati Charlie Chan of Lainee, Robertson & Gresham
  RWD—Primavera's Devil Made Me Do It, O'Neil & Gurin
  WB—Chaka Khan di Visconti, Crissman
  RWB—Emperor's Confederate Jasmine, Simartan
1979—Long Beach, CA, June 28-29. Judge, Dogs & Inter-Sex Competition, Mrs. M. L. Billings. Judge, Bitches, N. Calicura.
  BOB—Ch. Ying Su Johnnie Reb (D), Miller
  BOS—Lou Wan Slate of Li Ming (B), Tendler
  WD, BOW—Jazmins Maxi-Million, Peterson
  RWD—Bel Air Matinee Idol, Chadwell
  WB—Pen Sans Peaches N Cream, Christensen & Busselman
  RWB—Dragonwyck Danielle, Burger
1980—Miami, FL, June 11-12. Judge, Dogs & Inter-Sex Competition, P. J. Federico. Judge, Bitches, Mrs. J. W. Penta.
  BOB—Ch. Jolei Chinese Checker (D), Stearns
  BOS—Ch. Charjalongs Kiko Kidd (B), Long
  WD—Ti Gis Hotten Blue Blazes, Glavan
  RWD—Wendav's Razzmataz, Brewer & Lehmann
  WB, BOW—Wenricks Miss Tiffany Sou Yen, Paquette
  RWB—Lou Wan Lucky Lady, Gec

Cabrand's Devil's Desciple, owned by Daryl Martin.

Ch. Hapiours Swing On A Star O'Copa, bred and owned by Patsy Williams and Coni Nickerson.

Above: Ch. Chaka Khan di Visconti, Winners Bitch at the 1978 ASTC National Specialty over the largest entry of bitches in the history of the breed. Owner, Jon Ferrante.

Above: Ch. Erincroft Qu Ti Pi of Jazmin, owned by Jackie Peterson.

Above: Ch. Bel Air Gamblin Man of Mei San, Best in Sweepstakes, 1978 ASTC National Specialty. Owner, Betty Meidlinger. Handler, Linda Miller. Judge, Mary Wood.

Below: Ch. Wingate's Debutante, owned by Jody Neal.

Above: Ch. Jazmin's Maxi-Million. Owned by Jackie Peterson. Handled by William Cunningham.

Below: Ch. Vilenzo Red Rover, Red Rover, owned by Sally Vilas; Ch. Choo Ling's Red Royalty, owned by Bill and Dottie Campbell; and Choo Ling's Lil Red Riding Hood, owned by Olla Conway.

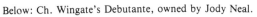

1981—Fort Worth, TX, March 18-19. Judge, Dogs & Inter-Sex
   Competition, R. R. Reedy. Judge, Bitches, R. C. Graham.
BOB—Ch. Lukens All Fired Up (B), Guggenheim
BOS—Ch. Hodari Lord of The Rings (D), Battey
WD—Ch'ang Ch'u Apollo, Barrand
RWD—Happi's Perfect Clown, Archer
WB, BOW—Charlens Dragon Lady, Davis, Conrad & Busselman
RWB—Nova's Miss Dee Fying Min Dee, Perlmutter

1982—Trevose, PA, May 6-7. Judge, Dogs & Inter-Sex
   Competition, G. S. Kahn. Judge, Bitches, Mrs. M. L.
   Billings.
BOB—Ch. Fancee Heir Mhale Bon D'Art (D), Alverson &
   Wheeler
BOS—Ch. Nova's Magnificent Obsession (B), Novak
WD, BOW— Din Ho Ma Tu Great Balls Afire, Strom
RWD—Debelles Hikaru of Mei Ting, Cacciotore
WB—Rambutan Sabrina Fair, Francis
RWB—Bon D'Art Fancee Leggs, Wheeler & Guggenheim

1983—San Mateo, CA, June 23. Judge, Dogs & Inter-Sex
   Competition, Mrs. G. Busselman. Judge, Bitches, C. S. Long.
BOB—Ch. Lou Wan Rebel Rouser (D), Gec
BOS—Ch. Ah So Sue Suki (B), Ledoux
WD, BOW—Anh Wei Heirrogant Snob, Kim
RWD—Shen Wah's For Members Only, Walton
WB—Wingates Debutante, Neal
RWB—Sharn's Marquisa Of Zorro, Utstein

1984—Worcester, MA, May 30. Judge, Dogs & Inter-Sex
   Competition, E. E. Bivin. Judge, Bitches, R. Tendler.
BOB—Ch. Wen Shu's Mona Lisa (B), Bartlett
BOS—Ch. Emperors Top Line Designer (D), Jordan
WD, BOW—Anjuli's Dan Dee Lyon, Parker
RWD—Jolanes All American Boy, Boyles & Wheeler
WB—Hodari Mercy Me O Clary Tang, DeVoll
RWB—Woodsmoke's Before Yesterday, Miller

Ch. Erincroft Qu Ti Pi of Jazmin, owned by Jackie Peterson.

Ch. Geodans Ron Eric, owned by Garrett Crissman.

1985—Beaverton, OR, July 11. Judge, Dogs & Inter-Sex
   Competition, N. L. Patton. Judge, Bitches, Jay Ammon.
BOB—Ch. Cabrand Agent Orange v. Lou Wan (D), Koeppel
BOS—Ch. Tu-Mac's Phoebe Shou (B), Atchley
WD, BOW—San Yen Lei Ning, Barr
RWD—M And R's Jual Hill Billy, Rukavina & Graber
WB—Halcyon's Rona Bear-it, Dishman
RWB—Pan Sans That Girl Nordii, Hortung

1986—Romulus, MI, May 29. Judge, Dogs & Inter-Sex
   Competition, W. N. Brewer. Judge, Bitches, Frank Sabella.
BOB—Ch. Lou Wan's Rebel Rouser (D), Gec
BOS—Ch. Billies Follie Little Shaver (B), Shaver
WD, BOW—Moonglow's Smooth As Brandy, Beaurine
RWD—Tu Chu Take It To The Limit, Kwait
WB—Loubren Pretti Sassy Of Toma, Meltzer & Webb
RWB—Lou Wan Fancee Gunning, Wheeling & Gunning

1987—Fort Worth, TX May 18-19. Judge, Dogs & Inter-Sex
   Competition, B. L. Guggenheim. Judge, Bitches,
   June Penta.
BOB—Ch. Cabrand Agent Orange v. Lou Wan (D), Koeppel
BOS—Ch. Wenshu's Mona Lisa (B), Crosby & McMichael
WD, BOW—Paramount Trivial Pursuit, Moncion
RWD—Sabar's Goin' In Style, Craig
WB—Wenrick's M's Kelly N' Sou Yen, Paquette
RWB—Quin-Don's Faith Hope and Charity, Burchi

1988—New Carrollton, MD, April 20-21. Judge, Dogs & Inter-Sex
   Competition, Jane Forsyth. Judge, Bitches, Martha Olmos-
   Ollivier.
BOB—Am. & Can. Ch. Shente's Brandy Alexander (D),
   Ehricht & Brown
BOS—Ch. Dragonfire's Shot Gun Bunny (B), Nelson
WD—Szechuan Man In Command, Hollenbeck
RWD—Wingate's Never Say Dare, Wharton
WB, BOW—Dragonfire's Marim Muffin, Jacobson
RWB—Shalimar's Fatal Attraction, Thompson

Ch. Luken's All Fired Up, owned by Bonnie and Len Guggenheim.

AMERICAN CHAMPIONS, 1969-1987

The information in the following listing was first published in *Pure-bred Dogs/American Kennel Gazette*. The dates shown here are the dates of the issues of the magazine in which the information appeared. The name(s) following the dog's name is (are) the person(s) who owned the dog at the time the championship was attained.

11/69	Bjorneholms Pif		Tacksamycket Uchi Oui		Ca Pi of Dreghorn (D)
12/69	Carrimount Ah-Chop-Chop	7/70	Aa-Pi-Wang De Kleine Ooosterling		Chin Chin of Aurigny (D)
	Chumulari Li-Tzu		Deer Run Tien		Kapena (D)
	Chumulari Ying Ying		Hui Tu Uchi Oui		Ku Che Toi of Antarctica (D)
	Lakoya Princess Tanya Shu		Imperial Ping Tan		Mariljac Ta-Kuai (D)
	Si Shu V.D. Oranje Manege		La Gai Sampan of Llonnee Lane		Paisley Petronella (B)
1/70	Bill-Oras Kwin-Ni		Mar Del's Samantha		Taramont Tiger's Urchin (D)
	Bom Shu's Dee Dee		Shan Soo of Rawstock	4/71	Bom Shu Empress Su-Ling (B)
	Chumulari Hih-Hih		Si-Kiang's Jenn-Wu		Cho Gyo Uchi Oui (B)
	Mai-Lyn Gold Nugget Of Barusann		Str-Range It's Wen Dee		Dan-Dee-Wang De Kleine Oosterling (D)
	Mar Del's Guy Pan		Talifu Bobby Dazla		De Amo I See Astra (B)
	Taramount Champagne Mist	8/70	Avalon's Chou Chang		Hee Shee's Wee Wee (B)
	Witch's Wood Soket Tumi		Chumulari Yu Lo		Joclif's Ah-Fu-Ee of Mariljac (D)
2/70	Aga Lynn's Chen Hei Chu		Graywood's Merry Christmas		Mar Del's Tempel Bells (B)
	Char-Nicks Sam Chu		Mar Del's Moo Goo Gai Pan		Mei Tu of Holli Ro (D)
	Chumulari Hsuan Shou		Mar Del's Titwillow		Pentara's Mi-Guy (D)
	Imperial Pong Tan		Mariljac Mr Boogie Bear		Petwill Ah Mei of Brynhall (B)
	Jin Chi Of Shu Lin		Mariljac Tinker Town Tidbit		Sangchen Chai of Rennard (D)
	Kathway's Lee Toi		Pentara's Miss Petty Coats		Shou Jen Ai Kuoche (D)
	Llonnee Lane's Tango		Si-Kiang Jody's Tidbie Toodle		Starline's My-Gy-Hotai (D)
	Mar Del's Ring A Ding Ding		Si-Kiang's Mayfair Geisha		Taramont Ah So Herbie (D)
	Mariljac Cee Wind Up Toi		Silver Nymph's Top Secret		Witch's Wood T'Ang Shui (B)
	Mariljac Friskie		Taramont Ah So Ho Bo	5/71	Chumulari Jen Tung (B)
	Mariljac Tinker Town Toi		Willows Jin Che		Emperor's Golden Fizz (B)
	Mariljac Tinker Town Tom	9/70	Chumulari P'Eng Yu		Glenarden Emperor Tse Jee Tao (D)
	Sitsang Whiz-Bang		Fan-Ci-Mei Tu		Lau Rin Jasmine Of Shang T'ou (B)
	Taramont Firefly		Ho Tai of Greenmoss		Lynncrest Suzuki (B)
	Taramont Moon Flower		Joclif's Taf-Fi		Mar Del's Kwai-Nine (B)
	Wedgewood's Signature		Roku's Charlmaine		Mariljac Kwang Ming (B)
	Yoshi's Ah So Omar		Royale Hu Lu		Pentara's Ting Ling (D)
3/70	Bom Shu Van De Oranje Manege		Taramont Ah So Onions		Sam Sun Spoo (D)
	Geojan Samitode	10/70	Darlyn's China Doll (B)		Seen-Haou Of Marlen (D)
	Hee Shee's Wee Bel Ange		Singsong Son's Boy (D)		Thalia's Sidney-Sidney (D)
	Hotai Uchi Oui		Toomi Of Lhakang (D)	6/71	Bluemarking Lalae (B)
	Mar Del's King Kanishka		Witch's Wood Mai Tai of Camelot (B)		Bom Shu's Fling Ling (D)
	Mariljac E's Mi Boi	11/70	Adair's Tek of Paisley (D)		Chun Cha Chong Lee (D)
	SaraA-Lee Ho-Chim-Wali-Du		Bom Shu's No Qwai Baby (B)		Emperor's Ha-Ta-Dee (B)
	Si-Kiang's I Ko Tien Shih		Greenmoss Golden Frolic of Elfann (D)		Golden Royalist of Elfann (D)
	Si-Kiang's Say It Again		Jade Lily of Elfann (B)		Hee Shee's Min-Dreh (B)
	Taramont Rickshaw Sam		Lil' Minx Alii (D)		Kharlan's Golden Condor (D)
	Taramont Tong		Long's Little Lick (B)		Ku Tee of Greenmoss (B)
4/70	Fran-Oaks Fu-Wi	12/70	Anibes Satru (D)		Sangchen Wuji (D)
	Mar Del's P'An Ku		Barnstorm Inferno (D)	7/71	Bernett's Ming Toi (D)
	Sangchen Christmas Angel		Bel-Air's Tinker Toy (D)		Captain Kidd of Nor-Ton's (D)
	Tin-Sel of Greenmoss		Copper Penny's Sun Mai (B)		Chumulari Ping Chu (B)
5/70	Bambu Sassy Saboo		Llonnee Lane's Gumdrop Gus (D)		Chumulari Ping Shan (B)
	Bill Ora's Ching-Ching		Sangchen Spring Song (B)		Fluff and Stuff Of Paisley (D)
	Bom Shu's Rockette Ting		Vams Joss Hotei (D)		Me John Henry's Folly (B)
	Choh-Non Uchi Oui		Wyllson's Saki-Tu-Mei (D)		Nanjo's Ah So Mi-Tee Wun (D)
	Mai Ling of Mountainside	1/71	Bom Shu's Earth Ling (D)		Shang's Marco Polo (D)
	Mai Lyn Mai Kwan Yin		Chumulari Sheng-Li Che (D)		Talifu Lianee (B)
	Peersun's Always Amber		Heeshee's Golden Shoestring (B)		Winddrift's Mai-Li Of Highland (B)
	Taramount Sampan Joe		Mariljac Jhon-Nhee Rheb (D)	8/71	Bel Air Bronze Boo-Dah (D)
	Teen Sih Shu		Pentara's Warrior of Lanbur (D)		Bom Shu's Kan Du No Wong (B)
6/70	Choo Lang Of Telota		Sopon Vom Tschomo-Lungma (D)		Emperor's Golden Rule (B)
	Dougal Of Telota		Tiko Ling of Antarctica (D)		Greenmoss Gilligan (D)
	Emperor's Bronze Gong	2/71	De Amo Golden Fan (B)		Greenmoss Golden Talon Of Elfann (D)
	Mariljac Ebony Emperor		Jo-Elz Topaz of Fifeshire (B)		Mariljac Twinkle Toes (B)
	Mariljac Kwang K'Whae		Lakoya's Jo-Jo (D)		Marinas May-Be-He (D)
	Mariljac Tinker Town Tot		Mariljac Chatterbox (D)	9/71	Anjos Yu Tu (D)
	Mariljac Tish-A-Mingo		T'ien T'an's Moon Ling (B)		De Amo Mee Tu Of Cherry Hill (B)
	Misty Isle Tashi Shu C.D.		Westmount Lady (B)		Emperor's Silver Fizz (B)
	Paisley Ping Pong	3/71	An-Ge-Lih (B)		Gamburg's Ku Ku Kutie (B)
	Pentara's His Nibs		Bambu Jacinth Jong (B)		Mai-Lynn Lum Lin Yue (B)
	Sangchen Christmas		Bel Air's Smoke By George (D)		Valimar Ming Chu Chi (B)

Vitahund's Hsi-Wang (B)
Willows Dan-Di-Lion (D)

10/71 Avalon's Mr. Woo (D)
Bela-Mia Tzu (B)
Bom Shu's Win Dsong (B)
Carrimount Ah Tiko Tiko (D)
Chumulari Tzu Yu (B)
Cresswood Son-Ata (B)
Emperor's Rascali Wag (D)
Emperor's Tiny Toe Tickler (B)
Golden Oscar (D)
Kathway's Sui-Yan (B)
Misty Isle Fei Ying (D)
Misty Isle Number One Son (D)
Pierrot's Wei-Shu Tre'zure (B)
Tzi Tzi Shu (D)

11/71 Aga-Lynn's Ying Yang (D)
Chang Of Kandu (D)
Fooldja (B)
Ken Mors' Ming Toi (B)
Mar Del's Chow Mein (D)
Mariljac Tattle Tail (B)
Taramont Maya (B)
Valimar Ming Yuin (D)
Windsor My Rimpoche (D)

12/71 Bom Shu's Moon Blossom (B)
Char Nick's Sesame Of Sam Chu (B)
Dun-Kee-Wang De Kleine Oosterling (D)
Mandarin's Buttercup (B)
Mar Del's Flutterby (B)
Parquins Sarrtezza (D)
Petwill Suzy Wong Of Kenmor (B)
Talifu Starlight (B)
Witch's Wood Yum Yum (B)

1/72 Chekenda Lady Gay (B)
Hee Shee Little Albert (D)
Jaisu Ting-Ling (D)
Khr-Ushe-Hev Uchi Oui (D)
Lakoya Momotaro-Asian Peach (D)
Sitsang Black Lace O'Ambrosia (B)
Taramont Miko of Fifeshire (D)
Ti-Ki-Rum-Pu (D)

2/72 Choh-Choh Uchi Oui (B)
Chumulari Chin-Te (B)
Chumulari Mei-Mei (B)
Emperor's Tea Taster (B)
Hayohan V Buruf (D)
Hee Shee Smudge Of Pinafore (B)
Huck-Elle'-Buck's Diamond (D)
Mar Del's Har-Tosie (B)

3/72 Bill Ora's Fancy Panys Of Po-Yen (B)
Bill Ora's Ruffles Of Mar-Jim (B)
Bomshu's Olletime Gorgeous (D)
Bomshu's Qwaier Boy (D)
Char Nick's Chun King Louie (D)
Chumulari Li Liang (D)
Chumulari Mei Lite (B)
Curzon Colkock (D)
Hatch's Makin Wu Pi Of Tien Tan (D)
Jaisu Hum-Dinger Of Loriel (D)
Jody's Jing Sik Ho (D)
Legend's Sakee Tu Yu (D)
Mai-Lyn Kwan Tu (B)
Northshire's Bit O'Honey (B)
Peersun's Day Dream (D)
Pentara's Sir Moto (D)
Shaadar's Lady Sha-Sheen (B)
Shaadar's Yan-Kee Doll (B)
Shang's Wu Wong (D)
Su-Le's Here Tiz (B)
Taramont Cokishin (D)
Tucker Of Fiddler's Green (D)

4/72 Bel Air Mik-Kie Toi-Sho (B)
Chumulari Chung Hsia Te (D)
De Amo Akachan (D)
Durga v d Blauwe Mammouth (B)
Greenmoss Saki Tuo (B)
Long's Chiny Chin Ah Chop Chop (D)
Mar Del's Sugar Tong of Copa (B)
Mariljac Kwang Tung (D)
Mariljac Superstar (D)
Northshire's No-Foo-Lin (B)
Peersun's Evening Echo (B)
Silverheel Su Jon Ko·v (D)
Taramount Samantha (B)
Taramount Wang Chi (D)

5/72 Antarctica Yang Koo-Chung (B)
Bomshu Hi Ho Geronimo (D)
Christamon's Pei Loo (D)
Echodale Flower Power (B)
Emperor's Copper Show Stopper (D)
Hale Koa's Sherry Spumone (B)
Kathway's Tong De Amo (D)
Little Lyin Moonmaid Mist (B)
Nanjo's Ah So Sweet-Sum-Wun (B)
Willows' Marionette (B)

6/72 Bomshu Kimba (B)
Char Nick's I Gotcha (D)
Ching Tsu of Marlen (D)
Elfann Golden Sunmaiden (B)
El Greco Soket Tuya (D)
Little Lyin Fuli Moonbeam (D)
Lyneva's Gold Sheba (B)
Royale White Tie And Tails (D)
Sitsang Chin-Chin (D)

7/72 Carrimount Ah-Crepe-De-Chine (B)
Citri Nessa Of Kansu (D)
Char Nick's My Sin (B)
Emperor's Adoring Amah (B)
Fei-Koo-Wang De Kleine Oosterling (D)
Floridonna Mil-Yen-Aire (D)
Gin Doc's Fortune Cookie (B)
Gin Doc's Golden Image (D)
Greenmoss Dainty Della (B)
Hee Shee's Ett Mia (B)
Hee Shee's George (D)
Long's Bedeviled Bedazzled (B)
Mar Del's Poppy Seed (B)
Meadowbrook Pudee Fu (D)
Mister Wang (D)
Shaadar's Mhaskarde de Cave (D)
Shangti Of Lhakang (D)
Shan Su Of Khamba (B)
St. Aubrey Greenmoss Beau Geste (D)
Yosha Toddie Mikko Bear (D)

8/72 Bluemarking Yana (B)
Chumulari Shen-Shih (D)
Emperor's Ebony Bla-Ka-Moor (D)
Emperor's Golden Buddha (D)
Gambrel's Farm Fair Suzuki (B)
Hee Shee's Mr. Bullwinkle (D)
Joclif's Sum Ting Lse (D)
Little Lyin Sami Shu Wong (D)
Sefai Ku Ching (B)

9/72 Aagalynn's China Doll (B)
Bel-Air's Gentle Char-Ming (B)
Greenmoss Golden Garter (B)
J.S. Sun-Tu (D)
Lau Rin Destiny of Shang T'ou (D)
Lyckobringarens Guy of Vita Hund (D)
Mariljac Maripet (D)
Moon-Ling's Tamanika (B)
Pen Sans An Lu Shan (B)
Si Kiang's Aff-Kins Kee (B)

Sitsang Wild Witch (B)
Tunxis Valley Thai Phichit (D)

10/72 Antarctica Kimiko (B)
Bel Air Ku Che Toi (D)
Bel Air Tigherson of Shang T'Ou (D)
Bernett's Wee Toi (D)
Char Nick's San Fu Li-Po (D)
Lansu Magnolia Time (B)
Lilly Loo of Myarlune (B)
Long's Heidi-Ho Ah Chop-Chop (B)
Lotus Blossom of Lyre (B)
Rebecca of Myarlune (B)
Splashdown of Greenisle (B)
Starfell Solitaire (B)
Tien Tan's King Po Tu (D)
Vitahund's Fu-Jen (B)

11/72 Charing Cross Ching El Chang (D)
Chin Yu Honeybee (B)
Copper Penny Charlen Bow Ku (B)
Din Ho Chi Ki of Copper Penny (B)
Emperor's Ping Pong Partner (D)
Golden Lotus Blossom of Elfann (B)
Long's Hi-Sacke Ah Chop Chop (D)
Madamar's Gladly (B)
Nanjo Kan-Do (D)
Sangchen Muffin (D)
Spring Valley Sure Fire Fat Al (D)
Yoshi's Wu-Chen (D)

12/72 Bernett's Shangri La (B)
Gamburg's Number One Son (D)
Gin-Doc's Tiger Lily (B)
Hee Shee's E.H.J. (D)
Li-Sa-Mor De Neergaard (B)
Loui Sing (D)
Oates Sumi Loo (B)
Raina's Dandelion (D)
Sho Mei Keibo (B)
Winemakers Tiz Tuo Flintrock (D)

1/73 Bill Ora's Char Li Brown (D)
Cresswood Mok-Tai (D)
Darlyn's Little Miss Muffitt (B)
Hol Lee Tui Son Uchi Oui (D)
Seng Fu Jazzy Tu (D)
Shaadar's The Yan-Kee Dollar (D)

2/73 Bel Air's Silver Ching A Ding (D)
Bernett's Sun Toi (D)
Chateau's Golden Dandy (D)
Chin Yu Firstborn (B)
Cresswood Pir-Anha (B)
De Amo I Mandy's Son (D)
De Neergaard's Tao (D)
Le Chateau's Mee-To Shih-Kai (D)
Mariljac Lotus Blossom (B)
Mattlen's Price-Patrick Am-A-Do (D)
Royale Mandarin Buttons Up (D)
Sam Tsu's Kim Sue Ling (B)
Thompson's Tun Pu (B)

3/73 Aga Lynn's Ying Yum of Gin Doc (D)
Bluemarking Lande (D)
Bomshu Fui Manchu (D)
Bomshu Imperial Matisse (B)
Bon D Art Aramus of Parquins (D)
Darlyn's Von-Twiggie of Geodan (B)
Emperor's Dancing Star (B)
Greenmoss Honey Bee (B)
Heavenly Dynasty's Olivia (B)
Kathway's Too To (B)
Luv-Li Sunflower a La Ming (B)
Mar Del's Golden Sunset (D)
Mee Ming Tuo Of Greenmoss (D)
Mo Yeh of Brynhall (D)
Phee's San Ko of Zijuh (D)

Am. and Can. Ch. Bilor's Pepsi Generation, owned by Lorraine De Salvo.

Judge Jay Ammon awarding BW to Ch. Mit-zu's Royal Grand Prix, owned by Floyd and Jackie Sable.

Left: Bilor's Golden Duster Buster, owned by Lorraine DeSalvo.

Right: Ch. Imua's Wicked Wahine, owned by Ginger Schedlbauer Buis.

Ch. Wingates TKO, owned by Jody Neal.

Ch. Lainee Chopped Liver, "Choppy," an example of correct liver pigmentation. Owned by Elaine Meltzer.

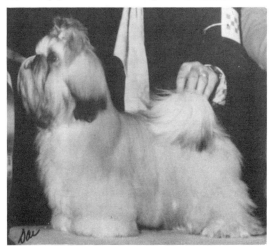

Roark's Fu Man Chu (D)
Su-Le's Ono (D)
Vams Benjamin Queue (D)
Willows' Miss Pitty Pat (B)
Wun Dey Atta Tyme of Cannonade (B)
4/73 Aagalyn Lion of Joppa (D), Kellogg
Mei-Tu of Lou Wan (D), Gec
Moonlighter So Sweet Sum Wun (B), Burch
Silverheel Aa-Li-Shang T'ou (B), Phillips & Mills
Wein-Man Mai Tai Dan-Di (D), Weinman
5/73 Carlee's Bey Be (B), Whitlock
Chumulari Leidza (B), Tranquillo & Skeffington
Gardner's Geisha Girl (B), Gardner
Gin Doc's Pirates Gold (D), Stoughton
Greenmoss Jezebel (B), Naegele
Monki Doodle of Midhill (B), O'Donnell & Phillips
Stentaway's Butterfly (B), Sicker
6/73 Ambrosia Tutt Tutt Tootsie (B), Jones & Mahy
Bluemarking Jia (D), Gajniak
Bon D Art Emperor of Parquins (D), Guggenheim
Din Ho Pong's Shu Ting Star (D), Strom
Encore Suki Tong (B), Hopkins
Li Po of Chasmu (B), Peisel
7/73 Aagalynn's I'm A Dandy (D), Lee & Keenan
Asian Peach Chin Chin (B), Leder
Dand Po Kyi (D), Baker
Din Ho Pong's Moon Beam Boe (D), Strom & Preston
Emperor's Lord Exchequer (D), Edel
Feather's Chiny Chile (B), Wilson
Garvins Topaz of Runkel (B), Busselman
Hee Shee's Miss Miller (B), Schoel
Kathway's China Doll (B), Hertel & Walker
Kathway's Mee Kylie's Sun Top (D), Hertel & Walker
Komorr's Hey Minx (D), Morrison
Latoba's El Tiger (D), Baker
Lee Way's Boo at Chantel (D), Forbes
Miss Peach of Sitsang (B), Salo
Nanjo Happi Yakki (D), Smigley
Shaadar's Marquis De Midas (D), Smithburn & Ray
Taramont Genral Su Wu (D), Brown & Bolus
8/73 Charjalong's Lotus Flower (B), Camberis
Conwynn's Tabetha (B), Smart
Emperor's Strawberry Blonde (B), Edel
Encore Flower Child (B), Fitts
Gin-Doc's Golden Nugget (D), Strait
Heavenly Dynasty's Yeh Shou (D), Noble
Highlands Ky-Ky of Winddrift (D), Barber & Stone
Hilton's Fortune Cookie (B), Hilton
Kee Lee's So Chee (B), Lee & Keenan
Lansu Blossom Time (B), Quillen & Warner
Little Lyin Pretti Penni (B), Robins & Pardon
Lorrac Nel Ray Chrys (B), Spong & Miller
Perry's Ming Chu (D), Perry
Sangchen's Little Man (D), Michael
Town Hall's Dragon Flower (B), Schielke
Town Hall's Dragonfire (D), Steapp
Witch's Wood Muy Muy (D), Murphy
Ying Ling of Mountainside (D), Lombardi
9/73 Bao Bay of Loriel (D), Jones
Bel Air Bali Hai (B), Atkinson
Char Nick's High Time of Nanjo (D), Sanfilippo
Char Nick's Mr. Chit Chat (D), Cowie
De Ville's Tu Ling (B), Emmell
Floridonna Sexa-Peal (B), Ellis
Hee Shee's Mr. Treek (D), Chapin
Ma-Tu's Most Happy Fella (D), Hanson
Pentara's Trinka (B), Rust & McKew
Quisang Van De Blauwe Mammouth (B), Dudgeon
Rani Victoria (B), Camarest Kennels & Ricefields Kennels
Silverlidens Marlboro Moppet (B), Novick
Sitsang Evening Star (B), Wright & Brisell
Taramont Ah-So Sebastian (D), Warner

Tasmin Puppity (B), Hegyes
10/73 Bel Air Sunsation of Gil Mar (D), Veniey & Washington
Carrimount Ah Flip Flop (D), Lambert & Repice
Charing Cross Hih Tsung (D), Kahn
Emperor's Favorite Son (D), Edel
Hillside Acres Simon Legre (D), Rudacille
Hodari Tam Lin of Moonling (B), Battey & McClarnon
Joclif Tami (B), DeArman
Kathway's Drummer Boy (D), Hertel & Walker
Long's Kiko Man of Tovar (D), Long
Mi China Doll of Drenthe (B), Hopkins
Shaw's Ping Wing Amee (D), Shaw
Shor-Ts-Nort of Al-Mar (B), Korotev
Willows the Golden Fleece (D), Easton
11/73 Chateau's Push-Ting (B), McGratty
Imperial Mikko Ling Chan Bear (D), Hein & Donleavy
Kee Lee's Yen Chen Yi (B), Lee & Lombard
Mister Chan II (D), Pearsall
San-Yen's Chang (D), Rust & McKew
San-Yen's Shanna (B), Rust & McKew
Tuf-Fee of Uchi Oui (D), Thornton
Vip's Confusious (D), Paulus
Vita Hund's Sheng-Chang (D), Bergman
Zizi's Twan (D), Easton & Wegmann
12/73 Bernett's Ky Lynn (B), Hertel & Walker
Bom Shu Bacardi of Moon Ling (D), Kendall
Brownhills Yolan of Greenmoss (B), Carrique
Dun Kee Wang Socket Tu Ya (B), Marcum
Ima Dandy of Drenthe (D), Wieda
Lau Rin Poke A Long (B), Riney
Mai-Lyn Pun-Kin-Puf (B), Seydel
Nodla Ayron Samantha (B), Dunmire
Raina's Moonglow (B), Parasiliti
1/74 Affinity's Hotie Idol (D), Robinson
Ah So Yen Of Chan Ju (B), Garrett
Bobbie's Brandy B-Bomb (D), Franklin
Cabrand's Lou Wan V Alarickhan (D), Von Ahrens & Gec
Char Nick's Be Wit Ching Of Copa (B), Davis
Chateau's Lan-Sing O'Briarhill (B), Craddock
Geodan's Ron Eric (D), Kendall
Heavenly Dynasty's Pasha (B), White & Elliott
Highfalutin (D), Crisp, Cookingham & Preston
Mar Del's Tempel Chimes (B), Edel
Nan-Cee's Saucy San-San (B), Tripp
Nanjo Ping's Pa-Ti-Cake (B), Cowie
Rosemar Very Bismark (D), Warner
San Yen-Ming Toi Ja-Shu-Wa (D), Donleavy
2/74 Bali Hai Huffin Puffin (B), Voss
Emperor's Flutter Ying (B), Edel
Emperor's Thing Ah-Ma Ying (D), Dinelli
Hee Shee's Ko Yin Ski (D), Schoel
Lakoya's Gi Gi (B), Hoffman
Sparkle Plenty for David (B), Raker
Thunderhills Bombay Budda (D), Grimes & Nagle
Vams Yuan Don (D), Duckworth
Witch's Wood Na-Ta-Sha (B), Kabel
3/74 Chateau's Desiree Of Diandee (B), Allen
Chin Ki Wun Of Greenmoss (D), Neagle
Hai-Du's Honey Bear (D), Miller & Haiducek
Heavenly Dynasty's T'ai Tzu (D), Wong
Mandarin's Royale Rhapsody (B), Di Nicola & Meltzer
Nanjo Oh Mai Gosh Of Char-Nick (D), Cowie
4/74 Car-Lyn's Foxy Lady Of Cambalu (B), Koeppel
Obie Is My Delight At Nobah (D), Hall & Michalinos
5/74 Charnick S'Wing Erh Of Copa (D), Nickerson
Emperor's Quapaw Dakota Sioux (B), Core & McCarty
Gin-Doc's Suzy Wong (B), Weber
Lou Wan Casinova (D), Gec
Mar Del's Chiajen Of Copa (D), Nickerson
Paradises Silver Lining (D), Starwalt & Becker
Sonja Of Marlboro (B), Novick
Town Hall's Hallelujah (B), Patton

6/74 Amricks San Tana (B), Wilson
Antonidorn Chip's (D), Schoberlin
Christamon's Tai-Pan (D), Lucchina & Hudson
Mistybank Ouzo V Zervlistan (D), Zervoulis & Banga
Shazam (D), Knight & Ellis
Spring Valley Lynncrest Loui (D), Wright & Brisell

7/74 Bomshu No Stuffed Toi (D), Kaye & Gadberry
China Seas Monsoon (D), Beauter & Parry
House Of Wu Tiz Tu (B), Eckes
Joclif Hi N Mi Ti Of Lake (D), Rovill & Busby
Nanjo Hi-Hope Of Joy-Fu-Li (D), Dean & Stratton
Parquins Pretty Boy Floyd (D), Ammon
Shang's Mie Tu Of Sue (B), Clark
Vitahund's Tiang-Chang (B), Harris

8/74 Charjalong Mr. Flip Of 'Afmoon (D), Repice & Lambert
Chumulari Chin-Tan (B), Gec
Elfann Golden Beau Brummel (D), Smart
Emperor's I Has Pizazz (D), Wheeler
Joart's Goldstrike (D), Davison & Orlando
Laineux Wunh Hungh Loh (D), Hansen & Kelly
Mistybank Santi Sen (B), Banga
Noble's J-Son (D), Noble
Seng Fu Ding A Ling (D), Seng
Vip's Quenni-Lyn (B), Arnold

9/74 Bel Air Tai-Son (D), Daniels
Charjalong's Ah Chit-Chat (D), Long
Chen Yu (D), Zidanowicz
Chin Yu Brindala (D), Wisser
Emperor's My Doll (B), Edel
Highlandell Golden Persimon (D), Hansen
Hodari Sheng Li Of Moonling (D), Toliver
Johmar's Doodle Bug (B), Potis
Long's Kiko Lady (B), Long
Misty Isle April Morn (B), Jorgensen
Nanjo's Good As Gold (B), Cowie
Nanjo Suki Sue (B), Riggi
Sanchi's Kokutan Of Si-Kiang (B), Selfon
Si Kiang's Lady Bug (B), Burt
Silverheel Amida (D), Veniey
Winemakers Pla-Boi (D), Wine

10/74 Beedoc's Chueh Shih Mei Jen (B), Stubblefield
Bel Air Fantasia (B), Daniels
Chumulari Yu-Yu (B), Stone & Barber
Emperor's Quapaw Quarter Emp (D), Core & McCarty
Jan-Pat's Soo Ling Of Nanjo (B), Shackelford
Johmar's Pahko (D), Potis
Lillico's Mi Toi Ro Byn (B), Lillico
Mariljac Long Shot (D), Schaefer
Nanjo Yung Ping (D), Edge
Vitahund's Lin-Jen (B), Bergman
Wyesarge Jade Butterfly (B), Greggans

11/74 Ambrosia Poco Dot (B), Maly
Blantyre Hsiao Hu Chia Pao (D), Inglis
Bojang Dixie Dewdrop (D), Phillips
Del Wood Regent Kali-Li-Lee (B), Goodwin & Thompson
Dragonwyck Sugar Cookie (B), Johnston
Dun-Kee-Wang Sissy Pissy (B), Marcum
Emperor's Bloody Mary (B), Crissman
Gin Doc's Hiawatha Of Lou-J (B), Rees
Lilibet Dhan Boi Of Shang Tou (D), Riggi
Loto's Panda Bear Of Nanjo (D), Cowie
Lyckobringarens Iona (B), Wisser
Marlboro's Autumn Leaf (B), Novick
Nanjo's Little Rag A Muffin (D), Weberg
Northshire's Bruno Bear (D), Naegele
Thinge-Wingh (D), Mariljac Kennels, Riggi & Anzese
Town Hall's Huette O'Shartrina (B), Steapp
Vitahund's Szu-Wen-Jen (D), Lindblom

12/74 Ah-Kamas Jasmin (B), Novick
Aja Shu Van De Oranje Manege (B), Aja
Char Nick's Star Of Sharn (B), Utstein
Cinnabar Golden Pirate (D), Malone

Cresswood Tourmaline (B), Cress
Dashi's Chin-Tan (B), Pouliot
Emperor's Cheer Leader (B), Higman
Gunning's Kismet Of Shang T'ou (B), Gunning
Hei Lein's Mr. Bojangles (D), Adams
Hidden Coves Golden Pendant (B), Ward
House Of Wu Wing-Wa Of Sheng-Ti (B), Baker
Mariljac Marilyn Of Chusanho (B), Coolina
Moon Ling's Wu Tai Shan (D), Zervoulis
Northshire's Q-T-Pye Of Nan-Cee's (B), Tripp
Parquins Egyptian Magic (D), Antonucci
Sam Tsu's Tam-E (B), Stubblefield & Carroll
Sumi's Sum Wun Tu Luv (B), Oates & Callaway
Thompson's Hsi Tse (B), Thompson & Miller
Town Hall's Trude (B), Marcum

1/75 Ewan Tiko Fu Ling (D), Plewa
Marlima Chi Lin (D), Walsh
Pen Sans Cinnamon Toast (D), Busselman & Brown

2/75 Dolmar So-Su-Mi (B), Martin
Dunklehaven Luv-Li-Ladee (B), Bogner
Emperor's All That Glitters (D), Edel
Ewan Chin Chih Kei (B), Dehring
Gim Ling Tianna Of El Greco (B), Craddock & Henderson
Highlandell Gold Tiger Tail (D), Hansen
House Of Wu Mimosa (B), Eckes
Kwitcherkidden (D), Brinlee
Largyn Forget-Me-Not Of Nanjo (B), Smigley

3/75 Fou Ts'ong Of Antarctica (D), Thornton
Chasmu Solo (D), Frothingham & Nugent
He's My Guy Of Drenthe (D), Wieda
Hodari Ying Su Of Moonling (B), Battey
Ima Slick Chic Of Drenthe (B), Wieda
Jilga Shu Van De Oranje Manege (B), Aja
Link's Bamboo Too Too (B), Deering & Link
Moon-Ling's Hop Sing (D), Tolliver
Ramblewood's Ring-Go (D), Alexander & Cole
Shamisen's Number One Son (D), Herbst
Tricina Corol (B), Koch
Windsor Gayelyn Ra-Sa-Ruck (D), Knoche

4/75 Almont's Richard J Levy (D), Teitelbaum & David
Barbara's Mr. Tu Ling Sing (D), Henderson
Bel Air Koochi Ku (D), Deering
Charjalong's Little Iodine (B), Long
Ding-A-Ling The Emperor's Ying (D), Edel
Hajji Baba Of Floridonna (D), Ellis
Heavenly Dynasty's Hochi (D), Perretz
Hsing Ch'i Ssu Yeh Uchi Oui (D), Thornton
Jac-Lyn's San Yen Chinny Chin (D), Walter
Jatsu Rallyround Smoo-Ching (B), Kazar
Lainee's Holly Golightly (B), Meltzer
Nan-Cee's Apricot Nectar (B), Tripp
Stumpy Acres Sandalwood Fan (B), Blanco
Winemaker's Fire Bomb (D), Batley

5/75 Bom Shu Nine Lyves Of Moon Ling (D), Gadberry
Char Nick's Executive Action (D), Sanfilippo
Dragonwyck The Great Gatsby (D), Patton
Emperor's Sweet Harlequin (B), Linden
Fang Of Shang T'ou (D), Hollingsworth
Nanjo's Haiku Dragon Brat (B), Schedlbauer
Tipton's Lady Jen-Mi (B), Tipton
Winemakers Oriental Poppy (B), Laughter

6/75 Bom Shu Kahlua Of Moon Ling (B), Steapp
Car-Lyn's A Touch Of Class (D), Morgan
Deray's Our Gal Pentara (B), Anderson & Johnson
Emperor's Dynamic Darrette (D), Andersen
Emperor's First Lady Ch'Eng (B), Heilman & Strapp
Jaisu Ling Ho X-Rated Of Lainee (D), Meltzer
Kee Lee's Le-Pre-Chaun Sundae (B), Lee & Keenan
Malone's Le-Jil Mop See Aa Lei (B), Malone
Marco Polo Di Visconti (D), Ferrante
Meili Dikang Lilyang (B), Jamison
Nanjo Toby Ty Of Tywood (D), Graney

Jaine and Impal vom Tschomo-Lungma, owned by Trudy Kerr.

Ch. Robara's Domino Monkeydo (center) with Bobo and Teddy. Owners Barbara and Robert E. Flaharty, Jr.

Conwynns Beau Geste and Ch. Elfann Golden Beau Brummel, owned by Constance Smart.

Jap. and Am. Ch. Lainee The Raven Maniac, owned by Elaine Meltzer.

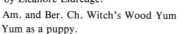

The King of Siam and Shang T'ou, owned by Eleanore Eldredge.

Chinai's Pretty Penny, owned by Chris and David Jones.

Ch. Lainee Racy Lady, owned by Rose Marie Boggess.

Am. and Ber. Ch. Witch's Wood Yum Yum as a puppy.

Ch. Lainee Sigmund Floyd at 5-1/2 months. Owned by Elaine Meltzer.

Nat-Sam's I Can Too (B), Marcum
Nat-Sam's Mister Shih Tzu (D), Marcum
Tien Tan's Mei Jen Of Su-Le (B), Bouchard
Tien Tan's Tai Li Chu (D), Bouchard

7/75 An Wu's Lion Of Nanking (D), Rothleder
Beedoc's Yu Mei Te Jen (B), Stubblefield
Emperor's Thunderhill Buddah (D), Tarallo
Fancee Chances R (D), Wheeler
Highlandell Sun's A Blazin (D), Russell & Marshall
Mahjong Artemus (D), Washington & Veniey
Mar Del's Mei Lan Of Kee-Lee (B), Lee & Keenan
Peers Hall Gunga Din Din (D), Pearsall
San Yen Tang Ku Hai Sing (B), Hayward
Stentaway's Too-Kee (B), Seger & Hechinger
True Blue's Goodi Tu Shooz (D), Hopkins
Winward's Tami Tu (B), Gardner
Witch's Wood Ching Ching (D), Winslow & Guiraud
Yum Pin Yim An Nee (B), Merrill

8/75 Bel Air's Check-Mate (D), Cole
Bobbie's Hunk I Dor I Do (D), Franklin
Bom Shu Nine Lyves Of Moon Ling (D), Graver
Din Ho Merry Sun Shine (B), Strom
Emperor's Bee Witch Ying (B), Edel
Emperor's Favorite Bannerman (D), Wayne
Faerie Dean Fleur-De-Chine (B), Thompson
Sevarg's Chang Tzu Mi (D), Graves
Tsma's Peter Pumpkin (D), Weber
Twan Pun Kin (B), West & Danleavy
Victor Of Starhaven (D), Warner

9/75 Chin Yu Boybaby (D), Wisser
Tahanni's Dragon Eater (D), Lowell

10/75 Conwynn's Glory Bee (B), Smart
Copper Penny Happiness Is (B), Pennington
Emperor's Life Of The Party (D), Hickey
Encore Golden Girl (B), Fowler
Encore Golden Suyen (B), Fitts
Fang's Chang Tzu Of Shang T'ou (D), Hollingsworth
Gamburg's Shazzam Of Nikko (B), Gamburg
Jaisu Pitchin Wu Of Din Ho (D), Strom
Kum Tims Eeyore Of Ram-Sita (D), Hutchins
Maricam's Tiki Tiki Tembo (D), Benanti
Su Chan's Gol-Ee-Shazam (D), Marker
Winemakers Tiz Ah Rumdinger (B), Pearsall
Winward's Lucky Charm (B), Bump
Zim Shu V D Oranje Manege (B), Miller

11/75 Ambelon Tick Tock (D), Long
Bon D'Art Petulant Paulette (B), Ray
Emperor's Something Else (D), Adshead & Andrade
House Of Wu-Hai-U (D), Eckes
House Of Wu Sam Ting (D), Lewis
Jaisu Play For Keeps Of Ling-Ho (D), Crissman
Lou Wan Mariposa Of Sarifan (B), De Stefano & Gec
Pinafore Ginger Bread Boy (D), Harney
Sanchi's Bekko (D), Miller

12/75 Bel Air Sa-Li (B), Phillips
Bojang Merrybelle Lee (B), Phillips
Car Lyn's Barcardi Barbarella (D), Roark
Car-Lyn's Kung Fu (D), Wicks
Carrimount Ah-Me-Jolly-Jo (D), Head
Chumlari Chin Te Jih (D), Joris
De Amo Dream Of Gold (B), Martin
Heavenly Dynasty's Hsi Hsi Te (B), Dziewit & White
House Of Wu Witch's Brew (B), Steapp
Lou Wan Tangra Ling (B), Gec
Mei San Saki Tuo Mee Babe (B), Meidlinger
Nanjo Tis Tu Pings (D), Cowie
Paisley Pong Of Davanick (D), Angelastro
Windsor Gayelyn Jade Of Nika (B), Hager

1/76 Elfann Golden Elegance (B), Di Nicola
Kublai Khan Di Visconti (D), Peace
Lansu Winter Time (D), Posateri
Wot-A-Bee Of Greenmoss (D), Schoberlein

2/76 Chateau's White Peony Of Arlys (B), Kijowski
Dragonwyck Miss-B-Havin' (B), Patton
Hullaballou J Ray Of Nanjo (D), Ballou
Jancy's Puff The Mi-Tee Dragon (D), Phipps
Nat-Sam's Hop-Sing (D), Luce
Pen San's Suzie Of Non Vel (B), Hood
Sam Tsus H B Calipso (D), Carroll

3/76 Abacus' Cn Di Lu (B), Basil & Smith
Briarhill Harley Davidson (D), Craddock
Char Nick's U Gotta Believe (D), Camileri
Emperor's Most Happy Fellah (D), Edel & Miller
Shanfu Chin Hui Hsing (D), Williams
Tori's Kimi Su (B), Rolle & Richards
Vitahund's A-Poll-O (D), Lindblom

4/76 Bel Air Stargazer (D), Crissman
Bitsy Bee Of Greenmoss (B), Brewer & Lehmann
Carrimount Ah-Chop-Chouee (B), Carrique
Char Nick Fantasy Of Gunning (B), Gunning & Arenz
Dynasty's Toi-Ying (D), Newkirk & Schmalhausen
Dynasty's Wind-Up-Toi (B), Alderman
Easy Ace Of Johmar (D), Berrier
Gin Doc's Champagne Ladi (B), Weber
Ming Toi P V Spunky (D), Boyles
Nanjo Domino (D), Allan
Nodla Ayron Blanchard (D), Gallucci
Pen-Sans Que Pee Doll (B), Walter
Sam-Tsus Marhia (B), Lewis
Vitahund's Hsien-Sheng C.D. (D), Winchell
Yang-Kee Clipper Of Langpur (D), Futterman

5/76 Ambelon Jewel (B), Long
Briarhill Ossa (B), Craddock
Car-Lyn's Dynamo Of Sanco (D), Cox & Morgan
Carrimount Ah-Chun-Ki (D), Johnstone
Char Nick's Legend Of Bon D'Art (D), Guggenheim
Mar Dels Chink Chink Chinaman (D), Edel
Missy Ling Franklin (B), Krusemark, Haskett & Teitelbaum
Nan-Ce's Vanilla Confection (B), Tripp
The Clown's First Hurrah (B), Chiochios
Von-Derfull Witch's Wood Chan-C (D), Vaughn

6/76 Arjun V Tschomo-Lungma (D), Lambert
Bel Air Ms Erica Beedoc (B), Stubblefield
Bomshu Luk Mah (D), Steapp
Encore Ming Huang Wing Tai (D), Lewis & Browne
Evanz Magnum Force (D), Pauley
Gin-Doc's Suzy Of Shanguish (B), O'Brien
House Of Wu Mai Mai (B), Warner
Pen Sans Crackerjack (D), Busselman
Shogun Kuro Kintaro (D), Sanchez

7/76 Aagalynn's Shanghai Lil (B), Grizzaffi
Cresswood High Fashion (B), Cress
Ding-A-Ling By Gosh Of Nanjo (D), Murphy
Elfann Golden Puff Ball (B), Kahn & Sanchez
Illenid's Liza Of Winsor (B), Dinelli
Kee-Lee's Om Tzo Tza Tzi (B), Ioia
Suki Mei Ling (D), Koch & Miller
Yin Shan Mi Sugar Pi (B), Hustler

8/76 Beedoc's Ku Che Kuo Wang (D), Stubblefield
Bel Air Tara Tu (B), Chapin
Chan Lan Nu Shen Of Kuei Tsu (B), Vander Weele
Charjalongs Bronze Bandit (D), Gunning
C's Gold Kung-Fu Of Tingerto (D), Sayres & Busselman
Dragonseed's Fu-Ke-Tu-U (B), Marsh
Fancee No Plain Jane (B), Thomas & Wheeler
Heavenly Dynastys Hsi Shih (B), Kerstein & White
Hodari Fuchsia Lin (B), Battey & McClarnon
Jaisu Ling-Ho Chinese Junk (D), Fritts
Whitethroat Shih Tsai (B), Kahn & Sanchez
Winwards Wheeler Delaer (D), Bump

9/76 Bomshu Born Flee (D), Zervoulis
Mar Del's U Betcha (D), Cannon
Marlboro's Marionette (B), Novick
Marya Winds Gilded Lady (B), Coolina

Ming Toi Miste Jen-Yuh (B), Boyles
Nanjo Cinder-Ella Of Largyn (B), Cowie & Smigley
Stumpy Acres Sandalwood-Man (D), Blanco
10/76 Bel Air Inspiration (D), Backovich
Bel Air Tif-A-Nee Of Bamboo (B), Backovich & Phillips
Capa's-Golden-Pandora Of Boru (B), Ballard
Crescendo Chan Tung (B), Tennant
Cresswood Breath Of Spring (D), Cress & Guzzy
Gin Doc's Huggy Bear (D), Karshner
Gin-Doc's Kubla Khan Of Lisel (D), Mickens
Heavenly Dynastys Mel Boi Toi (D), Johnson & White
Hil Tons' Rain Dragon (D), Hilton
Kee Lee's Munday's Child (B), Munday & Keenan
Marya Winds Tie-Dye Of Dynasty (B), Alderman & Winsemius
Mei San Chin-Tan (D), Krisko
San Tsu's Coco Puff (D), Carroll & Bobillot
Stentaway's Dragon's Seed (D), Hechinger & Calhoun
Willows Fancy Me (B), Gregory & Allen
11/76 Afshi's Gunther (D), Bowman & Charley
Ambleon Samantha (B), Frothingham & Lucchina
Amrick's Dar-Ling Puf Of Geodan (B), Wilson
Bomshu Contessa V Zervlistan (B), Zervoulis
Copper Penny Bar-Na-Bi Jones (D), Pennington
Gems Leonardo Di Visconti (D), Johnson
Hapi Our's Swing On A Star O'Copa (D), Williams & Nickerson
Highlandell Truly Terrific (B), Russel, Marshall & Hansen
Jaisu Cheesecake Of Ling-Ho (B), Williams
Mi Ti Wunurful Nuz Of La Ke (B), Rovillo & Busby
Nanjo Mystique (B), Cowie
Nat-Sam's Kwan-Yin' (B), Marcum
Rondelay Sheng Po (D), Deck
Sharn's Komik Kar-Ak-Ter (B), Utstein & Gunning
12/76 Bel Air Butterfly Of Bamboo (B), Backovich
Chiny Chin's Ah Ginseng (D), Mundy
Christamon's Kissy's Sissy (B), Pouliot
Din Ho Dapper Dan (D), Gilbride
Floridonna's Lucky Seven (D), Adshead & Andrade
Happi Showing Bandit (D), Archer
Hoppa Shu V D Oranje Manege (B), Miller
Jen-Mi Kis-Sing Kin Ming-Toi (B), Heuser
Johmar's Firefly Of Pashtun (D), Tunstall
Kara Lu's Rikety Rickshaw Man (D), Aronberg
Marlboro's Ashley (D), Novick
Nanjos Ruby Begonia Of Jolei (B), Kijowski
Pen Sans Flower Power Rime (B), Rime
Pine Haven's Chu Tzi Tzu (D), Huntsman
Rex Landor Di Visconti (D), Baker & Ferrante
Rockee-Vollee Kimko Of Luv-Tzu (D), Mueller
Shardeloes Emperor's Ti Kuote (D), Rodrigues
Stentaway Wo Shih Yuan (D), Hechinger & Seger
Talisman Charing Ching Toi (B), King
Ty Le (B), Newton
Winemakers Pla-Ting (D), Wine & McLister
Wunsum's Mr Uppity (D), Hagen, Cookingham & Preston
1/77 Bon D Art Adore Ring Of Fancee (B), Satelli & Satelli
Bon D'Art Amour Ring Of Fancee (B), Guggenheim & Wheeler
Chumulari Tai-Tai Of Aristo (B), Blanc
Dang Sai Vanilla Puddin (B), Rent
House Of Wu Outrigger (D), Eckes & Lamb
Lainee X-Tra Amorous (B), Gresham & Meltzer
Maralan's Chin P'Ing Mei (B), Blasinski & George
Mar Dels Golden Chimes (B), Arnett
Nanjo Sunshine (B), Cowie
Pen Sans Party Pooper (D), Baker & Donleavy
Te-Camp Smoki Kama Of Shirlynn (D), Thomas & Campbell
Urdu Vom Tschomo-Lungma (D), Rasor
2/77 Abacus' Little Red Waggin' (B), Basil & Smith
Charjalong's Party Doll (B), Long

Char Nick Forego Of Shirlynn (D), Parlak & Sanfilippo
Chin Yu Heaven Sent (D), Wisser
Dandy-Lion's Debutante (B), Arnold
Floridonna's Golden Primrose (B), Ellis
Jade Sun Nel Lee (B), O'Neil
Johmar's Cricket (B), Potis
Johmar's Yankee Doodle (D), Potis
Joya's Lill Ambsy Divy (B), Berrier
Mandarin's Mischief Maker (D), Regelman
Winemakers Taffi Candi (B), Mickens
3/77 Charjalongs Ah Lickey Split (B), Long
Chateau's Sans Souci Of Jolei (D), Kijowski
Chateau's Too-Tsi (B), Forsman & Kijowski
Chin Yu Daisi (B), Wisser
Emperor's Minstrel Man (D), Steapp
House Of Wu Tiana (B), Eckes
Li Ming's Ping Kan (D), Perreta & Tendler
Mariljac I'm A-Little-Devil-Too (D), Thomas & Wood
Mariljac Joey Of Jubilation (D), Crissman & Miller
Sheng'Ti's Ping Pong (D), Mantie
6/77 Abacus' Brutha Nutt (D), Smith & Basil
Hodari Chin Lin (D), Gambill
Hullaballou So Sumi (D), Oates & Ballou
Lotsa Sparkle Of Floridonna (B), Ellis & Tripp
Moonligher Daddy's Money (D), Burch
Nat-Sam's Sho Kiku (B), Volkstort & Marcum
Nodia Ayron The Great Gerald (D), Roberts
Spring Valley By By Bertha (B), Bellamy
Sun Canyon Hi Hopes (B), Goodwin & Thompson
Sun Canyon Stingray (D), Goodwin & Thompson
Willows Wizard (D), Bolsaks & Adams
7/77 Abacus Chairman Of The Board (D), Pier
Bee-Cee-Dee Of Greenmoss (D), Naegele
Briarhill Indian (D), Thornton
Capa's Sol-Del-Oro (D), Arcuragi
Evanz Dirty Harry (D), Ketchell & Pauley
Greg-Mar's Puff-N-Stuff (D), Stretch & Smith
Hal Sings Ho An Chu Of Pen San (B), Davidson
Hevnly Dynsty Ling Ki Kerijon (B), Woodward
Jondalin Fired Up (B), Thornton
Lillibet Golden Dawn (B), Kaye
Marya Winda Ja-Kai Jean Harlow (B), Means
Nanjo Ping's Free Spirit (D), Cowie
Tori's Gold Chrysanthemum (B), Tolle & Richards
8/77 Barbarella-Bellaire-Ming-Tzu (B), Roark & Gunning
Faerie Dean Hsiao Niao Fei (B), Miller
Irkoe Shu V D Oranje Manege (D), Keenan
Joclif Gentleman Jim (D), Miller
Kachina's Sugar N Spice (B), Kregar
Kaduna's Sewzi Q Lang-Sing (B), Sniderman & Corbett
Mariljac Mari-Ell (B), Wood & Johnson
Stylistic Barban Scarlet (B), Shepherd & Seranne
Tzu-Zi Foo Yung Of San Yen (B), McGill & Barr
Visconti The Enlightened One (D), Tripp
Visconti The Godfather (D), Crissman
Wynd Chumes Min Chieh (D), Ruskin
9/77 Magestic Mop-Ze Of Mudacres (B), Payne
Natasha Ling (B), Janson
Teddy Taurus Albert (D), Albert
10/77 Dragonseed's Wen-U-Hot-U-Hot (D), Marsh
Erincroft Qu Ti Pi Of Jazmin (B), Peterson
Ho Chi's Ring Leader (D), Alexander
Jen Sen Floyds Sweet Soo (B), Jensen
Jolei Annie Oak-Lei (B), Kajowski
Kee-Lee's Fine And Dandy (D), Simoes
Kee-Lee's Red Baron Of Mar-Del (D), Lee, Keenan & Edel
Malone's Mai-Tai Of Aurora (D), Mueller
Mandarins Oliver Twist (D), Crane, Pawelko & Barr
Pens Sans Dem Golden Slippers (B), Busselman
To Te Mei's Sundance (D), Caty
11/77 Blaze Saint 'N Satan (D), Fowler
Caralandra's Passing Fancy (B), Hogg

88

Ch. Janiric's Lorelei, owned by Jane McDaniel.

Ch. Ding-A-Ling By Gosh of Nanjo, owned by Sally Murphy.

Ch. Joylin's String of Pearls, dam of Ch. Joylin's Rebel Reflection. Owned by Hilde D. Pittelli.

Ch. Shen Wah's For Members Only, owned by Mr. and Mrs. Joe Walton.

Ch. Char Nick's Spiffy Laree, owned by Joe Walton.

Ch. Carefree Kid of Ju-I, co-owned by Nessa Gale and Louis Sanfilippo

89

Charing Cross Belinda Belle (B), Kahn & Sanchez
Chin Yu Brass Tacks (D), Wisser
Copper Penny Wil-Ee (D), Osborne & Pennington
Gunning's Highway Robbery (B), Utstein & Gunning
Kharisma Little Bo Peep (B), Nyberg
Lee-Joi's Peach Parfait (B), Whitman & Gunning
Wychmere's Ah Zalsa (B), Ellis & Tripp

12/77 Cabrand's High N Mighty (D), Gec & Tendler
Dashi's My My (D), Pouliot & Dullinger
Dynasty's Toi-Riffic (B), Alderman
Gardner's Yankee Doodle Dandy (D), Heinig
Jual's Imperial Winde Chime (B), Graber & Ammon
Lainee X-Tra X-Posed (D), Constantino
Lakewoods Kerijon Keemo (B), Hollingshead & Niedecken
Largyn Ping Pong Playmate (B), Smigley
Mandarin' Jet Set Di Visconti (D), Regelman & Regelman
Ming Toi Chase Manhattan (D), Rexroat
Sanchi's Shishi (D), Selfon
Sancos Sebastian Of Faro (D), Anderson & Johnson
Si Kiang's Chiang Tao Lipo (D), Gidusko
Sun Canyon Me A Boo Son (D), See & Goodwin
Sun Canyon Ming Lei (B), Goodwin & Thompson

1/78 Almont Chen Hy-Lan Chop Sa-Sao (D), Hylton & Chenoweth
Arbee's Chocolate Chip (D), Rukavina
Bel Air Ace Of Spades (D), Backovich
Fauntine Sunburst (D), Neugarth
Gunning's Frito Bandito (B), Gunning & Crane
House Of Wu Boi Named Tzu (D), Amonett
Jmua's Wicked Wahine (B), Schedlbauer & Spencer
Imu The Gatsby's Pride O' Ali-Aj (D), Castellano
Malone's Bronze Mer-Un-Dac (D), Malone
Pen Sans Ginger Bread Man (D), Jennings & Busselman
Philoore's Woo-Fie Do (D), Dommer
Silver Mist Shag (D), Thompson & Miller

2/78 Charing Cross Rising Star (D), Kahn & Sanchez
Jondalin Delilah (B), Lynn & Battey
Kay's Bim Bam O'Nat Sam (D), Gajniak
Kee Lee's Top Brass of Bar-Jon (D), Ioia
Li Ming's Cha Meng (B), Tendler

3/78 Balrath Honey Charm (B), Thompson
Cabrand's Temptress V Truro (B), Crane & Pawelko
Emperor's Hanky Panky Ying (D), Sturm
Ja-To-Mi-Kri-Fu Hi Ho Babe (D), Phillips
Jen-Mi Real McCoy Of Copa (D), Heuser
Joppa August Moon (D), Kellog
Mariljac Mari Samantha (B), Herbst & Patton
Nederlander's Baak-Yim-Jing (B), Tinsley
Ramurka's Cream Of The Crop (B), Murphy
San Su Kee Cabrand Clark Gable (D), Palmersten
Toshi's China Doll (B), Fotinakes
Zanadu Chantilly Lace (B), Sorem

4/78 Chumulari Ch'Un Chi (D), Malone
Entang Shu V D Oranje Manege (D), Lund & Merickel
House Of Wu Wee Ping (B), Eckes
Imua's Roots O Shurr's (B), Schedlbauer & Spencer
Nanjo Flippant Flirt (B), Hege & Hege
Sun Canyon Joy-Fu-Li (B), Goodwin & Thompson
Vitahund's Han-Full (D), Weil
Winemakers Huggy Bear (B), Crissman

5/78 Ah So Sue Suki (B), Ledoux
Emperor's Bee Devil Ying (D), Davidson
Granvilles Dar Din Sing (B), McDaniel
Lipo's Tiang Mei (B), Gidusko & Mauer
Paramount Lucky Lin Chu (D), Ikola

6/78 Bomshu Caralandra (B), Steapp
Carousel's Wee-O-Of Largyn (D), Lucchina
Davaniks Starduster (D), Himel
Lainee X-tra Daffy (B), Meltzer
Mundy's Ama Woo-Fie-Do Ranger (D), Mundy
Tahanni's Brazin Raisin (D), Gallaher & Gossman
Tumac's Hank (D), McIntee

Winward's Teddy Bear (D), Washington & Veniey

7/78 Encore Sun Flower Splendor (B), Fitts & Hoffman
Ho Chi's Belle Ringer (B), Alexander & Cole
Imua's Guava Jam (D), Hoo
Jen-Mi's Give Em Hell Harry (D), Heuser
Kee-Lee's Peke-A-Boo (B), Penn & Keenan
Kung Fu's Ha-Pi With Gunning (B), Brewer, Lehman & Gunning
Lainee X-Tra Exciting (D), Wells & Meltzer
Mei San Abracdabra (B), Hall & Miller
Mundy's Ama Yo Yo's Yum Yum (B), Mundy
Nanjo Breez E (D), Hege
Raintree's Promised Gold (D), Rainey
Winemaker's E'Zee Luvin (B), Ward

8/78 Beedoc's Ma Barker (B), Stubblefield
Charing Cross Peek A Boo (B), Kahn & Sanchez
Dot's Sacke Dancer Of Philadore (D), Gunning
Hoi Toi Rocky Mountain High (D), Voss & Roher
Sam Ting's Puying (B), Bossard
Sancos Mi Pretti Poppi (B), Buck
Sharn's Little Show-Off (D), Utstein
Zervlistan Impact (B), Zervoulis

9/78 Charing Cross Abigail Adams (B), Kahn & Sanchez
Copa Snow Baby (B), Luck & Luck
Mandarin's Salt N' Pepper (D), Regelman
Ming Toi Let Em Talk Of Yenvon (D), Carey

10/78 Beedoc The Floozy Of Lainee (B), Meltzer
Copper Penny Cur-I-Oh So (D), Pennington
Emps Cloisonne Glitter Ying (D), Marcum
Karo-La Snuffin Of Sonan (B), Richards & Smith
Lainee Sigmund Floyd (D), Meltzer
Lou Wan Cassandra Of Hapiours (B), Gec, Williams & Nickerson
Mar Dels Golden Lama (D), Edel
Mariljac Lolipop Of Joclif (B), Johnson

11/78 Ah So Geisha On The Go (B), Keith & Kennedy
Bon D'Art Tu Tone Of Fancee (D), Crissman
Caralandra Artu Of Bomshu (D), Steapp
Ch'l Feng Of Spruce Brook (D), Simoneau
Chin Yu Bumblebee (D), Heiney
Dragonwyck Miss-T-Fi-Ying (B), Patton & Constantino
Lisel's Eleanor Rigby (B), Miller
Ming Toi Bab-Ling Babs (B), Meltzer & Boyles
Miss M Monroe (B), Joris
Patie Charlie Chan Of Lainee (D), Robertson & Gresham
Rockee Vollee Valentino (D), Mueller

12/78 Abacus' Action Fraction (B), Basil & Smith
Akaba's Pinkerton Man (D), Burger
Beedoc's Bangaway (D), Stubblefield
Bel Air Proud Heritage (D), Rabell
Cha Ming Sugarplum Fairy (B), Merrill
Chandar Happi Munch-Kin (B), Bondar
Davaniks Stargazer (D), Angelastro
Dolmar My-T Barnum Of Din Ho (D), Martin
Encore Chan Lan (D), Hoffman & Fitts
Ho Chi's Follow The Leader (D), Smith
Joclif Satchmo (D), Miller
Largyn Could It Be Magic (B), Smigley
Largyn Daybreak (D), Smigley
Marya Winds Perri Como Hsing (D), Coolina & Keen
Mundy's Ama Little Ginseng (D), Hewitson
Pen San Pajamaparti O'Hai Sing (B), Hayward
Strawberry Blond Luvncare (B), Hoo
Tu-Mac's Sophistikate (B), McIntee
Wynn Dee's Leading Lady (B), Nissen

1/79 Ah So Candy Apple (B), Ledoux & Williams
Bel Air Gamblin Man Of Mei San (D), Meidlinger
Bel Air Irresistable O'Bamboo (B), Backovich
Dacun's Remote Control (D), Dailey & Cunningham
Hidden Coves Im' A Dan Dee Wun (D), O'Neil
Highlands Frosty Friday (B), Bogner
Janiric's Jumb-O-Laya (D), Long

90

Jen-Mi Sou Yen's Mr Wenrick (D), Paquette
Jolei The Artful Dodger (D), Kijowski
Jubilair Leif Ericson (D), Arnett
Mandarins Sassy Samantha (B), Harney & Di Nicola
Sweet Bee Of Greenmoss (B), Zinner
Wenrick's Miss Bobbin (B), Paquette

2/79 Bel Air Diamond Jim (D), Chadwell
Chandar Ginger Lei (B), Hollingshead
De Amo I Ching-Aye Aye-Tch (B), Kelly & Baxter
Jen-Mi's Spunky Lady (B), Heuser
Lainee X-Tra Daring (D), Robertson
Langpur's Gin And Sin (B), Papke
Mariljac Legend Of Bomshu (D), Steapp
Nederlander's Mr Cee (D), Keenan
Sho-Me's Dy-No-Might (D), Librach
Silver Mist La Dawn (B), Thompson & Miller
Sing Hi's Sweet Chariot (B), Hayward
Tradition's Beau Tzo (D), Marcum

3/79 Chow Lin Sug A Bear Di Visconti (D), Herndon
Gardners Sunshine Stepin Hi (B), Hilbert
Mandarin's Cinnamon Of Regal (D), Kwait
Pinafore Minstrel Mandarin (D), Poole
Pinafore Music Of Mandarin (B), Lynn & Battey
Raywin's Call Me Tousel Top (D), Winters
Sanchi's Suzume (B), Selfon
Sun Canyon Boo Print (D), Goodwin & Thompson
The Carefree Kid Of Ju-I (D), Gale & Sanfilippo

4/79 Chumulari Shen Te (B), Jacobson
Din Ho Willy Wagger (D), Mueller
Emperor's Confederate Jasmine (B), Simonton
Emperor's Heza Double Blaka (D), Edel & Simonton
Gin-Doc's Fu Manchu (D), Suarez
Hai Sing A-Hi-Song Of Pen Sans (D), Hayward
Hai Tai Chih Tsao Ching (D), Karelitz
Joclif Sun God Of Delphi (D), Levaque & White
Kharisma Sum Tuff Chop Suey (B), Martens
Luty Parti Mia Of Car-Sy (B), Syquia
Nanjo Hi-Point (D), Cowie
Paramount MGM Dragonwyck (D), Patton & Constantino
To Te Mei's I'm A Honey Bee (B), Wright

5/79 Beedoc's Floyd Jr (D), Stubblefield
Dang Sai Noon Time Spender (B), Krisko
De Amo I Obie (D), Toliver, Kelly & Baxter
Dynasty's The Great Escape (B), Gibson
Emperor's Confederate Jasmin (B), Adams
Hil Ton's Lollypop Lover (D), Hilton
Jolane's Hey Look Me Over (D), Mersol
Jolei Blazing Blanche (B), Kijowski
Joylin Sugarman Of Mahjong (D), Veniey
Kayesett Indo Gold (B), Kaye
Li Ming's Ameretta (B), Collins & Parker
Lou Wan Farrah Fawcet (B), Gec
Lyric's Lorelei (B), McDaniel
Phildore's Dream Weaver (D), Dommer
Sun Canyon Paper Tiger (D), Goodwin & Thompson
Sun Loon Ms Of Rockee Vollee (B), Heck
Vilenzo Hsing Ah Muk (B), Vilas
Wenrick's Happy Miss (B), Larsen
Westwood Amaretta (B), Buckner & Krasniewski
Winwards Wing Ding (D), Behrouzi
Wynn Dee's Darling Dotte (B), Hollingshead
Yatsen Bottoms Up Of Pem (D), Mushrush
Yatsen's Mi Cute As A Button (B), Buck & Cox
Zanzibaars Zany Zelda (B), Senske

6/79 Bel Air Elvis Of Luv Me Ten-Der (D), Arnold
Char Nick's Spiffy Laree (D), Walton
Emperor's The Gay Deceiver (D), Curtis
Gracelyne Joey Of Shang T'ou (D), Wilson, Fujita & Mesdag
Joclif Gemini Cricket (B), Winship
Largyn Kissin' Kate Of Nanjo (B), Cowle
Wendav Rugbee Of Hidden Cove (D), Ward

7/79 Barbara's Snow Bird (B), Henderson
Chin Yu Moonbeam Princess (B), Iliesco
Diaquiris Mad-About Manhattans (D), Hall & Miller
Gunning's Semi-Sparkle (B), Pittelli
Gunning's Semi-Tough (D), Gunning
Hai-Tai Honey Of Kathmandu (B), Karelitz
Moonlighter's Daddy's Darling (B), Burch
Pen Sans Parti Toi (D), Busselman

8/79 China Chimes Portrait Of Ping (D), Heilman & Strapp
Hai-U It Had To B-U (D), King & Kerfoot
Lainee Chopped Liver (B), Meltzer & Zanen
Lou Wan Scarlet Lady (B), Gec
Lou Wan Shanghai Lilly (B), Gec
Nanjo Dawn Of Largyn (B), Arnett
Sun Canyon The Barrister (D), Goodwin & Mabry
Wynndee Cheerleader Of Hochi (B), Meidlinger
Yingsu's Johnie Reb (D), Miller

9/79 Fancee Dari Heir Of Bon D'Art (B), Wheeler & Guggenheim
Gunning's Semi-Spunky Of Nova (D), Novak
Hai-U Chinese Trinket (B), Kerfoot
Hai-U Painted Lady (B), Kerfoot
Jen-Mi's Louie Primavera (D), Heuser
Johnson's Jac-Kee (D), Johnson
Lou Wan Slate Of Li Ming (B), Tendler
Mandarin's Nutmeg Of Regal (D), Wilus & Wilus
Mariljac Tiger Paws (B), Huffman, Herbst & Patton
Sun Canyon Autumn Gold (B), Anderson & Goodwin

10/79 Hoytoy's Larchmont Nick-Kee (D), Hess
Jazmin's Maxi-Million (D), Peterson
Loretlargent Honey Bear (D), Coughlan
Phildore's Kiss N' Tell (B), Dommer
Plesurs Shai Na Pu Chi (B), Ruppelt
Quang-Te Van De Blauwe Mammoth (D), Easton
Regal's Mark Of Excellance (D), Regelman
Royal Jade Rust-Ee Nail (D), Osbourne
Royal Jade Winn-Ee (B), Osbourne
Samurai Deja Vu Of Ling-Ho (B), Fritts & Green
Sun Canyon Brassy Lassy (B), Goodwin & Thompson
Winward's Hot Wheels (D), Downey

11/79 Charjalong's El Toro Bravo (D), Long
Chin Yu Son Of A Gunning (D), Lukenbach
Chin Tu Tinkerbell Chantyman (B), Bodarsky
Dang Sal Hot Sauce (B), Krisko
Greylock's Haram Scarem (D), Goldberg
Hodari Madame (B), McGill & Battey
Illenids Le-Pre-Chin Chiny (D), Buck
Kung Fu's Sassy Lassie (B), Tucker
Langpur Drambuie (D), Papke
Luvncare Buttercup Ring (Canada) (B), Hoo
Nanking Lucky Linda (Canada) (B), Ikola
Pagoda-Lion's Klassi Yingsu (B), Gibson
Pagoda-Lion's VIP of Gatsby (D), Gibson
Pen Sans Peaches N'Cream (B), Christensen & Busselman
Sabar's Snowfire Of Marcliff (D), Bresnahan
Sharn's Fredi-Ore-Knot (D), McKnight
Sparkle Plenty For Lou Wan (B), Gec
Tiffany Sparkler Of Shang Tou (B), Williams
Westwood's Bebe Wonderful (B), Hoffman

12/79 Bel Air Spring Fever (B), Phillips & Graham
Charjalong's Kiko Kidd (D), Long
Charlie Chan of Merry Ho (D), Hobs
China Chimes Cherokee Rose (B), Heilman & Strapp
Cookes Court Baby (B), Cookes & Cookes
Copper Penny Stargazer (D), Pennington
Emperor's Amulette Of Snofu (B), Edel & Burnett
Emperor's Drum Major (D), Edel
Hai-U Chinese Charmer (D), Durant
Joy Tu Ring Of Fire Of Luken (D), Lukenbach
Lou Wan Ruffian Of Hilaria (B), Collins
Muffin Boggess Ying Ming Chu (B), Boggess
Nat-Sam's Foxy-Lady (B), Marcum

Left: Ch. Elfann Golden Beau Brummel, owned by Del and Connie Smart.

Right: Gin Doc's Pocohanas, owned by Sue Miller.

Ch. Chinai's Tangoroo, owned by David and Chris Jones.

Ch. Nova's Magnificent Obsession, owned by Taunnie Novak.

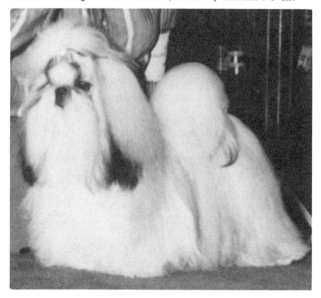

Left: Ch. Shih Chin's Piece of the Hunk, owned by Arlene Sprague.

Right: Garrett Crissman, Hilde Pittelli, Jon Ferrante, Margaret Edel MacIntosh, George MacIntosh, and John Ficerai.

92

Samurai Poppy Of Bon D'Art (B), Fritts & Green
Vitahund's Balder (D), Lindblom

1/80 Cheltenham Cricket Of Nanjo (B), Conlen
Jazmin's Drummer Boi Of Anh-Wei (D), Kim
Lisel's Lite N Lively (B), Miller
Mariljac Lady Kop Of Joclif (B), Johnson
Mee-Too's Capt'n Cave Man (D), Johnson
Mysty Dai Masumi (B), Poole
Nanking Cara Lin Madeley (B), Madeley
Pens Sans Hugger Bear (D), Libke & Busselman
Sun Canyon Huggin Muggin (D), Goodwin & Mabry
Truro's The Critic's Choice (D), Crane & Pawelko

2/80 Ali-Aj New York City Splendor (B), Castellano
Bel Fleur Hi Voltage Of Nanjo (D), Arnett
Bon D'Art Justintyme Of Fancee (D), Lemon & Thomas
Charing Cross Gentle Ben (D), Kahn & Sanchez
Char Nick's I'm No Snob (B), Sanfilippo
Dragonfire's I'm Annie (B), Iijima
Emperor's Ro-Ja's Bran-Dee (B), Foster
Jolei Chinese Checker (D), Stearns & Kijowski
Mundy's Ama Ginseng's Mai Gosh (D), Mundy
Shulee's Vs Apricot Brandee (B), Lemon

3/80 Bel Air Matinee Idol (D), Chadwell
Cantu's Million Dollar Stunt (D), Barr
China Chimes Dragon Bear (D), Heilman
Copper Penny Ah Gin (B), Pennington
Copper Penny Bittersweet (B), Osbourne & Pennington
Dragonwyck Desdemona (B), Burger, Patton & Constantino
Greylock's Rags to Riches (B), Goldberg
Hana Da-Ma-Su (B), Prato
Hana's Oh So Chu-Be (D), Prato
Jen-Mi's Four Wheel Drive (D), Connaughton
Timberlakes Rockyvolly Ki Ki (D), Heck

4/80 Chateau's Golden Bear (D), Vedder
Cloisonne Kaimacha Karaktr (D), Greer
Dalai Jackpot (D), Goodwin & Mabry
Dalai Razzl Dazzl (B), Goodwin & Mabry
Fashions J C Superstar (D), Kalina
Grenouille The China Doll (B), Blasinski & Sorth
Regal's Jack N' The Box (D), Kwait
Samurai Ko-Kane (D), King
Stylistic Artist Touch (D), Clay
Ti-Gi's Blazen Fury (D), Glavan
Wilkum's Bo Ti (D), Shire
Winemakers Stormee Night (D), Prillaman & Wine
Winward's Sly Fox (D), Frothingham

5/80 Charing Cross Peachy Keen (B), Kahn & Sanchez
Copper Penny Royal Jade An-Ge (B), Osborne
Dang Sai Snapshot (D), Krisko
Jolei Butch Cassidy (D), Thayer
Loubren Pippi Longstockings (B), McNight
Stylistic Ms Fiddle Dee Dee (B), Shepherd & Smith
Tenoma Ruffles And Flourishes (D), Amonett

6/80 Abacus' Brass Ring (D), Basil & Smith
Ah So Precious Rin-Po-Cid (B), Koch
Charjalong's Boo Boo (D), Long
Charjalong's Jumb-O-Jill (B), Long
Char Nick Mastapiece O'Sesame (D), Sanfilippo
Conwynn's Rolls-Royce (D), Fleener
Dansy's Kerijon Lil' Danny (D), Stewart, Griffiths & Nolan
Di Visconti Chaka Khan (B), Ferrante
Khantinkas The Great Pumpkin (B), Edwards
Nanjo's Hai-Ku OF Hornblende (D), Whiteside
Pen Sans Parti Pet (D), Busselman
San Yen Lai-Dee Of The Nite (B), Ormsby

7/80 Charjalong's Jumb-O-Jill (B), Long
Chateau Joly Roger (D), Guiraud & McGovern
Copa Sugar Babe Of Granville (B), Russell
Dragonfire's I'M Buckwheat (D), Christie
Jolei The Sundance Kid (D), Kijowski
Joya's Queen Of Hearts (B), Berrier
Kachina's Bright Autumn (B), Kregar

Lainee Hallucination (B), Meltzer
Lou Wan's Midnight Son (D), Gec
Ming Dynasty's Bamboo Shoot (D), Blackburn
Mundy's Ama Yummer's Bummer (D), Mundy
Winward's Free Wheeling (D), Strom

8/80 Dragonwyck Dragonfire (D), Patton & Constantine
Macada's Tribute To Char-Nick (D), Javier & Davis
Mandarin's Golden Fantasy (B), Di Nicola & Harney
Nanjo Moonshadow (B), Cowie
Rockee Vollee Velvetier (D), Mueller
Shen Wah's Ms Lib (B), Walton
Stylistic Good As Gold (B), Williamson & Shepherd
Sun-N-San Joi Of Phildore (D), Moser
Talywag's Terrific Troubles (B), Taylor & Wagner

9/80 Ashining Ms Josie (B), Korolak
Charing Cross Tropical Star (B), Kahn & Sanchez
Fancee Dear Me of Bon D'Art (B), Wheeler & Guggenheim
Freejanda Wai Ling Ban Chi (B), Brick
Gardner's Cameo Of Hodari (B), Gentry & Mantie
Gunning's Precious Gem (B), Hollingshead & Gunning
I'M A Pepper Of Bonsai (B), Himel
Jo-Ahn's Giorgio (D), Anthony
Lainee The Medicine Man (D), Kim & Meltzer
Mandarin Tantrum O Pinafore (D), Lynn & Battey
M And R's Glory Cheers (B), Norwood & Murray
Mei San Hey Checker Over (B), Meidlinger
Ming Dynasty's Fu-Manchu (D), Blackburn
Murr's Sun Yet Shines (B), Roberts
Rosemar Anything Goes (D), Warner
R-Own Sue Ling (B), Cecile
Silver Mist Sasi Woo D Tori's (B), Tolle & Richards

10/80 Abacus' Hazel Nutt (B), Spivey, Basil & Smith
Bar-Jon's Cute As A Button (B), Ioia
Beedoc's Honey Du (B), Stubblefield
Copper Penny In Cog Ni To (D), Pennington
Hidden Coves Robbee (D), Ward
Illenid's Licorice (D), Dinelli
Lainee Tung 'N Cheek Of Ming Toi (B), Meltzer
Luken's All Fired Up (B), Guggenheim
Macada's Wags To Witches (B), Davis & Javier
Pinafore Goldglo Mandarin (D), Kwait
Rogue's Little Lady Bug (B), Savio
Ti-Gi's Hotter'N Blu Blazes (D), Glavan
Wendavs Barbee (B), Brewer & Lehmann

11/80 Beedoc's Honey Du (B), Stubblefield
Charjalong's Ooo-La-La Yin Shan (B), Hustler
Faerie Dean Firefly (B), Miller
Hai-U Sheng Ti's Kiss (B), Young & Mantie
Highlandell Triple Threat (D), Hansen
House of Wu Benchmark (D), Eckes
Jazmin's Napoleon (D), Bump
Jubilation Constellation (D), Arnett
Kayesett Jung Tuck (D), Kaye
Lainee X-Tra Perpetual Motion (B), Wood & Meltzer
Luken's Four Alarm Fire (D), Lukenbach
Maryawinds Robert Redford (D), Caliento
Mundy's Ama Ranger's Riddle (D), Mundy
Pati's Hot Toddy (D), Parker & Gresham
Rosemar Void Wher Prohibited (B), Warner
Shen Wah's Quik Silver O Nanjo (B), Walton
Westwood's Sum Sirprize (D), Hoffman
Xanadu Is Mr Win-Dahl Walker (D), Walker

12/80 Ali Aj New York City Serenade (B), Wilus, Wilus & Castellano
Car-Lyn's Razzle Dazzle (D), Smith & Doherty
Charing Cross Belle Starr (B), Kahn & Sanchez
Copper Penny Royal Jade An-Ne (B), Anthony & Frank
Crown Jewels Kami Of Mi House (D), Alverson
Dragonwyck Desire ' (B), Caliento
Emperor's Honky-Tonk Cowboy (D), Adams
Illenid's Ms Ellie (B), Dinelli
Lai-Cyre's Lady-Paisley (B), Weberg

Lainee Tung-Tied Of Ming Toi (D), McCallion & Meltzer
Lisel's Moshe Dayan (D), Miller
Loubren's Trail Blazer O'Jolei (D), McKnight
Nova's Chantilly Lace (B), Novak
Nova's Takem Bi Surprise (D), Biller & Novak
Pen Sans Bedazzling Sparkler (B), Iseki
Shamisen's The Sorcerer (D), Herbst & Huffman
Truro's Command Performance (D), Wilus & Wilus

1/81 Chandar China Tiger Lily (B), Bondar
Gunning's Better Half (B), Wheeler & Gunning
Hai Sings Winahgin Of Sultan (B), Hayward
Heatherwoods Hot Deal (B), Hollingshead
Jazmin's Tiger Lily (B), Ikeda
Jolei Popp'N Fresh Of Sv (B), McKnight & Kajowski
Jolei The Jazz Man (D), Kijowski
Kayesett Mona Lisa (B), Kaye
Lainee Racy Lady (B), Boggess
Lipo's Ricmar Cracker Jack (D), Gidusko
Mar Dels Midgee Ming Of Kee-Lee (B), Whitney
Mundy's Ama Yumer's Bubble-Yum (B), Mundy
San Yen Ginger Snap (B), Ormsby
Si Kiang's Lil Devil (D), Durham
Stylistic Frankly I Do (D), Lijima & Shepherd

2/81 Arabah's Mi Tuf Toi Of Dynasty (D), Vogt & Bodin
Charing Cross Tee'D Off (D), Halpern
Din Ho Wind Jammer Of Ricmar (D), Banks
Emperor's Cameo Of Broomhill (B), Edel & Hauff
Faerie Dean Chantilly Lace (B), Miller
Gunning's Typografical Errer (B), Blackburn
Mundy's Ama Ginseng's Gee-Whizz (D), Mundy
Pen Sans Monkey Business (B), Wadsworth
Regals Sweet N'Spicy Mandarin (B), Regelman & Kwait
Sam Tsu's Dinah (B), Carroll
Springett Rejes Tomako (B), Pritchard & Wild

3/81 China Chimes Chinese Satin (B), Heilman & Strapp
Dalai Gin Tzu (D), Martell
Dalai Lil Copper Penny (B), Goodwin, Mabry &
    Pennington
Dragonwyck Danielle (B), Burger
Emperor's Jus A Li'L Mo Sherry (B), Edel & Adams
Fancee Put'N On Heirs Bon D'Art (D), Kim
Ho Chi's Ms Leading Of Wynn Dee's (B), Miller
Hodari Lord Of The Rings (D), Battey
Nanjo Avenger (D), Stroup
Nanjo Wild Honey (B), Cowie
Pagan's Johnie Come Lately (D), Gec
Rondelay Dee-Lite O'Gunther (B), Williamson &
    Williamson
Sabar's Starfire (D), Bresnahan
Shente's Mr Macbarker (D), Hollingsworth
Yen Den Hot Stuff Of Phildore (D), Deming

4/81 Ambelon's Son Of A Gunther (D), Nyberg
Beedoc's Four Point Two (B), Stubblefield
Crown Jewel's Tashu Of Go-Vel's (B), Vela & Gonzalez
Galaxy's Just A Sample (D), Voss
Highlands Twennty One Karet (B), Archer
Kayesett Michaelangelo (D), Kaye
Lainee X-Tra X-Tra Of Ming Toi (D), Tolle & Richards
Moonsong Fancee Chinwangtao (B), Mann
Mundy's Ama Ginseng's Ginger (D), Mundy
Pagan's Johnie Angel Wynn Dee (B), Pagan
Sabar's Scampi Of Ho Tai (B), Heinig
Wendavs Razzmataz (D), Brewer & Lehmann
Wen-Shu's Sin Gum Sze (D), Gerl

5/81 Bi-Wood's Hifalutin (B), Atwood & Caywood
Copper Penny Royal Jade An-De (D), Fleener & Osborne
Fancee Heirielle Of Bon D'Art (B), Wheeler &
    Guggenheim
Jazmin's Hi Calibre (D), Peterson
Jo-Ahn's Gisselle (B), Anthony
Jodon's Skip A Long (D), O'Neil

Lou Wan Lucky Lady (B), Gec
Lou Wan Rebel Rouser (D), Gec
Ming Toi Ful O Spunk (B), Boyles
Paramount Rhett Butler (D), Moncion, Constantino &
    Patton
Vilenzo Kenghis Khan (D), Vilas

6/81 Barbara's Pitti Pati Sing (B), Henderson
Calibre Tinkerbell Of Largyn (B), Hege
Char Nick's Studley Durite (D), Walton
Clarlen's Dragon Lady (B), Davis, Conrad & Busselman
Darrette's Glory Hallelujah (B), McDowell & Barr
Ding-A-Ling Lady's Delight (B), Dibeler
Dragonfire's Sara (B), Berry & Huston
Fancee Heir Mhale Bon D' Art (D), Alverson & Wheeler
Fran-Oaks Midnight Magic (B), Francis
Grenouille The Social Lion (D), Blasinski
Gunning Joint Venture Vtruro (D), Garrett & Gunning
Highlands Spice And Ice (B), Da Ponte
Lainee Dr C G Yung Of Zerox (D), Zerod & Meltzer
Lainee Tung Twister O'Ming-Toi (B), Hogg & Meltzer
Largyn Manilow Magic (D), Smigley
Li Ming's Coco Chanel (B), Tendler
Mundys Ama Yummers Summer (B), Mundy & Hewitson
Show Off's Serendipity (B), Williams

7/81 Copper Penny Ki-Mo (D), Pennington
Pekings Keely Smith Of Wen Shu (B), Connaughton

8/81 Ah So Peppermint Pattie (B), Ledoux
Ali-Aj Spectacular Bid (D), Semple & Castellano
Ambelon Annie Getcha Gunther (D), Weber
Ch'Ang Ch'U Apollo (D), Barrand
Charjalong's Jj Of Janiric (D), Logie & Long
China Chimes Chinese Gigolo (D), Heilman & Strapp
Frejanda Far East Fantasia (B), Janis & Brick
Hai Tai Mai Gai (D), Karelitz
Ho Leng's Carpetbagger (D), McDaniel
La En's Ah So Ruff And Ready (D), Neal
Lisel's Not Coffee But Sanka (B), Covey
Mei Shan Golden Sampan (D), Burley
Pinafore Mirage Of Mandarin (B), Harney & Di Nicola
PJ's Pajama Game Of Hai Sing (B), Hayward
Sir Winston Of Mount La Jolla (D), Hollenback
Zerox Shih-Nanigan (D), Sharpton, Dawson & Bridgeforth

9/81 Bar-Ro Charlie Chan (D), Becker
Dragonfire's Alfie Of Luty (D), Bryan & Hogg
Evanz Thunderball (D), Pauley
Joylin Golden Masterpiece (D), Pittelli
Li Ming's Pierre Cardin (D), Tendler & Niiyama
Lisel's Rock N Rye (D), Miller
Ming Dynasty's Hot-N-Spicy (B), Blackburn
Nat-Sam's Glitter-Bug (D), Graf
Pen Sans Sugartime (B), Busselman
Pen Sans Tecaro Capt Sunshine (D), Busselman
San Yen Masked Marvel (D), West
Tumac's Angie (B), McIntee
Vilenzo Miss Mavis Ming (B), Vilas
Wenshu's Ah-So Louie Of Peking (D), Gerl
Zerox Shih-Ah-Ten (B), Zerod

10/81 Chinoiserie-Chumulari Poupe (D), Ungaro
Fancee Cheir Ess Of Bon D' Art (B), Wheeler &
    Guggenheim
Kee Lee's Mai-Ling Lin-Lee (B), Matera & Lee
Kee Lee's Strut 'N Stuf Of Mar-Del (D), Mech
Lainee The Scatter Brain (B), Meltzer
Mandarin's Sunny Side Up (B), Di Nicola
Pekings Primadona Of Wen-Shu (B), Connaughton &
    Hewitson
Pen Sans Joy Tu The West (D), Busselman
Phildore's Zorro (D), Dommer
Vilenzo Nicely Of Glory (D), MacKay & Norwood

11/81 Anh Wei Dolly Parton (B), Kim
Bar-Jon's Brass Buttons (D), Ioia

Left: Ch. Dragon-fly's Dazz-Ling Toi, owned by Jacqueline Kraus.

Right: Ch. Joylin's Exstra Terrestrial, owned by Hilde Pittelli.

Left: Am. and Can. Ch. Kee Lee's Raisen Cain Of Ja-Ma, owned by Sandi Gibson.

Right: Ch. Mirra's Ceasar of Kee Lee, owned by Myriam Kogan and Tom Keenan.

Left: Chumulari Rev. D.A.E. Of Laksana, owned by Victor Joris.

Right: Ch. Mar Del's Har Tosie, owned by Margaret Edel MacIntosh.

95

Bel Air Cas Anko Tei (B), Brown
Bel Air Summer Storm (D), Gould
Brynmyr's Charlie Chan (D), De Bose
Carousel's Genuine Risk (B), Lucchina
Carousel's Second Hand Rose (B), Touzel & Edwards
Ho Chi Hit Or Miss (B), Cole
Jolei Lucille (B), Kijowski
Lakewood's A Blazin (D), Gangi
Luken's Kerijon Miss Fire (B), Lukenbach
Luken's Sand Pond Full Of Fire (B), Lukenbach
Lyric's Yankee Doodle Dandy (D), Robertson
Mei San Constant Comment (B), Meidlinger
Mi Clyde Chin Chiny (D), Buck
Parquins Lady Tangelo Of Snowfu (B), Burnett
Pen Sans Critics Choice (B), Busselman
Rockee Vollee The Empress (B), Pollak
Snowfu's Chilkoot Charlie (D), Burnett
Stylistic Bar None Prime Time (D), Perlmutter
Ti-Gi's Hot Cross Buns (D), Glavan
Winward's Napoleon Brandy (B), Bump
Zip The Tempest In A Teapot (B), Davis & Javier

12/81 Dang Sai Angie Dickens (B), Krisko
Dragonfire's I'M Darla (B), Tanida
Enchanted Dr Pepper Of Mei San (D), Meidlinger
Hai Sings Mee-Go-Too (B), Hayward & Cole
Happi's Perfect Clown (D), Archer
Lainee The Nympho Maniac (B), Di Vanni & Meltzer
Mar Dels Ring Leader (D), Edel & Lee
Nanjo's Devine Ms Wing (B), Cowie
Pen Sans Magical Madrigal (D), Young, Iseki & Busselman
Toryglen Alpha Khan (D), Vallee

1/82 Dalai All That Jazz (D), Goodwin & Mabry
Dragonfly's Cho-Ko Of Nanjo (D), Kraus
Kayesett Jasmin (B), Kaye
Mi I'M A Ten Too (D), Paulik
Nordli Buz Zin Comet (D), Hartung
San Yen Polly Pun-Kin (B), West & Donleavy
Shen Wah's The Argyle Kid (D), Walton
Vilenzo Mer-Tory-Us Action (D), Pennington & Vilas

2/82 Ah So He's My Man (D), Ledoux
Copper Penny Blatant Scandal (B), Pennington & Osbourne
Delray's Forever Amber Of T-Sun (B), Thompson
Forest Farm's Scheherazade (B), Burley
Kachina's All That Ping Jazz (D), Kregar
Kachina's Lockhart Chopstix (D), Lockhart
Kee Lee's Party Girl (B), Petrone & Keenan
Kee Lee's Showstopper Of Wei-Tu (D), Whitney
Lainee The Raven' Maniac (B), Meltzer
M and R's Big Bad John (D), Rukavina
Pen Sans Life Of The Party (B), Sprague
Romano Of Landor Di Visconti (D), Baker & Ferrante
R-Own Billy Boozer (D), Cecile
Wingates TKO (D), Neal
Yen Den Midnight Gambler (D), Deming

3/82 Barrington Animated Dustmop (D), Himel, Campbell & McDearmon
Hidden Coves Buz-Bee (D), Wilson
Jual The Fortunate Cookie (B), Graber & Reppond
Kee Lee's Munday's Fame (B), Munday & Keenan
Lainee The Compulsive Talker (B), Meltzer & Regelman
Mai Tai Dapper Dansin (D), Sinnamon
Raindance Hot Salsa (B), Vaughn
Regal's Cute Stuff Tu (B), Regelman
San Yen Grand Slam (D), West
Silver Mist Ruff'N Reddi (D), Scherer
Tenoma's Boi Ching Wu (D), Amonett
Tu Chu's Secret Dream (B), Kwait
Tumac's Pam (B), McIntee
Vilenzo Metaphor (D), Vilas & Savio

4/82 Anh Wei Sonic Boom (B), Kim
Che-Ro's One For The Road (B), Melder
Equinox Dang Sai Tribute (D), Krisko & Olson

Fang Chu's Sam I Am (D), Hollingsworth
Luken San Pon Roket Fire Ponte (D), Da Ponte
Mar Dels Red Baroness (B), Edel
Mundys Ama Yummers Blazer (D), Mundy
Russmar Becket (D), Martin
Shentes Brandy Alexander (D), Brown
Stylistic Tuff 'E Nuff (D), Shepherd
Woodsmoke's Enchantment (B), Miller

5/82 Barringtons Featherduster (B), Peterson
Bit's N Pieces Of Raintree (D), Rainey
China Chimes Changsha Charm (B), Heilman & Strapp
Grayarlin's Ginger Bread Girl (B), Forsyth
Highlandell Bet A Million (D), Hansen
Jo-Ahn's Jezebel (B), Anthony
Jolei Mint Julep Of Dansin (B), Sinnamon
Mundy's Ama Bummer's Charmer (B), Mundy, Harwell & Harwell
Mundy's Ama Yen-Si Of Ming-Ty (D), Verzi
Nova's Miss Dee Fying Min Dee (B), Perlmutter
Phildore's Red Light (D), Goodwin & Mabry
Sam Tsus Nefretete (B), Hansen

6/82 Barrington's Windsong (B), Campbell
Cabrand's Calliope (B), Gec
Dragonfire's I'M Crissy (B), Battey
Faerie Dean Afternoon D-Light (B), Miller
Gracelyne's Fantasy (B), Wilson
Kayesett Matisse (D), Kaye
Lainee The Brain Storm (B), Zanen & Meltzer
Nanjo King Of Swing O'Nan-A-Ju (D), Sirinsky
Nanjo Splendid Spike (D), De Carrie
Nova's Magnificent Obsession (B), Novak
Regal's Poppin' Fresh (B), Regelman
Sam-Tsus Foxy Lady Of O'Knoll (B), Carroll
Santini's Luciano Shubaru (D), Corbett & Sniderman
Shen Wah's Vanity Fair (B), Welch & Walton
Shin Chin's Jin Jiro Of Hojin (D), Sprague & Canales

7/82 Ah So Bobbin' For Apples (D), Ledoux
Centerfold's Helios Of Tu Chu (D), Moberly
Chi-Nees Sweet Music Man (D), Musselman
Dalai Sum Charmer (D), Goodwin & Mabry
Dang Sai's Sailor's Delight (D), Fjeseth
Dragonfire's I'M Mahalia (B), Hogg
Langpur Gin Swizzle (B), Papke
Mei Sans Queen High Cutie (B), Herman
Ming Dynasty's Blazing Bullet (D), Foster
Rockee Vollee Nantucket (B), Joens
San Yen Brass Button (B), Anderson
Shen Wah's On The Prowl (D), Walton
Tarma's Daring Deidra (B), Batchelden
Tu Chu's Patent Pending (B), Kwait
Wes Ro's KC Zig Zag (D), Rich
Winward's Senge Tashi (B), Bump

8//82 Bel Fleur Tiger Of Nanjo Dawn (D), Medellin
Brynmyr's I'M The Boss (D), Skidmore & Delp
Chaling Tickini Fancyv Che-Ro (B), Potts
Chi-Nees Sweet Temp-Ta-Tion (B), Musselman
Din Ho Me Tu Great Balls Afire (D), Strom
House Of Wu Fire Agate (D), Eckes & Williams
Kerijon Posy Of Bayou Bark (B), Friese & Griffiths
Lyric's Little Short Stuff (D), Schneider
Mandarin's Copyright (B), Krahn
Nanjo's Legacy Of Ping (B), Cowie
Tu Chu Golden Happines Marja (D), Puglise & Kwait

9/82 Bonsai's Ms Tuff (B), Gangi
Cenmar's Ready Or Not Of Macada (D), Javier & Davis
Devil's Own Of Sultan (B), Davidson
Dolmar Belle Star (B), Martin
Dragonwyck Lord Dragonfire (D), Patton
House Of Wu Quiz Kidd (D), Wild & Frambes
Jofins Do's Ta-Boo (B), Finney
Macada's Witch's Wish O'Hil-Ton (B), Hilton & Davis
Mundys Ama Bummer Pepper-Pot (B), Mundy

Rockee Vollee Woopie I'M Alive (D), Pipkorn
Shen Wah Knolland Tap Shoes (B), Jenner & Walton
Stylistic Make Mine Cashmere (B), Iliesco & Shepherd
Wes-Ro's Sunday Prime Time (D), Boggess
Zerox Shih-Duction (B), Zerod

10/82 Ali-Aj Holy Smoke O'Dragonfire (D), Castellano
Beedoc's Shooting Star (B), Stubblefield
Bon D' Art Fancee Footnote (B), Knoll, Gorgonio,
  Guggenheim & Wheeler
China Chimes Chunka Chang (D), Heilman & Strapp
Din Ho China Peach Blossom (B), Strom
Fang Chu's Five Card Stud (D), Hollingsworth
Kara Lu's Mikki Moto (D), Aronberg
Lainee Be Patient Of Nova (B), Gangi & Meltzer
Li Ming's Penny Andy (D), Tendler
Mar-Val-Us Oriental Lace (B), Wright
Taylwag's Kid Kiku (D), Devers
Willoway's Good Samaritan (D), Williamson & Williamson

11/82 Ah So Stocking Stuffer (B), Ledoux
Ali-Aj Diamonds N' Frills (B), Castellano
Anh Wei Lower The Boom (D), Kim
Anh Wei Rum-Pa-Pa-Pum (D), Kim
August Moon's Shadow Man (D), Nanni
Char-Ming Don Quixote O'Ali-Aj (D), Deleppo &
  Castellano
Chi-Nees Shome (D), Musselman
Dalai Hi Topaz (B), Goodwin & Mabry
Emperor's Precious Doll (B), Curtis
Gensing's Ten (D), Arnold
Hodari The Gremlin (D), Battey & Yuhl
Kam Tin's Struttin' My Stuff (D), Krajnak
Kayesett X Per Teeze (D), Kaye
Knottingham's Orient Express (D), Marder & Jacobsen
Linlee's Marquise Of KeeLee (D), Matera
Mo Tzu's Hsun Liu (D), Lovie & Thomas
Mundy's Ama An-Di Jax Son (D), Alderman
Mundys Ama Bummers Bobbi (D), Mundy & Papke
Paramount Krystal Kate (B), Patton, Constantino &
  Moncion
Pem's Pepp'O Mint Patti (B), Mushrush
Pen Sans The Cat's Meow (B), Busselman
R-Own Wendy Wong (B), Cecile
Sultan's Sassy Sherry O'Bar-D's (B), Davidson & Mills
Tori's Miss Piggy (B), Tolle & Richards
Wenshu's Mona Lisa (B), Thompson & Caroll

12/82 Briarhill Bing Kei (D), Hughey
Davanik's Classic Reflection (D), Cowie
Equinox Exotic Lover Oche-Ro (D), Meidlinger
Forest Farm Chinese Checker (D), Paquin & Regelman
House Of Wu U Know Who (B), Eckes
Jolei Gitter Bug (B), Kijowski
Jolei Over Easy (D), Kijowski
Jolei Southern Comfort (D), Kijowski
Li Ming's Carouser (B), Pennington
Lockhart's Toy Land China (B), Lockhart
Mar-Lin's Ginger Lee (B), Jones
Ming Dynasty's Show Gun (D), Wilson
Nanjo Cat Dancing (B), Cowie
Patrick's Sharon Share Alike (B), Savkov
Regal's Diamond Lill (B), Regelman
Taylwag's P B R Donimie (D), Taylor & Wagner
Wilkum's Ring Of Fire (D), Shire

1/83 Debelles' Sweet Honesty (B), Pagan, Torres & La Salle
Devil's Gotit Flauntit Of Murr (D), Roberts
Dragonfire's I'M No Lady (D), Hogg
Graebourne Traces Of Gold (B), Chapin
Hapiour's Gam Ling Gal (B), Hollingsworth
Jodon's Sexy Sadie Of Briden (B), O'Neil
Kinsa Tropo Grosso (D), Savio & Kinney
Lorien's MnM Caper (D), Taylor
Lou Wan Rebel Yell (D), Gec
Macada Lil-Bull Of Char-Nick (B), Fox & Davis

Mandarin's Chandra O Pinafore (B), Uckotter & Di Nicola
Pen Sans Plain Pockets (D), Busselman
Sumeng Hi Ping Doll Of Nanjo (B), McCarty

2/83 Bar None Wallace Beery (D), Perlmutter
Cabrand's Victoria J Lou Wan (B), Gec
Debelles' Hik'Aru Of Mei-Ting (D), Cacciatore
Emperor's Confederate Gold (D), Adams
Frejanda Disko Daffy (B), Brick
Gunning's Fancee Best Bet (B), Kraus
Lyric Tantrum's Phantum (D), Lynn & Alderman
M And R's Sweet Georgia Brown (B), Rukavina
Mi Fuchi Qo (D), Lucas & Buck
Mundy's Ama Ginger's Hi Tee (B), Battey & Mundy
Shente's Son Of A Gunther (D), Baker
Sho-Me's Getcha By Gotcha (D), Smith & Smith
Stylistic Frosting On The Cake (B), Vecchi & Shepherd
Ti-Gi's Raunchy Rumor (B), Glavan

3/83 Abacus Ichi Bon Of Jonea (D), Jones
Char-Ming Takara So Mer-Ri (B), Deleppo & Caouette
Fang Chu's El Toro Jr (D), Hollingsworth
Gensing Guchie Guchie Charo (B), Arnold
Kerijon Sweet Fire Rose (B), Griffiths & Bryant
Nanjo's Future Of Ping (B), Cowie
Shente's Ginger Rogers Benart (B), Stewart & Benner

4/83 Barrington's E Z Rider (D), Graf
Briarhill Heiso Gran Sun (D), Craddock
Char-Ming Emperor Tobias Chu (D), Medeiros
China Chimes Magnum P I (D), Heilman & Strapp
Chi-Nees Pit-Hei Patt (B), Musselman
Dang Sai Spinner V Tai Shan (D), Krisko & Pollak
Jo-Ahn's Dimitri (D), Anthony
Langpur Firewater (B), Martello & Papke
Li Ming's Rebellionne (B), Tendler
Ming Dynasty's Dragon Fire (D), Blackburn
Pen Sans Adida (B), Busselman
Pen Sans Parti Pinafore (B), Davis
Show Offs Swashbuckler (D), Williams
Sir Bellifur (D), White
Tou-Che Clearwater's Spitfire (D), Anderson & Murphy
Tumac's Hanky Panky (B), McIntee

5/83 Butterfly's Rusty J Rodrigues (D), Bartlett
Ch'Ing Fo Mai Toi Bear Of Joytu (D), Ruggiero
Diamond Jim Ponte (D), Da Ponte
Dorworth Apricot Confection (B), Armstrong
Emperor's Fashion Designer (D), Edel & Jordon
Gjinlo Super Sunday's Mvp (D), Price
Granville Rose Tatoo Of Copa (D), Russell
Gunning's The Eighth Wonder (B), Wheeler & Gunning
Jazmin's Hot Stuff (D), Gold & Ikola
Jennylyn Mini-Million (B), Le Croy & Turner
Loubren's Love Bandit (B), McKnight
Nanjo Jackie O Nan-A-Ju (B), Cowie & Sirinsky
Nanjo's Mia Honey (B), Smith
Nanking's Sprout (B), Ikola
Pen Sans Parti Pinafore (B), Davis
Phildore's Golden Memories (B), Dommer
Pinafore Katrina Of Mandarin (B), Harney
Regal's Florence Nightengale (B), Regelman
Sabar's That's Incredible (D), Craig
Yingsu's Ringmaster (D), Curry & Miller

6/83 Cabrand Agent Orange V. Lou Wan (D), Martin
Centerfold's Rumplestilskin (D), Moberly
Dansin Heart To Heart (D), Sinnamon
Fang Chu's Happi Hooker (B), McDearmon
Gracelyne Hula Of Shang T'Ou (B), Knoll & Gorgonio
Gunning's In The Buffnanking (B), Tarof & Gunning
Hai-Tai High Voltage (D), Karelitz
Koalin Tali Ho (B), Clay
Loubren's Tarsha Of Chin-Chu (B), Medeiros
Lou Wan Dixie Rebel (B), Gec
Lyric's Pipedream Of Phildore (D), Lynn
Nanjo's Hi-Fashion (B), McIntyre

97

Above: Ch. Mar Del's Ring A Ding Ding, bred and owned by Margaret Edel MacIntosh.

Above: Ch. Nanjo Tiz Tu Pings, owned by Joan E. Cowie. Handled by Jean Lade.

Above: Ch. Mar-Del's Tempel Chimes, owned by Margaret Edel MacIntosh.
Below: Ch. Marya Winds Tie-Dye of Dynasty, owned by Dynasty Kennels.

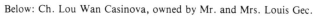

Above: Ch. Emperor's Quapaw Quarter Emp, owned by Dr. and Mrs. J. Wesley Edel. Handled by John Murdock.

Below: Ch. Lou Wan Casinova, owned by Mr. and Mrs. Louis Gec.

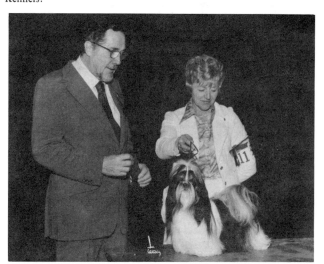

Ponte's Orloff Diamond (D), Da Ponte
Rojes Wildly A-May-Zing (B), McMichael & Crosby
Shen Wah's Sterling Silver (D), Walton & Kinowski
Shen Wah's The Idol Maker (D), Walton
Shih Chin's Piece Of The Hunk (D), Sprague
Zerox Purr-Suasive (B), Stone

7/83 Bon D' Art Fancee Leggs (B), Wheeler & Guggenheim
Dragonfire's Greatest Emily (B), Maehara
Galaxy's Coming Up Roses (B), Voss & Carrero
Jac-Len's Dancin' Man (D), Welch
Mundy's Ama Johnny (D), Downey
Regal's Sweet Tart (B), Paquin & Regelman
Tu Chu's Diamonds R Forever (B), Kwait

8/83 Briarhill So Lo (D), Craddock
Chi-Nees Princess Windsong (B), Haines
Din Ho Paddington Bear (D), Lawrence & Kolbert
Din Ho Rupert T Bear (D), Couch
Kinsa Impunity Jane (B), Savio & Kinney
Nanjo Touch Of Class (D), Cowie
Phildore's Zorena (B), Dommer
Qin Qin Yankee Boom-Boom (B), Covey & O'Leary
Rockee Vollee Cheeky Chick (B), Mueller
Shen Wah's A Piece Of The Rock (D), Bump
Show Off's Chiny Uppity (B), Williams
Taylwag's Tolkien (D), Campbell & McDearmon

9/83 Ali-Aj Double Dare Of Imua's (D), Castellano & Kurlander
An-Di's Venus De Wenshu (B), Alderman & Gerl
Beswicks Limited Edition (B), Waters
Heatherwood Victor Victoria (B), Guerra & Hollingshead
Loubren's Gretchen Barkhart (B), Barkley
Mejo's Heir-O-Dynamic (D), Wilson
Ming Dynasty's Ko-Motion (B), Blackburn
Ming Dynasty's Masked Bandit (D), Julian & Blackburn
Molnar's Colonel Rouser (D), Molnar
Pen Sans The Devil Made Me Do It (D), Tinsley
San Yen Gin-Gin Tu (B), Ormsby & Barr
Shamisen's Pepper Shaker (B), Morgan
Stylistic Miss Clairol (B), Rubino & Shepherd

10/83 A W Flytown Brass Band Drummer (B), Kim
Bilor's Stardust (B), Salvo & Fiedler
Bon D' Art Just Betwen Us (B), Guggenheim
Bon D'Art Rumor Has It (D), Guggenheim
Brynmyr's Chin Te Lung Hai (D), Webb & Luca
Ch'Ing Fo's Chang Ra La Of Joytu (B), Vinacco
Choo Ling's Windfall Profit (D), Campbell
Fancee Gunning Let's Face it (B), Snyder, Wheeler & Gunning
Gen Je's Eat Your Heart Out (B), Gentry & Mantie
Heatherwood Hot Sinful Sindy (B), Hollingshead
Jazmin's Everready (D), Arrington
Jolei Geronimo Of Cedarknoll (D), Jusey
Kai Shih's Call Me Paddington (D), Semple
Mi Lil' Bit O'Clover (B), Buck
Nanjo Classy Chassy (B), Cowie
Paje's Emperor Shogun (D), Fleming
Pem's Hots Si Tot Si (D), Mushrush
Shen Wah's For Members Only (D), Walton
Whirl Wind's Stormy Weather (B), Fjeseth

11/83 Beedoc's Smarty Pants (B), Stubblefield
Din Ho Koala T Bear (D), Strom
Dragonfire's I'M Bucko (D), Gidusko
Heatherwood's Fifth Wheel (D), Guerra
Hodari Baby-Face Nelson (D), Atkinson & Battey
Hodari Great Scott (D), Buis & Vierra
Joylin's Stolen Treasure (D), Pittelli
Kachina's Tribute Tu Ping (D), Burns
Lainee Edipus Complex Of Nova (D), Meltzer & Novak
Lantana's Leading Lady (B), Martin
Loubren Roustabout Of Sanyen (D), Barr
Mei Sans U Kno Who (D), Meidlinger
Mi Girl Named Sue (B), Buck
Pente's King Of Diamonds (D), Da Ponte

Regal's Dr Doolittle (D), Regelman
Regal's Dr Spock (D), Paquette & Regelman
Tu Chu's For Your Eyes Only (B), Puglise & Kwait
Varao's Teddy Bear (D), Varao
Vilenzo Polonaise (D), Vilas
Wingates Debutante (B), Neal

12/83 Ali-Aj Leading Lady At Imua's (B), Spencer
Anh Wei Crash Boom (D), Kim & Hewitson
Ballycastle's Chi-Chi Hai Sing (B), Jaramillo
Gunning's Fancee About Face (B), Wheeler & Gunning
Gunning's Henry The Eighth (D), Guggenheim & Gunning
Halcyon's Genie Of Mei Shan (B), Dishman
Indio's Classy Doctor (D), Frist
Loubren I'M A Billies Follie (B), Shaver & Shaver
Luken's Jack Frost (D), Lukenbach
Mei San Shindana (B), Potts
Mei Shan's Mariposa Gold Dust (D), Burley
Nanjo Suni Wun (B), Cowie
Oak Knolls Dandi Pandalion (B), Thomas
Rockee Vollee Grand Prix (D), Joens
Shan Ku Tu Ahn Khan (D), Vallee
Wes-Ro's Trapper John MD (D), Parker & Boggess
Wes Ro's Wonder Woman (B), Boggess
Winward's Elvira (B), Marcum

1/84 Anh Wei The Heirrogant Snob (D), Kim
Cedar Knoll's Copper Tone (B), Wall
Char Nicks Dapper Dan (D), Haines
Emperor's Burmese Dancer (B), Edel & Jordan
Ginkgo The Happy Hobo (D), Sproelich
Kayesett Xtra Special (B), Kaye
Kell's Mi Shou Chen (B), Keil
Lantana's Lover Boy (D), Oystrick
Le-Pre-Chaun Paper Doll O'Dashi (B), Pouliot
Luvncare Chopsticks (D), Hoo
Ponte's Ace Of Diamonds (D), Da Ponte
Rockee Vollee Cock Robin (D), Mueller
Sumeng Ms Oakley Of Nanjo (B), McCarty
Tai Shan's Dear Abby (B), Austin & Pollak
Tu-Su Larue Dan (B), Danielson
Wee Lee's Frosty Morn (D), Peterson

2/84 Ali-Aj The Lone Rranger (D), Castellano & Chinnici
Carousel Ten Speed (D), Lucchina
Fashions J C Gun Slinger (D), Price
Greylock's Smart E'Nuff (D), Goldberg
Heatherwood Chariots Of Fire (B), Friese & Hollingshead
Loubren Sweet N' Sassy (B), Spivey
LouWan-Ambiance Crowd Rouser (B), David
Mei Shan's Mandalay Mystique (B), Burley
Ming Dynasty's Chinese Silk (B), Blackburn
Mundy's Ama Magnificent (B), Bilicich
Mysty Dai Lone Star Mandarin (D), Poole
Shalimar Mint Julip (B), Black
Shen Wah's The Big Mac Attack (D), Seibel
Tu Chu's Golden Chip Ro Al (B), Savkov & Kwait
Windsong's Zephyr (D), Haines

3/84 Alba Golem (B), Kahn & Sanchez
Calibre Wind Storm (D), Hege
Choo Ling's Magic Wind (B), McDearmon
Choo Ling's Wind Chime (B), Campbell
Dazlen's Magnum PI Of Landor (D), Dudas-Balaze
Elusive Braggon Dragon (B), Schaffer
Emperor's Top Line Designer (D), Jordan
Hana-Kinsa Indiana Jones (D), Prato
Hu-Ber's Mr Pinkerton (D), Berry & Huston
Jolei Just For Laughs (B), Buis & Kijowski
Joylin's Spectacular Dream (D), Pittelli
Mandarin's Dragon Lady (B), Cooper & Di Nicola
Ming Dynasty's Chinese Sable (B), Blackburn
Ming Dynasty's Chinese Satin (B), Tomanica
Nanking's Maxwell Smart (D), Peterson
Pen Sans Patina Of Show Off (B), Williams
Shen Wah's Silver Streak (D), Hewitson & Walton

Left: China Trades Nicotine Fit and China Trades Hooked on Nicotine, with owner Mary Warren-Lea.

Right: Ch. Yoshi's Ah So Omar, owned by Richard Paisley.

Left: Ch. Dragonfly's Cho-Ko of Nanjo, owned by Jacqueline Kraus.

Right: Am. and Can. Ch. Chang Tang Sher Khan Tango, owned by Joyce DeVoll.

Left: Ch. Pen Sans Political Parti, owned by Gloria Busselman.

Right: Ch. Joylin's Stolen Treasure, bred and owned by Hilde Pittelli.

100

Taylwag's Gandalf (D), Devers
Tenoma's Kristen Of Karola (B), Smith & Amonett
Woodsmoke's Dashi Preview (B), Pouliet
Wychmere's Constant Comment (B), Thomas
Yingsu Grand Slam (B), Young

4/84 Fancee Gunning Re-Vival (B), Ammons & Venturella
Gensing Incredible Chi Chi (B), Arnold
Hidden Coves Golden Dream (D), McGonagle
Mo Tzu's Hellion Of Toi (B), Busselman
Regal's Perfectly Seasoned (B), Regelman
Rockee Vollee Honi Fire (B), Mueller
Sharn's Marquisa Of Zorro (B), Utstein
Shen Wah's Shoot The Moon (B), Walton
Tu Chu's Prim And Proper (B), Nicholas & Kwait

5/84 Ah So Dandy Andy Of La Ens (D), Neal & Ledoux
August Moon's Full Of Spunk (D), Nanni
Dragonfire's The Great Draco (D), Hogg
Hai Sings Nau Ti Kee Ho (D), Wood
Lainee The Doctor's Delight (B), Kotwitz
Mandarin's Eye Of The Tiger (D), Uckotter
Show Off's Just A Minute (D), Williams
Wendavs Sunblazer O'Tang Kou (D), English
Wingates Feather Fandancer (B), Goss & Neal
Wyn-Song Oliver Twist (D), Haines

6/84 Copper Penny Dalai Major Suit (D), Pennington & Machara
Dr Joyce Brothers (B), Regelman
Emperor's Gypsy Rosalee R and R (B), Cherry
Fancee Gunning Re-Pete (D), Olson & Wheeler
Gunning Fancee Re-Joice (B), Medeiros & Wheeler
Hai Sings Brass Buttons (D), Hayward
Hidden Coves Chewbacca (D), Murphy
Kuai Lo's Ultra Suede (D), Iliesco & Shepherd
Lainee The Liver Wurst Of Tyca (D), Meltzer, Zanen & Kotwitz
Lou Wan Tootsie (B), Gec
Macada's Mind Over Matter (B), Davis
Mandarin's Look Me Over (B), Gangstead & Di Nicola
Mei San's Dirty White Boy (D), Meidlinger
Mei Shan's The Golden Fleece (D), Burley
Ming Dynasty's Magic Samurai (D), Heckert
Pushkin's Ama Bummer's Yum-Yum (B), Cook & Smith
Raintree's Johnny Walker Red (D), Rainey
San Yen Marco Polo (D), Barr & West
Shen Wah's For Play (B), Walton
Show Off's Just A Minute (D), Williams
Stylistic Under A Kuai-Lo Tree (D), Podesto
Vilenzo Copper Penny Ruffles (B), Pennington & Goodwin

7/84 Akitzu Double Stuff (B), Wright
Dragonwyck Dominique (B), Patton, Constantino & Moncion
Emperor's Dixieland Delight (B), Adams
Gracelyne's Gemi-Jo Cricket (B), Hisaka
Kayesett Zebadiah (B), Kaye
Kee Lee's Raisen' Cain Of Ja-Ma (D), Keenan & Whitman
Lilibet Fyre Dragon (D), Hammond
Ming Toi Original Copy (D), Boyles
Mi Tenoma's Sunnee Daze (D), Buck
Shado's Hum Dinger (B), Hexom & Hewitson

8/84 Abacus' I Guess So (D), Basil & Smith
Beedoc's Mi Choyce (B), Stubblefield
Centerfold's Ex-Tra Ter-Rif-Ic (D), Moberly, Hollingshead & Ward
Grenouille Fastbuck Freddie (D), Weathers
Gunning Fancee Re-Cruit (D), Wheeler & Gunning
Hana-Kinsa Incredible Igor (D), Prato & Savio
Kayesett Zackary (D), Kaye
Laksanas Bubblin Brown Sugar (B), Joris
Langpur Oliver Oh Oliver (D), Papke
Pen Sans Spellbound (D), Wadsworth
Regal's Poppin' Jay Of An-Di (D), Regelman
Regal's Sweet N' O So Lovely (B), Regelman

Rockee Volly Gogetter Akitzu (D), Albrecht & Wright
Ti-Gi's Burning Ambition (D), Glavan
Tu Chu's Mesmerized (B), Kwait
Wingates Mandala Of Kailasa (B), De Angelis & De Angelis
Zalay Shogi (D), Cullen

9/84 Ah So Famous Amos Of La Ens (D), Neal
China Chimes Slew Of Gold (D), Heilman & Strapp
Choo Ling's Wind Warning (D), Campbell
Dang Sai Champagne Charlie (D), Krisko & Fjeseth
Dragonfire's I'M A Lady's Man (D), Hexom
Dragonfire's I'M Tiffany (B), Anthony
Lantana's Starlite (B), Montemurro
Mei San's Dynamite Damsel (B), Meidlinger
Pekings Secret Service (D), Imig
Pen Sans Truffles Of Edwin (B), Laughlin
Samalee's Reflections Of Baron (D), Oystrick
Terdel's Woodsmoke Chant (D), Miller
Ti-Gi's Burning Desire (B), Glavan
Vilenzo Red Rover Red Rover (D), Vilas & Savio
Zerox Shih-Ah-Sumtin (B), Fahnestock

10/84 August Moon Hearts'N Flowers (B), Nanni
Bilor's Flashdance (D), Desalvo & Shachat
Charing Cross Clown Prince (D), Halpern
Copper Penny Dalai Razmataz (B), Goodwin & Pennington
Dragonwyck's Spitfire (D), Hopkins
Hana Copper Penny Heather (B), Pennington & Prato
Jofins The Gambler (D), Lade
Jolei Margarita (B), Kijowski
Kachina's Designer Jeans (B), Kregar
Kam Tin's Goody Two Shoes (B), Krajnak
Kissme's Split Personality (B), Glavan, Krisko & Wheeler
Mandarin Sam Sun Of Pinafore (D), Delaney
Mei San's Great White Hope (D), Meidlinger
Pen Sans Eye Of The Thai-Ger (D), Busselman
Rambutan Sabrina Fair (B), Francis
R-Own Kam Chung (D), De Voll & Cecile
Sho-Bizz Silver Express (D), Jusay
Silky Acres Sumthing E T (D), Walton
Silwynd's Daffy Down Dilly (B), Smith
Tang Kou's Jaded lady (B), English
U-Tu's Striking Rezemblance (D), Finanger
Vandemere's Carawan Caraway (B), Lloyd
Willoway's Holiday Dee-Lite (B), Williamson & Williamson
Wyncrest Forget-Me-Not (B), Heckerman & Davis

11/84 Centerfold's Minute Maid (B), Goodman & Breaux
Centerfold's Orange Julius (D), Moberly & Goodman
Dragonfire's Antonia (B), Hogg
Dragonfire's Red Raider (D), Hogg
Dragonwyck Desperado (D), Morgan
Dragonwyck Roust About (D), Molnar
Faerie Dean Double Cream Oreo (B), Sylvia
Fashions Orange Of Benjerbo (D), Brooker & Blackburn
Hodari Mercy Me O' Chang Tang (B), Nelson & De Voll
Jolane's All-American Boy (D), Boyles & Wheeler
Jolei Jawbreaker (D), Kijowski
Loubren's Code Of The West (D), Gunning & Wheeler
Lou Wan Gunning Fancee Etc (B), Shaver & Shaver
Lou Wan's Jezebel Of Molnar (B), Molnar
Lou Wan's The Happi Dragon (D), Nichols
Pekings Tina Maria (B), Connaughton & Morgan
Ric-Shaw's Thunder'N Cannon (D), Foster
Shonaping's Argonaut Era (D), Cornett
Show Off's Buckshot (D), Bilicich
Szus Mitz Empty Pockets (D), Moody
Top Knots Brandi Amber (B), King
Woodsmoke's Before Yesterday (B), Miller

12/84 Arvind Vom Tschomo-Lungma (D), Kerr
Briarhill This Bud's For Me (D), Craddock
Centerfold's Lorien Oh Lordy (D), Moberly
Choo Ling's Wind Brook (B), Campbell
Genisa's Tin Pan Lizzy (B), Crooks & Crooks
Ginkgo My Fair Lady (B), Pipkorn

Heatherwood Din Ho Michael (D), Strom
Hu-Bers Glittering Peggy (B), Berry & Huston
Mei Shan Ambiance Demitasse (B), Cartwright & David
Nova's High Anxiety (D), Kotwitz
Pagoda's Kan-Dee Kiss (B), White
R Own Soft N Sleezy (B), Cecile
Tarma's Tu-Ling Of Jimijo (B), Adamson
Tasha Chisai Angel (B), Heath
Ty-Won-On's Images Of Kee-Lee (B), Pollina

1/85 Car-Lyn's Nutmegan (D), Justice & Tharp
El Frans Special T (B), Nasner
Fang Chu's Bueford T Justice (D), Hollingsworth
Lar-El's Tag-A-Long Of Sumhi (D), Ruggiero
Mejo's Frosty Heir (D), Wilson
Shadra Miracle Man O'Dewge (D), Clark & Dews
Ti-Gi's Warlord Of Woodrose (D), Oganeky
Tu-Mac's Phoebe Shou (B), Atchley
Zalay Here Comes Trouble (D), Cullen

2/85 Bar None Doctor Demento (D), Gec
Copper Penny Samantha (B), Pennington & Goodwin
Copper Penny Winsum Teddy (D), Pennington & Boynton
Emperor's Just A Li'L Mo Gold (B), Adams
Fang Chu's Lovett (B), Whitney
Shan Ku Kiku (B), Vallee
Taylwag's Silesia (B), Taylor & Wagner
T-Sun's Peppermint Patty (B), Sproelich & Thompson

3/85 Ali-Aj Sundance Kid Of Mer-Ri (D), Caouette
Anh Wei The Computer Boom (B), Busselman
Anjuli's Rhapsody In Blue (B), Madeley
Bar None Nurse Diesel (B), Wheeler & Gunning
Beedoc's Ms Genie (B), Stubblefield
China Chimes Miss Marker (B), Heilman & Strapp
Gunning' Lindee Yeller Ribbon (B), Shafer
Hai-Tai High Heritage (D), Karelitz
Hidden Coves Honey Bee (B), Ward
Kee Lee's Eclipse Of Mar Del (D), Laible, Nisbet &
  McIntosh
Lou Wan Jonathon (D), Williams & Gunning
Lou Wan The Fire Chief (D), Ammons & Venturella
Lyric's Limited Edition (D), Uckotter
Mei San Stage Door Johnnie (D), Alexander & Meidlinger
Ming Dynasty's Dragon Son (D), Ledbetter & Blackburn
Nanjo B J Honi-Cutt (D), Irvin & Stargel
Rockee Vollee Spiced Truffle (B), Finanger & Mueller
Shizzu's My Oh My Of Dashi (B), Zibel & Pouliot
Ta Ya Chai's Emeer Vom Arvind (D), Kerr
Taylwag's Bubbling Brew (D), Taylor & Wagner
Tu Chu's Flashdance-Marja (D), Kwait & Puglise

4/85 Ali-Aj Chin-Hua Kublai Khan (D), Nelson & De Voll
Dragonfire's Shirley Ann (B), Hogg
Langpur After-Dinner Special (B), Nyberg
Mei San Fancy Mi'E Ling (B), Potts & Meidlinger
Nanjo Honey Buns (B), Cowie
Nova's I'M No Puss-Over (D), Blackburn
Stylistic Willoway Good Memory (B), Shepherd
Tou-Che Winsum Happy-Go-Lucky (D), Anderson &
  Boynton

5/85 Ballycastle's Pla Misty For Me (B), Williams
Bel Fleur Yankee Doodle Boy (D), Medellin
Choo Ling's Win D (B), Kay
Dragonfly's Dazz-Ling-Toi (D), Kraus
Hodari Hai-U Hooligan (D), Vander Weele
Martin's Orange Ice Puff (B), Martin
Molnar's Miss Carousel (B), Molnar
Mo Tzu's Man About Town (D), Thomas
Mundy's Ama An-Di's Bumper Jax (D), Helmick & Mundy
Mundy's Ama Riddle's Koz-Mo (D), Mundy
Shan Ku Kung Chu (B), Whitehead
Shansi's Brandywine Pla-Boi (D), Shada
Tu Chu's You Only Live Twice (D), Nicholas & Kwait

6/85 An-Di's Lucky Lady L (B), Alderman
Fancee Gunning Up Start (B), Biller & Wheeler

Ming Dynasty's Plum Sassy (B), Blackburn
Sanchi Dyan Of Mi House (B), Selfon & McIntyre
Show Off's Minute Waltz (B), Williams
Webbs Lo Ling (D), Webb
Wingate's Coppelia (B), Williams

7/85 Ali-Aj Wildfire Of R And R (B), Cherry
Bel Fleur Taylwag's Oreo (D), Taylor & Wagner
Beswicks Brandy Alexandria (B), Horton
Fancee Gunning Get Up N Glow (B), Meideiros & Wheeler
Jana's Toot Toot Tootsie (B), Awtrey
Langpur Knikerboker Special (D), Papke
Macada's State Of Mind (B), Davis
Pe-Kee's Ron Wan (D), Arrington
Shawnakin Sting Like A Bee (D), Gerrior
Tu Chu's Could It Be Magic (B), Nicholas & Kwait

8/85 Bar None Nurse Rerhyme (B), Bryant
Bobests E'Zee Duz It (D), Bean
Bon D'Art Today's Headlines (D), Deleppo
Dragonfire's Lady Rebecca (B), Moore & Gossett
Faerie Dean Devil In Disguise (D), Sylvia
Fancee Gunning Up Roar (B), Eshelman, Connaughton &
  Wheeler
Foxfire Tunz-A-Fun (D), Fox
Gunning's BitoyellTai Shan (B), Pollak
Jac-Len's Rich And Famous (D), Kelly, Toliver & Welch
Jen-Mi's Gee Whiz (D), Tipton
Mundy's Ama Bummer's Bon-Bon (B), Stock
Show Off's Wat's Not To Love (B), Williams
Suncrest's Cute Stuff (B), Krahn

9/85 Akitzu General Rebel (D), Wheeler
Ali-Aj Smokey Penney Of Lomel (B), Fahnestock
August Moon's Sugar Daddy (D), Nanni
Centerfold's Cap'N Pierce MD (D), Moberly
Dark Decon Of El-Fran (D), Nasner
Granville Sno Dancin (B), Russell & Fox
Gunning's Juan N Only Tu Chu (D), Kwait
Jolei Bubblicious (B), Kijowski
Lainee Devilish Dream Of Jba (B), Meltzer
Lou Wan's Regal Rebel (D), Moore
Luken's The Eyes Have It (B), Lukenbach
Nanjo Classablanca (D), Cowie
Nanjo Honey Nut Cheerio (D), Cowie
Pao Pel's James Bond Of Camelot (D), Brink & Fishler
R And R Major Motion (D), Cherry

10/85 Akitzu Mis-Fire (B), Wright
Bel Fleur Bonsai Rocket (D), Gangi
Bing's Rowdy Rebel (D), Bingaman
Bon D'Art Nose In The Heir (D), Guggenheim
Copper Penny Music Man (D), Alderman & Pennington
Dragonfire's Dang Sal Dickens (B), Hogg
Fan Chu Happiour (D), Frenklin
Fang Chu's Bodacious (D), Burchi & Hollingsworth
Kayesett Grand Prix (D), Kaye
Lainee Just Pretending (D), Oganeku
Luken's Kee Largo Of Din Ho (D), Goss
Marja Gold Hooker Of Happiness (B), Puglise
Me Ling's Good Time Charlie (D), McDearmon
Pen Sans Thai Dyed (B), Nowatzki & Busselman
Regal's Elusive Escapade (D), Schaffer & Regelman
Rockee Vollee Irish Red Bayly (D), Mueller
Rockee Vollee Tawny Tansy (B), Gallion
Rosemar Ima Lure (B), Warner
Sam Tsus Lady Pao Kuei (B), Carroll
San Yen Yoda Sun Of Sing-Yu (D), Rager
Tai Shan's Power Of Magic (D), Lageman & Pollack
Terribrooke's I'M Irresistible (B), Wharton
Willoway's Dee-Lite Of Zorro (B), Williamson &
  Williamson
Wingate's Aka Tattletail (B), Stone & Neal
Wyn-Song Midnight Lace (B), Haines & Kijowski

11/85 Abacus' Small Wonder (B), Basil & Smith
Akitzu Yankee Rebel (D), Wright

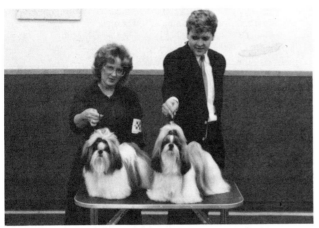

Jeannette Forcier with Rockee Vollee U-Tu In Feathers and Greg Larson with Ch. Rockee Vollee Banshee No. Both owned by Jeannette Forcier.

Ch. Bel Air Tigherson of Shang Tou, owned by Cathie Phillips.

Emperor's Bamboozle Ying and Emperor's Gossip Ying with Mrs. J. Wesley Edel.

Ch. Bon D'Art Adore Ring of Fancee, owned by Marilyn Sue Woodward.

Can. Ch. Bilor's Golden Elegance, owned by Lorraine De Salvo.

Ch. Bjorneholm Pif (on left) and his daughter (center). Owners Jack and Mary Wood.

Ali Aj Puttin On The Ritz (B), Cacciatore
Ambiance-A Head Of The Crowd (D), David
Anh Wei Baby Babble (B), Kim
Centerfold's Touch 'O' Sunshine (B), Moberly
Charing Cross Rotten Ralph (D), Kahn & Sanchez
Chinai's Galaxy Gal (B), Jones
Dragonfire Golly G Chang Tang (B), Devoll
Dragonfire's I'M Major Of Sujo (D), Irey & Watson
Dragonwyck Dramatique (B), Patton, Melvin &
    Constantino
Emperor's Top Priority (D), Adams
Genlea's Miss Rosie O'Grady (B), Crooks & Crooks
Ginkgo Blame It On Rio (B), Pipkorn
Halcyon's Rona Bear-It (B), Dishman
Hun Fu Flash Dance (D), Watts
Kallusa A-Ku-Ta (D), Joris
Kar Tin's Bubblin' Over (B), Krajnak
Lar-El's Ebony'N'Ivory (B), Ruggiero & Ruggiero
Li Ming's Bristol Beaufighter (D), Terkildsen
Ming Dynasty's Snow Crystal (B), Daniels
Nat-Sam's Angelica (B), Marcum
Nova's Mistress Of The Rings (B), Novak
Qundon Nichols Of Nanjo (D), Burchl
Regal's Bit O'Honey (B), Regelman
Regal's Hello Dolly (B), Regelman
Rockee Vollee Scarlet Angel (B), Mueller
San Yen Black Magic Of Donalen (B), Cullen
San Yen Buttons N Bows (B), Barr
San Yen Rusty Bayonet (D), Barr
Sehing Yu Pandy Lion (D), Horwitz
Shen Wah's By Request Only (D), Moody & Walton
Sumeng Gi Gi (B), McCarty
Tanna's Tip's N Noodles (B), Batchelden
Tiara's Stylistic Cover Girl (B), Rubino & Shepherd
Tov-Che's Breazy Copper Penny (B), Anderson, Boynton &
    Pennington
12/85 Ah So Amazing Amanda (B), Ledoux
Ali-Aj Syn-T-Lai-Ting Of Lilibet (D), Hammond
Ambelon Tuff Cookie (B), Flynn & Larick
Foxfire Sid E Slicker (D), Fox
Gunning Fancee All The Rags (D), Wheeler & Gunning
Hideaway's Mel Ah Winemaker (B), Shada
Loubren's Ms Bee-Hav'N O' Halsing (B), Hayward
Lou Wan Daphne (B), Olin & Wheeler
Luken's Red Rose (B), Lukenbach
Ming Dynasty's Snow White (B), Blackburn
Ming-Ty Woodlands Chein-Si (D), Verzi & Resnick
Nanjo Forever Amber (B), Cowie
Pen Sans The Devil Made Me Do It (D), Busselman, Iseki
    & Hirahara
Ric Shaw's Hi Clas Captivator (D), Foster
Sa Lu Se Danteinferno (D), Gibson
Shen Wah's Turn it Loose (D), Walton
Stylistic Tiara Jumping Jack (D), Stubblefield
Sumeng Gentle Ben (D), McCarty
Tara Tzu Merry Sunshine Vi Jeh (B), Vela-Roberts
Tu Chu Gunning In The Ruff (D), Nasner & Wheeler
Willoway Stylistic Smak'Ngood (D), Ehricht
1/86 A-May-Zing Red Reuben (D), McMichael & Crosby
Ambiance Crowd Stopper (D), David
Bonsai's Ha Ha Ha (B), Gangi
Cane's Ama Sugar Cane (B), Cane, Craig & Craig
Centerfold's Gosh Almighty (D), Moberly
Chi-Nees Bo Dar Ik (B), Burchi & Musselman
Dragonfire's Lady Sunshine (B), Curry
Galaxy's Cobblestone Spanky (D), Craig & Craig
Gensing Incredible Red (D), Arnold
Jolei Jack Daniels (D), Blasinski
Jolei Presenting Priscilla (B), Stearns & Kijowski
Kachina's Autumn Mist (B), Kregar
Lainee Lord 'N Master (D), Smith
Mei San Afternoon Delight (B), Meidlinger & Potts

Mei San Tuff E Nuff (D), Meidlinger
Mo Tzu's Raggedy Annie (B), Thomas
Mundy's Ama Bumer's Bib'N-Tucker (D), Mundy
Regal's Specially Packaged (B), Regelman & Regelman
Ric-Shaw's Hi Tone Topsy (B), Foster
San Yen Lei Ning (B), Barr & Ormsby
Tu Chu's Major Motion (B), Kwait
2/86 Amaryllis' Sweet Dreams (D), Macintosh & Keenan
Anh Wel Heirrospace (D), Kim & Connaughton
Billies Follie Little Shaver (B), Shaver & Shaver
Choo Ling's Desert Wind (D), Campbell & Campbell
Choo Ling's Wind Bluff (B), Campbell & Campbell
Dalai Delta Breeze (B), Mabry
El-Fran Gunning A W O L (D), Schaffer & Wheeler
Ginkgo Steamboat Willie (D), Pipkorn & Pipkorn
Gunning Fancee All's Fair (B), Wheeler & Gunning
Jhen-Lee's Broker's Delight (D), Jones & Jones
Kachina's Mystic Warrior (D), Kregar
Kual-Lo Stylistic Golden Ring (D), Iliesco & Shepherd
Mei Shan's Star Dust (D), Burley
Ming Dynasty's Suthern Melody (B), Blackburn &
    Blackburn
Mundy's Ama Amanda (B), Mundy
Nanjo Simply Sinful (B), Cowie
Nanjo Trade Secret O Shenwah (D), Cowie & Cowie
Pen Sans Magic For Karola (D), Smith & Armstrong
Pen Sans Parti Cheer (B), Gerrior
Shalimar's Bear Elegance (B), Bilicich & Bilicich
Tiffany Toi Golden Lady (B), Saunders
Wes-Ro's Fall Guy (D), Boggess
Woodsmoke's Dragon Lace (B), Miller
3/86 Briggan Ard Ri O'Connemara (D), Larick & Flynn
Chinawood Jih-Lo (B), Sutay & Hainline
Ginkgo Glass Slipper (B), Pipkorn & Pipkorn
Jo-Ahn's Truffles (B), Anthony & Gordon
Lindi's Rockum N Sockum (D), Sullivan
Lord Casey Ty-Ri Of Je-Mar (D), Medici & Medici
M And R's Just Hill Billy (D), Rukavina & Grabur
Mei San Theo-Dorable Cameo (D), Selvig
Nanjo Jezebel (B), Nielsen
Shali-Hi Kocachin Delite (B), Goss
4/86 Bonsai's Cheap Thrill (D), Gangi
Choo Ling's Tradewinds (D), Clemons & Clemons
Connemara's Llord Of London (D), Flynn & Larick
Elusive Lord Of The Dragons (D), Schaffer & Schaffer
Jana's Dutch Masters (D), Awtrey
Jen Len Magique Magpie (B), Olson
Langpur Tete A Tete (B), Papke & Papke
Lou Wan Gunning Tootsie Pop (D), Gunning & Wheeler
Mel Shan' Forest Farm Khamsin (B), Burley & Cartwright
Ponte's Mr Debeers (D), Da Ponte
Woodsmoke's Dragons Quest (D), Thompson
5/86 Bilor's Pepsi Generation (D), De Salvo & Fiedler
Bing's Hi-Jack (D), Bingaman & Bingaman
House Of Wu Cactus Flower (B), Eckes & Eckes
Loubren Sabar Mind Games (D), Craig & Craig
Lou Wan Gunning Fancee Ltd (B), Gunning & Wheeler
Shan Ku Kaldu Khan (D), Vallee & Vallee
Shen Wah's You Wanna Bet (B), Walton & Walton
Stylistic Tiara Loreal (B), Shepherd & Rubino
6/86 Billies Follie Red Raven (B), Shaver & Shaver
Char-Ming Veronica (B), Ptak & Wheeler
Chinai's Starlord (D), Jones
Choo-Ling's Wind Echo (B), Clemons & Clemons
Dang Sai I'M A Dickens Too (B), Krisko & Pollak
Dang Sallittle Jimi Dickens (D), Krisko
Granville Pud N Pie O'Hapiour (B), Russell
Grenouille Heartbreaker (B), Blasinski
Hai Sings N-Vee Of Shilo (D), Hayward
Ichiban Daphne Dee-Lite (B), Saunders
Je-Mar's Mighty Atlas V Ty-Ri (D), Medici
Langpur La Dee Da (B), Papke, Papke & Martello

Loubren's Lady In Red (B), McKnight
Maristo's Once In Love With Amy (B), Stock
Mejo's Little Red Waggin (D), Wilson
Mundy's Ama Peperminit Patrik (D), Mundy & Lane
Nanjo Classic Rhythm (D), Horwitz, Horwitz & Cowie
Pagoda-Lion's Han Sum Ting (D), Gibson
Red Raiders Cabbage Patch (B), Thomas
Regal's Chief Of Staff (D), Ford, Zimmer & Regelman
Regal's Corriander (B), Regelman
Ric-Shaw's Hi Test Car-Ling (B), Snyder & Foster
Shen Wah's Crazy Like A Fox (D), Walton & Walton
Stylistic Kuai-Lo Guther Tuch (D), Macaloney & Macaloney
Taylwag's Amaretto (B), Taylor & Wagner
Yi-Jing Sichuan Puppet Of U-Tu (D), Finager

7/86 Ali-Aj Briden Break My Stride (D), Vinacco & Vinacco
Anh Wei Boomin' Business (D), Kim
Centerfold's Robin Hood (D), De Voll & De Voll
Copper Penny Nutmeg (B), Pennington & Morrow
Emperor's Go For The Gold (D), Adams
Gen Je's Bette Shi Kan (B), Devoll & Gentry
Hun-Fu Klif's Karmel Kandi (D), Waits & Waits
Jo-Ahn's Validian Scoundrel (B), Rogers & Devens
Lou Wan's Fair Lady Of Miramar (B), Tripp
Mitsuli's Ode To Joy (B), McGonagle & McGonagle
Nanking's Lucky Seven (D), Ikola
Pen Sans Koosa Of Li Ming (D), Tendler, Tendler & Busselman
Pen Sans Toi Ing Around (B), Alderson
Prospect Hill's Pat'N Approval (D), Deputat
R And R Chariot Of Fire (B), Cherry & Cherry
R And R Golden Chablis (D), Kiesling, Cherry & Cherry
Regal's Elusive Danny Boy (D), Regelman & Regelman
Shan Ku Shang Ti Of Bubek (D), Whitehead
Shen Wah's Fast Forward (B), Walton & Walton
Willowind's Touch Of Mink (D), Johnston & Larson
Yu-Mei's Ho Chi Helen Wheels (B), Extest & Alexander

8/86 Bryant's Rebellion Of Lou Wan (D), Bryant
Ciarlen's Shady Lady (B), Conrad
Grenouille Hoodwink (B), Papke & Papke
Gunning Ti-Grr (D), Wheeler & Gunning
Gunning's On The Make O' Loubren (D), McKnight
Jo-Ahn's Rigaletto (B), Anthony
Jorel's Sagittarius O'Tyjoen (D), Freund & Thurston
Kai Shih Toast Of The Town (B), Semple
Lou Wan Cartier (B), Gec & Gec
Loubren Pretti Sassy Of Toma (B), Webb & Meltzer
Loubren's Dr. Ruth (B), McKnight
Lou Wan Eric (D), Seidl & Wheeler
Luken's Let The Light Shine (D), Lukenbach
Mundy's Ama Mum's The Word (B), Mundy
Protege's Afternoon Delight (B), Vander Weele
Sabar's All The Rage Of Galaxy (D), Craig & Craig
Shalimar Creative Evolution (B), Dishman
Shansi's Sheng Kam Winemaker (D), Shada & Shada
Show Off's Chiffon (B), Williams
Show Off's Kickapoo Karma (B), Williams
Tu Chu Lightnin Struck Twice (B), Kwait
Tyjoen's Fire 'N Ice O' Jorel (B), Thurston & Freund
Vilenzo Tuesday Ting (B), Vilas & Vilas
Wingate's Never Say Dye (D), Neal

9/86 Ali-Aj-Sumeng's Heidi (B), McCarty
Clearwater's Flashdance (B), Murphy & Anderson
Dashi's Sammy Sun (D), Cristaldi & Poulior
El Frans Charmed I'M Sure (B), Nasner & Nasner
Klassik Me Jane At Don Wai (B), Hansen & Wadsworth
Lar-El's Hum-A-Long (B), Ruggiero & Ruggiero
Lou Wan Alexander (D), Wheeler & Gunning
Lou Wan Gunning Fancee Et Al (B), Lane & Lane
Ming Dynasty's Saint He Ain'T (D), Blackburn
Ming-Ty Ching-Yea (D), Verzi & Resnick
Nanjo Absolutely (B), Cowie

Pen Sans Toi Fantasy (B), Busselman
Ponte's Diamond Prism (B), Da Ponte
Pre Dawn Kris Kringlo' Sumeng (D), McCarty & Mazar
Shar-Ming Clearwater Polo (D), Murphy & Bilicich
Shente's Puttin On The Ritz (D), Burchi & Hardy
Taylwag's Bit Of The Bubbley (B), Taylor & Wagner
Tu-Che' Clearwater Gold-Nugget (D), Anderson, Boynton & Murphy

10/86 Copper Penny Kahlua (B), Prato & Pennington
Gensing Red Rider (D), Hindman
Ginkgo Christie Brinkley (B), Pipkorn & Pipkorn
Je-Mar's Apollo Hellos V Lou Wan (D), Medici & Maloney
Je-Mar's Aurora Borealis V Ty-Ri (B), Whitehead & Whitehead
Julee Of Vandemere (B), Lloyd & Lloyd
Kuai Lo's All Wound Up (D), Iliesco
Mar-Lin's Doll E Of Paloma (B), Milstein & Milstein
Mei Shan's Star Dust Dancer (D), Burley & Burley
Mik-Lyn's Smuggler's Cove (D), Riggs
Regal's Diamond Crystal (B), Schoenfeld & Regelman
Rose Hill's Freedom Rose (D), Bryant
Ti-Gi's Kiss Of Dragonfire (B), Hogg
Yingsu's Carolina Rebel (D), Davis

11/86 Anh Wei Mightee Rebellious (B), Kim
Beswick's The Magician (D), Waters
Chisai Black Magic (B), Heath
Dijims Johni Walker Red (D), Ward
Hal Sings Ms Vish-Us Rumors (B), Hayward
Jofins Check It Out (D), Finney
Lomei Kaptin Kor-A-Jus (D), Fahnestock
Lou Wan Omar (D), Gec & Gec
Mei Shan's Star Dust Nugget (D), Burley & Burley
Mejo's Kerri's Bear (B), Hindman
Mirra's Ceasar Of Kee-Lee (D), Kogan & Kogan
Pagan's Free Association (B), Pagan
Shafers Cute As A Button (B), Shafer
Shan Ku Tartu Khan (D), Vallee & Vallee
Taylwag's Dilly Dally (B), Taylor & Wagner
Tu Chu Take It To The Limit (D), Kwait
Tu Chu's Ginger Snap (B), Nicholas & Kwait

12/86 Ahm Sugardolly Of Tara Tsu (B), Vela-Roberts
Akitzu Annabelle Lee (B), Wright, Wright & Wright
Bei Jing Appolo Of Shansi (D), Lewis & Martello
Don Wai Pardon My Dust (D), Lovie & Wadsworth
Faerie Dean's Velvet Villain (B), Sylvia
Gunning's Racheal Racheal (B), Gunning
Jolane Gunning Marsha (B), Wheeler, Gunning & Pollak
Joylin's String Of Pearls (B), Pittelli
Kell's Ying Ming O'Shou (D), Kell
Klassik's Rembrandt Of Samtsu (D), Hansen
Lomei Classic Sugar Bear (D), Fahnestock
Manchus Emperor Geisha Girl (B), Hawley
Maristo's Our Finest Hour (D), Kaiser & Stock
Pekings Just About Perfect (B), Bradshaw & Connaughton
Rockee Vollee Ginkgo Gigolo (D), Pipkorn & Pipkorn
Rockee Vollee Just Jenifer (B), Mueller
Se-Nan's Special Delivery (D), Sproelich
Sha Wis Jokers Are Wild (D), Wilson
Shado's Sakes Alive (B), Steffens
Taishan's Elliot Ness (D), Pollak
Taylwag's Mickey Finn (D), Taylor & Wagner
Wingate's Carrot Top (B), Neal

1/87 Car Ling's Let's Face It Again (B), Snyder & Snyder
Char Nicks Hi-Tone Crakajack (D), Jutzi, Bainum & Sanfilippo
Chinwangtao Gung Hoi Fet Toi (B), Mann & Mann
Copper Penny Peprika (B), Voll & Pennington
House Of Wu Windjammer (D), Eckes
Ichiban Cinnamon Spice (B), Saunders
M And R's Juais Winging Prince (D), Rukavina & Graber
Macada's Electric Company (D), Davis
Manchus Eastern Connection (D), Hawley

Ch. Pen Sans Koosa of Li Ming, owned by Gloria Busselman.

Ch. Copper Penny In Cog Ni To, owned by Bonnie Prato.

Ch. Mar Del's Chia Jen of Copa, owned by Coni Nickerson. Chia was by Ch. Mar Del's Chow Mein out of his daughter Ch. Mar Del's Samantha.

Ch. M&R's Big Bad John, owned by Bonnie Prato and Coragene Savio.

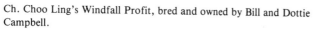
Ch. Choo Ling's Windfall Profit, bred and owned by Bill and Dottie Campbell.

Ch. Emperor's Fashion Designer, owned by Ornah Jordan.

Moonglow's Smooth As Brandy (D), Beauine & Beauine
Nanking's Broadway Joe (D), Ikola
Rosehills Rowdy Rose (D), Bryant & Wallace
Sehing Yu Ma Scarlet (B), Horwitz & Horwitz
Show Off's I've Got Rhythm (D), Lane & Lane
Show Off's Just A Tad (D), Watts & Williams
Swe-Chen's Good Times (B), Nyberg
Taylwag's Willie's Choice (D), Taylor & Wagner

2/87 Ambiance Chinese Rebellion (D), David & Williams
Artisan's Leonardo Da Vinci (D), Williams & Lane
Clarien's Murteza (D), Conrad
Dalai Copper Penny Scalawag (D), Mabry & Pennington
Dragonwyck Preferred Stock (D), Machara
Emperors Denim And Diamonds (B), Jordan
Forestfarm'Scrazy Like A Fox (D), Frothingham
Foxfire Born To Be Cherished (B), Fox & Heilman
Genisa's Puttin' On The Ritz (B), Crooks & Crooks
Jolei Bubble Yum (B), Kijowski & Kijowski
Kee Lee 'N' San Mar's Gizmo (D), Dellano & Keenan
Larue Dan Ryuko No (B), Danielson
Ming Dynasty's Chou Lee O' Re-Dan (D), Daniels & Blackburn
Prospect Hill's Pollyanna (B), Wilson
San Yen Gangbusters Windsor (D), Gordon
Sanchi Chumi Geisha (B), Acton & Acton
Shali-Hi Dancaway Duster (D), Lemire & Lemire
Shente's Christian Dior (D), Brown
Show Off's Just A Bit Uppity (B), Williams
Snobhill's Free Lance (B), La Salle
Taylwag's Tibi Kahn Du Sukara (D), Schwab
Tu Chu's Reached The Limit (B), Kwait & Di Giacoma

3/87 Ah So Diamond In The Ruff (D), Neal
Brandy Ice Of Bin Yunsi (D), Bouchard
Chin-chu's Red N' Rowdy (D), Medeiros
Dragonfire's I'M A Centerfold (B), Moberly
Dragonfire's Teddy 'O Nat-Sam (D), Marcum
Elusive Glory Be O'Chang Tang (B), De Voll & Schaffer
Fancee Gunning Priscilla (B), Gunning & Wheeler
Fancee Gunning Tom Foolery (D), Craig, Craig & Wheeler
Fran-Oaks Midnight Edition (D), Francis
Jen Len's Patty Cake (B), Olson
Lainee Make Believe (B), Meltzer
Mei San Dee O Gee (D), Peterson & Meidlinger
Mo Tzu's Gold Digger (B), Thomas & Easton
Mo Tzu's Marco Polo Ofweinric (D), Weinman
Six J's Jaqui's Joy Jal Wei (B), Gaffney & Pouliot
Skywalker Milinia (B), Kahn & Sanchez
Stylistic Kual-Lo Shalimar (B), Shepherd

4/87 Jo-Ahn's Alexis O'Munchkintown (B), Eckhardt
M And R's Jual Master Charger (D), Rukavina & Graber
Mei San Cameo's Raphael (B), Beiden & Potts
Pe-Kee's Char Gin Tu Win (D), Hyatt
Rockee Vollee Qp Cupcake (B), Mueller
Shados Ama Sheik Gentleben (D), Hazelwood & Mundy
Tumac's Epitimmy (D), McIntee & McIntee

5/87 CanAm's Sun Tu Vom Arvind (D), Kerr
Dragonfire's Mary Gold (B), Hogg
Lav's Cannon Ball Express (D), Hisaka & Wilson
Meeko's Kristal Reflections (B), Meek & Meek
Mei Shan's Tiffaney Chin (B), Burley & Cartwright
Ming Dynasty's Magic Moment (B), Blackburn & Blackburn
Mo Tzu's Tia Maria (B), Thomas
Pen Sans Cat's Got Your Tung (B), Busselman
Shado's MacIntosh (D), Hewitson
Shafer's Jazz O'Nat-Sam (D), Marcum
Shar-Ming's Pistol Pete (D), Bilicich
Ty-Won-On's Mischievous Megan (B), Hammond

6/87 Achilles Dang Sal Dragonfire (D), Cham
Akitzu Simply Sassafras (B), Piper & Piper
Bubeck Gang Sing V Shan Ku (D), Whitehead & Whitehead
Chinai's Chantilly Lace (B), Grasberger

Dashi's Abbey Dab-A-Do (B), Pouliet
Dragonwyck's Centerfold (D), Moberly
Indian Summer's Rebel Toot (D), Neal
Ka-Ja-Leens' Sha-Boo Magic Trix (D), Franklin
Kai Shih Talk Of The Town (D), Semple
Laksana's Li Ning (D), Shakofsky & Joris
Lipo's Knight Errant (D), Gidusko
Lou Wan Fancee Gunning Ad Lib (B), Wheeler & Gunning
Lou Wan Fancee Gunning Alibi (B), Wheeler & Gunning
Mei San O Dis Is Sum Wun (D), Meidlinger & Potts
Mundy's Ama Koz-Mo-Polly-Tan (B), Mundy
R And R Embers Of Fire (D), Cherry & Cherry
Regal's Road To Rio (D), Regelman
Robaras Domino Monkeydo (D), Flaharty & Flaharty
Shado's Ama Primadona Bouncer (D), Hewitson & Mundy
Shado's Fancy Free (B), Hewitson
Shihchi's Live Fantasy (B), Oystrick & Oystrick
Show Off's Daddy Tressed Me (B), Williams
Tang Kou's Mahogany Rebel (B), Martin
Tu Chu's Sky's The Limit (D), Kwait
Tumac's Theodore (D), McIntee
Vandemere's It Ain'T Ez B'N Ez (D), Lloyd

7/87 Akitzu Strawberry Bon Bon (B), Wright & Wright
August Moon's Sweet Cheeks (B), Nanni & Kennedy
Chang Tang's Elusive Jeffrey (D), Devoll & Devoll
China Chimes Shadow Of Slew (D), Heilman & Strapp
Fancee Gunning Fool Proof (D), Wheeler & Gunning
Gremar Teddy's Rough Rider (D), Calverase
Lainee Priority Parcel (B), Meltzer
Lou Wan Effervescent (B), Katz, Hermann, Guggenheim & Wheeler
Mandarin Purple Rain O Lyric (D), Di Nicola, Lynn & Poole
Ming Dynasty's Right Signal (D), Blackburn & Blackburn
Sheng Ti's Dreamy Drawers (B), Mantie & Gentry
Wenrick's Holly N-Rustinwood (B), Romano & Romano

8/87 J-Mor's Autumn Colour (B), Guerra & Friese
Joylin's Treasure Of Gold (D), Pittelli
Pen Sans Parti Caper (B), Busselman
R And R Hot Ta Trot (B), Cherry & Cherry,
Regal's Mr Ted E Bear (D), Regelman & Regelman
Ric-Shaw's Hi Fashion Boutiq (B), Foster
Rojacky's Special Edition (D), Henderson
Shafer's Cluny Lace (B), Shafer
Shou Mi In The Spotlight (D), Atchley
Shuzan's Fancee Beatrice (B), Ammons & Wheeler
Tru Gems Sugar Dragon (D), Acton & Acton
Wingates Juris Prudence (B), Williams

9/87 Billies Follie Burma Shave (D), Shaver & Shaver
Briden's Golden Hussey (B), Vinacco & Vinacco
Chang Tang Seven Come Eleven (D), Milligan
Chin-Chu's Risin' Son (D), Ikeda & Hall
Choo Ling's Red Royalty (D), Campbell
Dalai Copper Peny Fridalla (B), Pennington & Mabry
Dragonfire's Leading Lady (B), Hogg
El Jardin De Liberty's Tree (B), Martin
Faerie Dean Midas Touch (D), Sylvia
Genisa's Good Time Charley (D), Crooks & Crooks
Hei-Di's Desiderata (D), Selvig
Jolei Majorette (B), Kijowski
Kee Lee Deja Vu Moonlight Lady (B), Lee & Kiernan
Kuai Lo Stylistic Tapestry (B), Iliesco & Shepherd
Langpur Careless Whisper (B), Papke & Papke
Lomel Kandlekiss Of Tall Oak (B), Shaner & Shaner
Lou Wan Dorworth Mr Fridley (D), Doherty
Meekos Supercharged (D), Meek
Molnars Rich And Rare (D), Molnar
Pe-Kae's Sam-Sun (D), Smith & Arrington
Pen Sans Political Parti (D), Busselman & Nowatzki
Pen Sans Tuti Fruti Shalimar (B), Thompson
R And R Red Hot Sizzler (D), Cherry & Cherry
Shail-Hi Mischief Maker (D), Kong

Shail-Hi Ya-Si-Am Munchkintown (D), Eckhardt & Goss
Taylwag's Glitter Bug (D), Taylor & Wagner
Tiara Stylistic Twn-N-Country (D), Rubino & Shepherd
Tiara Stylistic Vogue (B), Rubino & Shepherd
Tu Chu's Fire Opal Kimiling (B), Raber, Feld & Koppel
Ultra's Only Make Believe (B), Nicholas
Woodsmoke Critics Choice (D), Shupe & Shupe
Woodsmoke's Simply Timeless (B). Miller

10/87　An-Di's Painted Lady (B), Milligan & Alderman
Anjuli's Tamara At Mei San (B), Meidlinger & Parker
Bing's A Head Of His Class (D), Bingaman & Bingaman
Boogen's Early Morning Frost (B), Paulsen & Paulsen
Cane's Sizzlin' Rose Of Sabar (B), Cane, Cane & Craig
Dexy Smart Alek Of Chi-Nees (D), Steinmiller &
　　Mussleman
Granville Yung Wip R Snap Erh (D), Russell
Gunning's It's A Wonder (D), Fletcher & Hoey
Heavenly Dynasty's Regal Duke (D), White & Lawall
Hun Fu Jr Gee Man (D), Lawrence, Webb & De Luca
Loubren's Saddle Tramp (D), Eckhardt
M And R's Jual Won Ton Woman (B), Rukavina & Graber
Mei San Sweet Daquiri (B), Meidlinger
Mi Heart Breaker (D), Buck
Shan Ku Chin Te (B), Vallee & Vallee
Sheng Ti's Mike Hammer (D), McQuade & Mantie
Shih Yeh Ah So Little Wascal (D), Hubbard & Hubbard

11/87　Beswicks Private Treaty (D), Waters
Dacun's Red-Hot Street Walker (B), Cass & Cunningham
Emperor's Nikki Fashion (B), McDonald
Ginkgo Nickelodeon (D), Pipkorn & Pipkorn
Lainee Out To Lunch (B), Meltzer
Lenacia's Careless Whisper (B), Charlebois & Charlebois
Lou Wan Rebel's Valley Girl (B), Gossett & Gossett
Mitsu's Rainy Day Rainbow (B), Joens
Mundy's Ama Classic Case (D), Rogers & Rogers
Nanjo R Gyle Sox Of Jj (D), Schloz
Pen Sans All Dolled Up (B), Reiling & Reiling
Rockee Vollee Banshee-No (B), Forcier & Mueller
Rockee Vollee Masterpiece (D), Wilson & Mueller

Sabar's Goin'In Style (D), Craig & Craig
San Yen Kojac (D), Cham
Shado's Crystal Dynasty (B), Bachman
Shar-Ming Jost A Chatter Box (D), Bilicich & Gudgell
Show Off's Her Highness (B), Lane & Lane
Show Off's Just The Ticket (D), Milanich & Milanich
Sun-Che Golden Sun Of Wufpak (D), Riggs
Tu Chu's No Limit Munchkintown (B), Eckhardt
Wingate's T K Ritz (D), Frothingham

12/87　Bei Jing O Nathan Of Shansl (D), Shada & Martello
Bon D'Art Wheirs The Fire (D), Hammon
Cb's Marja Roses Are Red (B), Gerbe & Puglise
Chang Tang's Sky's The Limit (D), Collin
Don Wal Buttermilk Skies (B), Wadsworth
Dragonwyck Danielles Delite (B), Nichols & Patton
Granville Fa Pitti Sake (B), Russell
Jebar's Tribal Spirit (D), Gangi & Kotwitz
Kinsa Fancy Philamina (B), Savio & Kinney
Mai-T-Toi's Scorpio (D), Nisbet & Nisbet
Mei San Sizzling Si'Arra (B), Potts & Meidlinger
Ming Dynasty's Major Leader (D), West & Blackburn
Nemesis Of Woodrose (B), Oganeku & Oganeku
Pekings Maid To Order Wenshu (B), Connaughton &
　　Clough
Pem's Gotta Hugga Bunch (B), Mushrush & Reese
Pen Sans Arietta Of Yu Wang (B), Steffens
Pen Sans Sprout Of Li Ming (B), Nowatzki, Busselman &
　　Tendler
Quin-Don's Faith Hope And Charity (B), Burchi & Burchi
R And R's Fiery Rebellion (D), Cherry & Cherry
Regal's Black Eyed Tulip (B), Regelman & Regelman
Regal's Rum Collins (D), Canaan & Regelman
Rosehill's Rosana Dana (B), Bryant
Santini's Orion Belt (D), Montemurro & Montemurro
Shali-Hi's Tutu Much (B), Goss
Su Pan U's Dotz Kt Kiss N Tell (B), Biller
Tri-Na's Knight Rider (D), Hindman
Wenrick's M's Kelly N' Sou Yen (B), Paquette

Ch. Dragonwyck Dragonfire, co-owned by Norman Patton and J. Chip Constantino.

Ch. Encore Sun Flower Splendor, owned by Jane Fitts.

Ch. Hullaballou J. Ray Of Nanjo, owned by Jay and Linda Ballou.

Ch. House of Wu Mai Mai, owned by Ann A. H. Warner.

Ch. House of Wu Boi Named Tzu, owned by Harry and Charlotte Amonett.

Ch. Witch's Wood Soket Tumi, owned by Marilyn M. Guiraud and then Mrs. Dinelli.

Am. and Can. Ch. Elusive Glory Be O' Chang Tang, owned by Joyce and Hal DeVoll.

Ch. Hodari Lord Of The Rings, owned by Joyce Nelson DeVoll.

Pamela Chennels, former junior handler, daughter of Jackie Peterson of Jazmin Kennels. Pamela became a high fashion model in New York City and Milan, Italy.

Mar-Lin's Tien Wu Mo Kuei, C.D., with owner Kathleen Newman. Kathy is a former junior handler who has become a professional handler, as well as handling her own dogs in conformation and obedience competition.

Madeline Thornton handling Ch. Encore Siegen, bred by Jane Fitts and owned by Anna Cowie. Madeline was a junior handler before turning professional.

Anne McDaniel as a junior handler showing Lil Sing, winner of the Puppy Bitch Class, with Georgia Moore presenting the award. Georgia, also a former junior handler, went on to handling professionally.

Junior Showmanship

Junior handling classes are offered at most all-breed and Specialty shows, including the ASTC National Specialty. In these classes, juniors are judged on their abilities as handlers. Judging is based on finesse and professionalism, not the quality of the dog. It is helpful, of course, if the dog is well trained, but championship quality or even good show quality is not necessary.

Class divisions are Novice Junior, Open Junior, Novice Senior, and Open Senior. The winners of each class may compete for Best Junior. After three First Place wins in Novice classes, the handler progresses to Open competition. Thus, Novice Junior is for boys and girls ten to thirteen years of age on the day of the show, who have not placed First three times in a Novice class at a licensed show. Open Junior is for boys and girls ten to thirteen years of age who previously have placed First three items.

The Senior classes are for handlers thirteen to seventeen years of age on the day of the show, with other requirements the same as for Novice Junior and Open Junior classes.

The dog must be owned or co-owned by the junior handler or by the handler's father, mother, brother, sister, uncle, aunt, grandparent, or corresponding step- or half-relatives. The dog must be eligible for regular competition in AKC-licensed shows.

It is important for the dog to be well groomed. Nails should be trimmed, ears and teeth clean, coat shining and brushed. The dog should be in good weight.

Junior Showmanship competition can be stiff — especially for juniors who are not from a dog-oriented family. But the competition provides juniors with opportunities to learn about dogs in general and about their own breed in particular. Junior competition prepares participants for a future which may include breeding, professional handling, and/or judging. Even if a future in dogs is not the outcome, junior showmanship provides opportunities for learning responsibility and good sportsmanship, and acquiring self-confidence — which help in establishing a good foundation for a future in any field.

Bob Alexander, former junior handler, is shown here with Ch. Mei San Stage Door Johnnie winning the Toy Group. Bob, now a professional handler, is the owner of Johnnie. Betty Meidlinger is breeder and co-owner.

Diane Kijowski, professional handler, began her career as a junior handler. Here she is pictured with Ch. Chang Tang's Elusive Jeffrey, after handling him to a Toy Group First in May 1987. Jeffrey was bred by Joyce DeVoll and Bonnie Schaffer and is owned by Joyce and Hal DeVoll.

Tammy Tremont, now handling successfully as an adult, was a junior handler when she took Ch. Chaka Khan di Visconti to Winners Bitch over nearly a hundred bitches from the American-Bred Class. Jon Ferrante and Constance Smart are co-breeders of Chaka Khan.

Junior handler Sarah Miller showed her expertise in the ring with a favorite Shih Tzu.

Kathleen M. Newman handled Bilor's Golden Buster Duster to BOS in the 1981 Mispillion Kennel Club Show.

Michelle Miller was only 10 when she handled Yingsu's Strawberry Roan to First Place at the Greenville Kennel Club Show in July 1983—and it was Michelle's first show.

Ch. Rockee Vollee Velvetier with breeder/owner Helen J. Mueller.

Ch. Joylin's Rebel Reflection. Owned by Hilde D. Pittelli. Handled by Miwako Hosaka.

Am. and Can. Ch. Mei San O Dis Is Sum Wun, bred and owned by Betty Meidlinger.

Ch. Wenrick's Panda Bear, owned by Wendy and Richard Paquette.

Ch. Joylin's Treasure Of Gold, owned by Hilde D. Pittelli.

Ch. Pen San's Sprout of Li Ming, owned by Gloria Busselman.

113

Witch's Wood Sent RGM Pansy, C.D.X., and Witch's Wood Little Sister, granddaughters of Ch. Mar Del's Golden Sunset and Ch. Chumulari Li Tzu. Both are owned by Marilyn M. Guiraud.

Obedience Competition

For hundreds of years, dogs have been used in England and Germany in connection with police and guard work, and their working potential has been evaluated through tests devised to show agility, strength, and courage.

There was little interest in obedience training in the United States until 1933 when Mrs. Whitehouse Walker returned from England and enthusiastically introduced the sport. Two years later, Mrs. Walker persuaded The American Kennel Club to approve organized obedience activities and to assume jurisdiction over obedience rules. Since then, interest has increased at a phenomenal rate, for obedience competition is suitable for all breeds. Furthermore, there is no limit to the number of dogs that may win in competition, for each dog is scored individually on the basis of a point rating system.

The dog is judged on his response to certain commands, and if he gains a high enough score in three successive trials under different judges, he wins an obedience title. Three progressive titles are awarded: "C.D." — Companion Dog; "C.D.X." — Companion Dog Excellent; and "U.D." — Utility Dog. Another title, the "T.D." or Tracking Dog title, may be won at any time and tests for it are held apart from dog shows. In late 1979, the Board of Directors of The American Kennel Club approved the test for the Tracking Dog Excellent ("T.D.X.") title. Eligibility for this title is limited to dogs that already have earned the Tracking Dog title.

Effective July 1, 1977, the AKC approved the awarding of the Obedience Trial Champion ("O.T.Ch.") title. To be eligible for this title, a dog must have earned the Utility Dog title and then must earn one hundred points in competition, placing First three times under different judges.

Trials for obedience trained dogs, held at most of the larger bench shows and obedience training clubs, are to be found in almost all communities today. All dogs must comply with the same rules, although in broad jump, high jump, and bar jump exercises, the jumps are adjusted to the size of the breed.

The Novice class is for dogs that have not won the title Companion Dog. Novice competition includes such exercises as heeling on and off lead, the stand for examination, coming on recall, and the long sit and the long down.

In Open competition, the dog must perform such exercises as heeling free, the drop on recall, and the retrieve on the flat and over the high jump. Also, the dog must execute the broad jump. The dog must complete the long sit and long down with the owner out of sight.

In the Utility Class, competition includes scent discrimination, the directed retrieve, the signal exercise, directed jumping, and the group examination.

Tracking is always done out-of-doors, of course, and for obvious reasons, the competition cannot be held at a dog show. The dog must follow a scent trail that is about a quarter mile in length. He also is required to find a scent object (glove, wallet, or other article) left by a stranger who has walked the course to lay down the scent. The dog is required to follow the trail a half to two hours after the scent is laid.

Shih Tzu that have earned obedience titles are listed on the following pages in order of year and month of publication in *Pure-bred Dogs/American Kennel Gazette*. The name(s) following the dog's name is (are) the person(s) who owned the dog at the time the obedience title was earned.

Helen's Bit of Brandy, U.D. ("Scooter"), retrieves over the high jump in the Open exercise.

O.T.Ch. Helen's Brandy, T.D. ("Brandy"), goes over the broad jump in the Open exercise.

1966 Si-Kiangs Puddy-Kat (D), Clinch
      Da-Lu Of Brabania (B), Booth
1968 Chumulari Woo-Muh (B), Runkel
      Bambu Jubilee Jaz-Min (B), Seng & Fenton
      Bambu I Jaunti Tiger (D), Salo
1969 Chang-Hi Of Mem-Ten (D), Johnson
      Misty Isle Tashi Shu (B), Jorgensen
      Salween Ed Dzong (D), Crompton
1970 Silverheels Lei of Lotus (B), Stubblefield
      Dang Po Kyi (D), Baker
      Tohatsu Of Sherilyn (D), Heldman
      Wendy Wong of Myarlune (B), Fenton
      Caramont Dixie Darling (B), Crompton
1971 Lo Gay Kao (D), Hunt
      Ch Si-Kiangs Say It Again (D), Craig & Kellogg
      Ch Si Kiang's I Ko Tien Shih (B), White
      Ling Mai Chin (B), Warinner
      Senja Rimpache (D), Crompton
1972 Pat-Tez-Aloha (B), McCann
      Yum-Yum (B), Cowan
      Mogene's Nan Susui Yan (B), Blasinski
      Moko's Lo-Tsu (D), Thompson
      Omar Play Boy (D), Hollingsworth
2/73 Shao Mei Ai Chung (B)
3/73 Dugmore Hotsy Totsy (B)
      Ch. Ku Che Toi of Antarctica (D)
      Mai Tai Tasha (D)
      Mei-Hua Mai Minh of Leistraum (B)
      Sherilyn's Wan T'Ung (B)
      Tengri Nor of Brough (D)
5/73 Rim Po Che (D), Shapiro
6/73 Ho-Tai of Shamrock (D), Milton
11/73 Tasmin Puppity (B), Hegyes
5/74 Char Nick S'Wing Erh of Copa (D), Nickerson
      Emperor's Quapaw Dakota Sioux (B), Core & McCarty
      Gin-Doc's Suzy Wong (B), Weber
      Lou Wan Casinova (D), Gec
      Mar Del's Chiajen Of Copa (B), Nickerson
      Paradises Silver Lining (D), Starwalt & Becker
      Sonja of Marlboro (B), Novick
      Town Hall's Hallelujah (B), Patton
6/74 Snuffy Lou (B), Rascoe
7/74 Woo Muh Jade (B), Hegyes
9/74 Runkel's Ebony Yama (D), Williams & Runkel
      Top Dolly of Lexden (B), Schoberlin
12/74 Pat Tez Mia Ackiko (B), Fiskland
      Vitahund's Hsien-Sheng (D), Winchell
1/75 Fitzgerald (D), Carter
      Sandra's Yum Yum of Wildwood (D), Pederzini
      Yangtze Buster (D), Lockard
3/75 Chattee Cathee's Charlie Chan (D), Newman
      Foo Mahn Chow of Chu Ros (D), Haller
      Heavenly Dynasty Toy Tang Kou (B), Stansell
      Pat Tez Kung Fu Fredie (D), McDowell
      Rainey's Ah-So-Mi-Tee-Mo (D), Steel
      Thetzu Yi Xiong (D), Knoch
4/75 Shalimar Wang Hsuan Shou (D), Heldman
      Shangri La's Mai Tai (D), Immel
5/75 Pat Tez Po Go (D), McCann
6/75 Golden Girl Sandy (B), Titshaw
7/75 Odyssey's Miss-Priss Shelly (B), Hein
      Starfire Sun Kiang (B), Lockard
      Yen-Chi (B), Lockard
9/75 Chattee Cathee's Che Mo T'ien (D), Newman
10/75 Linglewood's Dusty Chan (D), Shuttleworth
11/75 Chadonn's Chin-Chin (D), Fetzer & Fries
      Kenmors' Kwan Yen (B], Dullinger

12/75 Mee Ko's Domino (D), Dayhuff
1/76 Fu Ming (D), Christensen
2/76 Mei Tu Vi (D), Ruskin
3/76 Laura's Skoshi Tomodachi (B), Topacio
      Mr. Ching of Red Bud City (D), Damm
5/76 Bogy's Mikiko Kiyoshii (D), Bogy
      Pat Tez USA Ko (B), Fiskland
      Pat Tez Yoshiko (B), McCann
6/76 A Bit of Flower Power (D), McAteer
      Heavenly Dynasty's Wynd Chyme (B), Stansell & Kerstein
      Keinan Cho-Cho (B), Criss
      Keinan Cyn-A-Mon (D), Criss
      Mariljac Millicent (B), Russell
      Mi Ti Fli N Mouse of La Ke (D), Johnson
8/76 Lyric's By Kirby (D), Falcone
9/76 Lady Lucy's Fancy Pants (B), Sicca
      Me Li Su Lin (B), Green
10/76 Kay Pierce (D), Montello
11/76 Beedoc's Hei Yeuh (D), Parashis
      Cooper's Fortune Cookie (B), Cooper
      Floridonna Chow Mein Noodles (D), Ellis & Lockard
      Lady Kismet (B), Hoban
      Lingchoo Woochin (D), Arnold
      Vitahund's Tu-Tzu (B), Whitman & Lindblom
12/76 Bickford's Kwang Lo Wun (D), Rosenthal
1/77 Ming Nan Ssu of Afmoon (B), Rohr & Rohr
2/77 Copa The Jasmin Patch (B), Densten
3/77 Poo Choo's Puff of Wind (B), DeSantis
6/77 Bellaire's Hawkeye Pierce (D), Rouanzoin
      Jerry's Choy Chen (D), La Peer
      Obilo Wong (D), Green
7/77 Benjamin Bartholomu Khaja (D), Ingram
      Madame Mystic Of Tian Shan (B), King
      Shansang Teko Of Timber Hills (D), Roeder
8/77 Chi Chi Ba Ba Ne Ha Wa (B), Kurimsky
9/77 Magestic Mop-Ze Of Mudacres (B), Payne
      Natasha Ling (B), Janson
      Teddy Taurus Albert (D), Albert
2/78 Cooper's Tong Shah Hai (B), Cooper
      Sunshine's Honey Bear (D), Prentice
3/78 Aagalynn's Rocky Road (D), Horowitz
      Fantail's Mai Tai Ling (B), Holtz
      H D's Forever-Amber (B), Doroff
      San Yen Ho-Chi Rea-Li Sumting (D), Christensen
4/78 Floridonna May Ting (B), Markowitz
      Milly J's Precious Pixie (B), Lumadue & Lumadue
      Wu-Ming Of Vandutchess (D), Van De Carr
6/78 Chateau's Ying Hao Ching (D), Ayanian
      Si Kiang's Fidget Fufu (D), Castellano
7/78 Helen's Brandy (D), Cash
      Pat Tez Chi I Sai Kohrogi (B), Fiskland
      Pat Tez Honalee (B), McCann
9/78 Chung Ho (D), Schuldt
      Miso Tse Sing (D), Benincase
      Pat Tez Dallas (B), McCann
      Pat Tez Tiffany's Lu Yen (B), Miller
11/78 Mai-Ling Molly (B), Bachman
      Mr. Chips VII (D), Skobjak
12/78 Ny Magdolin Wind Of Cho Sen (B), Coley
1/79 Chin Yu Farbin's Mahogany (B), Rice
2/79 Amapola Of Legibach (B), Leone
      Ch. Emperor's Thunderhill Buddah (D), Christensen
      Fang Chu's Lipton Chee (D), Hollingsworth & Brown
      Li Tsu (B), Neal
      Morgan's Chardonn Bernard (D), Eubanks
4/79 Kathy's Suzy Ssu Ling (B), Pearce
      Mei-Hua Iechibon (D), Whitman & Winchell
      Sen Sei's Stormi Weather (B), Berdeski
5/79 Sen Sei's Blackberri Brandi (B), Berdeski

6/79 Pat-Tez Aw Kumon Iwana (B), Fiskland
Su Roc's Sun Sauron (D), Perryman & Perryman
7/79 H. Bogart (D), Taylor
8/79 Joo-Ling Of Topaz (D), Munkers
Le-Pre-Chaun Happi-Hummer (B), Smith
Shang-Hi Flower Drum Song (B), Debus
Sir Charlie Chan II (D), Hurliman
9/79 Ch C's Gold Kung Fu Of Tingerto (D), Christensen &
Busselman
10/79 Hidden Cove's Sand Pebble (B), Young
Ling Su Ling (B), Burchi
12/79 Hai Sing Bah Sha Of Pen (D), Christensen
1/80 Portneuf's Pitti-Wun (D), Wadsworth
3/80 Chop Tzuzi (B), Vaughn
Hong Kong Holiday (B), Stein
Lolin (B), Smith
4/80 Ah-Fok (B), Donlon
Heavenly Dynasty's Bit O Venus (B), Hardy
5/80 Beedoc's Million Dollar Baby (D), Lursen
6/80 Syan Bai Gung Jru (B), Panuska
7/80 Cooper's Chann Yu Of Pat-Tez (B), Cooper
Mar Lin's Tien Wu Mo Kuei (D), Newman
8/80 Ch Imua The Gatsby's Pride O' Ali-Aj (D), Castellano
Pat-Tez Wojo Of Brighton (D), Bennett
Pen Sans Chimney Sweep (B), Marsh
Sunshine's Honey Bear (D), Prentice
Tchin-Tchin Dar Ling (B), Savitt & Boyd
Tilford Toe (B), Frantzman
9/80 Hua Siing Petey-O Torpedo (D), Hampson
Pat-Tez Kuan-Yen (D), Payne
11/80 Amanda Aurigna Joens (B), Joens
12/80 Hwa Ja Ming (B), Goodling
Vanhalen's You Really Got Me (D), Poe
1/81 Mister Ping Pong (D), Mathes
Santini's Big Guy From Cosenza (D), Montemurro
2/81 Ah So Khe-Mo Sah-Bi (D), Nadorff
Jingle Belles N Sunshine (B), Bruner
Mister Happy Of Campo Bello (D), Preston
5/81 Ali-Aj Tai Chin Shih (D), Jacobs
6/81 Diddle Bit Dust Ball (D), McCaffrey
St. Aubrey Garnet Of Elsdon (D), Van De Carr
Witch's Wood Bits N Pieces (D), Hawley
Witch's Wood Grizzly Adams (D), Hawley
7/81 Chiroyal's Song Of Spring (B), Strully & Boyd
Mariposa III (B), Barton
Pierponts Ti Ling (D), Pierpont
8/81 Little Gidget (B), Carter
9/81 Collets Toby Tyler (D), Dinardo
Jedcott's Chief Cooder (D), Sokal
Karen's Ma Choo Macho (D), Forehand
10/81 Prince Ace High (D), Berlin
Silver Frost Peppy (D), Mabry
11/81 Nanjo Amber Waves In Snow (B), McCans
1/82 Ch. Pen Sans Peaches N' Cream (B), Christensen
2/82 Charlie's Angel III (B), Hoffman
Tu De Live Wire (D), Dede
Yen Den Ixtapa Outlaw (D), Brennan
3/82 Pat Tez Lei Che (D), McCann
Witch's Wood Sent Rgm Pansy (B), Guiraud & Meyer
4/82 Shawn-Lee-Egan (D), Egan
7/82 China Bandit (D), Zankl & Zankl
Hsiao Kung Chu II (B), Dowke
Kee Lee's Double Fantasy (B), Petrone & Laible
Muppet XVIII (B), Zankl & Zankl
Nanjo's Whispering Wind (B), Rhein
8/82 Frederick (D), Berry
9/82 Bar-D's Dar-Ying O'sultan's (D), Mills
Ch Kee Lee's Om Tzo Tza Tzi (B), Ioia
Sunny Skies' J T (D), Ellis
Tzu-Ling-Ber-Ni-Malang (D), Seegmiller
11/82 Bel Air Trick-E-Wu Of Doncar (B), Hapke
Bright Soul Sister (B), Stephenson

Tu Chu Vardig Alf (D), Rohr
2/83 Cl's Montana's Koko Bear (D), Lindstrand
4/83 Baker's Twinkle Toes (B), Baker
Saucy Sugar (B), Cloutier
5/83 China Doll Ying Ming Suzi (B), Fowler
6/83 Godwin's Macho Len Shun (D), Godwin
Tcherri Juba-Lee (B), Boyd & Savitt
Wes Ro's Jolly Jason (D), Dorsey
7/83 Helen's Bit Of Brandy (D), Cash
9/83 Hi Ho Of Paloma (D), Hammond
10/83 Chumulari Ka Fai (B), Pletl
Kaduna's Santini Lan-Sing (B), Montemurro
Pat-Tez Paisley Skye (B), Atchley
11/83 Bar-D's Bee Daz-L-Ying O'sultan's (B), Bardee & Mills
Chi Chi Lee Pin Mei Chi (D), Vogel
Gwinn-Deli's Shang-Hai-Ku (D), Griffin
12/83 Chu Ti Ling (D), Aust
Toby Kin Tey (D), Seigfried
1/84 Bi-Wood's Valree Valentine (B), Martin
Mei San's Friend Jasper Jones (D), Carter
Pepper In Propria Persona (B), Saliano
Portneufs Disco Dani (D), Christensen
Regal Little Dawn (B), Dearringer
Ro Hu Ru's Kumo (D), Eveland
Tiki Poo (B), Theen
2/84 Faerie Dean Jabil's My-T-Genie (D), Sylvia
Manjusri I Ching (D), L'Heureux
3/84 Hodari Spiced Ice (B), Hoover
Shih Huang Ti Wu (D), Hurliman
6/84 Xiao Ting (D), Struthers
7/84 Ch Kachina's Sugar N Spice (B), Kregar
Ch Rockee Vollee Woopie I'M Alive (D), Pipkorn
8/84 Ben Je Fu Yung (D), Goole
9/84 Mei Sweet Kumiko (B), Pamperin
1/85 Phildore's Luk-E-Dixi Li (B), Hubbard
Who-Dat Ron Ko Samurai (D), Nickerson
2/85 An-Di's Sheide Of Wei Bear (D), Cornelius
Seiko Beene Mcdougal (B), Levy
3/85 Carolyn's Sami O (D), O'steen
Ragtime Cowboy (D), Rosenthal
Seigfreids Shan Dee Cane (D), Seigfried
7/85 Freddie Lai Foo (D), Cloutier
Rojes Wild Sin-Sa-Shon (D), Pritchard & Wild
Sunhigh's Brilliant Bo (D), Vorholt
Symans Ginger Snap Of Paloma (B), Hammond
8/85 Kiki's Stardust Morn (B), McCaffrey
Kim-Gay Yenta (B), Yoder
Tibetan Bear (D), Bortner
11/85 Hodari Hai-V Happiness Is (B), Hoover
Joy's Golden Genie (B), Treloar
Sam Aling-Meyer (D), Meyer
11/85 Bel Air Trick-E-Wu Of Doncar (B), Hapke
12/85 Cin-Cin May Ling (B), Simpson
Fanny Fu (B), Twinem
1/86 Ho Lang's Jennie Reb (B), Warren
Teddi's Fanci Tashi (B), Cornelius
Tomlin's Madame Sang (B), Durocher
2/86 Chans Chinny Pete (D), Jorgensen
Lin Sing Tu-Tu (B), Jorgensen
Ming Su's Precious Pandora (B), Laboar
5/86 Ma Crystal Starfire (B), Stark & Sabol
6/86 Sa Lu Se Abigail (B), Ainscough & Ainscough
Shar's Golden Dragon (D), King
7/86 Chu's Dottie Ling (B), Martinka
Ch Mei Sans Dirty White Boy (D), Meidlinger
8/86 Arca Sunn-Shyner (B), Watson
Pekay's Move Over (B), Drobac
9/86 Tien Chin Ssu War Lord (D), Jeffries
10/86 Baffles Chin Su (B), Coleman & Coleman
Skeeter Vi (D), Best
11/86 Toranaga's Kubilai Khan (D), Rossier & Rossier
12/86 Charlotte's Sasha Lu (B), Kirkegaard

Left: Brandy finds the article in the scent discrimination exercise. Right: Brandy retrieves over the high jump in the Open exercise.

Left: Brandy finds the glove in the Tracking exercise. Right: Brandy retrieves it.

Left: Brandy jumps the high jump in the directed jumping exercise, Utility Class. Right: Brandy retrieves over the high jump in the Open competition.

Companion Dogs Excellent

Utility Dogs

Utility Dogs Tracking

Obedience Trial Champions

Am., Can., and Ber. Ch. Winemaker's Pla-Boi, owned and handled by Fay Wine.

Am. and Can. Ch. Shente's Christian Dior, owned by Margaret Brown.

The Shih Tzu in Canada

The best Shih Tzu from Canada compete very successfully with the best from the United States. Canadian-bred Shih Tzu have been among winners at the American Shih Tzu Club Specialty Shows, Westminster Kennel Club Shows, and many other major shows in the United States. Canadian Shih Tzu fanciers have contributed heavily to breed improvement in the Americas, and exchanges of stock across borders are common occurrences today.

In Canada the Shih Tzu competes in the Non-Sporting Group, where, after a Best-of-Breed win, the Shih Tzu competes with the Lhasa Apso and other breeds that are included in the Non-Sporting Group in the United States as well as in Canada. The American Kennel Club recognizes the Shih Tzu as part of the Toy Group, but the difference in Group does not affect comparative breed characteristics of dogs bred in the United States and those bred in Canada. It probably is true, though (as some contend), that larger outstanding Shih Tzu from the United States have won more Groups in Canada as "Specials" than they might have done in the United States because of their size.

American and Canadian Ch. Mar Del's King Kanishka, an American-bred son of Ch. Mar Del's Ring A Ding Ding out of Aagalynn's Water Chestnut, is cited as an example. A fine specimen, Kanishka was bred by Margaret Edel of Mar Del fame. He was sold to Bonnie Miller, D.V.M., and was campaigned by her in the United States, "finished," and then sent to Canada to be campaigned, "finished," and "Specialed" in the Non-Sporting Group. Kanishka was considered large by judges in the United States. Bonnie's decision to send him to Canada proved wise. He became a top Shih Tzu winner in Canada in the early 1970s. His son, bred by Bonnie, became American and Canadian Ch. Sanchi's Vhima after he was sold to Winemakers Kennels. Vhima was a small male and eventually was bred to Ch. Lansu Magnolia Time, an English import. From this breeding came American Ch. Jaisu X-Rated of Lainee, bred by Jay Ammon and owned and campaigned by Elaine Meltzer.

Another American-owned English import who became a top Canadian winner in the early 1970s was Ch. Choo Lang of Telota. Choo Lang (as was discussed elsewhere in this book) was Best in Show at the prestigious Canadian "Show of Shows," for which the entry is limited to Canadian Best-in-Show winners. Choo Lang was imported to the United States by William Guzzy and Peter Federico. Both Kanishka and Choo Lang were outstanding movers, and although Choo Lang was much smaller than Kanishka, his movement surely made him a noticed contender among the larger dogs also competing in Canadian Non-Sporting Groups.

Mr. and Mrs. Jeffrey Carrique's "Carrimount" influence was tremendously important. They imported the bitch Ch. Brownhills Yolan of Greenmoss from England. When she was bred to American and Canadian Ch. Chumulari Ying Ying, she produced American, Canadian, and Bermudian Ch. Carrimount Ah Chop Chop, who sired Janet and Charles Long's Ch. Long's Chiny Chin Ah Chop Chop, producer of twenty-seven American champions.

Carrique-bred Shih Tzu won in Canada and took many top honors in the United States. Ch. Carrimount Ah Tiko Tiko was Best of Breed and Fourth in the Group at the 1975 Westminster Kennel Club Show; Carrimount Ah Chun Ki was Reserve Winners Dog at the 1976 Westminster Kennel Club Show; and Carrimount Ah Flip Flop was Reserve Winners Dog at the 1973 American Shih Tzu Club National Specialty.

Patricia Dickinson piloted her Canadian Ch. Carrimount Ah Ting Ting to tops in the breed in Canada. Patricia seems to be the standard bearer of the line and the record keeper of the years the Carriques were breeding.

American and Canadian Ch. Greenmoss Golden Frolic of Elfann was brought to Canada from Greenmoss Kennels in England. He was bred by Freda Evans of English "Elfann" fame. English Ch. Greenmoss Chin-Ki of Meo was the top producing Shih Tzu stud in England. He was bred to Golden Bobbin of Elfann to produce Golden Jasmine of Elfann — another Shih Tzu brought to Canada and shown to the championship title there. Pedigrees prove that the English "Greenmoss" with the English "Elfann" produced outstanding and influential Shih Tzu.

Fortunately, the Leadbitters (Greenmoss) and Freda Evans (Elfann) parted with some of their best when requests for their stock were received from Canada and the United States. The beautiful heads and expressions of the Greenmoss/Elfann imports, along with nice substance in body, have carried through into the many outcrosses to Canadian and American lines. One of today's outstanding examples of the Carrimount/Greenmoss/Elfann combination bred to a basically American combination of lines is Canadian and Bermudian Ch. Rambutan Sabrina Fair, bred and owned by Canadians James and Jane Francis. Sabrina was sired by American Ch. Lainee Sigmund Floyd out of Canadian Ch. Rambutan Jubilation, a granddaughter of both Chin-Ki and Golden Bobbin. Sabrina was Winners Bitch at the 1982 American Shih Tzu Club National Specialty Show.

Carrimount stock from Canada, brought into the United States, affected the American Shih Tzu in very positive ways overall. Nice heads, balance, substance, and movement have been the pluses. And American stock has been interbred with Shih Tzu in Canada.

Cathie Phillips competed very successfully for years with her Bel Air dogs, taking her stock into Canada. Bel Air appears as a prefix in many Canadian-bred Shih Tzu pedigrees, as does Gloria Busselman's Pen Sans prefix. Ruth Di Nicola (Mandarin Kennels) and Jo Ann Regelman (Regal Kennels) have shown various American winners in Canada, as did Faye and Ray Wine. The Wine's American and Canadian Ch. Winemakers Pla-Boi was Winners Dog and Best of Winners at the 1974 American Shih Tzu Club National Specialty. Pla-Boi, from the United States, was sired by American Ch. Greenmoss Gilligan out of a bitch with a Mariljac background. He won many Best-in-Show awards, both in the United States and in Canada, and had a lasting impact on Canadian Shih Tzu.

A number of bitches were sent from Canada to the United States to be bred to Ch. Dragonwyck The Great Gatsby and to Ch. Parquins Pretty Boy Floyd. They, also, had great impact on Canadian Shih Tzu.

Jackie Peterson (Jazmin Kennels), in Ohio, purchased Best-in-Show winning American Ch. Erincroft Qu Ti Pi of Jazmin from Gerry Ikola, of Ontario, Canada. Gerry (now using the prefix Nanking instead of Erincroft) combined Gatsby and Floyd in her line to produce Qu Ti Pi. When bred back to her grandsire, Gatsby, Qu Ti Pi whelped one puppy who became American Ch. Jazmin's Maxi-Million, owned as well as bred by Jackie Peterson. Maxi sired many Canadian-bred Shih Tzu.

Cabrands Ciara of Lou Wan, a champion producing bitch both in the United States and Canada, is another example. She was sired by American Ch. Paisley Ping Pong, a Ringy son.

Canadian Ch. Copa's Cherish of Samalee was bred by Coni Nickerson of Virginia. Amilous Shesadandi, sired by Chow Mein out of Chow Mein daughter Ch. Mar Del's Samantha, was bred to Ch. Aagalynn's I'm a Dandy to produce Cherish.When bred to Ch. Kee Lees Red Baron of Mar Del (a Ringy Son), Cherish produced Canadian Ch. Samalee's Black Omen.

The Gatsby infusion into Diane Moncion's line produced several dogs which were exported from Canada into the United States and became top winners. Included was American and Canadian Ch. Paramount Rhett Butler, a Best-in-Show winner. Diane has been successful in incorporating Gatsby and others to produce dogs exported to Japan and France. Paramount Krystal Kate is one of the newer, lovely Shih Tzu in Diane's kennel, which is located in Ontario.

Canadian breeder Rosemary Hoo (Luvncare Kennels) has bred some excellent Shih Tzu. She purchased Ch. Imua's Guava Jam from American breeder Ginger

Schedlbauer. Guava Jam won the championship title in Canada, then came to the United States to win his championship title here (including points at Westminster). He returned to Canada, where he placed Best in Show. His gorgeous daughter (exported to Japan) is Ch. Luvncare Strawberry Blonde. In Guava Jam's background are Bobby Dazla, I Gotcha, and American Ch. Nanjo's Ah So Sweet Sum Wun, the Nanjo bitch sired by Ping Pong.

Many of the Shih Tzu who have attained fame in Canada have been of outstanding quality. Canadian Ch. Golden Royalist of Elfann, an English import to Canada, was top winning Shih Tzu in 1971. Choo Lang, also imported from England, was tops in 1970. Although an American-bred Shih Tzu, Ch. Mariljac Damn Yankee was Number One in 1967. Kanishka and Pla-Boi also were American bred. Many of the top winning Shih Tzu in Canada have been Canadian bred. Included among them are Chop Chop, top winner in 1969, and American and Canadian Ch. Kaduna Sewzi Q Lansing, Kanishka's gorgeous granddaughter, the top winner in 1977, 1978, and 1979. Canadian Ch. Samalee's Reflections of Baron had many Canadian Best-in-Show wins. Reflections was sired by Ch. Kee Lee's Red Baron of Mar Del.

Among other Best-in-Show winning Canadian-bred Shih Tzu are Marilyn Corbett's American and Canadian Ch. Santini's Luciano Shubaru, and Paquette's Ch. Wenrick's Tini Tina.

American and Canadian Ch. Shente's Brandy Alexander, at nine and a half years of age, was Best-in-Show (from the Veteran's Class) at the 1988 American Shih Tzu Club National Specialty Show. He made the win in

Can. Ch. Wenrick's Care Bear, owned by Jim and Cora Lee Romano, Ontario.

Can. Ch. Wyvern The Master Mariner, owned by Mr. and Mrs. R. Jodoin.

very stiff competition from a very large entry. Probably one of the greatest showmen in Shih Tzu history, Brandy made all Canadian owners of Shih Tzu very proud — as well as almost everyone else who attended the show and who really loves the breed. Soon thereafter he won Best-in-Show at the Canadian Kennel Club Centennial All-Breed Show.

Trudy Kerr (Ta Ya Chai Kennels), gifted spokesperson for the breed, has imported many fine Shih Tzu from Europe — mainly from Erika Geusendam. Her articles in various publications have been informative and inspiring. Heartbreak along with great success have made Trudy a respected figure not only in Canada but also around the world.

Can. and Ber. Ch. Wenrick's Against All Odds, owned by Wendy and Richard Paquette.

Int. and Can. Ch. Dhuti Vom Tschomo-Lungma, owned by Elaine Mawson and Margaret Easton.

Richard and Wendy Paquette are consistently producing outstanding specimens. Their winning in the United States and Canada proves it. Wendy was selected by the ASTC to judge the Sweepstakes at the ASTC National Specialty Show in April 1988.

Canadians unquestionably have bred some of the finest Shih Tzu in the world. Major successful strains influencing Canadian Shih Tzu include the following combinations (expressed as groups of kennels and stud dogs): Greenmoss/Elfann/Carrimount; Chow Mein/Ringy/Kanishka; Mariljac/Greenmoss/Winemaker; Ying Ying/Gatsby mixed with Floyd; and Char Nick/Ping Pong/Bobby Dazla.

The list that follows includes all Shih Tzu who have been awarded the title of champion in Canada from the time the breed was first permitted to compete in 1959 through those confirmed as of December 31, 1987. It must be emphasized that the title of Canadian Champion is conferred by the Canadian Kennel Club only to dogs who have finished the requirements AND who are officially registered with the Canadian Kennel Club.

CANADIAN CHAMPIONS, 1959-1987

1959 King Chan of Clarebrand
    Roadedge Yin-Yo
1960 Ching Janmayen
    Fiona Janmayen
1961 Yo-Yo of Clarebrand
1962 Metropolitan Mario
    Metropolitan Stella
    Satterleigh Todi
1963 Satterleigh Khazana
    Satterleigh Li-Tien
    Wynn-Hollow's Shan Wang
1964 (None)
1965 Lili Shu Van De Oranje Manege
1966 Beldams Kanshung Ling
    Celestial Jade of Elfann
    Isis Shu Van De Oranje Manege
1967 Tangra Vom Tschomo-Lungma
1968 Balkaren Nan Kara Shan C.D.
    Chumulari Ying Ying
    Khazana Tu Show
    Khazana Yul Chan
1969 Bambu Jenni Jang
    Bambu Sassy Saboo
    Brownhills Yolan of Greenmoss
    Carrimount Ah Chop Chop
    Carrimount Tai-Tai Chumulari
    Ching-Hi of Leskips
    Fu Shu Van De Oranje Manege
    Khazana Tu Tu
1970 Balkaren Kim Yin
    Bambu Kwan Yin
    Chiltonways Chwan-Choo
    Chumulari Sheng-Li Che
    Greenmoss Golden Frolic of Elfann
    Shan Soo of Rawstock
1971 Carrimount Ah Chou Chou
    Carrimount Ah Suki Su
    Chumulari Jen Tung
    Chumulari Ping Shan
    Ewan Kotow of Bashi
    Golden Royalist of Elfann
    Khazana Tul Choo
    Mariljac Tish-A-Mingo
    Nancarrow's Ho Tai Foo-Chee
    Shiva's Empress Tara
1972 Chumulari Leidza
    Chumulari Li Jen
    Ewan Tsun Tsan Fu-Hi
    Filicia Ah Hope So
    Filicia Natasha
    Judlu's Chung Kee
    Mai Ling of Mountainside
    Mai-Lyn Gold Nugget of Barusann
    Mai-Lyn Lum Lin Yue
    Mar Del's King Kanishka
    Misty Isle Jon Jon
    Pentara's Annabella
    Shou Jen Ai Kouche
    St. Aubrey Greenmoss Beau Geste
    St. Aubrey Jeff of Carrimount
    Willows The Golden Fleece
1973 Balkaren Fara Fhai

Bluemarking Simon
Carrimount Ah-Crepe De Chine
Carrimount Ah Ting Ting
Cedarglen Framberley's Hsi-De-Ho
Chen Yu
Chu Min of Alabouche
Chun King of Shang T'Ou
Darlyn's Von-Twiggie of Geodan
Dun Kee Wang Socket Tu Ya
Ewan Cho Cho Tsan
Ewan Tiko Fu Ling
Gin Doc's Pocohanas
Greenmoss Bumble Bee
Greenmoss Cherub
Greenmoss Honey Bee
Hale Koa's Sherry Spumone
Khr-Ushe-Hev Uch Oui
Lunar's Shen Yutang
Luv Lees Wee Pandy Bear
Michaels Geisha Wampus Ba-Bie
Nancarrow's Cha Tui
Nancarrow's Wo-Te Chu
Northshire's Jaded Lady
Pompano's Ching Tsu
Raina's Dandelion
Seng Fu Luv Lee Pooh Bear
Seng Fu Me-Tu Suzi-Q
Si Kiang's Aff-Kins Kee
Su Shan
Whinbrae Fei Tsaow
Whinbrae Won Ton Chan
Whinbrae Yeng Sing
1974 Ahsoluvlee's Teddi Berra
Bali Hai Huffin Puffin
Balkaren Dalai Kuri
Balkaren Thara Shan
Bomshu Hi Ho Geronimo
Carrimount Ah Chip Chip
Carrimount Ah Chun Ki
Carrimount Ah Tina Tina
Fang of Shang T'Ou
Filicia's Mei Kuan Te-Niki
Filicia's Suki Won Ton
Gratom Chuan T'Sun
Hale Koa Mahalo Nui Pane
Hee Shee Si Wang Mu of Yingsu
Lejusand Yung Mang of Gweekwood
Li
Lindi-Lu of Akaben
Nancarrow's Sah-Tseye Pif
Nancarrow's Tai Tai Tieh-Hu
Pompano's Ki Che Ki
Pompano's No Musuko Ringo
Raina's Moonglow
Royale Mandarin Buttons Up
Sanchi's Vhima
Sang Chen Christmas Beauty
Shang's Wu Wong
Sitsang Whiz-Bang
St. Aubrey Antarctica Jen Nai
Taipan En Lai
Town Hall Me Jolli Dragon

Vitahund's Hsien-Sheng
Whinbrae Tashi Tu
Winemaker's Pla-Ting
1975 Ahsoluvlee's Cinnamon Candi
Ahsoluvlee's Golden Babe
Ahsoluvlee's Lil Gigi
Ahsoluvlee's Lil Pooh
Bel Air Infanta
Bel Air The Candyman
Bobette's Moon Yee
Carrimount Ah Ching A Ling
Carrimount Ah Flip Flop
Carrimount Ah Me Jolly Jo
Carrimount Ah Me Saucy-Su
Carrimount Ah-Shen Li
Carrimount Ah Shu Shu
Chiltonways Choo Ming
Chinshan Muy Guy of Kaduna
Chumulari Liu Ling
Emperor's Kiss O'Yap Yap
Filicia's Chin Te Nu Shen
Golden Jasmin of Elfann
Greenmoss Casanova
Greenmoss Georgina
Guyden Black Magic
Gweekwood's Lui Ping Yeit C.D.
Handsworth Su Lung Lee
Jaisu Play Boy of Ling-Ho
Jo Jo's Ping Pong Tascha
Kaduna's Ming-Ling Lan-Sing
Keytor Witch Hazel
Kuri Ssu-Ki
Lil'Gilly Ahsoluvlee
Lillibet Shugar Shag
Ma-Tu's Most Happy Fella
Mandarin's Ching Ling Soo
Maui's Ping Kan
Nancarrow's Huang-Hou Jih
Nancarrow's Ki-Ki
Nancarrow's Rimpoche
Pompano's Golden Girl
Pompano's Suki San
Shaing Hi Sam of Yingsu
Shang's Kubla Khan
Silver Nymph's Magic Touch
Summerfield's Kueilan
Ti-Zu's Chang Hu Ling
Tu Shing's Zsa Zsa of Shang T'Ou
Wenrick's Tini Tina
Whinbrae Chen Yuan Chi
Whinbrae Fei Ying
Winemakers Cotton Candi
Winemakers Toi Toi Peershall
1976 Ahsoluvlee's Glowin' Ember
Ahsoluvlee's Kleewyk
Ahsoluvlee's Q-Tas A Button
Carrimount Ah Chop Chouee
Carrimount Ah Mei Chi
Char-Re Golden Dragon
Charing Cross Golden Star
Charing Cross Lan Su So Luv Lee
Chumulari Ho Li

Chumulari Pao Mu
Conwynn's Golden Jason
Daybreak At Wyvern
Elfann Golden Adonis
Gayholme's Yangtze
Gweekwood's Tu Yung Mi
Heavenly Dynasty's Ho Chi
Hodari Shan Shuo
Jancy's Puff The Mi-Tee Dragon
Kaduna's Jak-Ling Lan-Sing
Kaduna's Sewzi Q Lan-Sing
Kalidan Hsuan Tse
Kalidan Sukee Cayenne
Kow Choo
Kwieyang Yheti Aqsu
Lillico's Mi Toi Ro Byn
M'Lady Marina of Wyvern
M'Lord Ashley of Wyvern
Mandaren's Number One Son
Mei-Hua Mai Minh of Leistraum
Miss Tzuzzie Q of Chru-Ling C.D.
Nancarrow's Jung-Ying
Nancarrow's Kuo-Wang
Pen Sans Cinnamon Toast
Pepper VII
Pick-A-Dilly of Cheekee
Rambutan Kiss Me Kate
Rambutan Yin Yan
Sam Tsu's H B Calipso
Sam Tsu's Tam-E
Seng Fu Superstar of Mica
Shaggihi's Cha Chi Woo
Shou Mei Little Beauty of Marz
Wenrick's Miss Bobbin
Wenrick's Sou Leng
Wenrick's Sou Son Sin
Wenrick's Sweet Jai Son
Wenrick's Tini Stacy
Whinbrae Suzey Wong
Winemakers Chinky Won
Winemakers Pla-Boi
Wyvern M'Lord Ainslie
Yingsu Sparkler
Yingsu's Dragon Rouge
Zalay Mo See Ho Lang

1977 Atina Tiger Lily Maderly
Bel Air Ee-Tu of Tiki Wan
Bonnibell Ting's Tien-Liang
Carrimount Ah-So-Mr. Chan
Char-Re Especially For Richie
Chin Yu Rubber Ducki
Chumulari Yang
Emperor's Ebony Bla-Ka-Moor
Evanz Magnum Force
Fang's Chang Tzu of Shang T'Ou
Gin Doc's Kuhla Kahm of Lisel
Gregar Paquetbot of Sussie
Gregar Tun Chung
Guesstzu Sarge Of The Crest
Gunning's Magic Touch
Gweekwood's Ky Win Pooh
Gweekwood's Yung Dominic
Hale Koa Oahu Kula
Jack O'Diamonds
Jaisu Ling-Ho Chinese Junk

Jancy's Ming Jade Figurine
Janiric's Jumb-O-Laya
Kabuki's Jolly Jo's Ephine
Kaduna's Jak-Ling San-Sing
Kalidan Sang Chun Tse
Kee Lee's Munday's Child
Knolland Tashi Ling
Lee-Joi's Peach Parfait
Maui's Mai Jen
Mei-Hua Elegance of Yingsu
Minimoto's Tong-Lee
Paramount Lucky Lin Chu
Pen Sans Chim Chim Cheree
Quang-Te Van De Blauwe Mammouth
Rambutan Jubilation C.D.
Rutherends Sassy Geisha Girl
Tashi Chinshan Kaduna
Ti-Zu's Mi-Shaun Pan
Tushing's Avalanche
Wenrick's Miss Ta Cha Min
Wenrick's Misty Morning
Wenrick's Mr. Muffin
Wenrick's Sweet Jai Jai
Wenrick's Wee Tam Ting
Whinbrae Tien Fu
Winemakers Oriental Jewel
Winemakers Top
Wishmeluk Huggy Bear
Wyvern M'Lady Melissa
Wyvern M'Lord Chin-Key
Yingsu Bren Dee Lee of Gralee
Yingsu Crepe Suzette
Yingsu Ling Po Ching
Yingsu Lucky Finger
Yingsu Lucky Lindy
Yingsu Paquerette of Jaymar

1978 Beedoc's Yu Mei Te Jen
Bel Air A Taste of Honey
Bel Air Proud Heritage
Bonnibell Khigh Dhiegh
Cec Nich Kasha
Cec Nich Me-Lah
Char-Re Truly Scrumptious
Chieh-Chi Hsing Ming
Chieh-Chi Ping Pong
Chinshan D-Rek-Lyn To Kaduna
Chintan's Ying Su
Chumulari Ai Jen
Chumulari Feng Yeh Kalidan
Copa's Cherish of Samalee
Crowvalley Llewelyn
Dhuti Vom Tschomo-Lungma
Daiquiri's Mad-About-Me
Dunklehaven Luv-Li-Ladee
Emperor's Sunshine Band
Emperor's Sweet Daiquiri
Fang Chu's Lipton Chee C.D.
Fauntine Sunburst
Gweekwood Ky Tomi
Heeshee's Mee Mee
Ho Chi's Follow The Leader
Illenids Lei Sun Kee
Imua's Guava Jam
Jabil's Faerie Dean Filligree
Janiric's Charmin Chessa

Janiric's Chelsea Morn
Janiric's Rockin' Robin
Jen-Mi Sou Yen's Mr. Wenrick
Joli's Li'l Annie Laurie
Kaduna's Kong-Ling Lan-Sing
Kaduna's Santini Lan-Sing C.D.
Karmicki's Ding-A-Ling
Kee Lee's Butterfly O'Samalee
Li Ming's Ping Kan
Lousann's Madam Flutterby
Mahjong Lao Yen
Mandarin's Salt N' Pepper
Mar Dels Ring Ling
Maui's Mai China
Maui's Tzu Hsi
Murray's Chipper Dan
Nancarrow's Fli-Ying-Hi
Paramount Just By Chance
Paramount Motion Picture
Rambutan Impenitent Sinner
Rutherends Chee-Kee Boy
Samalee's A Thimbleful
Shellaureven Solitaire
Shonaping's Sabrina Wenrick
Sou Yen Number One Wenrick Son
Sou Yen's Silver Tin Wing
Strawberry Blond Luvncare
Sun Chine Loli Pop
Treecroft Wotzu Kailash
Treecroft Wotzu Sen-Ta-Fold
Tushing's Shan Too Khan
Vic-Torin's Sugar Daddy
Viva Chiquita
Wenrick's Happy Miss
Wenrick's Ho Leng Sou Yen
Wenrick's The Great Mikado
Winemakers Country Girl
Wishmeluk Joker's Wild
Wyvern M'Lord Asquith
Wyvern This One's For Leechee
Zalay A Star Is Born
Zalay Golly Miss Molly
Zalay Sweet Lil Maggi

1979 Ashining Ms. Charisma
Ashining Ms. Josie
Bamboo Grasshopper Jewel
Bel Air Heart Throb
Bel Air Royal Heritage
Cabrand's High N Mighty
Char-Nick's Mister Wise Guy
Char-Re Giant Killer
Char-Re Love A Lot
Chieh-Chi Enchantment
Chieh-Chi Hitman
Chieh-Chi Short and Sassy
Chintan's Chu Chu
Chintan's San Se Chin
Danca's Chi-Chi-Lin
Dashi's My My
De Ray's Here's My Heart
Gaya Vom Tschomo-Lungma
Gralee Vegas Jokers R Wild
Gunning's Semi-Precious
Gweekwoods Suki Tong
Hai Sing Bah Sha of Pen Sans

125

Can. Ch. Bilor's Princess Dominique, owned by Lorraine De Salvo and Sharon and Bob Young.

Can. Ch. Jancrest Luvncare, top winning Shih Tzu puppy in Canada in 1979 with 6 wins as Best Puppy in Show.

Can. Ch. Imua's Five-O Of Alethra, owned by Mr. and Mrs. R. Jodoin.

126

Hai-Tai High Hope
Hornerbrook's Toba
Imua's Director of Luvncare
Imua's Five-O of Alethra
Jancrest Luvncare
Jancrest The Aristocrat
Janiric's Chili Sauce
Jazmin's Drummer Boi of Anh-Wei
Johnson's Jac-Kee
Joli's Li'l Dusty Miller
Karmicki's Kooper
Karmicki's Misty Mahnchu
Karmicki's Sassi Missi
Lainee X-Tra Arrogant
Lichee's Mi Chin Mia
Lou Wan Farrah Fawcet
Lou Wan Slate of Li Ming
Luvncare Buttercup Ring
Luvncare Kimitzu
Mei San Abrac' Dabra
Nancarrow's Chan Lan Hu
Nancarrow's Yu Yen Te Hua
Nanking Lin Tzi Tamawae
Pan Lu's Lang Jai
Paramount Extra Special
Paramount Lucky King Presley
Paramount Madam X
Pen Sans Peaches N'Cream
Samalee's Crackin' Rose
Samalee's Precious Golden Girl
Samalee's Reflections of Baron
Samalee's Sweet Desire
Seng Fu Feelin Groovy
Seng Fu It'll Do
Shamisen's Number One Son
Shellaureven Pha-Nci Kaduna
Shente's Trick Or Treat
Shonaping's Argonaut Era
Shonaping's Brilliant Supernova
Shonaping's Gold Crown of Midas
Sou Yen's Wenrick Parkers Yumyum
Tailspin's Mr. Bo Jingle
Tailspin's Witchy Woman
Tamawae's Tzu An C.D.X.
Tiffany Sparkler of Shang T'Ou
Wenrick's Copper Penny
Wenrick's Jung Ming
Wenrick's Madam Zu Zu Jolterra
Wenrick's Rainshadow Poppy
Wenrick's Yasmeen
Winemakers Chinese Tiger
Winemakers Silver Jingle
Wyvern M'Lord Shaugnessy
Yingsu's Johnie Reb
Yingsu's Tangarine of Jay Mar

1980 Arvind Vom Tschomo-Lungma
Ashining Wee Willie
Bar-Ro's Charlie Chan
Bel Air Kristi of Terribrooke
Cec Nich Topaz
Char-Re Star Fire
Charjalong's JJ of Janiric
Cheekee's Wind Song
China Chimes Portrait of Ping
Chop Tung Lee

Daiquiri's Southern Nights
Dragonfire's I'm Buckwheat
Gralee Nanking Goodtime Charli
Gralee Travis James
Janiric's Rerun-Ah-Ching
Janiric's Yeung Chou
Jen-Mi's Louie Primavera
Kabuki's Bronx Bomber
Kabuki's Jimmy Cricket
Karmicki's Mia Melodie
Klaumar Burlington Bertie
Ky Karmicki's Kimi
Li Ming's Annie Hall
Luvncare Cherry Red
Luvncare Red Pepper
Luvncare The Director's Choice
Luvncare The Wiz
Luvncare Tiny Tim
Marya Winds Paramount Krissy
Nancarrow's Chi P'u Sai Jen
Nanjo Winter Star of Chin Shan
Nanking Gunnings Aunt Jemima
Nanking Lucky Linda
Nanking Mari Lu Tamawae
Nanking Mari Melody
Omni Top Dollar
Paramount Award Winner
Paramount Madam Mindy
Pen Sans Parti Pet
Pen Sans Parti Toi
Pen Sans September Song
Pen Sans Sweet Ting
Pen Sans Tecaro Capt Sunshine
Pen Sans Who-Dat of Xalmes
Pinafore Minstrel of Mandarin
Portneufs Disco Dani
Primavera's Yo Yo
Rainshadows Penny Lane
Rambutan MacGonichle
Rambutan Rejoicing
Rockee Vollee Charisma
Samalee's Black Omen
Samalee's Crystal Mist
Samalee's Teaken Silhouette
Santini's Kaduna Phat-Choy-A
Shente's Brandy Alexander
Shente's Mr. MacBarker
Shente's Tidbits
Shentes Pina Colada
Shonaping's Aria Shalimar
Shonaping's M's Domese Wenrick
Sou Yen's Xmas Angel Tai'Shan
Sou Yen's Xmas Eve
St. Aubrey Poesy of Elsdon
Taisoolyn's Bad New Reb
Tamawae's Happi Hustler
Ta Ya Chai's Tou Wan
Terribrook's Pi-Ku Luv
Vegas High Roller
Wenrick's Just Like Bobbin
Wenrick's Miss Fluffy
Wenrick's O-By-Jingo
Wenrick's Pocket Money
Wenrick's Sindy Sou
Wynndee Cheerleader of Hochi

Wyvern Janz Che-Wei
Wyvern The Master Mariner
Wyvern The Sea Witch
Wyvern's Jewelled Butterfly
Yah-Sue Mai-Ling

1981 Ashining Ms. Peppi
C's Parti Angel Of Pen Sans
Carousel's Lucifer
Din Ho China Pansy Petal
Heavenly Dynastys Panda Bear
Jen-Mi's Great Balls of Fire
Kabuki's Grand Illusion
Lainee Saturday Nite Fever
Lantana's Sassafras Tea
Liche's K'O Chu
Luvncare Chopsticks
Luvncare Panama Red
Luvncare Sweet Cher-Rity
Luvncare The Director's Image
Luvncare William The Conqueror
Nanjo Bizzy Lizzie
Paramount Rhett Butler
Pen Sans Foolish Pleasure
Royal Jade Rust-Ee Nail
Santini's Luciano Shubaru
Shente's Cin Cin
Shentes Snowflake
Shonaping's Aurora Borealis
St. Aubrey Miss Crissy O'Elsdon
Tailspin's Lucinda Chen-Chu
Ta Ya Chai's Chang Sheng
Ta Ya Chai's Shih Huang Ti
Ta Ya Chai's Wu Tse T'ien
Vegas Star Attraction
Wenrick's Miss Tiffany Sou Yen
Woodsmoke's Hoot N' Tell
Woodsmoke's Loose Change
Wyvern Oh Abraham
Wyvern The Admiral
Yingsu Lucky Lady Of Nanking

1982 Ah-Suki T'ou
Ashining Ms. Maygen
Ashining Ms. Tiffany
Beedoc's Bangaway
Beedoc's Four Point Two
Brighten's Famous Amos
Brynmyr's I'm The Boss
Can Am's Sun Tu Vom Arvind
Carousel's Second Hand Rose
Ch'ang Ch'u Apollo
Chinshan's Another World
Chosunfu Cha Cha Cha
Consolnor Chen Chu
Dancara's Main Event
Double Daiquiris On The Rocks
Faerie Dean Afternoon D-Light
Fanci-Pant's Mai Tamawae
Fang Chu Hapiour
Graerose Misti Morn
Gunning's Jackpot in Vegas
Heavenly Dynasty's Bit O Venus
Impa Noble Sun
Jadesong's Tequilla Sunrise
Janiric's Boo Gee Boo Gee
Janiric's Chanel

Jazmin's Hi Calibre
Jazmin's Hot Stuff
Klaumar Spun Sugar
Korolaki Ms. Fanci Pants
Korolaki Ms. Smarti Pants
Kristeva's Apollo
Lainee Buster Brown
Lainee Flying High
Lainee The Brain Storm
Li Ming's Coco Chanel
Luvia Good Man Friday
Luvia Happy Hour
Luvia Twilight Time
Luvncare Eric The Red
Luvncare Etc.
Luvncare I'm Buckshot
Luvncare Promise To Shente
Luvncare The Love Bug
Madelay's Mr. Beau Brindle
Madelay's Tabatha
Marya Winds John Travolta
Mi Clyde Chin Chiny
Milo's Classy Benjamin
Moonglow's Pride And Joy
Moonglow's Something Special
Moonsong Fancee Chinwangtao
Na-Tasha Golden Heart Throb
Nancarrow's Hsing Ta Shih
Nancarrow's Huan Le Te Er
Nanchi's Creme O Wheat
Nanchi's Master Spy
Nanking Kamira Body on Tap
Nanking's Sprout
Nanking's The Butler Did It
Omni Dream Merchant
Paramount Krystal Kate
Pen Sans Ima Topaz Tu
Pinafore Goldglo Mandarin
Pinafore Master Charge-A-Long
Portneuf's Pride N Joi
Rambutan Royal Deja Vu
Rambutan Sabrina Fair
Rembrandt
Rockee Vollee Bionic Wizard
Rockee Vollee Woopie I'm Alive
Samalee's Black Forest Slice
Samalee's Chariot of Fire
Samalee's Charlotte Russe
Samalee's Chincerely
Samalee's Lady Marmalade
Samalee's Rodes Windwalker
Samalee's Sweet Inspiration
Santini's Big Guy From Cosenza
Shente's Ginger Rogers Benart
Shente's Omni Tequilla Punch
Shentes All That Jazz
Shihchi's Midnight Madness
Shoamai Tiko Mi Lou
Sun Loon Padi of Rockee Vollee
Tamawae's Christmas Holly
Tamawae's Daiquiri Dancer
Tamawae's High Voltage
Tamawae's Hunki Munki
Tamawae's Raindance Renegade
Tasheen's RJ's Imperial Jade

Vegas Show Stopper
Vegas Star Celebrity
Wen-Shu's Sin Gum Sze
Wenrick Tia Maria
Wenrick's Kamira Fortune Cookie
Wenrick's Miss Klaumar
Wenrick's Miss Mindy Sou Yen
Wenrick's Miss Molly
Wenrick's Super Trouper
Wenrick's Top Banana
Winward's Sly Fox
Woodsmoke's Before Yesterday
Woodsmoke's Enchantment
Woodsmoke's Mad Money
Wyvern Cueh Shih Mei Jen
Wyvern Wands Me Tu Pj
1983 Ambermoon of Chinwangtao
Anjuli's Vegas Arrogant Beau
Anjuli's Vegas Camomille
Anjuli's Vegas Dainty Lady
Beswicks Limited Edition
Chieh-Chi Inch to A Foot
Dancara's Champagne And Caviar
Dragonfire's Terribrooke
Dragonwyck Lord Dragonfire
Faerie Dean Devil in Disguise
Ginal's Heart Stealer
Glaranik Paramount Caesar
Hidden Coves Chewbacca
Hidden Coves Golden Dream
House of Wu U Know Who
Impa Moon Shadow
Impai Vom Tschomo-Lungma
Jadesong's Jazz Man
Jaina Vom Tschomo-Lungma
Janiric's Kelley Louise
Joli's Li'l Peppermint Patti
Karmicki's Ming Toi
Lantana's Leading Lady
Lantana's Lover Boy
Lenacia's Sunshine In Luvncare
Lou Wans Dixie Rebel
Luvia Dancara Easter Angel
Marxim J. J. Jr.
Mawwilli Shogun Chan Shih
Mei San Shindana
Mindy's Ty-Nee Bear
Moonglow's China Doll
Nancarrow's Yu Mei Te Ying
Nanking's Tojo
Omni Vegas Command Performance
Panda's Duchess Bear
Paramount Fille Mignon
Ponte's Orloff Diamond
Regal's Dr. Spock
Samalee's Bobby Sue
Samalee's Mark of Distinction
Samalee's Star Gemini
Shente's Bit of Brandy
Shente's My My Terri Brooke
Shente's Mr Macho of Fang Chu
Shihchi's Scarlett The Harlett
Shihchi's Tim Sheen
Sho Tru Fox Fire of Forestfarm
Shubaru's Gorgeous Gussy

Taisoolyn Tailspin's Rebecca
Tamawae's Precious Tiffany Ginal
Tamawae's Ring Master
Terdel Woodsmoke Magic
Terribrooke's I'm A Hot Pepper
Tora Shogun of Kiku-Uye
Vegas Anjuli Queen of Hearts
Vegas Tamawae Show Girl
Wades Mi-Lo Bubbling Bibette
Wee-Luv'Em's Shantilly Lace
Wenrick's Panda At Luvncare
Wenrick's Sweet As Sugar
Wenshu's Mari Ginseng
Woodsmoke's John Hamilton
Woodsmoke's Pick Pocket
Woodsmoke's Ruffle's Rate
Zalay In A Frenzi
Zalay Shogi
1984 Anjuli Shimizu In Vegas
Anjuli's Dan Dee Lyon
Anjuli's Rhapsody in Blue
Bel Air Summer Storm
Beswicks Brandy Alexandria
Blair Alexander
Brighton's Ravishing Rachael
Ch'ing Fo Mai Toi Bear of Joytu
Dancara's Cover Girl
Diaquiri's Bottoms Up
Diaquiris Touch Of Brandy
Fang Chu's Ms Elly Of Shente
Genisa's Tin Pan Lizzy
Ginal's Silver Enchantress
Ginal's Tamawae Shadi Ladi
Glaranik Anastasha
Hana-Kinsa Incredible Igor
Here Comes Trouble Of Lou Wan
Hodari Mercy Me O'Chang Tang
Jadesong's Lil Ms Muffin
Jadesong's Ms Ritz Bitz
Jadesong's Rotsa Ruck
Janiric's Cherries Jubilee
Lainee Edipus Complex Of Nova
Lantana's Starlite
Lenacia's Golden Cadillac
Leolynne's Truly Tasha
Lou Wan Chin Tan Beau Geste
Lou Wan Tootsie
Mandarin Sam Sun Of Pinafore
Mei San U Kno Who
Mei San's Dynamite Damsel
Molnar's Colonel Rouser
Moonglow's Secret Vision
My Nanchi Sand Pebble
Nancarrow's Chen Chu Yun
Nancarrow's Chin Te Yu Chung
Nancarrow's Rustinwood Shadow
Nancarrow's Ying Erh Hai Li
Nanjo's Young Ping At Klaumar
Nanking's Mari Melanie
Nanking's Maxwell Smart
Oak Knolls Black-Gamin
Odeon's Tailor Made For Patme
Palacepride's Genuine Jewel
Paramount Precious Princess
Pinafore No Trouble At All

R-Own Kam Chung
Saddlebrook's Yum Yum
Shente's Checkmate Beswick
Shente's Rich And Famous
Shihchi's Love N Kisses
Shihchi's Private Eye
Shonaping's Aureus Darius
Stormy Weather Chinwangtao
Tailspin Blue Smoke
Tamawae's Challenger
Tamawae's Hi-Struttin'
Tamawae's X-Otic Spice
Ta Ya Chai's Emeer Vom Arvind
Tenoma's Boi Ching Wu
Tenoma's Kristen Of Karola
Terdel's Page One
Terdel's Woodsmoke Chant
Terribrooke's I'm Irresistible
Tochi's Ideal Whiskey
Tu Chu's Double Stuff Oreo
Tu Chu's White Lightning
Vegas Playboy
Vegas Strikes It Rich
Vegas Tropicana Star Debut
Wee-Luv'Ems Rebel Echo
Wenrick's Pandamonium
Wenrick's What's Up Doc
Willoway Stylistic Smak'N Good
Woodsmoke's Flute Of Gold
Woodsmoke's Shonaping Tune
Wyvern Here Comes The Son
Yingsu's Charleston Blue
Yours By Woodsmoke Design
Zalay Here Comes Trouble
Zalay Sassie Pants

1985 Ali-Aj Chin-Hua Kublai Khan
Anh Wei Heirs Enuff
Chieh-Chi Dom Perignon
Copper Penny Kahlua
Dancara's Dream Weaver
Dancara's Go For Gold
Dancara's Hard To Be Humble
Dazlens Magnum P I of Landor
Daiquiri's Proud Appeal
Donalen Ms Pammy
Dragonwyck Dominique
Dragonwyck Roust About
Duchess Teejay Bear
El Frans Special T
Elusive Braggon Dragon
Fancee Gunning Re-Pete
Fang Chu's Irish Cream
Flandair's Miss Sou Yen
Glaranik Meadowmorn
Hai Sings Brass Buttons
Hana Jumping Jack Flash
Impa Bobby Dazzler
Impa Chinese Ginger
Jadesong's Lil' Gizmo
Jofins Kno-Peking
Joffins Shian Mee Hu
Joli's Li'l Luci
Kamira's I'm Just Jemima
Lar-El's Ebony'N'Ivory
Lenacia's Maria Christina

Lenacia's Pretty Mandy
Louwan's Jezebel of Molnar
Luvtu's Quiet Riot
Marxim Pyjama Parti In Vegas
Mavarick Chang Lee
Mei San Fancy Mi'e Ling
Mik-Lyn's Golden Sunset
Mik-Lyn's I'm A Storm Too
Ming Shih's Tiffany
Molnar's Miss Carousel
Mysty Dai Lone Star Mandarin
Nanking's Edward C. Bear
Omni Night Fever In Vegas
Palacepride's Oriental Jade
Palacepride's Precious Gem
Paramount Call Me Krissy
Pen Sans Chintan Fire N Ice
Rambutan Ulterior Motive
Rojacky's Blue Angel
Samalee's Facelle Royale
Samalee's Midsummers Dream
Shente Flash Dance Bennart
Shente X-otic Singapore Sling
Shente's Fred Astair Bennart
Shihchi's Love Fantasy
Shimizu White Lightening
Shonaping's Myth Of Theseus
Sumeng Gi Gi
Ta Ya Chai's Dalai Vom Arvind
Ta Ya Chai's Eeshta Vom Arvind
Terdel's Thomas Jefferson
Terribrooke's Ki Kel-See
Terribrooke's Tada Of Karmicki
Tu Chu's Could It Be Magic
Tu-Mac's Phoebe Shou
Tyc's Farah Vom Arvind
Wee Luv'Ems Rebels China Dance
Wee Luv'Ems Rebels Ruffle
Wenrick's Brooke In Rustinwood
Wenrick's Care Bear
Wenrick's Delice
Whinbrae Velvet Pinafore
Woodsmoke Dragons Breath
Woodsmoke's Dandino
Woodsmoke's Declaration
Woodsmoke's Dragon Lore
Woodsmoke's Ring Of Lords
Woodsmoke's Who's Who
Wyn-Song Oliver Twist
Wyvern's Jonathon
Zalay Formal Attire

1986 Ahchoy's Miss Goodie Two Shoes
Ali-Aj-Sumeng's Heidi
Anjuli's Blue Gizmo
Anjuli's Blue Trinket
Anjuli's Stardust
Anjuli's Twylight Magic
Ashining Ms. Special K
August Moon's Sugar Daddy
Beswick's The Magician
Bilor's Pepsi Generation
Crown Royal Of Shente
Dark Decon Of El-Fran
Desmann's Dynamite
Diaquiri's Very Preppy

Don Wai Pardon My Dust
Dragonfire Golly G Chang Tang
Dragonfire's Great Santini
Glaranik Ms. Fancy
Goldwin's Raz Mamataz
Halcyon's Rona Bear-It
Hodari Hai-U Hooligan
Hodari Stir Crazy Of Lainee
Jazmin's Victoria
Jewel's Of Shente
Jofins Black Eyed Susan
Joylin's Impossible Dream
Karmicki's Holli Houhou
Klusive Lord Of The Dragons
Lar-El's Tag-A-Long Of Sumhi
Lenacia's Careless Whisper
Lou Wan Boom Boom
Lou Wan Ginger
Loubren's Jiminy Cricket
Mi Lo's Bits And Pieces
Mi-Lo's Bims Justawee Gizmo
Milo's Little Bailey Quarters
Ming Shih's Amanda
Ming Shih's Enchantress
Molnar's Brandy On The Rocks
Momni's Innovation Of Louwan
Moonglow's Cover Girl
Moonglow's Smooth As Brandy
Mysty Dai Satin Doll
Nancarrow's Shen Te Hu
Nancarrow's T'ing Ling
Nanking's Broadway Joe
Nanking's Flowering Fushia
Nanking's Lucky Seven
Nanking's Melinda
Nanking's The Showgirl
Palacepride Beijing
Palacepride's Ebony N Ivory
Palacepride's Treasure
Paramount Finesse
Paramount Ricochet Romance
Patme's Custom Taylor Made
Pen Sans Koosa Of Li Ming
Pen Sans Toi Fantasy
R And R Golden Chablis
Rambutan Ardent Spirit
Regal's Elusive Escapade
Regal's Rum Raisen
Samalee's Billie Jean
Samalee's Easy Lover
Samalee's Lovin Spoonful
Samalee's Squire Of Desmann
San Yen Black Magic Of Donalen
Santini's Cuylony Boy By Cozzi
Shimizu Master Moonraker
Shimizu Rising Sunburst
Shonaping Jayvee Gilded Lady
Shonaping's Midas Monte
Shonaping's Primo Vere
Sou Yen's Taylor Made
Sumeng Gentle Ben
Sweettzu's Vagabond Lover
Ta Ya Chai's Geeta Von Emeer
Ta Ya Chai's Gelaen Von Emeer
Tailspin's Blue Stratos

129

Tamawae's Cla-Mal Dreamweaver
Tamawae's Firemouse
Tamawae's Kinas Moor Kimi Sin
Terdel's Simon Chang
Terribrooke's Cute As A Button
Terribrooke's I'm A Fantasy
Tu Chu Gunning In The Buff
Ty's Freeway Bear
Wenrick's Ebene Et Ivoire
Wenrick's Gizmo
Wenrick's Holly N'Rustinwood
Wenrick's M's Lindsay
Wenrick's Panda Bear
Wenrick's Sweet Pea Ginseng
Woodsmoke Dragon's Quest
Woodsmoke With Style
Woodsmoke Wrinkle In Time
Woodsmoke's Heir Apparent
Woodsmoke's Keep Th' Change
Wunan's Jazz Ma Tazz
Wyvern Diamonds And Daisies
Yolan's Fancy That Of Shente
Yolan's Huggy Bear

1987* Achilles Dang Sai Dragonfire
Anjuli's Autumn Splendor
Anjuli's Dandy Tigger
Artisan's Toulouse Lautrec
Beswicks Pennies From Heaven
Beswicks Private Treaty
Beswicks Seventh Delight
Bilor's Golden Elegance
Bilor's Princess Dominque
Centrefold's Robin Hood
Chinadoll's Maid By The Butler
Dragonfire's Cg of Terribrooke
Dragonfire's Dee Dee

Elusive Glory Be O'Chang Tang
Gen Je's Bette Shi Kan
Goldwin's Ming Dynasty Of Yolan
Jenric's Sassette
Josol's High And Mighty
Kailasa East Of Eden
Karmicki's Shades Of Tada
Karmicki's Shogun
Lady Francesca of Momi
Linven's Marcus Welby
Linven's Simon And Simon
Luv Tu's Madonna
Marcus' Hot Toddy
Marcus' Princess Daisy
Mei San's Cheers At Anjuli
Mei San O Dis Is Sum Wun
Mei San Sweet Daiquiri
Mei San Theo-Dorable Cameo
Mei-Ting's Risky Business
Mysty Dai Southern Comfort
Nanking Kamira's Secret Agent
Nanking's Rockton
Nanking's Seven Up
Odeon's Just A Delight
Palacepride's Classic Charm
Paragon Elegant Lady
Paramount Gorgeous Gidget
Paramount Modern Medicine
Paramount Trivial Pursuit
Pensans Holy Smoke
Rojacky's Elegance For Palme
Rojacky's Special Edition
Royal Manor Primadonna
Rustinwood's Bearly There
Sabar's All The Rage Of Galaxy
Samalee's Affair Of The Heart

Santini's Dark Star
Santini's Orion Belt
Shali-Hi's Image Of Raider
Shente's Apricot Brandy
Shente's Christian Dior
Shente's Shining Star
Shimizu Nicki Nine Doors
Shimizu Princess Mikaela
Shimizu Sparkling Stardust
Shimmilee's Now More Than Ever
Shimmilee's Tamtan Trucker
Shonaping's Halley's Comet
Shonaping's Midas Marigold
Shonaping's Serene Highness
Shou Mi Black Belt Shimmilee
Talasin Draco's Bucky Tyler
Tamawae's To Ta Lee Ah Sum
Ta Ya Chai's Indira Von Arvind
Ta Ya Chai's Jasmine Von Arvind
Terribrooke's Papa Smurf
Ty-Won-On Mischief Maker
Webbs Lo Ling
Wenrick's Against All Odds
Wenrick's Apache Gold
Wenrick's Boys Will Be Boys
Wenrick's Casinova N' China Doll
Wenrick's Mr. Peppy C.D.
Wenrick's M's Kelly N' Sou Yen
Wenrick's Toby Tyler
Williwig's Kami Kaze Kid
Woodsmoke's Time Will Tell
Yolan's Michaelangelo

* As confirmed in "Dogs in Canada"
magazine.

Can. Ch. Yingsu Lucky Lindy, owned by Sue Miller.

TOP PRODUCERS IN CANADA

Based on number of champions confirmed through December 1987.

Sires	Number of Champions
Ch. Shente's Brandy Alexander	34
Ch. Samalee's Reflections of Baron	21
Ch. Carrimount Ah Ting Ting	20
Am. Ch. Lainee Sigmund Floyd	17
Am. Ch. Lou Wan Rebel Rouser	16
Ch. Wenrick's Sweet Jai Son, C.D.	15
Ch. Regal's Dr. Spock	14
Ch. Dragonfire's I'M Buckwheat	12
Ch. Sanking Lin Tzi Tamawae	12
Ch. Carrimount Ah Chop Chop	11
Am. Ch. Dragonwyck The Great Gatsby	11
Ch. Nancarrow's Ki-Ki	11
Ch. Nanking the Butler Did It	11
Ch. Arvind Vom Tschomo-Lungma	10
Am. Ch. Dragonfire's The Great Draco	10
Ch. Golden Royalist of Elfann	10
Ch. Gralee Vegas Jokers R Wild	10
Ch. Greenmoss Golden Frolic of Elfann	10
Ch. Yingsu Lucky Lindy	10

Can. Ch. Can Am's Sun Tu Vom Arvind, owned by Trudy Kerr.

TOP-WINNING SHIH TZU IN CANADA

All-breed System: One point for each dog of any breed defeated, including from Best of Breed up.

Year	Dog
1967	Ch. Mariljac Dham Yhan Kee
1968	Ch. Khazana Yul Chan
1969	Ch. Carrimount Ah-Chop-Chop
1970	Ch. Choo Lang of Telota
1971	Ch. Golden Royalist of Elfann
1972	Ch. Mar Del's King Kanishka
1973	Ch. Carrimount Ah-Ting-Ting
1974	Ch. Carrimount Ah-Ting-Ting
1975	Ch. Winemaker's Pla-Boi
1976	Ch. Winemaker's Pla-Boi
1977	Ch. Kaduna's Sewzi Q Lan Sing
1978	Ch. Kaduna's Sewzi Q Lan Sing
1979	Ch. Kaduna's Sewzi Q Lan Sing
1980	Ch. Santini's Kaduna Phat-Choy-A
1981	Ch. Samalee's Reflections of Baron
1982	Ch. Samalee's Reflections of Baron
1983	Ch. Shente's Brandy Alexander
1984	Ch. Shente's Brandy Alexander
1985	Ch. Shente's Brandy Alexander
1986	Ch. Shente's Brandy Alexander

Can. Ch. Wyvern M'Lord Shaugnessy, owned by Mr. and Mrs. A. Dickson.

Can. Ch. Nanking's Mari Melanie, bred and owned by Mrs. Gerry Ikola.

Dams	Number of Champions
Ch. Carrimount A-Chou-Chou	9
Ch. Copa's Cherish of Samalee	9
Ch. Pentara's Annabella	9
Ch. Gaya Vom Tschomo-Lungma	7
Ch. Nanking Mari Melody	7
Ch. Wenrick's Pocket Money	7
Ch. Brownhill's Yolan of Greenmoss	6
Ch. Chumulari Li Jen	6
Fang Chou's Ms-A-Sissi of Shente	6
Ch. Keytor Witch Hazel	6
Luvncare Miss Clairol	6
Ch. Wenrick's Tini Tina	6

Ch. Bilor's Flashdance, owned by Lorraine De Salvo.

Ch. Sanchi's Bekko, owned by Bonnie Miller, D.V.M.

Foxhall Floydian Flirt of Copa, owned by Coni Nickerson.

Ch. Char Nick's I'm No Snob, owned by Mr. and Mrs. Louis Sanfilippo.

Dog Shows and Breed Standards

Centuries ago, agricultural fairs were held in conjunction with spring and fall religious festivals. To these gatherings, various agricultural products and animals were brought for exchange. As time went on, it became customary to provide entertainment, too. Dogs often participated in such events as bull baiting, bear baiting, and ratting. The dog that exhibited the greatest skill in the arena was usually the one that brought the highest price when time came for barter or sale. These fairs may seem a far cry from today's highly organized dog shows and obedience and field trials. But they were the forerunners of modern dog-show competition and played an important role in shaping the development of purebred dogs.

The first organized dog show was held at Newcastle, England, in 1859. Later that year, a show was held at Birmingham. The first dog show in Germany was held at Apoldo in 1860. Interest expanded rapidly, and by the time the Paris Exhibition was held in 1878, the dog show was a fixture of international importance.

The first organized show in the United States for judging the physical structure of dogs was held in 1874 at Chicago in conjunction with the meeting of the Illinois State Sportsmen's Association. Interest spread quickly. Before the end of the year, similar "conformation" shows were held at Oswego, New York; Mineola, New York; and Memphis, Tennessee. The latter show combined competition in conformation with the first organized field trial ever held in the United States. In January 1875, the first all-breed show in the United States was held at Detroit, Michigan.

Rules at early shows were not uniform. John Henry Walsh (1810-1888), editor of the sporting magazine *The Field* published in England, was among the first to campaign for uniformity of written descriptions by which dogs could be judged. Under his pseudonym, "Stonehenge," Walsh wrote *The Dogs of the British Islands*, in which each breed was described in some detail. This first edition of detailed "Standards" for dog breeds was so successful that four additional editions were published. The first book of Standards published in the United States was *The American Book of the Dog*, by G. O. Shields. In the United States there was no organization through which to coordinate dog-show activities until September 1884, when The American Kennel Club was founded. Through the ensuing years the AKC has grown to become the largest dog registering organization in the world. It is an association of several hundred member clubs, including all-breed, specialty, field trial, obedience, and national "parent" breed clubs for individual breeds. It is under the auspices of the parent club that the Standard for the particular breed is written. Then the Standard is submitted to the AKC's Board of Directors for approval. Any later additions or revisions also are prepared by the parent breed club, and such changes also must be submitted to the AKC's Board of Directors for approval. A similar process is followed for breeds eligible for registration with the governing organizations of other countries.

The Standard for the breed does not describe a particular individual dog, but, rather, a concept. The purpose of the Standard is to serve as a word pattern by which the breed is judged at shows. Consequently, the Standard serves as the primary guide for breeders seeking to produce outstanding dogs that will contribute toward long-term improvement of breed characteristics.

Although there may be minor variations from country to country, Standards for the Shih Tzu are much the same regardless of the country where the breed may be entered in show competition. Despite the general uniformity of requirements for breed type, a Shih Tzu that is a top winner in one country may not be a top winner in other countries — assuming similar promotion of that dog. Individual breeders and judges interpret Standards differently — and such variation is magnified when it comes to interpretation from country to country or from continent to continent. Although a dog may be selected as "Best" in both American and Canadian shows (because of the doubling-up of various lines in breeding programs), that same dog may not be among the winners in competition with dogs in countries on different continents. Styles and trends vary. A stud dog that has great impact on the breed on one geographical area may never influence breeding on another continent. Therefore, because the type of dog being shown in a country tends to be "trendy," a dog, despite his individual excellence, perhaps would have done more winning had he been shown ten years earlier. Or that dog might have been more successful as a winner or producer of champions if shown on another continent.

The American Standard, the Canadian Standard, the English Standard, and the F.C.I. Standard are included here. Study and comparison of these documents will show that throughout the world, breeders and exhibitors are working together to produce outstanding Shih Tzu that encompass almost identical characteristics.

THE AMERICAN STANDARD

General Appearance

The Shih Tzu is a sturdy, lively, alert toy dog with long flowing double coat. Befitting his noble Chinese ancestry as a highly valued, prized companion and palace pet, the Shih Tzu is proud of bearing, has a distinctively arrogant carriage with head well up and tail curved over the back. Although there has always been considerable size variation, the Shih Tzu must be compact, solid, carrying good weight and substance.

Even though a toy dog, the Shih Tzu must be subject to the same requirements of soundness and structure prescribed for all breeds, and any deviation from the ideal described in the standard should be penalized to the extent of the deviation. Structural faults common to all breeds are as undesirable in the Shih Tzu as in any other breed, regardless of whether or not such faults are specifically mentioned in the standard.

Size, Proportion, Substance

Size—Ideally, height at withers is 9 to 10-1/2 inches; but, not less than 8 inches nor more than 11 inches. Ideally, weight of mature dogs—9–16 pounds.

Proportion—Length between withers and root of tail is slightly longer than height at withers. *The Shih Tzu must never be so high stationed as to appear leggy, nor so low stationed as to appear dumpy or squatty.*

Substance—Regardless of size, the Shih Tzu is *always* compact, solid and carries good weight and substance.

Head

Head—Round, broad, wide between eyes, its size *in balance* with the overall size of dog being neither too large nor too small.
   Fault: Narrow head, close-set eyes.

Expression—Warm, sweet, wide-eyed, friendly and trusting. An overall well-balanced and pleasant expression supercedes the importance of individual parts. *Care should be taken to look and examine well beyond the hair to determine if what is seen is the actual head and expression rather than an image created by grooming technique.*

Eyes—Large, round, not prominent, placed well apart, looking straight ahead. *Very dark.* Lighter on liver pigmented dogs and blue pigmented dogs.
   Fault: Small, close-set or light eyes; excessive eye white.

Ears—Large, set slightly below crown of skull; heavily coated.

Skull—Domed.

Stop—There is a *definite* stop.

Muzzle—Square, short, unwrinkled, with good cushioning, set no lower than bottom eye rim; never downturned. Ideally, no longer than 1 inch from tip of nose to stop, although length may vary slightly in relation to overall size of dog. Front of muzzle should be flat; lower lip and chin not protruding and definitely never receding.
   Fault: Snipiness, lack of definite stop.

Nose—Nostrils are broad, wide, and open.

Pigmentation—Nose, lips, eye rims are black on all colors, except liver on liver pigmented dogs and blue on blue pigmented dogs.
   Fault: Pink on nose, lips, or eye rims.

Bite—Undershot. Jaw is broad and wide. A missing tooth or slightly misaligned teeth should not be too severely penalized. Teeth and tongue should not show when mouth is closed.
   Fault: Overshot bite.

Neck, Topline, Body

Of utmost importance is an overall well-balanced dog with no exaggerated features.

Neck—Well set-on flowing smoothly into shoulders; of sufficient length to permit natural high head carriage and in balance with height and length of dog.

Topline—Level.

Body—Short-coupled and sturdy with no waist or tuck-up. The Shih Tzu is slightly longer than tall.
   Fault: Legginess.

Chest—Broad and deep with good spring-of-rib, however, not barrel-chested. Depth of ribcage should extend to just below elbow. Distance from elbow to withers is a little greater than from elbow to ground.

Croup—Flat.

Tail—Set on high, heavily plumed, carried in curve well over back. Too loose, too tight, too flat, or too low set a tail is undesirable and should be penalized to extent of deviation.

Forequarters

Shoulders—Well-angulated, well laid-back, well laid-in, fitting smoothly into body.

Legs—Straight, well-boned, muscular, set well-apart and under chest, with elbows set close to body.

Pasterns—Strong, perpendicular.

Dewclaws—May be removed.

Feet—Firm, well-padded, point straight ahead.

Hindquarters

Angulation of hindquarters should be in balance with forequarters.

Legs—Well-boned, muscular, and straight when viewed from rear with well-bent stifles, not close set but in line with forequarters.

Hocks—Well let down, perpendicular.
  Fault: Hyperextension of hocks.

Dewclaws—May be removed.

Feet—Firm, well-padded, point straight ahead.

Coat

Coat—Luxurious, double-coated, dense, long, and flowing. Slight wave permissible. Hair on top of head is tied up.
  Fault: Sparse coat, single coat, curly coat.

Trimming— Feet, bottom of coat, and anus may be done for neatness and to facilitate movement.
  Fault: Excessive trimming.

Color and Markings

All are permissible and to be considered *equally*.

Gait

The Shih Tzu moves straight and must be shown at its own natural speed, *neither raced nor strung-up,* to evaluate its smooth, flowing, effortless movement with good front reach and equally strong rear drive, level topline, naturally high head carriage, and tail carried in gentle curve over back.

Temperament

As the sole purpose of the Shih Tzu is that of a companion and house pet, it is essential that its temperament be outgoing, happy, affectionate, friendly and trusting towards all.

Can. and Am. Ch. Santini's Luciano Shubaru, owned by Marillyn Corbett and Mildred Sniderman.

Ch. Visconti The Enlightened One, owned by John Bohm.

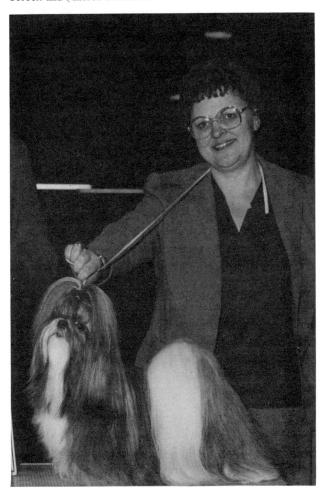

135

THE ENGLISH STANDARD

Adopted 1985

General Appearance: Sturdy, abundantly coated dog with distinctly arrogant carriage and chrysanthemum-like face.

Characteristics: Intelligent, active and alert.

Temperament: Friendly and independent.

Head and Skull: Head broad, round, wide between eyes. Shock-headed with hair falling well over eyes. Good beard and whiskers, hair growing upwards on the nose giving a distinctly chrysanthemum-like effect. Muzzle of ample width, square, short, not wrinkled, flat and hairy. Nose black but dark liver in liver or liver marked dogs and about one inch from tip to definite stop. Nose level or slightly tip-tilted. Top of nose leather should be on a line with or slightly below lower eyerim. Wide open nostrils. Downpointed nose highly undesirable, as are pinched nostrils. Pigmentation on muzzle as unbroken as possible.

Eyes: Large, dark, round, placed well apart but not prominent. Warm expression. In liver or liver marked dogs, lighter eye colour permissible. No white of eye showing.

Ears: Large, with long leathers, carried drooping. Set slightly below crown of skull, so heavily coated they appear to blend into hair of neck.

Mouth: Wide, slightly undershot or level. Lips level.

Neck: Well proportioned, nicely arched. Sufficient length to carry head proudly.

Forequarters: Shoulders well laid back. Legs short, and muscular with ample bone, as straight as possible, consistent with broad chest being well let down.

Body: Longer between withers and root of tail than height at withers, well coupled and sturdy, chest broad and deep, shoulders firm, back level.

Hindquarters: Legs short and muscular with ample bone. Straight when viewed from the rear. Thighs well rounded and muscular. Legs looking massive on account of wealth of hair.

Feet: Rounded, firm and well padded, appearing big on account of wealth of hair.

Tail: Heavily plumed carried gaily well over back. Set on high. Height approximately level with that of skull to give a balanced outline.

Gait/Movement: Arrogant, smooth-flowing, front legs reaching well forward, strong rear action and showing full pad.

Coat: Long, dense, not curly, with good undercoat. Slight wave permitted. Strongly recommended that hair on head be tied up.

Colour: All colours permissible, white blaze on forehead and white tip to tail highly desirable in parti-colours.

Weight and Size: 4.5 to 8.1 kgs (10–18 lbs.) Ideal weight 4.5–7.3 kgs (10–16 lbs.) Height at withers not more than 26.7 cm (10-½ ins), type and breed characteristics of the utmost importance and on no account to be sacrificed to size alone.

Faults: Any departure from the foregoing points should be considered a fault and the seriousness with which the fault should be regarded should be in exact proportion to its degree.

Note: Male animals should have two apparently normal testicles fully descended into the scrotum.

Eng. Ch. Firefox of Santosha, owned by Mr. and Mrs. D. Crossley.

Eng. Ch. Greenmoss Chin-Ki Of Meo, top producer of English champions, owned by Mr. and Mrs. Arnold Leadbitter.

FEDERATION CYNOLOGIQUE INTERNATIONALE STANDARD

The national kennel clubs of every European country (with the exception of England), every South American country, Japan, and South Africa are members of the Federation Cynologique Internationale (F.C.I.) This organization licenses certain shows to award international championships. In order to earn the title of international champion, a dog must be awarded a specified number of certificates (called CACIBS, or Certificats d'Aptitude au Championat Internationale). Following is the Standard by which Shih Tzu are judged in F.C.I. licensed shows:

General Characteristics: Very active, lively and alert, with a distinctly arrogant carriage.

Weight and Size: Weight range, 10–18 lb, with ideal weight 10-16 lb; height at withers not more than 10-1/2 inches; type and breed characteristics are of the utmost importance and are not to be sacrificed to size alone.

Head: Broad and round, wide between the eyes. Shock-headed, with hair falling well over the eyes. Good whiskers and beard. The hair growing upward on the nose gives a distinctly chrysanthemum-like effect. Muzzle square and short, but not wrinkled like a Pekingese's; rather, it is flat and hairy. Nose black preferably, with about 1 inch from tip to stop. Mouth level or slightly underhung.

Eyes: Large, dark and round, but not prominent.

Ears: Large, with long leathers, carried drooping. Set slightly below the crown of the skull. So heavily coated that they appear to blend with the hair of the neck.

Body: Between withers and root of tail, body should be longer than height at withers; well coupled and sturdy; chest broad and deep, shoulders firm, back level.

Tail: Heavily plumed and curled well over back; carried gaily, set on high.

Forequarters: Legs short and muscular, with ample bone. The legs should look massive because of the abundance of hair.

Hindquarters: Legs short and muscular, with ample bone. They should look straight when viewed from the rear. Thighs well rounded and muscular. Legs should look massive because of abundance of hair.

Feet: Firm and well padded. The abundant hair should make them look big.

Coat: Long and dense but not curly, with good undercoat.

Color: All colors permissible, but a white blaze on the forehead and a white tip to the tail are highly prized. Dogs with liver markings may have dark liver noses and slightly lighter eyes. Pigmentation on muzzle as unbroken as possible.

Faults: Narrow head, pig jaws, snipiness, pale pink nose or eye-rim coloring, small or light eyes, legginess, sparseness of coat.

German Bundessieger, World Champion (F.C.I.), and Int. Ch. Al Jarreau of Jenshu, owned by Jens Niedergesaess, West Germany.

German Bundessieger, 1975, World Champion (F.C.I.), Paris, 1974, and Int. Ch. Quang-Te van de Blauwe-Mammouth, owned by the Reverend and Mrs. D. Allan Easton.

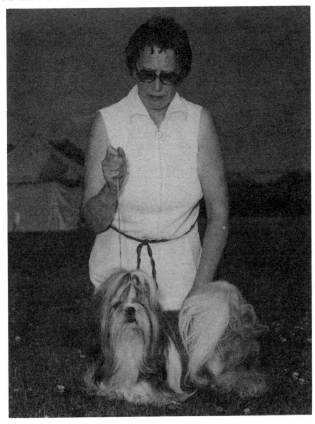

THE CANADIAN STANDARD

General Appearance: Very active, lively and alert, with a distinctly arrogant carriage. The Shih Tzu is not a toy dog.

Size: About 11 in. (28 cm) at the withers, but considerable variation from this standard is permissible, provided other proportions are correct and true to type.

Coat and Colour: Coat long and dense, but not curly; looks harsher than it feels to the touch. All colours; but a white blaze on the forehead and white tip to tail are highly prized. Dogs with liver markings may have liver noses and lighter eyes.

Head: Head broad, round, and wide between the eyes, shock headed, with hair falling well over the eyes; good beard and whiskers; the hair growing upwards on the nose gives a distinctly chrysanthemum-like effect. *Muzzle* square, short, but not wrinkled like a Pekingese, flat and hairy. *Mouth* level or slightly underhung — overshot jaws undesirable. *Eyes* large, dark and round, but not prominent. *Ears* carried drooping, so heavily coated that they appear to blend with the hair of the neck.

Forequarters: Legs short, straight, and muscular. The legs should look massive on account of the wealth of hair.

Body: Body between withers and root of tail should be considerably longer than the height of withers; well ribbed up.

Hindquarters: Legs short, straight, and muscular. The legs should look massive on account of the wealth of hair. Feet should be big with hair between the pads. The feet should look massive on account of the wealth of hair.

Tail: Heavily coated and curled well over back; set on high.

Am. and Can. Ch. Arvind Vom Tschomo-Lungma, owned by Trudy Kerr, Canada.

Above: Am. and Can. Ch. Mar Del's King Kanishka, owned by Bonnie Miller, D.V.M. Kanishka was the top winning Shih Tzu in Canada in 1972.

Above: Am. and Can. Ch. Nanking's Broadway Joe, owned by Gerry Ikola and David and Mary Robertson.

Below: Can. and Ber. Ch. Carrimount Ah Ting Ting, owned by Mr. and Mrs. A. Dickson.

138

Ch. Romano of Landor di Visconti, owned by Jon Ferrante and Mary Warren-Lea.

Ch. Mariljac Joey of Jubilation, owned by Garrett Crissman and Linda Miller.

Martin's Black Magic Puff, owned by Daryl Martin.

Ch. Wyvern Oh Abraham, owned by Mrs. A. Dickson.

Can., Am., and Ber. Ch. Wenrick's Holly N' Rustinwood, owned by Cora Lee and James Romano.

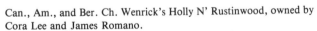

Ch. Chateau Joly Roger, bred by Billie Forsman and owned by Marilyn M. Guiraud.

Ch. Lou Wan Casandra of Hapiours, owned by Ted Gec, Patsy Williams, and Coni Nickerson.

Copa Made In The Shade of Granville, owned by Marion Russell.

Ch. Hillside Acres Simon Legree, owned by Louise Rudacille, who was one of Ingrid Colwell's original "disciples." Robert Sharp handled Simon to his championship.

Ch. Mandarin's Nutmeg Of Regal, owned by John and Pam Wilus.

Variations Within and Beyond the Standard

Although there are resemblances to the Pug, the Pekingese, the Lhasa Apso, and the Maltese, the Shih Tzu overall is unique in personality, structure, and movement. The very essence of breed temperament, along with structural peculiarities, is what makes the breed the Shih Tzu.

The aforementioned breeds doubtless figure in the ancestry of the Shih Tzu, but there is no need to compare the Shih Tzu with them in order to comment on the Shih Tzu Standard.

The American Kennel Club approved the original Shih Tzu Standard in 1969 and approved the revised Shih Tzu Standard in 1988. The new English Standard, the F.C.I. Standard, and the Canadian Standard are all very similar. Despite the fact that the Shih Tzu has been approved to be shown in different Groups in different countries, size and weight have become stabilized to the point where there is surprisingly little variation in size and weight in different locations in the world. Great diversity in size and weight is more the exception than the rule. From the time of breed acceptance by the AKC, America's greatest winners have ranged from as low as ten pounds to as high as eighteen pounds. But such variances among winners are becoming less and less frequent.

Prominent Shih Tzu breeders throughout the world are communicating with each other through magazine articles, books, and personal correspondence. Importing and exporting of breeding stock and valuable show stock are constantly going on among breed owners in the United States, Canada, Europe, and Asia. Logically, because of quarantine regulations, few importations to the British Isles occur in any breed. The six months' quarantine can cost upwards of one thousand pounds, or approximately $2,000.

The implications of few imports of outside breeding stock into England is not a subject of discussion in this book except to state that any New World trends in "type" would be least likely to affect the Shih Tzu in England. In years past some of England's finest were exported around the world to improve the breed. The Shih Tzu is evolving, nonetheless, somewhat differently in the United States and Canada. Because of the simplicity of the Shih Tzu Standards throughout the world in comparison to, let us say, the Great Dane (*Deutche Dogge*) Standards throughout the world, there appears to be more room for interpretation of the Standard by breeders who visualize the Shih Tzu in different ways in different areas of the world.

1. The Shih Tzu Standards state that the Shih Tzu should be "slightly" longer, "somewhat" longer, or just "longer" than the height at the withers. How long is "slightly," or "somewhat," or "longer"? Whatever the length of the Shih Tzu, a square body is, at least, not correct.

2. Most Shih Tzu Standards call for a short leg. The new AKC Standard does not, but legginess is faulted, and anything less could be considered relatively short. If a Shih Tzu is square, its legs cannot be considered short. In comparison, a Great Dane should be square — as should many other breeds — and "squareness" excludes the term "short legs."

3. All Shih Tzu Standards require that the dog be "well boned," with "ample bone." That, by definition, should preclude "slightness of bone." Variations on this term visually and by actual examination are possible considering the condition of the dog at a particular time. A Shih Tzu in good weight and condition would conform to the Standard even if it tended to be somewhat "slight of bone." The Shih Tzu is not intended to be "coarse," and a dog which is too heavy in bone cannot be conditioned to disguise that structural exaggeration.

4. A "broad and round" head is essentially characteristic of a good Shih Tzu. The professional cosmetic grooming of a narrow head that creates the illusion of "broad and round" does not replace what should be present structurally. Judges should take care not to be fooled by exaggerations of grooming which substitute hair for actual skull. Beautiful, careful grooming is always appreciated. But why create dishonest illusions? Why not breed for beautiful heads?

5. The eyes of a Shih Tzu should be filled with "mystery, warmth, sweetness, depth and the wisdom of a thousand sages." Standards are *very clear* in saying large and round but not prominent. That means that the eyes should *not* be bulging or protruding. "Very dark" eye color (lighter on liver pigmented and blue pigmented dogs) precludes blue, green, and light brown, as well as too much white in the eyes. In the new AKC Standard, excessive eye white showing is listed as a fault. There appears to be reason to suspect that exaggerated white markings on the face, as attractive as they may be, sometimes go hand in hand with light colored eyes and large white areas in the eye or eyes. A black masked solid is rarely if ever seen with an abnormal amount of white showing in the eyes. This is an important reason to include the solid colored Shih Tzu in the ring and in breeding programs.

6. Length and placement of the nose seems to represent a very personal issue with breeders, even causing great and emotional controversy. Since this is intended to be an accurate and reasonable treatise on the breed,

Ti Mull Ling's Chi Chi Mei, owned by Laura Gidusko.

Can. Ch. Santini's Kaduna Phat-Choy-A, owned by Marillyn Corbett.

Father and son: Am. and Can. Ch. Fauntine Sunburst, owned by Patricia Neugarth, and Ch. Joylin's Masterpiece, owned by Hilde Pittelli.

Ch. Emperor's Ebony Bla-Ka-Moor, bred by Dr. and Mrs. J. Wesley Edel, handled by Cathie Phillips.

Am. and Can. Ch. Bel Air Stargazer, owned by Garrett Crissman.

Ch. Kee Lee Eclipse Of Mar Del, owned by Warren Lee and Margaret Edel MacIntosh.

142

let us say that muzzle length "may vary slightly in relation to overall size of dog" does not mean two inches of nose length. The nose should never be downturned.

7. While it is best to strive for a broad under jaw with six incisors between the canines, as is stressed in England and on the Continent, let us be reasonable and realistic. The Shih Tzu was not bred for Terrier activity, herding sheep and fighting off wolves, guard and attack work, or coursing game. Doubling up on breeding stock that have missing teeth is not wise. But judges who overscrutinize bites to the exclusion of other more pertinent structural characteristics are either misdirected or do not have the required "eye" to see overall structure and movement. Such judges can count teeth and therefore seem to use such counting as their only criterion in judging quality. The overall balance, structure, condition, and movement of the Shih Tzu are of far more importance than the bite, unless it is overshot or terribly undershot.

Before the reign of the Dowager Empress it was stylish to breed the Imperial Palace Guardian Dogs to appear ferocious. Certainly, greatly undershot dogs with double rows of teeth were the vogue. Such was not the case after breeding came under the scrutiny of the Dowager Empress. A sweet-faced, amicable Shih Tzu, Oriental in appearance, was her requirement.

8. The AKC-approved Standard for the Shih Tzu calls for the gait to be smooth, flowing, and effortless, with good front reach and equally strong rear drive. As is true in all breeds, the movement of the Shih Tzu is indicative of the structure of the dog. That is why it is essential to recognize the Shih Tzu which moves properly and to use that recognition as a basis for comparison. Fast movement is not necessarily correct movement. Slow movement is not necessarily improper movement. In Group and Best-in-Show competition, it is the combination of proper speed and correct gait that observers must recognize. Sheer speed is oftentimes erroneously praised with no concern or knowledge of what is proper.

To understand correct movement in the Shih Tzu, try to visualize a "sailing ship" or a "sword brandishing, belted, swashbuckling musketeer or pirate" in motion. This is the essential Shih Tzu gait, unique among all breeds of dogs. All of the elements of Shih Tzu conformation described in the Standard are inherent in this phenomenon. The sailing ship floats in a rhythmically flowing, slightly hesitant way. The musketeer complete with sword and trappings moves in a rhythmically flowing manner on a sturdy and well built frame which is capable of doing great damage to the enemy. With head well up, the Shih Tzu with such carriage is distinctly arrogant and proud of bearing, as befits noble ancestry.

9. Legs must be set well apart, both in front and rear, providing a complement of driving power, and connecting to a sturdy, tight body with a level topline and well set tail that is carried properly. This correct outline has a "forward look" of *avanti* and *elan*. Any looseness or exaggeration in structure detracts from the overall balance described in the Standard. It is lovely indeed to see well-let-down, perpendicular hocks and well-angulated, wide rears typical of the Shih Tzu. Weak, narrow, straight-stifled rears cannot provide the proper drive, nor can they contribute to the correct movement.

10. A front that is too narrow, shoulders too straight and not set back properly, and a chest so narrow as to preclude the slight curvature of the shoulder that is needed with relation to the forearm — all contribute to what is known as a "Terrier front." This type of front is not characteristic of a good Shih Tzu but is truly an abomination. It is the broad chest, well-laid-back shoulder blades, slight curvature of the upper arm, a straight lower arm (or leg) fitting smoothly to the broad chest, along with proper movement of the thighs, which combine to produce the gait that is characteristic only of the Shih Tzu. Legs should be as relatively short and straight as possible, consistent with good spring of ribs. The length from the withers to the ground should be not quite as long as the distance from the withers to the root of the tail. Stilted movement in front from side to side is to be abhorred, for it is indicative of loose shoulders.

11. The temperament of the Shih Tzu is a phenomenon. Impressing observers as extraordinary beings, these intelligent yet independent fluffy clowns are capable of winning highest honors in such exacting competition as obedience and tracking exercises. So beware, ye people who would be nonparticipants in the Shih Tzu world. These courageous and sturdy little dogs are capable of conquering the coldest of hearts. Perhaps even King Richard I, despite his "lionheart," would have succumbed to the enchanting eyes of a Shih Tzu — had he owned one. Perhaps he would have remained in "Merry England" rather than wreaking havoc on the Continents of the East during his Crusades to win the Holy Land.

Many a lonely heart has found fulfillment, and many an uneasy spirit has been quelled through companionship with a Shih Tzu. That is the basis for the growing popularity of the breed. Owners often find themselves increasingly involved in the quest for broadened knowledge of all things Oriental — Chinese art, Eastern literature, and Buddhist symbolism. Meditating on the intrinsic character of the Shih Tzu, the introspective owner finds an ever deepening answer to the obvious question, "Why was the Dowager Empress so jealous of her ownership of these dogs?"

12. In the paragraph dealing with eyes, the new American Shih Tzu Standard states that the eye color is to be *very dark*, but may be lighter on liver pigmented

Mei Sans Friend Jasper Jones, Am. and Can. C.D.X. Owner, Terry Carter. Jasper, liver colored, is a producer of champions.

Foxhall Floydian Flirt of Copa, owned by Coni Nickerson.

Ch. Sun Loon Ms of Rockee Vollee daughter, owned by Molly Heck.

Eng. Ch. Golden Heidi of Elfann, owned by Tom and Sylvia Hoyle.

and blue pigmented dogs. When it comes to coat color and markings, however, the new AKC Standard states that "*All* are permissible and to be considered equally." This long-overdue anti-discrimination clause should encourage serious breeders, fanciers, and judges to find the real value in specimens they might previously have overlooked. Nevertheless, there is no realistic way to prevent judges and breeders from favoring certain colors and from seeing special aesthetic value in symmetrical markings on the parti-colors.

Certainly, the Dowager Empress loved her best specimens regardless of their color. The only photograph known to exist of the Dowager Empress with a Shih Tzu is reproduced in this book. A favorite, Sea Otter, was a solid black. But a rainbow of Shih Tzu colors existed in the Imperial Palaces in the Forbidden City, including solid blacks, brindles, sables, silvers, golds, and whites, as well as parti-colors with white markings in all of these colors.

The writings of the Dowager Empress's beloved attendant, the Princess Der Ling, are extensive. Written in Chinese, they later were translated into English. The entire collection of her writings has been noted and reviewed by this author. There is no mention of the Dowager Empress's having a color preference in any of her Shih Tzu.

The fact that the Dowager Empress valued the symmetrically marked Shih Tzu above those not so perfectly marked should not influence modern-day judgment of quality in conformation. The heraldic significance accorded the white forehead blaze, two white whiskers, and perfectly marked saddles by Forbidden City aficionados was influenced by Buddhist (and earlier Hindu) symbolism. Such religious connotations should not be considered in assessing Shih Tzu quality in fairness to less flashy specimens that may be of superior quality structurally.

Me Ling's Me & My Shadow, owned by Dottie Campbell.

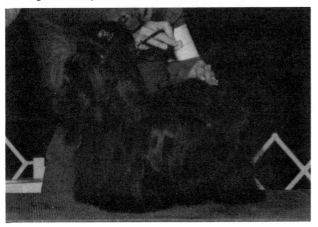

Chumulari San Pai Yinte Yen, owned by Sissi Loo Kennels.

The liver color has been recognized and accepted in Shih Tzu Standards around the world. This color is no novelty and there should be no discrimination against it. Pigmentation of eye rims, lips, and nose should be dark liver or brown and should be unbroken. Any area that is flesh colored represents an absence of pigment and should be faulted.

Liver puppies may be whelped when least expected. And when expected, from breeding a liver to a non-liver with liver ancestors, liver puppies may not be included among the progeny.

Dominant and recessive genetic color inheritance laws may govern the production of blue Shih Tzu puppies more than the production of livers. A blue carries *no black-pigmented hairs*. At birth, the blue or parti-color blue with white markings is (except for white portions) a mouse gray, slate, Weimaraner-color, blue gray, silver gray, or steel blue. With maturity, the blue gray or variance of it may turn dark silver or pastel gold, or it may remain steel blue.

Certain lines produce more blues than do others, and blues may produce black pigmented puppies. At adulthood, the nose pigment of blues may be so dark a gray as to appear black until the dogs are compared closely with Shih Tzu that have black nose pigment. The difference can then be appreciated. Blues *never* mature to have black hairs or nose pigmentation.

Breeding blue to blue is *not* recommended by this author. Experiences over the years suggest that the blue color *may* be linked to a semi-lethal gene that creates problems when doubled by mating blue to blue.

Blue Shih Tzu are sometimes almost lavender in color. Some such blues have finished championships in easy stride against the toughest of competition. Their full acceptance should be welcomed by breeders and exhibitors when their characteristics and possible genetic potential are realized.

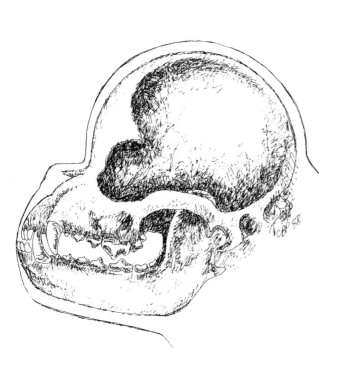

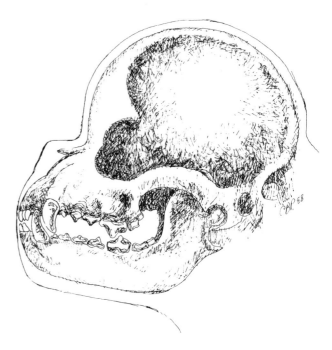

The flat muzzle, square and unwrinkled, the straight nose, neither too long *nor too short,* the definite stop, the slightly undershot bite, the round, domed skull—all contribute to proper expression and to the likelihood of adherence to the Standard.

The level bite was preferred in the previous American Standard. The revised Standard does not mention the level bite either as a virtue or as a fault. The level bite in a breeding program can be useful to correct badly undershot bites. Yet, doubling up on the level bite is not recommended because that may lead to seriously overshot bites and receding skulls.

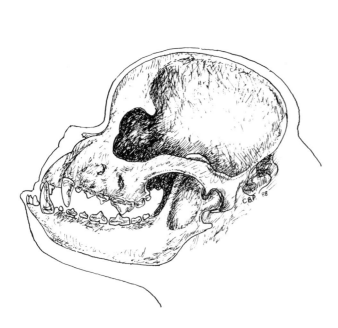

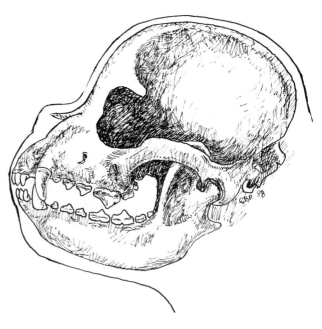

Here, the front of the muzzle is not square; the lower jaw and chin protrude; and the skull is not round or domed.

The skull sometimes recedes when the bite becomes overshot; the muzzle becomes downturned; the stop becomes less than definite; and the skull flattens. Consequently, unsightliness occurs. Nature tends to push the genes toward "canine normalcy," although typical Oriental Shih Tzu characteristics then begin to disappear.

146

Expression should be warm, sweet, wide-eyed, friendly, and trusting.

Of utmost importance is an overall well-balanced dog with no exaggerated features.

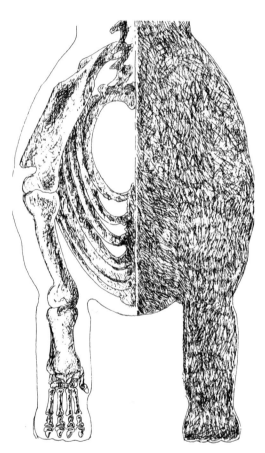

Sound front assembly.

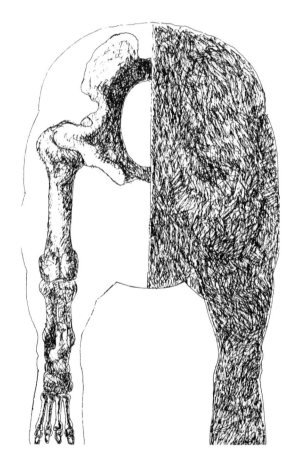

Sound rear assembly.

The Shih Tzu is proud of bearing, has a distinctly arrogant carriage with head well up and tail curved over the back.

Feet, bottom of coat, and anus may be trimed for neatness and to facilitate movement.

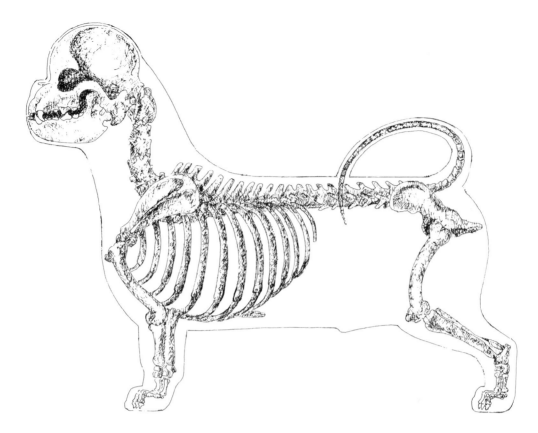

Correct skeletal structure.

Ch. House of Wu Mai Mai (bitch), all-breed Best-in-Show and all-Toy Best-in-Show winner. Breeder, Mrs. Charles Eckes. Owner, Ann Hickok Warner.

STRUCTURE OF THE SHIH TZU

The following comments on the structure of the Shih Tzu conform with the provisions of the Standard and represent the author's verbalization of what he looks for when he judges the breed. The skeletal drawing and the photograph on the opposite page illustrate the author's comments.

Head: round, broad but not flat, skull domed. Balanced with size of body. Carried proudly.

Eyes: large, round, wide set, unobtrusive. Very dark, no excessive white showing. Liver pigmented and blue pigmented dogs have lighter eyes.

Ears: nicely formed, large, set high. Appear long and drooping because of length of coat fringes.

Stop: well defined.

Nose: not exaggerated. About an inch in length. Turned up, never turned down. May appear slightly turned up because of texture of nose leather. Balance between length of nose and head size may be considered.

Muzzle: unwrinkled, square, broad, and cushioned. Tongue and teeth are not exposed, and lips meet neatly when mouth is closed.

Underjaw: strong, broad, never receding.

Neck: neither too long nor too short. Slight arch at crest. Sloping smoothly and flowingly into withers and back. Carried elegantly.

Withers: smooth as result of well-fitted blades meeting closely.

Back: strong, level, free from dip behind shoulders.

Shoulders: well-laid-back, contributing to nicely formed neck and overall balance. Sloped well into back, meeting snugly at withers.

Chest: broad, rounded, drops to slightly below elbows.

Loin: level with back. No higher than back. Strong. Level at croup.

Croup: flat at base of tail.

Tail: growing directly off a flat croup. Set high. Forming lovely arch over back, with teacup-handle appearance.

Elbows: well fitted against body.

Pasterns: strong. Perpendicular.

Feet: strong, well padded, of good size. Moderately arched. Turning neither in nor out.

Body proportions: *slightly* longer from withers to root of tail than from withers to ground.

"Look alikes." Statue of Foo Dog with Yum Yum of Dragons, owned by Mr. and Mrs. George Graine.

Typical puppies from Anibe, shown with their dam's prize from winning the Tibethund show.

Reproduction of Indian painting titled "Noah's Ark," attributed to Miskin ca. 1590. The lions depicted here became a focal point of Oriental imagery for many breeds of dogs.

Glossary of Genetic Terms

Aberration. A variation from normal in some basic hereditary factor, such as the number or the arrangement of chromosomes.

Allele. Shortened form of the word *allelomorph* and generally used instead of allelomorph.

Allelomorph. Any alternative form of a gene inherited according to Mendelian Law, influencing the same developmental process or processes of any given trait, but in different ways.

Autosomal chromosome. An ordinary body chromosome — one that is not a sex chromosome.

Back cross. Mating of a hybrid or outcrossed offspring back to one of its parents.

Blending. Combining of opposite genetic extremes, resulting in phenotype that is neither extreme but a compromise.

Break-through. The partial expression of a recessive trait. Also referred to as "incomplete masking."

Carrier. An individual who possesses and transmits an unseen recessive genetic characteristic.

Cell. The basic unit of living tissue.

Character. Demonstrable or observable attribute of an individual resulting from genetic similarities or differences.

Chromatid. A half-chromosome, the result of the splitting of a chromosome during cell division.

Chromatin. A granular protoplasmic substance in the nucleus of an organic cell.

Chromosomes. Any of the microscopic, rod-shaped bodies into which the chromatin separates during mitosis or meiosis. Chromosomes carry the genes that convey hereditary characteristics and are constant in number for each species. (Human cells contain twenty-four pairs of chromosomes; canine cells contain thirty-nine pairs of chromosomes.)

Crossing over. The exchange of minute particles, including genes, by chromosomes during synapsis.

Cytoplasm. The protoplasm of a cell other than the nucleus.

Cytoplasmic inheritance. A rather new branch of the science of genetics which holds that in addition to the genes of the nucleus, the cytoplasm of cells contains material contributing to heredity.

Deletion. A condition in which a piece of a chromosome becomes detached and ceases to exert any function.

Dihybrid cross. Breeding or reproductive cross in which the action of two heterozygous pairs of genes is considered.

Diploid. Literally, two-fold. Having twice the number of chromosomes normally occurring in a germ cell. Most somatic cells are diploid. Opposed to haploid.

Dominant. Designating or relating to that one of any pair of opposite inheritable characteristics which, when factors for both are present in the germ cell, excludes the expression of the other and appears in the organism's phenotype. Opposed to recessive.

Embryo. An organism in the early prenatal (before birth) stage of its development.

Enzyme. An organic substance which accelerates chemical transformation without itself undergoing change.

Epistatic. Literally, placed above. Applied to a gene that conceals the expression of one or more other genes. Dominant. Opposed to hypostatic.

Eugenics. The science devoted to improving hereditary qualities of a breed or race.

Filial. Designating any generation following the parental generation. Symbol used is F with subscript numeral. (F_1 represents first filial generation; F_2 represents second filial generation; etc.)

Fluctuation. Variation attributed to non-genetic factor or factors, usually to the environment.

Gamete. A reproductive cell that can unite with another reproductive cell to form the cell that develops into a new individual. Also called the germ cell (example, sperm or ovum).

Gene. Any of the units by which hereditary characteristics are determined and transmitted. Each mature reproductive cell is believed to carry a gene for every inheritable characteristic. Thus, an individual receives a complete set of genes from each parent.

Gene pool. Genes available in any given geographical area or breeding program.

Genetics. The science of heredity (inheritance) and variation (inherited differences), and related phenomena.

Genotype. The fundamental constitution of an organism in terms of hereditary factors which may or may not be apparent in physical appearance because of the dominance or recessiveness of individual traits. See also phenotype.

Germ cell. A gamete.

Get. Progeny, offspring, children.

Gonad. An organ in which reproductive cells are proliferated and developed. In the female, the ovary, and in the male, the testis.

Haploid. Having the number of chromosomes characteristic of the mature germ cell after meiosis. Opposed to diploid.

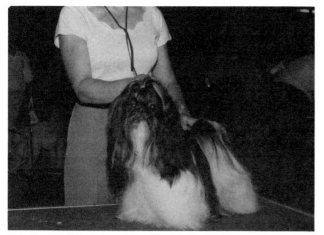

Ch. Chateau Joly Roger, owned by Marilyn Guiraud.

Ch. Nanjo Hi Hope of Joy Fu Li, owned by Joan E. Cowie.

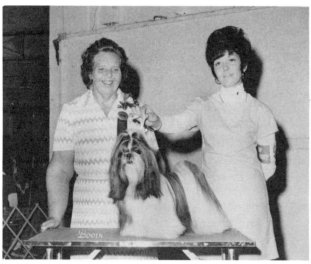

Ch. Nanjo's Oh Mai Gosh of Char-Nick, owner Nanjo Kennels.

Ch. Chumulari Hih-Hih, owned by Richard Bauer.

Ch. Sanchi's Shishi, owned by Bonnie Miller, D.V.M.

Ch. Chow Lin Sugar Bear Visconti, bred and owned by Beth Herndon.

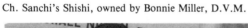

Heredity. The transmission from parent to offspring of certain characteristics. The tendency of an organism to reproduce itself.

Heterosis. Phenomenon referred to as hybrid vigor, and occurring when a cross is made between strains, breeds, or varieties, resulting in offpring which exhibit qualities superior to those exhibited by either parent.

Heterozygote. An organism producing two kinds of germ cells with respect to a particular gene, or two different alleles of the same gene, and therefore not breeding pure or true for a given factor. Opposed to homozygote.

Homozygote. An organism having duplicate genes for a particular character and producing only one kind of germ cell with respect to that character, and therefore breeding pure or true for that factor. Opposed to heterozygote.

Hormone. Internal secretion of endocrine (ductless) gland. This secretion then activates other organs.

Hybrid. The offspring of two animals or plants of unlike genetic makeup for one or more characters. A heterozygote.

Hypostatic. Literally, placed under. A factor masked or suppressed by another factor. Recessive. Opposed to epistatic.

Inbreeding. Continual mating of individuals of the same or very closely related stocks. Opposed to outcrossing or outbreeding. By common usage, inbreeding usually is regarded as mating together more closely related individuals than in linebreeding.

Incomplete dominance. The situation in which a recessive trait shows through the expression of the dominant trait. A break-through.

Interaction. The combined influence of two or more gene pairs.

Lethal. Term applied to a gene causing death at an early stage of development, often while the organism is still in the embryonic stage.

Linkage. Transmission en bloc of genes occurring on the same chromosome. Crossing over would prevent linkage.

Linebreeding. Continual mating of succeeding generations of individuals of somewhat related stock. Opposed to outcrossing or outbreeding. By common usage, linebreeding usually is regarded as mating together individuals not so closely related as those mated together in inbreeding.

Locus (plural, loci). A particular point or location on any given chromosome which is occupied by any particular gene group or allele.

Mask. To conceal or cover the influence of a gene. For example, as a dominant characteristic conceals a recessive one.

Meiosis. The process of cell division in which the number of chromosomes is reduced from the diploid number to the haploid number. Also called reduction division.

Mendelian trait. That which is inherited in accordance with Mendel's Laws.

Mendel's Laws. The three principles of hereditary phenomena discovered and formulated by Gregor Mendel, as follows:

1. Law of Segregation: genes exist in pairs in individuals, and in the formation of gametes each gene separates or segregates from the other member of the pair and passes into a different gamete, so that each gamete has one and only one of each kind of gene; thus characteristics are inherited separately as units and equally from each parent.

2. Law of Independent Assortment: the distribution of each pair of genes into gametes is independent of the distribution of any other pair.

3. Law of Dominance: when two factors for the alternative expression of a given characteristic are brought together in one individual, one may be expressed completely and the other not at all.

Mitosis. The process of cell division in which the chromosomes split lengthwise, the halves forming a new cell having the diploid number of chromosomes.

Mutation. A sudden, spontaneous variation in some heritable characteristics of an individual organism, as distinguished from a variation resulting from generations of gradual change. Once a mutation has occurred, it is heritable. After a gene has undergone mutation to a new form, this new form is stable and usually has no greater tendency to change again than the original gene. The mutation may result in only a minor variation or may result in stock dissimilar from ancestral stock.

Natural selection. Nature's regulation of survival and capability of carrying on succeeding generations through adaptation to environmental factors.

Nick. A breeding that produces desirable puppies.

Nucleoplasm. The substance within the nucleus of a cell.

Nucleus. The central mass within the cell, containing the chromosomes and genes.

Offspring. Children, descendants, progeny.

Outcrossing (also called outbreeding). The mating together of unrelated stocks, individuals, or lines. Opposed to inbreeding or linebreeding.

Ovary. The female organ in which reproductive egg cells or ova develop.

155

Ovum (plural ova). An egg or female germ cell which (generally only after the act of fertilization) develops into a new member of the same species.

Pathogenic. Disease producing.

Penetrance. Relative frequency with which a gene or combination of genes for a given factor proves effective.

Phenotype. The visible characteristics of an individual, resulting from the interaction of its genotype and its environment.

Polar body. The nonfunctional cell cast off by an ovum following meiosis.

Polygenetic. A trait inherited through the interaction of more than one gene, each ordinarily with relatively small effect.

Probability. A prediction of the likely frequency with which any of several possible heritable combinations can be expected to occur, under a known set of circumstances.

Probable error. A computation of reasonable divergence from expected frequencies of heritable combinations, under a known or presumed set of circumstances.

Progeny. Children, descendants, offspring, get.

Progeny selection. A method of deciding which adults to use for further breeding, based on the offspring they produced in a reasonable number of breedings. A method used to develop a breeding program.

Progeny test. A method of determining the genotype of an adult by breeding to another adult of known genotype, then tracing back on the basis of the resulting offspring. Breeding for the specific purpose of determining whether or not a particular recessive trait is carried by the offspring of any given breeding.

Protoplasm. A semifluid, viscous, translucent colloid, the essential matter of all animal and plant cells. Protoplasm consists largely of water, proteins, lipoids, carbohydrates, and inorganic salts.

Punnett square. A visualization tool used to help determine the theoretical mathematical probabilities of inheritance of any given trait in any given breeding.

		A	a	SIRE
DAM	A	AA	Aa	
	a	Aa	aa	

PROBABILITY: 25% AA, 50% Aa, and 25% aa; 25% homozygous dominant; 25% homozygous recessive; 50% heterozygous dominant carrying recessive.

Quantitative inheritance. The cumulative hereditary effect of multiple genes, particularly on measurable characteristics such as speed, size, weight, etc.

Random assortment. The chance way in which genes of a pair (or of pairs) divide and form into gametes and then recombine in the fertilized egg.

Recessive. Designating or relating to that one of any pair of opposite heritable characteristics which, when factors for both are present in the germ cell, remains latent. Opposed to dominant.

Reversion. Reappearance of ancestral traits not seen in the immediately preceding several generations. An offspring evidencing such traits is often referred to as a "throw back."

Secondary sex characteristic. Trait associated with one sex or the other, beyond the basic differences in sex organs. For example, a higher voice range for a woman.

Segregation. The manifestation in the F_2 (and later hybrid generations) as the separation and distribution to different individuals, of heritable traits in which the parents of the F_1 hybrid generation differed.

Selection. The process of picking certain individuals for their presumed qualities, particularly for future breeding programs. The process may be accomplished by phenotype (physical appearance) or by genotype (determination of genetic makeup). The latter method is the more effective if it is correctly applied.

Sex-influenced genes. Genes in which the precise effect depends on the sex of the individual. For example, in body and pubic hair, the pattern expressed differs greatly between male and female humans.

Sex-linked traits. A trait for which the gene is attached to one of the chromosomes that determines sex. Therefore, the trait tends to manifest itself only in one sex or the other.

Sib. Shortened form of sibling.

Shih Tzu Fanciers of Greater Baltimore Specialty, 1987. Kathleen Britton with Can. Ch. Bilor's Golden Elegance; Lorraine De Salvo with Dominique di Visconti; judge Robert Tendler; and Hilde Pittelli with Bilor's Golden Duster Buster and Can. Ch. Bilor's Princess Dominique.

Sibling. One of two or more individuals born of the same parents: brothers or sisters, littermates, or progeny from repeat breedings. Those offspring which have one parent in common, but the other parent is not the same, are referred to as "half-siblings," or "half-sibs."

Somatic cells. Any of the cells of an organism that become differentiated into body cells — tissues, organs, etc. Opposed to germ (reproductive) cells.

Sperm. The male germ (reproductive) cell which unites with the ovum to form the zygote.

Synapsis. The pairing of the chromosomes prior to reduction division (meiosis).

Test cross. The mating of two individuals selected by phenotype in an effort to determine their genotypes from the appearance of the offspring thus produced.

Testis (or testicle). The male sex gland or gonad.

Test mating. The mating of a hybrid (heterozygote) back to a recessive to determine whether or not the individual being tested carries the recessive genotypically.

Trihybrid cross. A breeding or reproductive cross in which the relative action of three pairs of heterozygous genes is considered.

Unit character. A quality in which the difference between one manifestation and its opposite is determined by a single pair of genes.

Variation. A trait which varies between siblings or between siblings and parental types, but which nevertheless is a heritable trait.

X-chromosome. The kind of chromosome of which the female germ cell in higher animals possesses two, while the male germ cell possesses only one plus a Y-chromosome.

Y-chromosome. In male germ cells in higher animals, this is the chromosome that is paired with the one X-chromosome present. The germ cells of females normally do not have a Y-chromosome, having instead two X-chromosomes.

Zygote. The primordial cell, formed by the union of two reproductive cells (gametes, or germ cells), one male and one female.

Ch. Chang, owned by Peggy Rust.

Am. and Can. Ch. Chumulari Li Liang, owned by the Reverend and Mrs. D. Allan Easton.

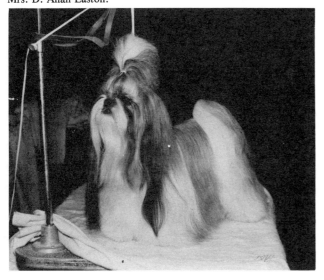

Ch. Chumulari Li Tzu, owned by Marilyn M. Guiraud. Li Tzu, by Ch. Chumulari Ying Ying out of Eng. Ch. Katrina of Greenmoss, was one of the first to attain championship status after AKC recognition.

157

Wei Honey Gold of Elfann, owned by the Reverend and Mrs. D. Allan Easton. Imported from England by the Eastons, Wei Honey Gold became a favorite at Chumulari Kennels. She is the dam of Chumulari Trari.

Ch. Bon D'Art Tu Tone of Fancee, owned by Bonnie Guggenheim and Dolly Wheeler. "Tony" was co-owned during his Specials career by Garrett Crissman. Handled by Sandy Tremont, he was a multiple Group winner.

Ch. Gunning's Semi-Spunky of Nova, owned by Taunnie Novak. He was sired by Ch. Ming Toi's P.V. Spunky and became the sire and grandsire of several Specialty winners.

Ch. House of Wu Hai U, owned by Max Kerfoot. Hai U was one of the best moving Shih Tzu of all time.

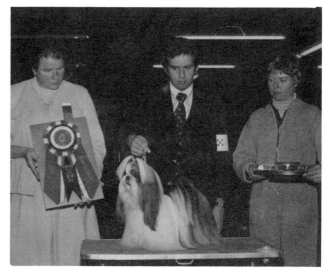

The Science of Heredity

Heredity is the process by which physical and mental traits of parents are transmitted to their offspring. At best, the process is difficult to predict or control. For centuries Man has been trying to solve the puzzles of heredity. During much of that time Man has had a general understanding of hereditary principles and has applied them, with results that have ranged from poor to excellent. Perhaps the poorest results have come from the idea (which probably dates to prehistoric times) that leadership ability could be passed intact from father to son through many succeeding generations.

The assumption was rationalized in various ways. A popular theory that persisted for centuries was that in the process of procreation a father implanted a tiny replica of himself in the mother's womb. The function of the mother was simply to protect and nourish this little fellow until he became big enough to be born.

Another widely held misconception was that characteristics were passed on to the offspring through the mixing of the blood of the mother and father. This idea is perpetuated today when it is said that someone is a full-blooded Indian, of royal blood, or of a good or bad bloodline.

Gregor Johann Mendel, an Austrian monk, is usually given credit for the earliest serious work in the field of heredity. He published the results of his findings in 1866, but little attention was given to them until the same results were obtained in three independent research projects about 1900. The word "gene" was coined after Mendel's time, but he concluded correctly that some factor transmitted from generation to generation regulated specific characteristics.

Mendel studied at the Augustinian Monastery in Brun and then at the University of Vienna. He graduated with an outstanding record, and upon the suggestion of a professor, he entered the Augustinian Monastery at Brun as a teacher of science. Being the son of a farmer, Mendel had a strong interest in botany. He was assigned only a small strip of ground for a garden, but he managed to grow great numbers of plants. His interest and curiosity were so strong that he was prompted to keep careful records of each generation of plants he produced. He focused his interests on the ordinary garden pea. In all, he grew twenty-two different varieties: some with tall stems, some with short; some with purple flowers, others with white; some with smooth seeds, others with wrinkled seeds.

Then Mendel started to hybridize the plants. He cross-pollinated tall plants with short ones; purple blossoms with white ones; those that had smooth seeds with those that had wrinkled seeds; and so on. During the spring blooming season, Mendel would patiently cross-pollinate the blossoms and cover each bloom with a tiny fabric bag. As the pods would ripen, he would carefully collect the seeds and package and label them. The next spring he would plant these hybrid seeds and record the results.

As his studies continued, Mendel found that when he crossed two varieties, one trait was always "dominant," and its opposite was always "recessive," and that the dominant trait was always shown in the first generation. He also found that the opposite trait (the recessive trait) was always carried unchanged from one generation to the next, even though it was hidden in the first generation.

For example, when he crossed a tall plant with a short one, in the first generation all of the plants were tall. There was no haphazard mixing of the characteristics that resulted in a plant that was of intermediate height. When he crossed the plants with white blossoms with those with purple blossoms, the resulting plants had purple blossoms, not a mixture of purple and white.

Then Mendel observed that when he crossed two plants of that first-generation cross, the resulting second generation included some plants that had short stems and some that had long, some that had white blossoms and some that had purple. Thus, he concluded that both of the opposite hereditary characteristics of the parents were transmitted to the first generation offspring, even though only one trait showed, and that in the next generation the hidden characteristics could become evident again. And further, that these characteristics passed on as a unit did not undergo change even though they had been concealed for a generation. The short plants of the second generation cross were identical with the earlier generation insofar as that trait was concerned. The degree of shortness was not changed even though it had been concealed for a generation.

As the study of inheritance progressed, it was discovered that individual characteristics are passed on from one generation to the next through "genes." Genes are likened to beads clustered on strings situated on chromosomes. What are chromosomes? They are thread-like structures within each cell of a living being. It is the total number of chromosomes and the genes on them that make each species different from all others. That is why two different species cannot reproduce if they are mated.

There are hundreds of thousands of genes and each gene can be different. Association does not blend them, but each remains true to its own identity. Some bacterial viruses are known to possess only eight to ten genes per chromosome, while other viruses may have one to two hundred. Mammals or other higher organisms may have one thousand to ten thousand genes per chromosome. The fruit fly has only eight chromosomes, but man has forty-eight and the dog has seventy-eight. It is obvious, therefore, that it is extremely difficult to predict what characteristics will appear in the offspring even when parents are similar in appearance.

The cells that make up a living being are of two types: "germ" cells and "body" cells. The germ cell is the beginning cell. It is created by the union of two half (or "haploid") germ cells — one haploid cell contributed by the male parent and one haploid cell contributed by the female parent. These haploid cells are derived from the splitting of germ cells that contain the full (or "diploid") number of chromosomes. This process is known as "reduction division," or "meiosis." When the germ cells of male and female split and the haploid cells join to form the beginning cell for a new being, the other two halves — one half from each parent — become nonfunctional and are cast off.

In the dog, this beginning cell now has the full number of chromosomes, seventy-eight, with thirty-nine coming from the dam and thirty-nine from the sire. When the sire's contribution merges with the dam's, it is the sire's genetic material that determines the sex of the puppy that eventually evolves. In this original cell containing seventy-eight chromosomes, each parent contributes thirty-eight that seek a partner. These partners line up as pairs along the thread-like chromosome, to resemble two strings of beads, side by side. The thirty-ninth pair also line up side by side, but they are different from all of the other chromosomes. The dam's member of the pair is always a so-called X chromosome. The sire's may also be an X chromosome, or it may be what is termed a Y chromosome. The dam's X chromosome may be paired with an X chromosome from the sire, in which case the resulting puppy will be a female. Or the dam's X chromosome may be paired with a Y chromosome from the sire, and then the resulting puppy will be a male. Chance seems to determine whether the sire will contribute an X or a Y chromosome.

Body cells split in a different way — by a process known as "mitosis." In this process the original cell splits into two identical cells. Those two cells each split into two identical cells, to make a total of four. Each of the four splits to make a total of eight. And so on, eventually forming a complete new organism.

At an early stage of cell division following conception, one of the cells and its subsequent subdivisions become germ cells for future reproduction — egg cells in a female, sperm cells in a male. In dogs, this occurs at about the sixth division. Thus this cell and its subsequent subdivisions become the vehicles not only for giving life to the next generation, but also for determining that next generation's hereditary potential through the chromosomes and genes it contains.

In the process of growth of the foetus (the unborn puppy) the genes, hormones, and environment work together. That is, the development of the puppy is regulated by the material inherited through the genes interacting with the cellular material around them. This interaction is extremely intricate and still only partially understood. Nevertheless, some growth factors can be examined independently of others.

Some traits are known to be genetically determined and to be influenced very little if at all by the environment surrounding the embryo. Blood type and eye color are examples. These characteristics are known to be influenced by only a small number of genes.

Other traits are known to be strongly influenced by prenatal environment as well as inheritance. Body build and intelligence as well as rate of growth are examples. These traits are influenced by a relatively large number of genes, and the effects of genes and environment are so intertwined that even a skilled geneticist may be unable to prove what is genetic in origin and what results from environmental influences.

The science of genetics resembles the science of mathematics in that when a breeder has a firm grasp of a few basic principles, he can solve a wide variety of problems. The basic principles include the following genetic concepts of proven practical value.

1. Inheritance is biparental. Both parents contribute an equal number of messages to the genetic constitution of the offspring.

2. Genes are not altered by existing together in a pair. A "recessive" gene existing alongside a "dominant" gene is not changed by that relationship.

3. Each individual has two of each kind of gene, but a "gamete" (mature germ cell) has only one of each kind (the "haploid" number).

4. Two pairs of genes located in different chromosomes are inherited independently, even though their action is linked. For example, straightness or curliness of the coat and color of the coat are not inherited together. In one puppy the coat might be black and straight and in a sibling, black and curly — or an entirely different color, and either straight or curly.

5. Gametes unite at random. There is neither attraction nor repulsion between a particular female cell and a particular male cell.

6. Some traits are controlled easily because only a single pair of genes is involved. Others are difficult to control because they are the result of "quantitative" inheritance — that is, the interaction of many genes.

7. Even in quantitative inheritance, important improvements can be made by application of selection methods.

8. The three major types of selection are natural selection, selection by phenotype, and selection by genotype.

9. Natural selection is basically nature's way, wherein

160

the strong survive and the weak perish. Survivors are not necessarily the best individuals from the viewpoint of seeking types desired for show-ring conformation. Thus, this method has no place in breeding purebred dogs.

10. Selection by phenotype has been for centuries the major tool of breeders of purebred dogs. It involves visual selection for desired types and elimination from breeding programs of poor individuals or those which have major faults. It is obvious that selection by phenotype alone utterly fails to eliminate individuals that are phenotypes for a desired dominant trait but carry an unwanted recessive.

An example is monorchidism, an inherited trait which may result even if it is not visually apparent in the sire. And there is, of course, no visual evidence that a female may or may not be able to pass on this fault to her offspring.

11. Selection by genotype obviously is the best choice. How to select by genotype requires a practical answer. Breeding tests are part of that answer, since the final criterion of the value of a dog or bitch is the kinds of pups he or she will produce. From a practical viewpoint, it is not possible to conduct breeding tests on a large scale. It is possible, however, to make genetic deductions from a regular breeding program by keeping complete records of the results.

12. Eradicating faults should be the primary objective. Producing superior offspring should be a close second. The major factor in establishing certain dogs as breeding favorites is their show records — and dog shows are, after all, only a method of selection by phenotype. It is wise to choose a sire on the basis of his production record — that is, whether he produces champion offspring.

If conformation only is the objective for future generations, a dog with a good show-winning record probably has a better chance of contributing good type in puppies than does a dog unable to win in shows. But even for consistent winners, the ability to transmit good conformation qualities consistently will depend in part on whether the individual is homozygous or heterozygous for genes affecting specific qualities — and in part on the mate's genetic makeup for the same qualities. Thus, progeny results provide a better clue to the individual's transmitting ability than do show winnings.

Some show champions and some non-champions are far above average in the production of show-winning progeny, proving a "prepotency" for passing on important conformation qualities because they are homozygous for many of those qualities.

When a dog, whether a champion or not, is able to produce progeny with a better than average conforma-

tion record, the first-generation offspring may be heterozygous for the good qualities for which the prepotent parent is homozygous. Whether this is the case will depend on the contribution of the other parent. But if the progeny are highly heterozygous, they will have lost much of the prepotency of the prepotent parent, and later generation pups will regress toward the breed average, with wide variation between individual progeny.

13. For certain qualities valued in some breeds, there is little or nor correlation between conformation and the trait under consideration. Examples in the Shih Tzu include vigor, fertility, viability, tractability, and sound temperament. Selection for these traits must be among a Shih Tzu breeder's major objectives.

14. Uniform genotypes may be produced by *judicious* use of three types of selective breeding: inbreeding, linebreeding, and outcrossing. All include certain risks.

Ch. Rex Landor di Visconti, owned by Billy L. Baker, bred by Jon Ferrante. By Ch. Marco Polo di Visconti out of Mar Del's Wind Chimes, Rex was one of the breed's finest movers, with a flowing, slightly swashbuckling, powerful gait.

Ch. Jaisu Ling-Ho X-Rated of Lainee, whelped January 1974, died August 1988. He was owned by Elaine Meltzer and Mrs. A. H. Warner. An outcross, he was a top Specialty winner and a top producer.

Int. Ch. Sopon v. Tschomo-Lungma, owned by Jean Gadberry

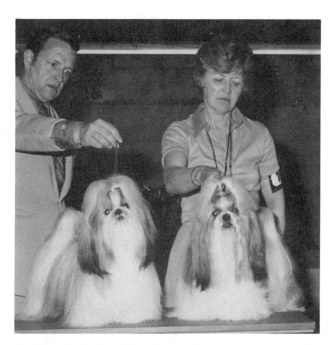

Am. and Int. Ch. Bjorneholm Pif with owner/handler Mary Wood, and Ch. Mar Del's Ring A Ding Ding with owner/handler Margaret Edel MacIntosh. Progenitor of both dogs in this treasured photo is Int. Ch. Bjorneholm Wu Ling.

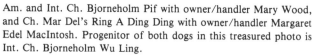

Ch. Erincroft Qu Ti Pi of Jazmin, owned by Jackie Peterson; and Ch. Dragonwyck The Great Gatsby, owned by Robert Koeppel.

Variations on the Themes of Inbreeding, Linebreeding, and Outcrossing

The subjects of inbreeding, linebreeding, and outcrossing are discussed often in current dog publications, and there are more than a few books on the market which deal thoroughly yet simply with genetics and different ways to approach the programs of breeding dogs. Many champions were whelped by chance, but it is a fortunate breeder who has a sound knowledge of the laws of genetics, and it is likely that his kennel frequently produces winners as well as breeding stock that can produce winners!

A breeder not only is breeding dogs; he actually is joining together sets of genes which are bound together into chromosomes. With this knowledge in the workings, it becomes evident that the terms inbreeding, linebreeding, and outcrossings are used too loosely by far too many breeders, and that some important variables should be discussed to clarify these terms that are so frequently used incorrectly.

Inbreeding is the breeding together of very closely related individuals, such as mother to son, father to daughter, and, closest of all, full brother to full sister. Linebreeding is the breeding together of relatives not quite so closely related, such as uncle to niece, or first cousin to first cousin. Outcrossing is generally accepted as the breeding together of individuals who have few if any common relatives in, let us say, five generations of breeding.

Although not usually the case, it is possible to breed together two dogs whose pedigrees show the breeding to be very loose linebreeding, when actually the breeding is as close genetically as full brother to full sister. The same, but reversed, can occur, although, once again, it would not usually be the case, that two dogs could be bred together, full brother to full sister, when genetically an outcross takes place. The type of breeding that actually takes place thus depends entirely on the genes which the individuals inherit from the ancestors' genebanks and then are paired when the individuals are bred together and fertilization takes place.

Why not breed for dominant genes, not only hybrid dominance, in those characteristics which need improving? Why inbreed, except to discover recessive faults and faults to breed out of one's line — when the particular line may need the influence of better characteristics from an outcross? Sometimes an outcross, properly made, can produce what is known as "heterosis" or "hybrid vigor" and give vitality to the offspring of that cross. Then again, why not breed

brother to sister if both brother and sister very closely parallel the Standard of the breed, are fertile, have outstanding temperaments, have no obvious genetic defects, or if unwanted and distressing recessives have been virtually bred out prior to that breeding?

What we are saying is simply, why not inbreed or outcross — depending on what is needed to improve the breed? If a characteristic is desired and can be obtained (all other variables being equal) in linebred union, why outcross for that characteristic? Why not save a generation in time and breed to an individual who can further the accumulation of dominant genes or the desired recessive genes by being a product himself of an outcross union with half of his pedigree already in the line? And then again, why further mediocrity by linebreeding or inbreeding a mediocre bitch to a mediocre stud, only so that we can say we have "linebred"?

The work of breeders who possess extensive personal knowledge of breeding and genetics is sheer artistry. Imagine the knowledge that breeders must have possessed in the formative years, as compared with the knowledge we as breeders have today. Imagine the patience of years of trial and error in developing new breeds — including our own inimitable Shih Tzu. Let us remember how breeds have been greatly improved and/or totally destroyed because of change — and how great a responsibility we as breeders have as we strive for the perfection of our breed.

Ch. Lainee Sigmund Floyd, owned by Elaine Meltzer. Sigmund Floyd was Number One top producer for several years. A multiple Specialty winner himself, he produced many Specialty winners.

Ch. Yingsu Johnie Reb, owned by Sue Miller. Johnie Reb is a multiple Specialty and all-breed Best-in-Show winner. He is the sire of Ch. Lou Wan's Rebel Rouser.

Am. and Can. Ch. Chumulari Ying Ying, owned by the Reverend and Mrs. D. Allan Easton. Whelped in the United States only hours after his dam Tangra's importation from West Germany, Ying Ying became world famous as the first Shih Tzu to go Best in Show in the United States on the first day of AKC breed recognition.

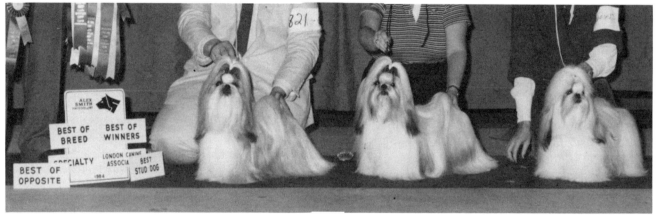

Am. and Can. Ch. Shente's Brandy Alexander, owned by Margaret Brown and Luke Ehricht. Brandy won more Best-in-Show awards in Canada than any other Shih Tzu. In 1988 at the age of 9, Brandy won Best-in-Show awards at both the ASTC National Specialty and the Canadian Kennel Club Centennial All-Breed Show.

Am. and Can. Ch. Mi Clyde Chin Chiny, owned by Joan M. Buck.

Shaadar's Happi Boi Sam, owned by Jim and Joyce Jeppesen and Mrs. Charles R. Eckes.

The Stud Dog

Owning a stud dog is an important responsibility. It is a responsibility to the betterment of the breed, because the offspring of a dog that is siring puppies for possible competition in the show ring, or of one that is siring pets that may eventually be bred, affect the quality of the breed for, potentially, many years.

Although it is advisable that a top stud be exhibited and that he prove his worth in the show ring, many factors contribute to the attainment of the title of champion. Among those factors are proper conditioning, expert handling, good timing in view of the competition during the exhibition period, and, of course, the innate quality of the dog from a conformation standpoint. One thing that must always be remembered is that the dog's winning does not affect his genes. Nevertheless, a relatively well-known dog who is successful in the show ring and who is producing quality puppies is likely to have a large number of bitches sent to him for breeding. He will be attractive to owners of high quality bitches and thus be more likely to produce quality puppies. Consequently, a popular stud dog's chances of success as a financial investment and as a producer of show-winning offspring are increased.

Although good structure is of utmost importance and should be a prime requisite of a popularly used stud dog, a pedigree replete with champions and top producers often is a major factor considered by owners of bitches. One never knows with certainty what the quality will be until the puppies mature into adulthood, but a stud dog owner should have knowledge of pedigrees in the breed in general in order to advise use of a particular stud dog on certain bitches, or to advise against his use on bitches where complementary breeding would not occur.

A fault of a serious nature is likely to be reproduced in a litter if that fault is outwardly apparent in both the stud dog and the bitch to be bred together. Consequently, in addition to the producing record of a stud, his pedigree, and his show record, consideration should always be given to the quality of the dam.

A level topline is an important structural characteristic for which to breed. Let's say that a major fault of a well-known Shih Tzu stud dog is a topline that obviously is not level. It would not be wise to breed that stud to a bitch that also has a poor topline. Neither would it be wise to breed that stud to a bitch that has an acceptable topline but whose pedigree is laden with ancestors who have poor toplines. In the latter instance, pedigree knowledge is of prime importance. If pedigree knowledge is not initially available, it is advisable that it be procured from reliable authorities. All aspects of conformation must be evaluated, since some faults are concomitant with others. For example, characteristics such as poor shoulders and poor rear angulation affect topline. Therefore, these qualities also must be taken into consideration.

Although breeders have varying reasons for breeding dogs, the basic theme throughout this book is breeding for breed betterment. That can mean trying to improve structure, temperament, coat, or movement through a single bitch producing high quality pets. It can also mean that a breeder who is on record for a particular year as breeding the highest number of champions or as breeding the Number One winner in the show ring for that year, tries with the next litter to breed even better Shih Tzu. In both instances, the breeder is continuing to improve quality as described in the Standard for the Shih Tzu.

It is unrealistic to assume that breeders never breed to a particular dog for the sake of convenience — that is, to breed to an in-house stud dog or to one within close driving distance — even though a better choice of stud dog can be found but his use involves more effort and expense. It is unrealistic to hope that Shih Tzu breeders will not breed to fulfill public demand and to realize financial gain. But if ideals are expressed, breeders will give thought to being discriminating in breeding plans and to continuing the trend toward excellence.

Individuals often buy pet quality males with hopes that the dog will be used at stud. Owners should realize that a pet male, unless of exceptionally good quality structurally, should be thought of only as a pet, and that prospects of his being used extensively at stud are minimal. It makes sense to breed a bitch to an experienced stud dog or to a champion of record so that the breeder might have better chances of success. A breeder using a proven stud dog is likely to give up a puppy in lieu of payment of a stud fee. Shih Tzu stud fees traditionally have been reasonable in price when compared to some breeds where there is a huge difference in the cost of using a local pet and using a proven stud that is a champion of record.

It was stated earlier in this chapter that the title of champion does not improve the genes or the ability of a stud dog to produce quality puppies. And keeping in mind that the stud dog contributes only half of the genetic input to a litter of puppies, it is well to remember that a male who has proven himself in the show ring is not necessarily in increased demand by serious breeders for use on their bitches.

Many males, not only in the Shih Tzu breed but also in all other breeds, acquire the championship title but never produce any puppies. The reasons for their lack of use at stud are many and varied. Even if the dog is of exceptionally outstanding quality, the owner may choose

165

not to offer him at stud, so the opportunity to sire puppies may never arise. Considering the effort and expense in campaigning a dog to the title, it is wise for owners who have aspirations to further the new champion's career as a producer of quality puppies, to continue his exposure to the public in varying ways. (We assume at this point that the male is capable of breeding. Artificial insemination and natural breedings will be discussed later in this chapter. It is rare, however, that an otherwise healthy young male is not fertile.)

PHYSICAL EXPOSURE

No one can be expected to consider using a stud dog with his bitch if he does not know that the animal exists. Usually, the greatest concentrations of potential users are breeders and fanciers who are at dog shows, either exhibiting or in attendance to view judging procedures.

If a male puppy is outstanding, is in good condition, and is well presented at puppy shows, he will be noticed by breeders and watched through various stages of his development. He may acquire a following, and breeders may consider him for future use with their bitches. If he continues to develop properly from the conformation standpoint and continues to do well in the show ring, more than likely breeders will begin to inquire about his pedigree, will consider his structure, and perhaps will lay plans to breed particular bitches to him. The psychological elements of good public relations on the part of the owner or handler are extremely important, and an agreeable attitude toward those who show interest in the dog makes far more sense than an aloof or unfriendly attitude.

A breeder should fault his own stud dog honestly. No dog is constructed perfectly, and people resent deception and exaggeration when considering a potential stud. Physical presence and personality will be obvious, but potential clients should be provided pedigree data pertinent to their own bitches and breeding programs.

Shih Tzu breeders and owners appreciate literature relevant to the breed, so it is wise to have professionally printed brochures or stud cards that include vital statistics, a photo, the pedigree of the stud, and any other information that seems pertinent. Such material should be available to give out to interested individuals at dog shows or to send by mail in response to inquiries by telephone or through correspondence.

THE POWER OF ADVERTISING

Individual breed publications, all-breed publications (especially of a national scope), or other magazines (distributed nationally or internationally), are by far the best means by which to inform the general public that a dog or a bitch is being campaigned or that a dog is at public stud. Photos should be of the very best quality obtainable, and copy should be submitted continually, with new highlights of the dog's prowess and progress as a winner and as a producer.

Any photographs used for serious promotion should be scrutinized by the owner of the dog and by honest authorities in the breed. The best attributes of the dog must be represented accurately so that a worthy dog is not discarded mentally by serious breeders for reasons unfair to the dog's reputation and true potential for breeding.

Originality in format, in type, or in presentation of information is important so long as the promotional material is accurate, honest, and professional in appearance. Too much information in an ad or a cluttered display of print and photographs usually decreases the impact of the presentation. Considering the escalating costs of printing brochures and stud cards as well as the increasing costs of advertising, any presentation must be designed with a view to realizing the greatest return possible in the way of public awareness.

TRAINING AND CARE OF THE STUD DOG

If it is intended that an outstanding young male Shih Tzu be promoted eventually as a stud dog, he should be deliberately and carefully trained to develop his prowess as a reliable stud. It is wise to select an in-house bitch with whom to prove the potency and fertility of the young male, if at all possible. Depending on the physical maturity of the individual male, it should be possible to use him for the first time when he is between seven and twelve months of age. At the time selected, he should experience a session with a bitch who is easily bred, who is receptive, and who will contribute to a successful and relatively problem-free breeding.

Mature Shih Tzu males between seven and twelve months of age should not be overused despite the fact that they may be able to breed. If a male has sired two litters from two quality bitches of different backgrounds and the resulting puppies are of good quality, the indication is that the young stud's potential as a producer of merit may come to fruition provided he is promoted properly.

Although planned and even unplanned breedings often occur naturally and accidentally with no harm done physically and emotionally to the dogs and bitches, care generally should be taken that the two dogs be watched continuously during the entirety of the actual breeding and throughout the period when the stud and bitch are tied. Carelessness on the part of owners of stud dogs during the breeding cycles of either in-house or visiting bitches can result in unwitnessed breedings and possible injury to stud dogs or bitches. Stud dogs and bitches in season must be maintained separately until the proper breeding days when supervised breeding can take place. Owners must train stud dogs to accept physical guidance and handling during breeding sessions, so that the success of breedings may be optimized.

Stud dogs, especially in the later years of life and consequent lessened productivity, should be fed as fine a diet as can be found, with a concentration of a high quality kibble. Meat and vitamin supplements may be used in moderation. Parasites, external or internal, should never be permitted to interfere with the vigor and vitality of any dog. A stud dog in generally poor condition may be seriously handicapped when it comes to productivity, so care must always be exercised to keep stud dogs in excellent health.

ARTIFICIAL INSEMINATION

Instances sometimes arise where artificial implantation of semen into the bitch is necessary or desirable. A stud dog who is being campaigned extensively on show circuits may be used with the artificial process in order to decrease stress on the stud's system. Sometimes a male will not breed naturally, and some bitches refuse to be receptive to the natural breeding attempts of a particular male or of males in general.

Unless the stud dog owner is expert at the artificial breeding process, a veterinarian or other experienced person should be sought to assist safely and effectively with the breeding.

The American Kennel Club is funding studies to perfect various techniques of artificial insemination in

Ch. Parquins Pretty Boy Floyd, owned by Jay Ammon.

dogs, using frozen semen. These techniques, which have been used successfully to breed horses and cattle, will result in means by which highly intelligent dogs and top champion-producing show dogs will be able to influence breed characteristics over long periods of time. Semen from such dogs will be extracted and frozen, then thawed and used effectively. That means that in many instances bitches will not have to be shipped long distances to studs. It also means that excellent linebreeding practices can be continued long after such practices normally would be impossible.

Currently, The American Kennel Club sanctions twelve centers in various parts of the United States for collecting semen, freezing and storing it, and performing artificial insemination. Such breedings are acceptable to The American Kennel Club, so resulting offspring may be registered with the club.

From time to time, breeds change in type, in size, and in other characteristics. A particular trait in any breed may have been popular many years ago and may be more true to the approved breed Standard than what is being bred presently. That trait may swing back into vogue. Imagine being able to breed a sound bitch to a long deceased dog who was known to be a prepotent producer for the trait now almost non-existent. That is only one example of the pluses of frozen semen and artificial insemination. With skyrocketing costs for dog-show participation, for promotion, and for handling fees, why not preserve the genes of top-quality dogs for generations and then be able to tap these valuable resources years on into the future?

Ch. Ming Toi P.V. Spunky, owned by Judy Boyles. Sired by Ch. Parquins Pretty Boy Floyd, Spunky is also descended from Ch. Talifu Bobby Dazla.

Ch. Car-Lyn's Foxy Lady of Cambalu, owned by Mrs. Robert A. Koeppel.

Ch. Shaadar's Yan-Kee Doll, owned by Mrs. Charles R. Eckes.

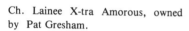

Ch. Lainee X-tra Amorous, owned by Pat Gresham.

Four offspring of Ch. Taylwag's PBR Donimie out of Ch. Barrington's Windsong of Choo Ling. From left, Ch. Choo Ling's Desert Wind, owned by Bill and Dottie Campbell; Ch. Choo Ling's Tradewinds, owned by Dr. Roy and Sara Clemons; Ch. Choo Ling's Wind Bluff, owned by the Campbells; and Ch. Choo Ling's Wind Echo, owned by the Clemonses.

The Brood Bitch

The selection of a bitch puppy or adult bitch intended for eventual breeding is an extremely important procedure. Regardless of one's aspirations, whether as an owner of one Shih Tzu or of great numbers of dogs, the first step is acquisition of the best bitch possible. Determination, patience, bargaining power, and financial resourcefulness combine to effect such a purchase.

Although many breeders prefer to own their bitches free of any financial obligations or obligations to give up puppies in lieu of cash, co-ownership of stock may prove more beneficial for some breeders. Payment by sharing the offspring for a set number of litters can benefit both seller and purchaser provided a written contract sets out details of the agreement specifically.

Many successful and ethical breeders who have larger than average breeding programs do not sell outright the best Shih Tzu they own or breed. Financial obligations that prevent campaigning of outstanding homebreds, or lack of sufficient kennel space may justify their parting with outstanding specimens on a co-ownership basis with serious and potentially show-minded partners.

Often the price of an outstanding specimen is less with a co-ownership agreement than it would be if the Shih Tzu were offered for direct sale. Without a co-ownership agreement, puppies or stud services might constitute payment or partial payment for the dog or bitch desired.

Suppose the bitch you own or co-own has finished her championship, and you are considering breeding her. If she is of outstanding quality, it is hoped that in return for the investment, she will produce her own quality or better. The bitch contributes half the genes which will make up the puppies she produces. The stud dog contributes the other half. His genetic contribution determines the sex of the puppies.

The bitch determines the number of puppies in the litter — that is, she is responsible for the number of egg cells which are available for fertilization at the time of breeding. Should the bitch be bred too early in her breeding cycle, or too late, fewer puppies may result than what nature could intend if she were bred at the optimum time. The optimum time is usually, but by all means not always, around the eleventh through the thirteenth day of the breeding period. Even at the optimum time, which is scaled by the number of egg cells ready to be fertilized, the number of puppies whelped may vary each time the bitch is bred, depending on the physical condition of the bitch, the age of the bitch, etc.

SELECTING THE STUD

There is no way of knowing each time your bitch is bred what quality puppies she will produce. A bitch may prove to be a top producer, one who consistently produces potential champions no matter what stud she is bred to. Or she may produce inferior quality puppies most of the time. In order to upgrade the quality of her puppies, she may need to be bred to a stud consistently producing outstanding offspring. On the other hand, a well-bred bitch of only mediocre appearance but good background, may produce excellent puppies if she is carefully bred to a stud whose structure complements hers, and who has the genetic capability to override her faults.

THE NUMBERS GAME

There is a science to dog breeding. Each time your bitch is bred, the results of that breeding are tempered by laws of chance. Breeding the bitch to a certain stud dog the first time may result in an outstanding litter of the highest caliber. You may repeat that combination at the bitch's next season and the resulting puppies may all be of inferior quality. There are so many hundreds of thousands of possible combinations of genes that each time a Shih Tzu bitch is bred, some of the resulting offspring may not be of desirable quality.

IMPROVING CHANCES FOR SUCCESS

Breeders who have a number of good, well-bred, healthy bitches, and who own or have access to studs whose outward characteristics and temperaments complement those of the bitches, stand excellent chances of breeding winners consistently. Don't think that high-profile breeders don't have disappointments in the whelping box. But numbers offset problems so that it appears to the public that excellence is the rule. Breeders who have only one or a few bitches may not have the desire to conquer the Shih Tzu world with winners and record-making producers. But if the rules, policies, and procedures they observe in their work of bettering the breed are inherent and are maintained at all costs, they can experience the satisfaction of seeing high-grade returns. Eventually, even small numbers can compete with the puppies produced by breeders with numerous bitches. The proof of the breeding program comes with satisfied purchasers of puppies and consistent winners in the show rings.

Much-sought-after stud dogs usually produce winners as good as or better than themselves when bred to sound, producing bitches that have regular breeding seasons, that produce respectable numbers in litters of strong, healthy, uniformly superior puppies, and that have plenty of milk to feed them.

Am. and Can. Ch. Wyndee Cheerleader of Ho Chi, owned by Betty Meidlinger.

Ch. Gunning's Semi Sparkle, owned by Hilde D. Pittelli.

Madonna di Visconti, owned by Jon Ferrante.

Ch. Billie's Follie Little Shaver, owned by Dr. and Mrs. Sam Shaver.

Ch. Gunning's Fancee Best Bet, owned by Jacqueline Kraus. Best Bet is a daughter of Ch. Gunning's Better Half, the top producing bitch of American champions.

Ch. Wychmere's Constant Comment, owned by Nina A. Thomas.

170

GUIDELINES FOR BREEDING YOUR BITCH

1. Never breed a bitch that is in poor condition, that is infested with internal parasites, or that is known to have had problems in the whelping box which cannot be remedied. Breeding such a bitch without concern for her and her probable suffering is an abomination.

2. There is no set rule which says an older bitch should not be bred. If the older bitch has been an easy whelper in previous whelpings, is healthy, and has suffered no recent infections, there is no reason she should not be bred. Keep in mind that litters from such a bitch may be smaller than in the past, and that her nutritional needs may increase during the gestation period and while she is nursing her puppies.

3. Monitor your bitch continually so that you recognize the beginning of her breeding cycle. "Hit and miss" and "accidental" breedings have produced some great winners, but such *modus operandi* is unprofessional, and success for careless breeders is the exception — not the rule.

4. Breed your bitch when she is "ready" to be bred for optimum conception of maximum size litters. Learn the peculiar signs of your bitch's "breeding readiness." It may be necessary to consult a veterinarian to determine "readiness" by making a test called a "vaginal smear," since some bitches don't show the usual signs and are reluctant to be bred — "ready or not." Some breeders who accept bitches on regular bases for their popular studs wisely acquire the knowledge and invest in the equipment necessary to do vaginal smears routinely to help ensure conception in bitches sent to them for breeding. Costs of travel and shipping are high and stud fees may also be high. Woe to stud owners who do not control every aspect of breeding procedure. A negligent owner whose stud otherwise might contribute to the advancement of the breed may be guilty of mismanagement of breedings. Stars that rise to their zenith may fall quickly if an owner is guilty of mismanagement.

5. A cardinal rule espoused time and time again is, "Don't breed your bitch to a stud simply because it is convenient to do so." There are many ways to interpret that rule. Although going to the stud which may be best for a particular bitch for optimum results is a golden rule, the key idea is *may be best*. The stud dog in one's own kennel or in one's own geographic area may produce lovely, show-quality puppies. So might the top-producing stud of all time, whose services might be quite expensive. Adding shipping expenses if that stud is in a distant location may make the total financial outlay very, very expensive. Trying to excel by breeding to the best and keeping one's goals at a high level will pay off generally.

6. When using an outside stud dog on your bitch, try to find out what that particular stud is producing when outcrossed, inbred, or linebred. Many a popular stud is a top producer because very good bitches have been bred to him, and consequently the breeders of the litters campaign his get. That stud may have sired many puppies in a particular year, and consequently chances of his get being shown are increased significantly over the get of a stud who produces better overall quality but may not be as popular or famous. The best producing studs may not be in the official "top-producer list" in a particular year. Also, it may even be that the best producer for your bitch is the pet Shih Tzu on the next block because he has structural pluses which your bitch may not have outwardly or genetically.

7. The pedigree should never be more important than the individual. An impressive pedigree is highly desirable, especially if the Shih Tzu reflects the genes of the great ones in the background. But breeding a bitch to a stud because of his pedigree, without concern for his phenotype (outward appearance), is foolhardy if he shares the same faults with the bitch. Linebreeding and inbreeding a Shih Tzu stud to bitches who carry common faults is like cementing the bad characteristics into the offspring, or even augmenting the faults. Such procedure is very sad but is true of many breedings. As prepotent as a bitch or a stud may be for excellence, so may they be for mediocrity, and also for producing disasters.

8. Be objective and critical not only of your own Shih Tzu but also of her immediate family. You may like what you see in your bitch but not want to linebreed or inbreed her to any stud within her family because she may be a "fluke," a "throwback," or a "blend." She may be unusually good, yet totally unlike her siblings, considering the mediocrity of all Shih Tzu closely related to her. In that case, consider an outside dog, an outcross whose phenotype (outward appearance) matches his genetic makeup and the get he is producing.

Ch. Hodari Tam Of Moonling winning the Brood Bitch Class at the first Southern California Specialty in January 1975. Owner, Laurie Battey.

171

Ch. Choo Ling's Wind Chime, owned by Bill and Dottie Campbell.

Ch. Choo Ling's Magic Wind, owned by Ann McDearmon.

Ch. Parquins Sintez, owned by Raymond Antonucci.

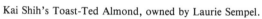

Kai Shih's Toast-Ted Almond, owned by Laurie Sempel.

Contractual Agreements for Breeders

A contractual agreement between the owner of a stud dog and the owner of a bitch is a necessary part of the transaction when a stud and bitch are to be bred, whether naturally or artificially. If a service is received and if that service is paid for by a fee or a choice puppy, consideration is evident. Both owners must have a clear understanding of the important elements of the transaction before the breeding of the two dogs takes place. Pre-printed forms are available, with blank spaces for filling in details of the transaction. Any deviation from the basic elements of a pre-printed agreement form must be written into the contract or added to the form as a separate statement or addendum.

Both the stud dog owner and the bitch owner should keep a copy of the agreement. The most important reason for keeping the copies is that the agreement constitutes a declaration that a breeding has taken place between two specifically named dogs. This declaration, attested to by the signatures of both owners, is protection to both owners and to the credibility of the resulting pedigree of the puppies from the breeding.

Should a dispute arise between the owners for any reason, the registering kennel club (assuming both stud and bitch are purebred and registered) has a positive reference upon which to base registration of the litter.

The owner of the bitch usually is responsible for providing the litter registration form, which will be available from the kennel club that has registered both the sire and the dam. The stud dog owner should be prompt and responsible in filling in and signing the application after the owner of the bitch has filled in and

Ch. Regal's Jack N' The Box, owned by Kathy Kwait. He is the sire of Ch. Mandarin's Sunni Side Up.

Int., Am., Mex., and Can. Ch. Dashi's My My. Owned by Catherine Pouliot. Co-owned and handled by Mary K. Dullinger.

signed the litter registration application and presented it to the stud dog owner.

Among the conditions and issues which should be discussed, agreed to, and put into contractual form before the breeding takes place are the following: whether return stud services will be provided at no charge should no litter result from a breeding; whether a partial stud fee is to be paid at some stipulated time; whether future breedings may be arranged at future breeding seasons of the bitch; the minimum number of puppies to be expected from the breeding; whether the service is to be paid for by a set fee or with a choice puppy (or puppies); and if the payment is to be a puppy (or puppies), who makes the selection, at what age, whether with or without canine inoculations, wormings, and health certificates.

In addition, the stud dog owner may set conditions that must be expressed contractually and agreed upon mutually. Naturally, conditions must not violate the codes regulating registrations by the sponsoring kennel club.

Suspicion that an accidental breeding may have occurred, that the bitch may have been bred by more than one stud dog during a particular season, non-payment of expected stud fees (whether cash or puppies), doubts on the part of the stud dog owner as to the authenticity of the total number or the number of each sex in the litter — all are incidences where disputes may arise between breeders. Although the existence of a comprehensive stud dog contract is not necessarily a panacea for a dispute, a dispute can be resolved more easily if a contract exists.

Can. Ch. Chumulari Feng Yeh Kalidan, owned by Elaine Mawson.

Kirin Georgia On My Mind, owned by Ruth M. Michael and Sharon Crosby.

Am. and Can. Ch. Paramount Rhett Butler, owners George and Diane Moncion, Norman Patton, and J. Chip Constantino.

174

Breeding the Shih Tzu

A Shih Tzu bitch usually comes into season for the first time at the age of about eight months. Following that first season, she will come into season at intervals of roughly six months. Her maximum fertility builds up from the time of her first season until she reaches full maturity. It then declines gradually until she becomes totally sterile in old age. It is difficult to determine exactly when total sterility occurs, for a bitch still may evidence signs of being in season but be incapable of reproduction.

The first indication that the bitch is coming into season is a pronounced swelling of the vulva, with bleeding — called "showing color" — for seven to nine days. Gradually the discharge turns to a creamy color. This stage (called the "estrus") lasts from about the tenth to the fifteenth day. It is during estrus that the bitch is ovulating and is receptive to the male.

Unfertilized ova survive only for about seventy-two hours. If fertilization does not occur, the ova die and are discharged the next time the bitch comes in season. If fertilization does occur, each fertilized ovum attaches itself to the wall of the uterus, a membrane forms around each ovum to seal it off, and a fetus develops from it.

The bitch's season continues to follow estrus until about the twenty-first day after she first shows color. She continues to be attractive to males throughout her season, but following estrus she usually fights them off, as she did prior to the beginning of estrus. To avoid accidental mating it is essential that the bitch be confined for the entire period. Male dogs have uncanny abilities in their efforts to reach a bitch in season, so it is necessary to exercise extreme precautions to make sure the bitch does not become the victim of an accidental mating. Virtual imprisonment of the bitch is necessary.

It is the odor present in the bitch's urine during her season that attracts males. Consequently, it is advisable to take her a good distance from the house before permitting her to relieve herself during her season. Otherwise, males from blocks around will create a nuisance by congregating around your house or yard. Your veterinarian can prescribe a preparation that will disguise the odor throughout the bitch's season. This preparation will not interfere with breeding when the time is right. Owners and handlers who use the preparation find it totally effective. Nevertheless, it is not advisable to permit the bitch to run freely even if she has been given the preparation, for during estrus she actively seeks male dogs and an accidental mating could occur.

The Shih Tzu must be physically mature before being bred. She must be beyond the puppy stage, and have ample breadth and depth of ribbing, good bone, and adequate room in the pelvic region. If the bitch is well beyond the puppy stage, she may be bred at her first season. Many Shih Tzu breeders feel it is wiser always to delay breeding until the second or a later season. Even though it is possible for a bitch to conceive twice a year, she should not be bred oftener than once a year. A Shih Tzu bitch that is bred too often is likely to have puppies that lack vigor, and she herself is likely to lack vitality because her body will not have had time to return to its normal functioning between pregnancies that are close together. This is especially true of a dam who has nursed a large litter.

Any mating should be planned well in advance. The stud dog should be selected only after careful consideration as to just which sire is likely to complement the bitch's genetic makeup, resulting in what seems potentially the best possible litter. The bitch's physical condition must be assessed carefully two or three months prior to onset of her season. If she is too thin, changes in her diet should be considered, but guidance on this should be sought from your veterinarian. All Shih Tzu need regular daily exercise in order to develop and maintain strong, supple muscles. For the too-thin bitch exercise is essential, as it is for the too-fat one. The latter should have more exercise and at a more rapid pace, as well as a reduction of food. Any Shih Tzu bitch should be brought to optimum condition prior to breeding.

A Shih Tzu bitch must have had booster shots as well as rabies vaccination prior to mating. A veterinarian should examine a stool specimen for worms a month before the bitch's season is expected to start. The bitch should be wormed if there is evidence of infestation of internal parasites. External parasites, of course, should never be tolerated. If fleas, lice, or ticks are noted either on the Shih Tzu's coat and body or in the area the dog frequents, steps to eradicate them should be taken immediately.

The first time your Shih Tzu bitch is bred, it is preferable that you select as sire a dog that already has proven his ability by having sired successful litters. The stud should be the one you feel to be most suitable from a genetic standpoint. This requires intensive study of both pedigrees, and thoughtful evaluation of the conformation of both your bitch and the potential sire. In order to have your bitch mated with a popular sire or one whose owner resides some distance from you, you must negotiate arrangements well in advance. It may be necessary for you to ship your bitch by air some distance in order to have her mated with the sire of your choice. (For later breedings, artificial insemination may prove a practical substitute for long-distance shipping.) All

Ch. House of Wu Benchmark, owned by Gay D. Eckes.

Ch. Long's Little Lick at 9 months. Owners Charles and Janet Long.

Ch.Fancee Gunning—Re-Pete, owned by Jean A. Olson. His parents are the top producing stud and bitch of American champions.

Ch. Dragonfire's Greatest Emily. Owned by Katsutoshi Maehara. Bred by Peggy Hogg and Elaine Meltzer.

aspects of the physical arrangements for the mating usually require planning months in advance.

You may wish to consult your veterinarian concerning preparations for inhibiting the onset of your Shih Tzu's season, should it develop that the sire you prefer is not going to be available when your bitch comes into season. Using special preparations, with the guidance of your veterinarian, you can delay the bitch's season indefinitely.

Always remember that the purpose in breeding your bitch is to produce the best puppies possible. Therefore, your selection of a sire should not be influenced by the fact that a particular male Shih Tzu is readily available. The best possible combination of genetic factors for what potentially will be the best possible litter must always govern the selection of the stud dog.

The first service usually is successful. If it is not, an additional service usually is provided without further charge. This, of course, assumes that the stud dog is still owned by the same person. As discussed in an earlier chapter, all details of all aspects of the arrangements should be understood by both the owner of the bitch and the owner of the stud, and should be included in a written agreement signed by both.

If the bitch does not conceive, it may be because her cycle varies widely from normal. By microscopic examination it is possible to determine exactly when a bitch is entering the estrus phase, and thus, when she is likely to conceive. Most veterinarians and some owners of stud dogs have the equipment necessary to make such an examination. Particularly for the first time a bitch is bred, it is well to have the examination made in order to ensure the success of the mating.

There usually is visible enlargement of the abdomen by the end of the fifth week following conception. A veterinarian may be able to distinguish developing puppies by palpation (feeling with the fingers) as early as three weeks after breeding. It is unwise for an inexperienced breeder to attempt to make such a determination, for it may result in serious injury either to the puppies or to the bitch.

The normal period of gestation (pregnancy) is nine weeks (sixty-three days). It may vary from sixty-one to sixty-five days. If sixty-five days elapse and there is no evidence that whelping is imminent, you should consult your veterinarian.

Throughout the first four to five weeks, the bitch should be permitted her normal activity. As her pregnancy progresses beyond that time, she is likely to be less agile than she is normally, so strenuous running and jumping should not be permitted. You should continue to exercise her moderately, however. Her diet should be well balanced and your veterinarian may recommend addition of vitamins, minerals, and calcium. Such dietary supplements should not be given without consultation with your veterinarian.

The bitch's abdomen will undergo a definite change in shape about forty-eight to seventy-two hours before whelping is to commence. The surest sign is a drop in temperature of two or three degrees about twelve hours before labor begins.

A careful reading of the chapter on whelping a Shih Tzu will impart a feeling of confidence in even the totally inexperienced breeder. Of particular significance is the advice on equipment needed. These items must, of course, be secured well in advance of the date whelping is expected to take place. Remember too that a breeder who is well prepared through advance consultation with his veterinarian is going to feel confident in the new role of serving as "midwife" to his Shih Tzu bitch.

Owners sometimes decide to have a bitch spayed or a male castrated simply as a matter of convenience. This is to be commended if the Shih Tzu has a serious inheritable defect and if an abnormality of the reproductive system develops. In sound, normal, purebred Shih Tzu, spaying a female or castrating a male may have decided disadvantages. These surgical procedures automatically bar the dogs from competing in shows as well as preclude use for breeding. They should not be performed without serious consideration of these facts.

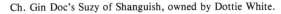

Ch. Gin Doc's Suzy of Shanguish, owned by Dottie White.

Ch. Garvin's Topaz of Runkel, owned by
Gloria Busselman.

Ch. Billie's Follie Little Shaver, owned by
Dr. and Mrs. Sam Shaver.

Am. and Can. Ch. Bel Air Butterfly Of
Bamboo, owned by Diane Backovich.

The late Richard Paisley, owner/handler, with Ch. Yoshi Ah So Omar. Judge is Anna Cowie (Nanjo).

Whelping a Shih Tzu

by Richard J. Paisley

Personally, I do not like to see a pregnant bitch taken to a vet several days before she is due to whelp, inasmuch as most vets leave the office in the evening and do not return until morning. A Shih Tzu bitch generally does not remove the membranous sac which envelops the puppy. Therefore, if the puppy is born and no one is in attendance to assist the delivery, the puppy may drown in the sac. (A prenatal examination of the bitch is advisable, however.)

Some vets have attendants who are supposed to be on duty at night, but we know of several unfortunate incidents where the attendants either were not on duty or were not present when the puppies were born, and the puppies were suffocated in the sacs. A puppy must be removed from the sac *seconds* after it is born. Therefore, you can see why someone *must be* in attendance from the start of labor until the whelping is completed. Once in a while, that rare bitch comes along who will whelp her puppies and take them out of the sac and take over immediately, but these bitches are rare and far between.

If you are a novice breeder and have had no previous experience with whelping, the best method is to alert your vet that a litter is due on such and such a date and that you will contact him once you know the bitch is going into labor. Take the bitch to the vet at the first signs of labor and watch him deliver the litter. Then you will know what to do the next time your bitch whelps.

When a bitch is bred, the normal gestation period is sixty-three days from the date of mating. However, we have found that Shih Tzu bitches, especially those whelping the first litter, can be expected to whelp any day from the fifty-eighth day on from the date of the first mating. (By this, I mean breeders generally breed a bitch one day, skip the next day, and repeat on the third day. When this is done, you are not sure whether the bitch conceived on the first day or the third day. Therefore, it is best to count fifty-eight days from the first mating, so that someone will be with the bitch constantly from this date on.) A bitch can also whelp on the sixty-fourth or sixty-fifth day, but if she has not whelped by the sixty-third day, it is wise to have a professional examination by a vet to make sure all is going well and there are no complications.

The first question usually is "How will I know when my bitch goes into labor?" Usually, you will find that a bitch will scratch her bed and try to arrange it just the way she wants it several days prior to whelping. Not all bitches do this, however, so this is not a sure sign. Some bitches go into labor and just start dropping puppies like shelling peas. These bitches are in the minority, though, and, as a rule, a Shih Tzu whelping is spread out over a period of five or six hours — sometimes even more.

Usually, the day the bitch is going to whelp, she will refuse food. This, again, is not a sure sign, because some bitches can eat a pan of food and start dropping puppies immediately after walking away from the food pan.

We have found the first signs of labor consist of restlessness on the part of the bitch, with panting and labored breathing. The eyes become moist and glassy and have a staring expression to them. The bitch becomes very apprehensive of each little noise, such as the opening of a door or even the sound of a faucet being turned on.

In the very early stages of labor, contractions may not be in evidence. Accompanying the panting may be slight shivers or chills. Shortly thereafter, definite hard contractions will be noticed. Generally, the bitch will start with one or two hard contractions close together and then she will rest for a while. From the time the contractions start, there is no reason to be alarmed if the puppies do not appear for an hour or two. However, if the bitch seems to be having hard contractions and straining for two hours, it is wise to have a vet look at her to make sure she is not having undue difficulty which would require a Caesarean. This could be caused by an extremely large puppy, a small pelvic opening, the puppy being in a breech-first position, or a deformed or dead puppy. (Dead puppies are generally harder to deliver than live ones.)

Usually, a day or two before delivery, you will notice a small amount of mucus at the opening of the vulva. Shortly before actual whelping, the bitch will secrete a mucus plug. Again, unless close watch is kept on the bitch, this could easily go unnoticed.

Assuming your bitch is having a normal delivery and has reached the point where she is having steady contractions of three in a row every two or three minutes, a small "bubble" may appear just outside the vulva. This bubble looks like a large membranous marble with a little fluid in it. This is part of the sac of the first puppy. *Do not break or pull on this bubble.* (This is usually normal with the first puppy and generally does not appear with the following puppies.)

From the time the bubble appears until the puppy actually arrives, there again is no set rule. Sometimes it is only minutes and other times it can be an hour or more. Here again, if two hours go by and nothing has happened, professional help may be needed to get the puppy out.

At this point, perhaps a description may be helpful. The uterus of the bitch is like an inverted U with the birth canal coming down through the center.

The puppies are contained in the right and left horns of the uterus. The placenta or afterbirth is attached to the wall of the uterus and is the source of food and oxygen while the puppy is in the uterus. Usually the first puppy in either the right or the left horn of the uterus is lifted into the birth canal and that puppy is detached from the wall of the uterus. It is at this point that the puppy's oxygen supply from the bitch is ended, and it is imperative that the puppy be delivered and start breathing on its own. There is still a small supply of oxygen left in the placenta but not enough to sustain the puppy for more than a minute or two.

There is a hormone which may be injected into the bitch to stimulate or increase the contractions and induce labor. However, this hormone can be more dangerous than helpful. It should be left to the vet to determine whether or not it should be administered. Like a little knowledge being dangerous, laymen may be over-anxious to have the shot given, thinking it will speed up delivery. The cervix, the opening through which the puppy must pass, *must be* dilated before any injection of this type can be given. If an injection is given and the cervix is not dilated, the force of the contractions could possibly split the uterus, and the complications would be disastrous. Only a vet, at his discretion, should make any internal exploration of the vulva or genital area of the bitch. The uterus is extremely susceptible to infection at this time and sanitary measures should be employed to the fullest degree.

After the placenta has detached from the wall of the uterus, nature waits a reasonable period of time and then the next placenta becomes detached, and so on, until the delivery of all puppies is completed. Thus, one can see that if the first puppy is in the birth canal and has not been delivered and the next puppy in line to be born has its placenta detached and starts to move into the birth canal, the puppies will back up and all die unless they are delivered without delay. Sometimes the bitch will deliver all the puppies in the right horn of the uterus and then deliver the puppies from the left horn — or they may alternate, with one puppy from one horn, the next from the other, and so on.

Because of the size of the head of the Shih Tzu, delivery oftentimes is more difficult than in other breeds, but nature seems to make allowances for this, inasmuch as Caesareans are the exception rather than the rule.

Again, assuming all is going well, and the first puppy comes out of the vulva encased in the membrane, the umbilical cord is attached to the placenta, or afterbirth, which is still inside the bitch. The first thing you should do is either cut the membrane or break it with your fingers around the head of the puppy, then quickly strip back the membrane from around the puppy, allowing the fluid to come away from the puppy quickly. Puppies can be born either head first or hind feet first. If the puppy is delivered hind feet first, the head sometimes is stuck in the pelvic opening and gentle assistance on your part can help matters. The sac will be slippery and wet. Therefore, the bare hands are not as efficient as grasping the sac and puppy with a thin Turkish towel or rough paper towel. Grasp as much of the sac and puppy as you can and *gently* pull outward and *down. Never pull the puppy straight back or jerk it hard.* This could result in a broken neck for the puppy.

Usually, if the puppy comes head first, there is no problem, for once the head comes through the pelvic opening, the body follows. It is when the hind feet come first that assistance may be needed.

After you have broken the sac and quickly cleared the fluid and mucus from the mouth of the puppy, with one hand about one inch from the stomach of the puppy, grasp the umbilical cord and, with the other hand close to the bitch, gently try to pull the afterbirth down out of the bitch — but be sure you do not pull hard on the cord near the navel of the puppy. Oftentimes, a hernia is caused by too much pressure being exerted on the cord where it is attached to the puppy. It is wise to have on hand a professional hemostat or a pinch-type clothespin (which has been sterilized in boiling water or cleaned in alcohol). The hemostat or clothespin can be closed onto the cord about two inches from the puppy's navel, and the cord then cut on the puppy side of the clothespin. (Sometimes the bitch will expel puppy, cord, and afterbirth all in one effort and this will eliminate worrying about the afterbirth, etc. This procedure with hemostat or clothespin is intended only when the placenta seems to be stuck and will not come out with gentle pulling on the cord.) In any case, cutting the cord will leave you with a puppy in your hand with approximately two inches of umbilical cord dangling. It also leaves the bitch with part of the umbilical cord hanging out of her with a hemostat or clothespin attached, assuming the placenta did not come out with the puppy. This prevents the umbilical cord from slipping back up inside the bitch, and (once you have made sure the puppy is dried and breathing well) you can turn your attention to the bitch and getting the afterbirth out of her. Leaving the hemostat or clothespin attached, grasp the umbilical cord dangling from the bitch, and gently, but firmly, pull until the entire placenta or afterbirth comes out. If it still seems stuck after some effort, leave it alone for a few minutes and then try again. The placenta looks like a small chunk of "overripe" liver. Make sure an afterbirth accompanies each puppy, and keep count so that after whelping is completed, you know the bitch has not retained an afterbirth. If an afterbirth is retained, the bitch undoubtedly will develop a uterine infection. If the cord hanging from the puppy does not stop bleeding after you have pressed hard with your fingers on the end of the cord for several seconds, you can use another

Ch. Lyric's Lorelei, owned by Jane McDaniel.

Rockee Vollee Decidedly Ista, co-owned by Helen Mueller and Tammarie Gallion.

Ch. Rockee Vollee Orange Dumplin, owned by Helen Mueller.

Ch. Vilenzo Miss Mavis Ming, owned by Sally Vilas.

Ch. Dragonwyck Miss B-Haven, bred and handled by Norman Patton. Owned by Mrs. Dinelli.

Ch. Wychmere's Constant Comment, Ch. Miramar's Weekend Warrior, and Wychmere's Miramar At Liberty. All three are owned by Nina Thomas.

181

hemostat or clothespin to advantage by pinching it on the very tip of the cord for a minute or two. This should cause the blood to clot. Some people tie a piece of string or thread on the tip of the cord, but we find pressure with fingers or the hemostat or clothespin treatment does the trick. There are commercial blood-clotting agents on the market which may be obtained, although just plain cornstarch (cooking type) can be utilized. The cord will dry up and fall off eventually.

Some puppies will be very active the minute you break the sac — others seem lifeless. Regardless of either situation, you should have a rough Turkish towel or similar absorbent material on hand and rub the puppy briskly all over with the towel, tumbling and rubbing in all directions. Don't be afraid you will hurt the puppy. Just rub him until he yells. Also, with your forefinger make sure there is no fluid or mucus in the mouth of the puppy. If you have a small ear-syringe or baby-syringe on hand, it is ideal to use to suck out any fluid or mucus from the puppy's mouth. Also be sure the nostrils are clear of fluid.

Once the puppy is dry and breathing, let the bitch sniff it. More than likely, she will start licking it all over. This is nature's way of stimulating the puppy and making it yell and breathe better. Sometimes a bitch may be too exhausted or frightened to want anything to do with the puppy.

Here again, it is important that the novice learn that a newborn puppy is unable to urinate or have bowel movements unless stimulated by the bitch's tongue. If the bitch does not do this, you will have to use a piece of cotton or gauze which has been softened with a little baby oil, mineral oil, or vaseline. This is important to know in hand-raising a litter of puppies if the bitch is unable to take care of them or if they are orphaned at birth. Not only do you have to feed them, but also you must stimulate them artificially in order that they will have their natural body functions of elimination.

If the bitch accepts the puppy immediately and begins to lick it, you can leave it with her until the birth of the next puppy is imminent.

Once you notice contractions are indicating the appearance of another puppy, place the puppy already born in a box with either a heating pad or a warm-water bottle for warmth and protection until the next puppy is born. Repeat the process until all puppies have been born. If it seems there is a long time between births of puppies, it is wise to let each puppy nurse a few minutes. It is important that each puppy get some of this first milk (which is more a clear color than the later milk), because the first milk contains the antibodies which give the puppies natural immunity from many puppy illnesses and diseases. (Sometimes a bitch has milk several days before the puppies are born. Other times, a bitch doesn't have milk until the puppies are born, or shortly thereafter.)

It is wise to have a large paper bag or box and a supply of newspapers handy in which to place the afterbirths and fluid which accompany a whelping.

Some people let a bitch eat one afterbirth, saying it is good for her and starts some maternal functions. We have always disposed of all afterbirths and have seen no difference in our bitches, as compared with those who have been allowed to eat an afterbirth.

When you think the bitch has delivered all her puppies, you can place all the puppies with her in the whelping box. If she does not seem to accept them immediately, do not be alarmed. Some bitches are frightened or in a mild state of shock for a few hours. In this case, remove the puppies and place them in a box nearby on a heating pad or warm-water bottle. Place a towel over the heating pad or water bottle. At proper intervals, you can place the puppies with the bitch until she indicates that she will accept them. We have found many females are exhausted following a whelping and may inadvertently lie on a puppy and smother it if left unattended. Therefore, for at least six to twelve hours, we keep the newborn puppies in a box and place them on the bitch to nurse for a few minutes every three hours. This gives her a chance to accept them gradually and to get the rest she needs. An exceptionally good mother oftentimes will take over immediately and there then is no need to worry, but it is better to be cautious rather than overconfident. In the case of a highstrung or nervous bitch, it is sometimes three or four days before you can safely leave the puppies in the whelping box with her.

Following the whelping of the litter, it is always a good idea to take the bitch and her puppies to the vet within eight hours. This gives the vet an opportunity to make sure the bitch has not retained a puppy or an afterbirth. During the whelping, the uterus enlarges considerably, and, sometimes, even the vet is in doubt as to whether a bitch still has a puppy inside or whether the uterus is exceptionally thickened. But he would be a better judge than a novice breeder. More than likely, the vet will give the bitch an injection or two. One of these is a hormone which causes the uterus to expel any matter which could cause infection. Usually, an antibiotic also is given as a precaution against infection. Calcium pills and a small supply of antibiotics are good things to get and give the bitch orally for a few days to make doubly sure infection does not set in. The calcium should be continued until weaning has taken place.

The bitch may refuse to eat food for a day or two. This is not too serious, although she should be encouraged to eat as soon as possible because she will need food and strength for the nursing job ahead.

If the bitch has a long whelping, some broth or milk

may be offered to her between births. Also, she may not want to leave the puppies to go outside and relieve herself. If this is the case, she should be carried out so that she will relieve herself.

The hindquarters of the bitch can be cleaned with a damp towel and then should be dried thoroughly. It is not necessary to give a complete bath — in fact, is not recommended, for that might cause chilling — which should be avoided. She *will* have a certain amount of blood and mess on her hindquarters and genital area and it *should be* cleaned off.

It is normal for puppies to cry a little following delivery, but after they have nursed, this gradually stops. If puppies continue to cry for no apparent reason, you should contact your vet. If a puppy is warm and has a full stomach, it will sleep. Normally, the bitch will tumble the puppy around in cleaning it. Therefore, it will yell. This is normal. It is the crying for no apparent reason which must be watched. Sometimes a puppy will cry if it has not been cleaned by the bitch and needs to defecate and/or urinate. Hold the puppy's rear in front of the bitch's face and see if she will clean it. If she won't, use a piece of cotton as described earlier.

Remember, the puppies and the bitch must be kept warm and well fed. The bed should be in a place free of drafts, and it is wise to have it located where the bitch will have a certain amount of privacy. Some bitches do not resent visitors or strangers, but it is wise to avoid a lot of traffic the first few days.

The preceding may seem like a lot of trouble and hard to manage. Actually, it is not. It is all written to alert you to the fact that someone *must be* present to assist during the whelping. It is not hard if you remain calm. If you are an excitable person, it is best to have someone with you who can remain calm. If you cannot get your bitch to a vet, and it is your first whelping, perhaps you can get someone who has assisted in a whelping to come in to assist you when the bitch actually goes into labor.

In any event, GOOD LUCK.

MINIMUM MATERIALS TO HAVE ON HAND DURING WHELPING

An adequate whelping box.

Small cardboard box in which puppies can be placed while other puppies are being whelped.

Supply of newspapers (clean).

Pair of scissors (sterile).

Several small, pinch-type clothespins or a hemostat. (Thread, if you want to tie umbilical cords.)

Supply of rough towels, heavy paper towels, cheesecloth, or similar material.

Heating pad or warm-water bottle.

Small container of oxygen* (if you know how to administer it).

Pencil and pad. (Notes should be made of time contractions start, time of delivery of each puppy, etc., in the event you have to call the vet and he asks these questions.)

Pot of hot coffee or tea (for you).

* With regard to oxygen, we have never had need of it in whelping litters — although some other breeders find it useful.

A Jazmin litter by Maxi out of Bit O' Honey.

Once they have been weaned, puppies should not be permitted to nurse, for that could be harmful to the bitch's health.

Puppies owned by Trudy Kerr.

Puppies, Puppies, Puppies — Fluffy Clowns

Selecting a Shih Tzu puppy as a show prospect, as future breeding stock, or as a pet can be an exciting experience. Puppies that probably would develop into top-flight show stock, future champions, Group and Best-in-Show winners are available either from established breeders who have solid reputations for selling show prospects that mature into winners and producers, or from less well-known breeders who breed selectively on a small scale, or from new breeders who have bred their quality bitches very thoughtfully to excellent stud dogs. Sometimes it is possible to purchase a fine puppy from stock that is relatively unknown, but that option for finding a future champion is the least likely way to find exceptional quality.

Telephoning breeders who advertise puppies for sale in major metropolitan areas where there might be a density of established Shih Tzu breeders improves chances for newcomers to the breed to select good show and breeding stock. Breeders dedicated to the improvement of the breed frequently use the local newspapers to sell quality pets, quality breeding stock, and sometimes potential show specimens. Whether they have stock available or not, dedicated breeders are usually willing to help serious buyers locate the quality and type of puppy they seek.

Contacting members of local Shih Tzu clubs or local all-breed clubs is another excellent way of locating excellent puppies or older dogs that are for sale. It is possible to be very fortunate and naively purchase a puppy from an unlikely source, on first try, and acquire a quality Shih Tzu. But purchasers who "shop around" before purchasing their first Shih Tzu have better chances of success as future fanciers.

If AKC licensed all-breed dog shows are held within a convenient distance, contact can be made readily with professional handlers and serious minded breeders from many geographic areas of the country. And if Shih Tzu entries are high in number, various qualities of Shih Tzu being exhibited — from excellent to perhaps not really good quality — can be viewed so that an idea of the relativity of type can be ascertained. Eventually, or perhaps even at just one show, the prospective buyer can visualize the Shih Tzu he is interested in owning.

It must be remembered that it is natural for breeders to promote the virtues of their own stock. Although many knowledgeable breeders or handlers will verbalize their likes and dislikes of the structural qualities of their own stock and point out that which they admire in other lines, it is a good policy for newcomers to talk with as many people as are available before finally selecting a Shih Tzu puppy or adult.

The quality of puppies to be selected as show prospects should be close to the ideal described in the Shih Tzu Standard. Like generally produces like, and the characteristics and pedigrees of the sire and dam, in addition to the characteristics and pedigrees of grandparents, should be weighed heavily. Genetic pools involve countless chromosomes and genes, and, as discussed elsewhere in this book, it is possible that something great in the way of general conformation can be produced from parents of little outward consequence. That occurrence is rare, indeed. However, it does happen from time to time.

Shih Tzu puppies are more easily evaluated at twelve weeks of age than are some much larger breeds of dogs. Therefore, an outstanding twelve-week-old Shih Tzu that meets structurally empirical criteria will generally excel as an adult if accorded the proper care, conditioning, and training.

With knowledge of a puppy's pedigree, plus knowledge of the virtues and faults of his parents, and with careful examination of the puppy's structure as it conforms to the breed Standard — as to movement, coat factor, personality, and to some extent attitude, since that can be an environmental factor — we establish guidelines by which to make selection. Remember that selecting the best puppy from a given litter is not necessarily selecting a winner in the show ring. Some lines rightly have the reputation for innate showmanship and all the other elements of great vitality and plushness.

Records of show wins and production of champions by famous studs and bitches should be considered. But remember that advertisements and careful promotion, financial backing, and expert handling will never change the basic structure of even the most famous progenitor's offspring. Public opinion can be conditioned to mediocrity for a while so that attention may be drawn away from better lines that are not so heavily promoted. Selecting a puppy is a matter of selecting possible success or failure in the show ring for many years. So always buy the best you can find. Price does not indicate the quality of the purchase in many cases. Prices asked and received by some breeders may be out of line with proper ethical standards. The rule that one gets what one pays for does not always apply to quality in the Shih Tzu.

If a puppy of excellent conformation is kept by a breeder or is sold to a buyer who is likely to condition that puppy with a goal that the puppy is to be shown extensively, several things should happen. A puppy of high structural calibre, dazzling presence, and potential showmanship should be nurtured from an early age by careful lead training, by being worked a few minutes each day on a grooming table, and by exposure at puppy matches — either fun shows or AKC sanctioned matches.

Ch. Erincroft Qu Ti Pi of Jazmin at 9 months. Breeder, Gerry Ikola (Canada).

Fun matches offer exposure and practice for point shows. Pictured is Joe Cannon with his Cannonade A Chorus Line.

Am. and Can. Ch. Emeer Von Arvind, owned by Trudy Kerr.

Ch. Ta Ya Chai's Kerin von Emeer, owned by Trudy Kerr.

Ch. Choo Ling's Wind Warning, owned by Bill and Dottie Campbell.

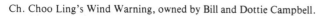

Madonna di Visconti. Owner/handler Jon Ferrante. Madonna is a great-granddaughter of Ch. Witch's Wood Yum Yum.

Promotion of an exceptional puppy from an early age is helpful if the owner has great expectations for the puppy's future. If funding is available, advertisements using good studio photos or photos of wins at point shows or matches can spark a great deal of interest. Remember that a photo not only must be of good photographic quality, but also must show the outstanding virtues of the dog. First impressions often are lasting in the eyes of fanciers, and positive public opinion is crucial. It is advisable that an expert groomer of Shih Tzu oversee final touches on a puppy before it is photographed.

One picture in an ad in a national Shih Tzu magazine helped to set off Ch. Dragonwyck The Great Gatsby as a puppy to astronomical success in later years. Ch. Witch's Wood Yum Yum was beautifully and deliberately advertised as a puppy, as was the gorgeous bitch Ch. Erincroft Qu Ti Pi of Jazmin. Ch. Parquins Pretty Boy Floyd, a top producer, and his prolific top producing son Ch. Lainee Sigmund Floyd were heavily advertised as puppies. Ch. Marco Polo di Visconti was seen in a national magazine as a puppy and won three all-breed awards as Best Puppy in Match and one Specialty puppy match. Ch. Hapiours Swing On A Star of Copa was a successful match and point winner as a puppy, and Ch. Char Nick's I Gotcha was Best of Winners at ten months

of age at the Westminster Kennel Club Show at Madison Square Garden and was beautifully advertised for that win.

The name for an outstanding puppy should be selected carefully and deliberately. The name selected should be one that appeals to the owner and other people and that fits the nature of the puppy, with the idea that the puppy one day will be adult and possibly a great winner and producer. Once the name is selected, it should be discussed with several people to learn their reaction before making a final decision.

Puppies often win points — even major points at AKC sanctioned point shows — and it is good to remember that compared to most other breeds, the Shih Tzu matures at an early age. The puppy must have sufficient coat and be of mature size to win over adults. Many handlers and owners of successful puppy winners believe that at the age of ten or eleven months, a Shih Tzu has an appeal in the way of plushness and attitude that is difficult for judges to resist. Be that as it may, a long maturing process is not necessary for outstanding Shih Tzu puppies if all conformation elements are apparent. And that means that care should be taken to make sure that an excellent puppy receives all the attention needed under all conditions, especially if the puppy is upward bound and show bound.

Count Dracula di Visconti, handled by John Ficerai.

Ch. Dragonfire's The Great Draco, owned by Peggy A. Hogg. Here, Draco is pictured winning an all-breed Best in Show as a puppy.

Choo Ling's Red Baron, owned by Jim and Tina Beller. Baron, the Bellers' first Shih Tzu, is strictly a pet and companion. His coat, however, is in plush show condition and is owner maintained.

Ch. Kee Lee's Strut 'N Stuff of Mar Del. His luxurious coat is carefully wrapped between shows to prevent tangles. Owner Julia Mech.

Conditioning the Coat — Grooming the Shih Tzu

by Peggy Hogg

Long-haired breeds seem to have been my fate for all the years that I have been handling dogs. I started with the long-haired varieties and, after a bit of success with them, became labeled as a handler of long-haired dogs. It would be a joy just once in a while to have a short-haired dog or two in my string to make the work a bit light. However, the long-coated ones are a definite challenge, and a great deal of satisfaction can be derived from conditioning and growing a lovely coat. So, you have chosen a long-haired breed, meet the challenge the best you can and you will be proud of what you have accomplished when the first show comes around.

Most everyone in show dogs realizes that you must start with a healthy specimen, so be sure your dog is free of parasites and eats a balanced diet. It is inexcusable today for a dog not to eat a balanced diet, with all the commercial meals on the market. Dog food companies spend thousands of dollars each year analyzing and improving their products so that you can feed a balanced diet to your dog. The dry meal that is available is by far the best balanced diet that you can buy and it is now offered to dogs of different ages, obese dogs, and dogs with kidney and heart problems. Although a balanced diet is important to healthy hair and to proper hair growth, a vitamin supplement may also be advisable for puppies, and for dogs which are being shown, because they are under a definite stress at this time. If your dog's coat is not as healthy or luxurious as you think it should be, an addition of Vitamin B and Zinc orally may well help your dog's coat. Also, Vitamin C is said to be beneficial as a daily supplement for eye strain; some maintain that Vitamin E is an important additive.

Good coats of hair are inherited in many lines, and unfortunately, in some lines dogs inherit coats that aren't so good. We do live in an age of science where specialists can tell us about diet and what to use on problem hair. Presuming the hair is fed properly, the greatest concern to us in conditioning hair deals with the epicuticle, which is the outer and protecting cloak of the main shaft of the hair. It is made up of flat, interlocking cells. The epicuticle is cemented onto the main body of the hair shaft by a thin layer of protein. Our main problem is that this protecting cloak can be rather easily damaged by combing, or by improper brushing or treatment of the hair. Many dogs are very hard on their own hair by being quite active, scratching, rolling, etc. This protective layer can be repaired by treatment with protein — namely, protein conditioners. If we can maintain the epicuticle in good condition, we will have hair that is healthy, beautiful, and of an even length, rather than broken with split ends. There are many good conditioners on the market, and many that can be made at home are just as good.

For dry or damaged hair, here are some home recipes that can be used very effectively. Hot Oil Treatment: warm olive oil applied after the hair is shampooed and lightly towelled; distribute oil near roots and work thoroughly, paying special attention to the ends; place entire dog, covered with a piece of plastic (garbage bag cut in half), under dryer for ten minutes; shampoo hair again and follow with a rinse. Corn oil may also be used, and with it use hot towels laid over the dog; wring out a very hot wet towel, place it over the dog, then cover with a dry towel to hold in the heat; follow with shampoo and rinse. Mayonnaise is an excellent conditioner and is primarily protein. You can use either commercially prepared mayonnaise or you can make your own, using two egg yolks, four tablespoons lemon juice, and one and three-quarters cup vegetable oil; beat egg yolks with lemon juice and add the oil, pouring in a thin stream while beating the mixture constantly until you have a thick mixture. Apply this directly to the roots and ends and cover with a folded hot towel, covered by a dry towel. Leave towels on for twenty minutes to a half hour. Shampoo and rinse. A conditioner applied once a week certainly will be worthwhile in maintaining and strengthening the coat.

If you buy a commercially prepared conditioner, beware of some of the fancy names in the ingredients. Some of the long names are not easy to comprehend, and, if you want to know what they mean, I advise you to invest in a copy of a *Consumer's Dictionary of Cosmetic Ingredients*, by Ruth Winter. It has complete information about the harmful and the desirable ingredients found in men's and women's cosmetics. The products we buy daily are sold in many countries by prescription only, because of harmful results or allergic reactions. The first ingredient listed on the label of the product is what it is primarily comprised of, and so on, in order listed.

I stay away from products containing mineral oil because it stays on top of the hair and will not penetrate into the hair shaft. Other oils will penetrate and not leave a coating on the hair which picks up dust, etc., making the coat soil faster and giving a drag to the coat when brushing it. In buying commercial products, I feel that Panthenol is a good ingredient. It does not flake or leave a film coating the hair. Panthenol, a provitamin of pantothenic acid Vitamin B5 (B complex group), has been proven effective in deterring hair loss and improving thin, brittle, and dry hair. Panthenol applied locally seems to have a favorable effect on cell growth by its regenerative action. In order to be effective, the product

189

Am. and Can. Ch. Bel Air Tif-A-Nee of Bamboo, owned by Diane Backovich.

Am. and Can. Ch. Hodari Hai-U

must be formulated with a 2% to 5% Panthenol solution. I have been using very successfully two products that contain the proper balance. There are many good commercial products, and, if applied faithfully and according to directions, they will give results that satisfy.

One of the most common problems in Shih Tzu coats is dryness and lack of elasticity. A moisturizer applied to the coat will prove to be very helpful for this. After conditioning the coat and rinsing out the conditioner, towel lightly and apply a moisturizer, as per instructions. You will notice a marked improvement in manageability and the way the coat lies. There is a great variety of moisturizers on the market — in packets, capsules, and bottles. Apply according to directions and you will be pleased. Always follow a shampoo with a rinse. Even if you use a conditioner, always pour a rinse through the coat afterward. It will restore the proper pH factor and also separate the hairs so that each hair can individually reflect the light and give a radiant luster.

In choosing a shampoo, you must realize that most shampoos have the same base, and the main thing to consider is the pH balance of the product you are using. The pH balance is a measure of the acidity or alkalinity of any substance. The pH balance can be checked easily by using nitrazine paper, available at the drugstore. Dip the paper into the shampoo, conditioner, creme rinse, or other substance you wish to test, and the paper turns color. There is a color scale on the package of paper, ranging from pH 4.5 to pH 7.5. Anything that registers 7 or below is acidic; anything that registers above 7 is alkaline. You want to maintain the proper acid-alkaline balance, and for good health, the balance should lean toward acidity. The average pH balance for dog hair hovers around a pH 5 level, whereas human hair has a higher level. It is good practice not to use products that are above the pH 7 level. There are a lot of good dog shampoos on the market. If you feel you need a shampoo to add body, soften the coat, etc., experiment to see which shampoo gives the best results on your dog's coat. You can check the pH balance with your nitrazine paper. Two shampoos or sudsings usually give a nicer effect; then rinse thoroughly — especially after the second sudsing — to remove every trace of shampoo. It is not necessary, as some believe, to have a high-sudsing shampoo in order to do a thorough job of cleaning.

We have discussed diet, conditioning, and shampoos — now we must say something about the way we brush our dogs and with what frequency. At our kennel we brush every other day, generally, but we brush some dogs every day — or at least check them every day. Frequency of brushing depends on the coat: how badly it mats; whether it is undergoing a change; etc. In other words, brush when needed. Brushing should always be done in a gentle but thorough manner. It is one thing that cannot be done in haste. As you learn to brush properly, you will find that with practice you can brush faster. After you have shampooed and conditioned the coat, used a humectant, and again towel dried the hair, you are ready to dry the coat thoroughly. This is a very important step in preserving the hair and also in obtaining the desired appearance. Wet hair loses some of its resistance and can be stretched and broken more easily. So do be careful as you brush your dog dry, and set the temperature of your dryer at medium. High settings on most dryers produce such intense heat that you can damage the hair. You should teach your dog to lie on his side. Beginning at the middle of the dog's chest, dry the hair thoroughly and carefully by layer-brushing each layer dry before proceeding to the next layer. For the Shih Tzu, we use a wire pin brush that has rather soft pins set in a rubber cushion. Dry the dog in layers until you reach the middle of the back, then turn the dog over and brush the coat in layers in the same way. If you do not know how to brush in layers, watch someone at a show or have someone instruct you.

Be sure you brush correctly: the pins of the brush should make contact at the skin at the beginning of each stroke and continue outward to the ends of the hair and right through the ends, using a straight stroke. Watch how you brush. You may notice that you have a slight upward lift at the end of the hair, in preparation for the next stroke. This is *not* correct, because you will break the ends of the hair by flipping them off in this manner. After the dog is completely dry, use a wide-tooth comb to restraighten the hair in the desirable show fashion. Use a small double-pointed knitting needle to get a good straight part. After the part is perfectly straight, use a mist of creme rinse diluted with water. Use a small amount and spray from about eight inches above the dog so that the mist falls gently down on the part. Then, using the palms of your hands, smooth down the hair on either side of the part and let dry, thus setting the hair to maintain the line of the part.

When you are preparing to show your dog the next day, use a creme rinse (no more than two tablespoons of creme rinse to one quart of water) misted lightly above the dog's coat just *before* brushing. This aids in brushing without breaking or pulling so much on the hair, and it also helps to eliminate static electricity. If you have a problem with static electricity, even though you have used a conditioner, humectant, and creme rinse, there are other aids you can use. Tressemme makes an excellent aerosol spray that is sprayed onto the brush and eliminates electricity in the hair. (This is a product made for humans, so consult a beauty supply store about it.) Lambs wool worked in over the pins of your brush and down to the rubber cushion also helps to control static electricity.

Practice brushing your dog with gentle but thorough strokes of the brush, remembering to use long straight strokes from beginning on through the ends of the coat. Brush as though you were brushing each hair individually, thinking about what you are doing and how you are supposed to do it, and before long it will come naturally. Lay your dog in a position vertical from your body, so that when you are brushing you have plenty of room to finish with a straight stroke of the brush. If you lay the dog horizontally to your body, you have a tendency to flip the end of the brush upward.

The ear fringes and the beard of the Shih Tzu are groomed to the body and add to the smooth outline of the dog. One method for setting the topknot is to part the hair horizontally from eye to eye, brushing the head hair back to form the topknot. Then part the hair from the outside corner of the eye to the inside corner of the ear, and from this point across the head to the inside corner of the other ear. This will make the base of the topknot into a square.

Some groomers feel that this will make the topknot too large and will give a bulky appearance to the head. These groomers will part the hair between the eyes as in the description above. They will start at a point at the outside corner of the eye and make a diagonal part to the center of the head at a point about one-half inch behind an imaginary line drawn between the forward at-tachment points of the ears. This top point can be moved either forward or to the rear to modify the illusion of head shape that the topknot will create. While some groomers use the triangle, others make the diagonal line into an arc when moving the top point, thus creating a semicircle rather than a triangle. You will want to experiment with these possibilities, for what will look right for one dog may not look right for another.

No matter which parting method is used, the final treatment for the topknot will be the same. The hair should be gathered around an imaginary center located about two-thirds of the way back on a center line between the eyes. A white dental rubber band should be slipped over the hair and placed about one-half inch away from the head. With the hair held loosely in this fashion, it is possible to pouf the topknot around the edges, keeping the center shorter to give strength to the finished hair set. Once the pouffing has been completed, the rubber band should be twisted and lapped over one or two more times so that the hair cannot slip out.

The final step in finishing off the topknot is to allow the hair above the rubber band to cascade gently down the back and sides in a semicircle, allowing none of the hair to hang forward over the front of the head. The topknot can be sprayed lightly with coat dressing to hold it in place. A small bow or a pompon may decorate the rubber band that has been twisted around the topknot.

Ch. Kayesett Zebadiah going through last-minute preparations for the ring at the 1986 Westminster Kennel Club Show.

Ch. Kayesett Zebadiah, owned by Mr. and Mrs. R. Flaharty and groomed and handled by Miwako Hosaka. Zebadiah is a daughter of Ch. Lainee Sigmund Floyd.